Partners in O&M

Supporting Orientation and Mobility for Students Who Are Visually Impaired

Rona L. Pogrund and Nora Griffin-Shirley
Editors

AFBPress
American Foundation for the Blind

Printed in the United States of America

Library of Congress Cataloging-in-Publication Data

Names: Pogrund, Rona L., editor. | Griffin-Shirley, Nora, 1954- editor.
Title: Partners in O&M : supporting orientation and mobility for students who are visually impaired / Rona L. Pogrund, Nora Griffin-Shirley, editors.
Description: First Edition. | New York : AFB Press, American Foundation for the Blind, [2018] | Includes bibliographical references and index.
Identifiers: LCCN 2017019200 (print) | LCCN 2017038073 (ebook) | ISBN 9780891287674 (epub) | ISBN 9780891287681 (mobi) | ISBN 9780891287940 (pdf) | ISBN 9780891287650 (pbk. : alk. paper) | ISBN 9780891287667 (online subscription)
Subjects: LCSH: Children with visual disabilities—Education. | Children with visual disabilities—Orientation and mobility.
Classification: LCC HV1631 (ebook) | LCC HV1631.P37 2018 (print) | DDC 371.91/1—dc23
LC record available at https://lccn.loc.gov/2017019200

The mission of the American Foundation for the Blind is to create a world of no limits for people who are blind or visually impaired. We mobilize leaders, advance understanding, and champion impactful policies and practices using research and data.

It is the policy of the American Foundation for the Blind to use in the first printing of its books acid-free paper that meets the ANSI Z39.48 Standard. The infinity symbol that appears above indicates that the paper in this printing meets that standard.

To all the children and adults with visual impairments we have had the privilege to educate, to the university students who inspire us to share our passion for teaching, to all the partners, including families, who have supported orientation and mobility in multiple ways, and to our colleagues, past and present, who have contributed and continue to add to the research and knowledge base that inform the daily practice of our field.

Important Notice

Dear reader of *Partners in O&M*,

The American Foundation for the Blind has developed an online learning center to accompany this book. Access to the AFB Learning Center is complimentary for purchasers of the book, but registration is required. If you purchased an online subscription of this book, you will be able to access the full text through the Learning Center as well.

Registration for the AFB Learning Center is fast and simple. Just follow these steps:

- Go to www.afb.org/PartnersOMRegister
- Complete the short registration form by entering your name and e-mail address, creating a username and password, and entering the code **PartnersOM**.
- Submit the form.

To access the AFB Learning Center once you have registered, go to www.afb.org/PartnersOM. Choose the link to log in and enter the username and password you created during registration.

If you experience technical problems or have any questions, contact AFB at afbpress@afb.net.

Contents

Foreword

Partners in O&M: Supporting Orientation and Mobility for Students Who Are Visually Impaired, edited by Rona Pogrund and Nora Griffin-Shirley, is a timely and important new resource for those interested in helping students achieve one of life's most essential skills, that of independent travel in the environment. Almost all aspects of daily life depend upon being able to move from place to place efficiently, safely, and with self-direction. Our work and leisure times are highly connected to movement, and the degree to which students can develop agency over where they need and want to go will have much to do with their quality of life. This view of independent movement is about practicality and joy, and students with visual impairments should have access to it in a way that aligns with the life they aspire to live.

Partners in O&M is a new take on what professionals needs to know to enter into the occupation of working with students who are visually impaired. My own training as an orientation and mobility specialist in the late 1970s was excellent, but focused heavily on the teaching of cane skills in a variety of environments as a solo act. Our profession has grown tremendously in the ensuing decades, and among the most valuable developments has been the recognition that our students need support from all the key adults in their lives in order to maximize their indepen-

dence. The goals of O&M instruction cut across all aspects of a student's day, making time with families, teachers, and related service personnel opportunities for skill attainment that an orientation and mobility specialist should actively cultivate through collaborative partnerships. This is the key concept that makes *Partners in O&M* such a good match for informing how our profession should work today when it is at its best.

Rona Pogrund and Nora Griffin-Shirley have long and distinguished careers working directly with students with visual impairments and preparing new professionals to enter the field. Their concept for the development of *Partners in O&M* is informed by their expertise and by the many leadership activities they pursue that puts them in contact with our field's best thinkers. They have assembled a group of writers with outstanding knowledge and experience, and with the ability to organize and share their information with clarity. I encourage you to read this book and to share its ideas with all your partners who are similarly striving to ensure that students with visual impairments achieve their highest level of independence.

William E. Daugherty
Superintendent
Texas School for the Blind and Visually Impaired
Austin, Texas

Preface

A longtime need has existed for a comprehensive book that can serve as an introduction to the field of orientation and mobility (O&M), with a focus on those who work in collaboration with O&M specialists to serve students who are blind or visually impaired. To fill this need, we envisioned and edited this book, whose primary target audiences are the preservice teachers of students with visual impairments and O&M specialists who attend a personnel preparation program to train for their careers. All these preservice educators take a basic O&M course that introduces them to the field of O&M, provides them with a foundation of information as future service providers serving students with visual impairments, and instructs them in basic O&M skills they will teach and reinforce with their students in the future. After surveying other personnel preparation programs in visual impairment, we received overwhelming support for a book such as *Partners in O&M: Supporting Orientation and Mobility for Students Who Are Visually Impaired.*

Previously, university students were required to purchase multiple books for their basic O&M course, yet they only utilized small sections of each because the books were primarily geared to O&M specialists. In their more advanced courses, students in O&M programs use additional books that are more comprehensive in scope and sequence, but the teachers of students with visual impairments or other professionals taking an introductory O&M course do not need a majority of the content of these more advanced books.

This book is geared to future O&M specialists and the partners who support O&M instruction. In addition to preservice professionals in the field of visual impairment, partners include related service personnel such as occupational therapists, physical therapists, and speech-language pathologists; special education teachers who have students with visual impairments and additional disabilities in their classes; general education teachers who have students who are blind or visually impaired in their classrooms; paraeducators; interveners; early childhood interventionists; school nurses; physical education teachers; music therapists; recreational activity directors; administrators; and other personnel who work with students with visual impairments. All these specialists will benefit from the content of this book. A theme of collaboration is highlighted throughout the book and focuses on how these O&M partners can support and reinforce the skills their students are learning during O&M instruction. Through this book, these collaborative partners will learn about the basic skills (e.g., guide techniques, protective and alignment techniques, room familiarization, and so on) taught to their students by O&M specialists as well as basic information about the field of O&M that they can use daily to support their students with visual impairments.

Family members of children with visual impairments and other caregivers will also find the information in this book valuable. There are no partners more important in supporting O&M skills than the individuals who spend most of their time with their children. Parents, other family members, and caregivers play a critical role in reinforcing the O&M skills and concepts taught in O&M lessons if these skills are to be integrated into the children's daily routines and generalized to new environments. Family members as O&M partners are central to the theme of this book.

Although the primary focus of this book is on working with children, much of the information can also be applied to working with adults. The foundational information about O&M (e.g., the history of the field, O&M systems and tools, spatial awareness, use of secondary senses, environmental accessibility and modifications, current issues in the field) applies to O&M specialists and their partners working with adults as well as children, so the value of the book goes beyond the content that only applies to children. Much of the information is primarily applicable to working with children from birth through age 22, such as the chapters on concept and motor development and working with students with multiple impairments, but the basic O&M skills included in Chapter 6 apply to individuals of all ages. This book also offers valuable information for future adult service providers such as vision rehabilitation therapists and low vision therapists, so it can be used in these preservice programs as well.

At the beginning of each chapter, readers will find a list of questions to guide their reading of the chapter to help them focus on some of the key issues and content of that chapter as well as key terms to provide a foundation of definitions for that chapter. Resources and suggested learning activities that can be used by instructors of a basic O&M course or for in-service training on any of the topics found in this book are provided in the online AFB Learning Center.

Partners in O&M is so much more than a textbook. Current philosophies in the field are included to make this book a relevant resource that reflects innovative current and future thinking in teaching O&M to children. It goes beyond traditional content on O&M services while still providing a solid foundation for professionals working with students who are blind or who have low vision.

We have talked about the need for such a book for a long time, and we are excited that this project has come to fruition. It would not have been possible without the support of AFB Press, particularly its director, George Abbott, and executive editors Ellen Bilofsky and Alina Vayntrub, who have patiently guided us through the publication process and supported our idea about the need for this book. We also extend tremendous appreciation and admiration to our chapter authors who have graciously shared their expertise and knowledge and who have shown commitment by meeting requested deadlines when asked. The collaboration that went into writing this book is an example of how effective joining together to meet a desired goal can be! As Helen Keller once said, "Alone we can do so little; together we can do so much!" Our hope is that through collaboration among O&M specialists, family members, and numerous partners, students with visual impairments will benefit most in attaining their individual O&M goals and will be prepared to reach their full potential.

Rona L. Pogrund
Nora Griffin-Shirley
Editors

About the Contributors

Editors

Rona L. Pogrund, PhD, is Professor, Special Education Program, College of Education, and Coordinator, Program for Teachers of Students with Visual Impairments, at the Virginia Murray Sowell Center for Research and Education in Sensory Disabilities at Texas Tech University, Lubbock. Dr. Pogrund is the coeditor of *Early Focus: Working with Young Children Who Are Blind or Visually Impaired and Their Families* and coauthor of *TAPS—Teaching Age-Appropriate Purposeful Skills: An Orientation & Mobility Curriculum for Students with Visual Impairments.* She has over 45 years of experience in the field of visual impairment as a teacher of students with visual impairments, orientation and mobility (O&M) specialist, and special education administrator. Dr. Pogrund is Associate Editor for Practice of the *Journal of Visual Impairment & Blindness,* previously served as associate editor of the journal *Insight: Research and Practice in Visual Impairment and Blindness,* and has published numerous journal articles and book chapters on the topics of service delivery and O&M for students with visual impairments. She is the recipient of the 2015 Distinguished Service Award from the Division on Visual Impairments and Deafblindness of the Council for Exceptional Children and served as chair of the subcommittee of the Texas Action Committee for the Education of Students with Visual Impairments, which developed *VISSIT: Visual Impairment Scale of Service Intensity of Texas* and *O&M VISSIT.*

Nora Griffin-Shirley, PhD, is Professor and Coordinator, Orientation and Mobility Program and TTU Graduate Certification Program in Sensory Impairments and Autism, and Director, Virginia Murray Sowell Center for Research and Education in Sensory Disabilities at Texas Tech University, Lubbock. Dr. Griffin-Shirley is coeditor of *O&M for Independent Living: Strategies for Teaching Orientation and Mobility to Older Adults* and coauthor of *Prescriptions for Independence: Working with Older People Who Are Visually Impaired* and *Strength-Based Planning for Transitioning Students with Sensory Impairments.* A certified orientation and mobility specialist and leader in the field with over 40 years of experience, she is the coauthor of book chapters, journal articles, and national and international conference presentations on the topics of orientation and mobility, strength-based planning, personnel preparation, and assistive technology competencies. Dr. Griffin-Shirley previously served as treasurer, chair of the Orientation and Mobility Division, and board member of the Association for Education and Rehabilitation of the Blind and Visually Impaired.

Chapter Authors

Laura Bozeman, PhD, a certified orientation and mobility specialist and low vision therapist, is Associate Professor and Director of Vision Studies at the School for Global Inclusion and Social Development at the University of Massachusetts, Boston. Dr. Bozeman is coeditor of *O&M for Independent Living: Strategies for Teaching Orientation and Mobility to Older Adults,* has authored and coauthored book chapters and journal articles and presented internationally at conferences and workshops on the topics of low vision, orientation and mobility, personnel preparation, and vision assessment, and has taught in the United States as well as in Taiwan, China, Saipan, Federated States of Micronesia, American Samoa, Australia, and New Zealand. Dr. Bozeman currently serves on the Board of Directors of the Association for Education and Rehabilitation of the Blind and Visually Impaired is past chair of its Personnel Preparation Division.

Jennifer L. Cmar, PhD, a certified orientation and mobility specialist, is Assistant Research Professor at the National Research and Training Center on Blindness and Low Vision at Mississippi State University. Dr. Cmar previously served as adjunct lecturer at California State University, Los Angeles, as an orientation and mobility specialist at the Department of Veterans Affairs and the Society for the Blind, and was a fellow of the National Leadership Consortium in Sensory Disabilities.

Shannon D. Darst, PhD, is an adjunct professor at Texas Tech University, Lubbock, and a teacher of students with visual impairments at the Elgin Independent School District in Texas. Dr. Darst is a board member of the Texas Association for Education and Rehabilitation of the Blind and Visually Impaired and served as a member of the subcommittee of the Texas Action Committee for the Education of Students with Visual Impairments, which developed *VISSIT: Visual Impairment Scale of Service Intensity of Texas.*

Vicki DePountis, EdD, is Program Specialist for the Blind and Visually Impaired at the Texas Education Agency, Austin, and an instructor at Texas Tech University, Lubbock. A certified orientation and mobility specialist and teacher of students with visual impairments, Dr. DePountis was previously Assistant Professor in the Visual Impairment Program at Stephen F. Austin State University in Nacogdoches, Texas, and served as director of the Division on Visual Impairments and Deafblindness of the Council for Exceptional Children. Her research interests focus on using technology to facilitate learning for students with visual impairments.

Tracy Hallak, MEd, is a certified orientation and mobility (O&M) specialist and teacher of students with visual impairments who taught in the vision and O&M programs at Stephen F. Austin State University in Nacogdoches, Texas. Ms. Hallak is president of the Texas Association for Education of the Blind and Visually Impaired and chair of the Itinerant Personnel Division of the Association for Education and Rehabilitation of the Blind and Visually Impaired. She served as a member of the subcommittee of the Texas Action Committee for the Education of Students with Visual Impairments, which developed *VISSIT: Visual Impairment Scale of Service Intensity of Texas,* as well as a member of the team that developed the *Texas Two-Steps: Successfully Teaching Early Purposeful Skills.*

Stacy M. Kelly, EdD, is Associate Professor in the Visual Disabilities Program at Northern Illinois University, DeKalb. Dr. Kelly is a certified orientation and mobility specialist and assistive technology instructional specialist for people with visual impairments, as well as a licensed teacher of students with visual impairments and school administrator. She has published book chapters, position papers, and journal articles on the topic of assistive technology for people with visual impairments and has been appointed cochair of the Certified Assistive Technology Instructional Specialist Subject Matter Expert Committee by the Academy for Certification of Vision Rehabilitation and Education Professionals.

Melanie Kalene Meeks, PhD, is a researcher and instructor at Texas Tech University, Lubbock, a scientific review officer at the Society of Research Administrators International in Arlington, Virginia, and a fellow at the Neuro-Optometric Rehabilitation Association. A certified orientation and mobility specialist and licensed medical technologist, Dr. Meeks served in the U.S. Army and has worked extensively with veterans and the agencies supporting them. She has published and presented nationally on the topics of traumatic brain injury, neuroplasticity, autism spectrum disorders, and sensory impairments.

Sandra J. Rosen, PhD, is Coordinator of the Orientation and Mobility (O&M) Program at San Francisco State University. A certified O&M specialist, vision rehabilitation therapist, and licensed physical therapist, Dr. Rosen developed

an approach to increase efficiency in teaching mobility techniques using proprioceptive neuromuscular facilitation and created an assessment and training approach to develop balance skills in preschool children who are blind. She is the author of *Step-by-Step: An Interactive Guide to Mobility Techniques*, an online curriculum used in the preparation of O&M specialists and related vision professionals, and has published numerous journal articles and book chapters on the topics of sensorimotor functioning, educating students with visual, multiple, and other impairments, and teaching various aspects of O&M. Dr. Rosen is the recipient of the 2016 Lawrence E. Blaha Award from the Association for Education and Rehabilitation of the Blind and Visually Impaired.

Wendy Sapp, PhD, is an educational specialist and consultant for Visual Impairment Education Services in Cohutta, Georgia, and a project director for Bridge Multimedia in New York. A certified orientation and mobility specialist and teacher of students with visual impairments, Dr. Sapp has conducted research, authored numerous journal articles, developed curricula, and presented nationally on the topics of communication and emergent literacy, assistive technology and accessibility, adaptive mobility devices, the expanded core curriculum, working with families, and audio description. She is a former board member of the Association for Education and Rehabilitation of the Blind and Visually Impaired and former chair of its Personnel Preparation Division.

Christopher Tabb, MA, is Statewide Orientation and Mobility Consultant at Texas School for the Blind and Visually Impaired Outreach Programs, a guest lecturer at Texas Tech University, and a private consultant through his company, Sensory Travel. A certified orientation and mobility specialist, Mr. Tabb has worked in California, Connecticut, Massachusetts, and Texas to provide orientation and mobility services in residential programs, as an itinerant, and as a private contractor to school-age students, adults, and seniors. He is chair-elect of the Orientation and Mobility Division of the Association for Education and Rehabilitation of the Blind and Visually Impaired a former president of the California Association of Orientation and Mobility Specialists.

Amy Van der Veer, BS, is a certified orientation and mobility specialist and occupational therapist with over 30 years' experience, based in Wyoming. Ms. Hadley specializes in sensory integration therapy, wheelchair seating and mo-

bility, and low vision and has presented on these topics at various conferences.

Other Contributors

Nouf M. Alzrayer, PhD, is an assistant professor of special education at King Saud University in Saudi Arabia. Dr. Alzrayer is a board-certified behavior analyst and has published journal articles on autism and augmentative and alternative communication.

Devender R. Banda, PhD, is a professor of special education at Texas Tech University, Lubbock. Dr. Banda is a board-certified behavior analyst and has published journal articles on individuals with autism and other developmental disabilities, communication systems, and meta-analyses.

1

Overview of Orientation and Mobility

Nora Griffin-Shirley and Rona L. Pogrund

Questions to Guide Your Reading of This Chapter

➤ How did the field of orientation and mobility (O&M) begin?

➤ What are the benefits of O&M instruction for students with visual impairments?

➤ What are the roles and responsibilities of different professionals in O&M service delivery?

➤ How are O&M skills evaluated?

➤ What are the current issues in the field of O&M?

We can draw lessons from the past, but we cannot live in it. (Johnson, 1965, p. 54)

Individuals who are blind or who have low vision need to learn to travel safely in their homes, schools, and communities to optimally function while in school and after they leave the educational setting and enter the adult world. As a component of the *expanded core curriculum (ECC)*, orientation and mobility (O&M) services teach individuals who are blind or who have low vision how to move purposely, safely, and as independently as possible. *Orientation and mobility specialists* are the primary individuals responsible for the evaluation, instructional planning, and implementation of O&M programs. Family members and other professionals, such as teachers of students with visual impairments, physical and occupational therapists, and eye care professionals, play important roles as partners in the instruction and support of children with visual impairments to allow them to reach their full potential in their travel abilities. The following case studies illustrate how O&M instruction is provided to Maria, a student who is totally blind, and to Larry, a student who is blind with additional disabilities.

Maria, a 14-year-old ninth grader, is totally blind and of above-average intelligence. She is in general education classes at her high school for most of the day. She has received O&M instruction from Mr. Todd, her O&M specialist, since she was in elementary school. Maria is a competent and confident cane user who can travel independently in her school and in the community near her home. During this academic year, Mr. Todd, Maria's educational team, and Maria have decided to focus on Maria learning how to use the city bus. This is an important goal because Maria has a job lined up for next summer, and she will need to take the bus from her neighborhood to her workplace.

1

During the school year, Mr. Todd will introduce Maria to the bus system by taking her to visit the bus depot, where Maria will become familiar with the parts of a bus as well as how to utilize it for travel. She will obtain information regarding the bus system (e.g., bus schedules, fares, transfers, routes) by going online or by calling the bus information number so she can independently plan her bus trips. Additionally, she will ride the bus with Mr. Todd until she has mastered bus travel, and then she will practice traveling independently on the bus to her future workplace in preparation for her summer job.

Larry, a 12-year-old student, is anxiously waiting for his O&M specialist, Ms. Davis, to meet him in his self-contained, special education classroom at Williams Middle School. He is very excited because he is going to learn how to travel to the principal's office. Once Larry can successfully travel to the office, his teacher, Mrs. Lucey, will assign him the task of taking the attendance sheet to the office daily. This task is very important to Larry because he enjoys interacting with the workers in the principal's office.

Larry is congenitally blind as a result of Leber's congenital amaurosis. He has cortical visual impairment (CVI), nystagmus, limited use of vision, and he is legally blind. Larry has been diagnosed with autism and has a severe receptive-language impairment with a profound impairment in pragmatic or social language. Larry exhibits the following behaviors: eye poking, self-stimulatory behavior (stamping feet, flapping hands), inappropriate hugging, and running away.

In the past, Larry received O&M instruction using a folding cane. To provide appropriate instruction, Ms. Davis conducted a preference assessment using five items (a clapper, noise putty, Play-Doh, a pair of magnets, and a rubber bracelet). The noise putty was Larry's preferred item, so Ms. Davis uses it as reinforcement during lessons whenever Larry meets a specific O&M objective. This reinforcer keeps Larry motivated to succeed during the lessons.

Larry has received O&M instruction in the use of a folding cane for over four years. He did not walk until he was 4 years old and did not initiate walking toward an object until the age of 5. During the past school year, school personnel have accompanied Larry and Ms. Davis on fewer O&M lessons. Larry is very motivated to reach his goal of learning to walk alone in the school since this is what his friends do all the time. O&M instruction will facilitate an increase in Larry's self-esteem and independence since he will rely less on other people as his own skills improve.

Definitions Related to Orientation and Mobility

Orientation is the ability to know "where you are, where you want to go, and how to get there" while *mobility* is "the act of going from one place to another safely and effectively . . . making full use of whatever mechanical, technological, or human resources needed" (Goodman, 1989, p. 3; see Sidebar 1.1 for definitions of key terms). In simple terms, orientation is knowing where you are in space, while mobility is safely and efficiently getting from point A to point B. The expanded definition of orientation for young children and individuals with multiple impairments includes the cognitive component of *purposeful movement,* while mobility is the motor component of purposeful movement (Anthony, Bleier, Fazzi, Kish, &

SIDEBAR 1.1

Key Terms

Accessible pedestrian signal (APS) Device that provides information (audible, vibrotactile, or both) accessible to pedestrians who are blind or visually impaired about when a pedestrian walk cycle at an intersection begins. Features may include a pushbutton, a tactile arrow, and volume adjustment.

Core curriculum General education curriculum that all students are expected to master, including reading and writing, language arts, science, mathematics, and social studies.

Expanded core curriculum (ECC) Concepts and skills beyond the general education core curriculum that often require specialized instruction for students who are blind or visually impaired to compensate for decreased opportunities to learn incidentally by observing others. The nine domains are compensatory access, sensory efficiency, assistive technology, orientation and mobility, independent living, social interaction, recreation and leisure, career education, and self-determination.

Familiarization Techniques used to systematically explore an environment independently or with support from another person providing verbal description or physical assistance.

Mobility Safely and efficiently getting from one point to another, or the motor component of purposeful movement.

Orientation Ability of an individual to know where he is, where he wants to go, and how to get there, or the cognitive component of purposeful movement.

Orientation and mobility specialists Professionals who teach concept development, sensory training, mobility skills, orientation systems, solicitation of assistance, use of community resources and public transportation, safety issues, decision making, and assistive technology to individuals with visual impairments.

Purposeful movement Intentional motor response or ambulation for a desired outcome.

Pogrund, 2002). Both orientation (*O*) and mobility (*M*) are important. If a person knows where he or she is and is well oriented but does not have skills to move about safely and efficiently, the person cannot be an independent traveler. Likewise, if the person has effective mobility skills but often becomes confused and disoriented, independent travel is also affected. *O* and *M* are both essential and work together. When integrated, O&M skills result in wayfinding (LaGrow & Long, 2011). An example of wayfinding, or spatial problem solving, is when Maria independently plans her bus route and

rides the bus from her neighborhood to her workplace.

O&M is one of the nine areas of the ECC, the cornerstone of instruction for students with visual impairments (Sapp & Hatlen, 2010). While the general education *core curriculum* refers to subjects such as math, science, and history that are taught to all students, the term ECC is used to define concepts and skills beyond the general education curriculum. These skills often require specialized instruction for students who are blind or visually impaired to compensate for decreased opportunities to learn incidentally by observing others, a common form of learning for children who are sighted. For children with visual impairments, O&M involves a broad range of skill areas, including

- concept development (e.g., knowledge of one's body, parts of a building, cardinal directions),
- motor development (e.g., reaching, crawling, walking, running),
- use of perceptual and sensory systems (e.g., using hearing to find a squeaky toy, reading a tactile map, orienting by the warmth of the sun),
- orientation skills (e.g., using a global positioning system to travel a route from home to a bus stop, planning alternate routes),
- mobility skills (e.g., use of protective techniques, use of a long cane or a wheelchair and a long cane),
- interpersonal skills (e.g., asking for help when disoriented, making a purchase in a store), and
- problem solving (e.g., What does a student do when he misses his bus stop? How does a student reorient after veering during a street crossing?).

Use of assistive technology to enhance O&M (e.g., using a monocular to read a bus number) is also an integral part of an O&M curriculum (Fazzi, 2014; Griffin-Shirley, Trusty, & Rickard, 2000; Jacobson, 2013). It is important to remember that O&M instruction is highly individualized, based on each student's needs at any given time (LaGrow & Long, 2011). Students with the same visual condition may not use their vision in the same way, and O&M needs change as students grow older. Therefore, O&M instruction should always be individualized to the specific strengths and needs of each student.

There are countless benefits of O&M instruction including stronger self-concept, greater performance of independent living skills, improved health and fitness from exercise, and increased social and employment opportunities (Bart, Katz, Weiss, & Josman, 2008; Cmar, 2015; Hill, 1986; Tuttle & Tuttle, 2004; Wolffe & Kelly, 2011).

Brief History of Orientation and Mobility

Individuals with visual impairments have been traveling for centuries using different tools (e.g., sticks, shepherd's staffs, canes, dogs, and guides). In the United States, the beginnings of O&M are rooted in the dog guide movement, the aftermath of the World Wars, civilian and government commitment and funding for veterans, and the efforts of influential, creative people. This section focuses on the history of O&M in the United States. In a historical sense, the field of O&M is relatively new, but it has been an ever-evolving field that continues to change and expand over time. Important milestones in the history of the field of O&M can be found in Sidebar 1.2.

Prior to the 1920s, there was little mobility instruction for individuals who were blind. Society did not see the role of a person who was blind as an independent one. Dorothy Harrison Eustis was an American heiress who bred German shepherds at her home in Switzerland and became interested in training dogs to serve as guides for people who were blind. She heard about a German doctor, Dr. Gerhard Stalling, who was training Army search and rescue dogs

Important Milestones in the History of O&M

1819	In Vienna, Johann Wilhelm Klein discusses use of a rigid harness handle for dog guides in his book, *Textbook for the Teaching of the Blind*.
1829	Perkins School for the Blind is founded. There, Francis Campbell uses a long cane and teaches a physical (body-training) class where he suggests putting the cane in front of the leading foot.
1872	W. Hanks Levy coins the term "typhlology"—the scientific study of blindness—in his book, *Blindness and the Blind: A Treatise on the Science of Typhlology*. He also mentions that mobility is enhanced by using a stick, a dog, or a gander.
1916	Dr. Gerhard Stalling opens the first dog guide school in Oldenburg, Germany.
1929	The Seeing Eye, the first dog guide school in the United States, is incorporated in Nashville, Tennessee, by Dorothy Harrison Eustis and Morris Frank.
1930	The first white cane ordinance is passed in Peoria, Illinois.
1931	Lions Club International supports a national program promoting the use of white canes by people who are blind.
1941–1945	Blind veterans are rehabilitated using Richard Hoover's cane technique.
1943	Valley Forge Hospital in Phoenixville, Pennsylvania, trains foot orientors.
1944	A social readjustment center for veterans is started at Old Farms Convalescent Hospital in Avon, Connecticut.
1948	Russell Williams appointed as chief of the Veterans Administration (VA) Hines Blind Rehabilitation Center. He begins training staff in the first blind unit devoted to rehabilitation of veterans with vision loss.
1950–1970s	Electronic travel aids are developed.
1952	*The Long Cane*, a film about O&M training at the VA, is developed.
1959	National conference on O&M, sponsored by the American Foundation for the Blind (AFB), is held to develop curriculum and recommend length of training, sponsorship, and selection criteria for O&M specialists. The results of the conference state that O&M instructors must be sighted and must be trained for one year in a university graduate program.
1960s	O&M programs begin in other countries.
1960	The Boston College Peripatology Program, the first O&M university-level training program in the United States, begins.

(continued on next page)

1961	The second O&M university training program, at Western Michigan University, begins.
1965	Interest Group IX of the American Association of Workers for the Blind (AAWB), which focuses on O&M, holds its first meeting.
1966	An undergraduate O&M program, funded by the U.S. Office of Education, begins at Florida State University.
1966	The Mobility Group is established by the American Association of Instructors of the Blind (AAIB).
1968	AAWB Interest Group IX adopts procedures for certification of O&M specialists.
1968	The Architectural Barriers Act (ABA), the first law addressing environmental accessibility, is passed.
1968	AAIB becomes the Association for Education of the Visually Handicapped (AEVH).
1969	First O&M certifications approved.
1969	Boston College and Walter Fernald State School develop a joint program to teach O&M skills to students who are blind and have intellectual disabilities.
1969	Dual-certification programs that prepare teachers of students with visual impairments and O&M instructors begin at the University of Pittsburgh and the University of Northern Colorado.
1971	First book focusing on O&M training for persons with low vision, *Distance Vision and Perceptual Training: A Concept for Use in the Mobility Training of Low Vision Clients* by Loyal Apple and Marianne May, is published.
1973	O&M Code of Ethics adopted by AAWB Interest Group IX.
1976	AFB publishes the first O&M text, *Orientation and Mobility Techniques: A Guide for the Practitioner* by Everett Hill and Purvis Ponder.
1978	A generic program to train professionals to provide O&M training to people with various disabilities other than blindness is funded at the University of Wisconsin.
1979	The first International Mobility Conference is held in Frankfurt, Germany.
1980s	O&M using a precane device for preschoolers is developed.
1980	The first edition of *Foundations of Orientation and Mobility*, edited by Richard Welsh and Bruce Blasch, is published by AFB.
1984	AEVH and AAWB merge to become the Association for Education and Rehabilitation of the Blind and Visually Impaired (AER).
1988	O&M Archives officially open at the Maryland School for the Blind in Baltimore.

1990	The Americans with Disabilities Act (ADA), the first comprehensive law to address the needs of individuals with disabilities, is passed.
1990	University Review committee is established by AER Division IX.
1990	AER publishes *Preschool Orientation and Mobility Screening*.
1992	Texas School for the Blind and Visually Impaired (TSBVI) publishes the first O&M curriculum for school-age students, *TAPS—Teaching Age-Appropriate Purposeful Skills: An Orientation and Mobility Curriculum for Students with Visual Impairments*.
1996	Certified orientation and mobility specialist (COMS) becomes a trademark.
1996	O&M is listed as one of the skill areas of the expanded core curriculum.
1997	Second edition of *Foundations of Orientation and Mobility*, edited by Bruce Blasch, William Wiener, and Richard Welsh, is published by AFB Press.
1998	Second edition of *TAPS—Teaching Age-Appropriate Purposeful Skills* is published by TSBVI.
2000	The Academy for Certification of Vision Rehabilitation and Education Professionals (ACVREP), which certifies COMS, is established.
2001	ACVREP develops a national O&M examination for applicants applying for O&M certification.
2001	The National Blindness Professional Certification Board is established by the National Federation of the Blind to provide the national orientation and mobility certification (NOMC).
2002	AER Division IX becomes the AER O&M Division.
2004	ADA and ABA accessibility guidelines are consolidated into one code of federal regulations.
2007	The American Printing House for the Blind in Louisville, Kentucky, becomes the new home of the O&M Archives.
2010	Third edition of *Foundations of Orientation and Mobility*, edited by William Wiener, Richard Welsh, and Bruce Blasch, is published by AFB Press.
2012	Third edition of *TAPS—Teaching Age-Appropriate Purposeful Skills* is published by TSBVI.
2017	Second edition of *Orientation and Mobility Techniques*, by Diane Fazzi and Janet Barlow, is published by AFB Press.
2017	ACVREP changes criteria for the number of hours of direct instruction required for O&M students completing an internship.

Source: Adapted from Wiener, W. R., & Siffermann, E. (2010). Appendix 14B: Dates and events that influenced the development of orientation and mobility. In W. R. Wiener, R. L. Welsh, & B. B. Blasch (Eds.), *Foundations of orientation and mobility: Vol. I. History and theory* (3rd ed., pp. 516–527). New York, NY: AFB Press.

to be guides for people who were blind. He started the first dog guide school, at the Oldenburg Society in 1916. In 1927, Eustis wrote an article for the *Saturday Evening Post* describing the training of this dog guide program in Germany for blinded veterans, titled "The Seeing Eye." Morris Frank, a man from Tennessee who was blind, read the article and corresponded with Eustis. Eustis and her trainer, Elliot Humphrey, trained a dog named Buddy for Frank. As a result of this successful venture, Frank and Eustis opened the first dog guide school in the United States, The Seeing Eye, in 1929, to train dog guides for people who were blind. They spearheaded the dog guide movement in the United States (Franck, Haneline, Brooks, & Whitstock, 2010). Dorothy Harrison Eustis became known as the mother of the dog guide.

After the World Wars, many soldiers went home blind, yet they wanted to become productive members of society. Following World War I, very little was done for the newly blinded veterans. They received medical treatment, and then most were sent home and did nothing after leaving the service. In 1930, the Lions Club of Peoria, Illinois, sponsored legislation that led to the passage of the first white cane law. This law guaranteed the right-of-way to pedestrians who were blind and carried a white cane with a red tip. The white cane law is still on the books in all states today, and National White Cane Safety Day is celebrated each October to increase awareness of independent mobility skills for individuals who are blind or visually impaired. In 1931, Lions Clubs across the country started distributing white canes as part of their national programs. Hundreds of thousands of short, white, wooden canes were given out free across the country to individuals who were blind. Unfortunately, no formalized

instructional program came with the cane, and the haphazard tapping and fumbling method that was generally used may have contributed to a negative stereotype of a cane user who is blind (Bledsoe, 2010).

After World War II, the road to independence began for veterans. As a result of veterans' desire for independence, Valley Forge General Hospital (commonly known as the "Army Hospital") in Phoenixville, Pennsylvania, developed a standard method of travel with a cane taught to veterans by foot orientors. Dr. Richard E. Hoover, Russell C. Williams, and C. Warren Bledsoe were employed at the hospital during that time. Hoover thought the wooden cane used by people who were blind was too short and heavy and that it created too passive a role for the user. Hoover, who became known as the father of modern cane travel, developed the long cane and the two-point-touch technique that is still used today. He also emphasized the importance of the rapport between the instructor and the veteran who is blind in contributing to the success of O&M instruction (Bledsoe, 2010).

Prior to World War II, Russell Williams was a teacher and an athletic director, but he was blinded during the war. At Valley Forge General Hospital, he was trained in the use of the long cane technique. In 1948, Williams became the first chief at Hines Veterans Administration (VA) Hospital in Illinois. He was instrumental in the establishment of the VA rehabilitation program for veterans who were blind, in which the staff were trained in mobility techniques under blindfold (Bledsoe, 2010).

Through his many publications, Warren Bledsoe became the historian for the field of O&M. The son of a former superintendent of the Maryland School for the Blind, he had been educated as a teacher of individuals who were blind, and as a soldier was assigned to the rehabilitation unit at Valley Forge General Hospital. He collaborated with Richard Hoover and Russell Williams on the refinement of the long cane and other techniques that veterans who were blind could use to travel independently (Bledsoe, 2010).

Several pivotal meetings were held in the 1950s that highlighted the viability of O&M. These meetings included the 1953 Gloucester Conference, where Reverend Thomas Carroll discussed the problems of untrained staff teaching travel skills to people who are blind, and there was a discussion that maybe other individuals besides veterans could benefit from O&M instruction. In 1959, the American Foundation for the Blind sponsored a national conference to determine the criteria for O&M personnel, develop the O&M curriculum, recommend the time needed to master the curriculum, and find potential funding sources. Conference participants identified major areas of study, including the physical O&M blindfold and the dynamics of human behavior related to blindness—how individuals relate to blindness, the functions of the human body, the study of the senses, and the cultural and psychological implications of blindness. The results of the conference were that: (1) O&M specialists should receive formal training of at least one year at a master's degree level, and (2) O&M specialists should be sighted (this decision was made by sighted VA personnel and by asking newly blinded veterans, who had their own fears and stereotypes about blindness, if they would prefer to be taught by an O&M instructor who was blind or one who was sighted). The federal government funded the first university training program in 1960 at Boston College and the second at Western Michigan University in 1961. Funding for these first personnel preparation programs came from the Vocational Rehabilitation Administration, now called the Rehabilitative Services Administration (Wiener & Siffermann, 2010).

The 1960s were known as a time of real growth for the field. Electronic travel aids were developed, undergraduate and graduate university training programs began, and accreditation for these programs was discussed. Funding for personnel preparation programs was expanded to include funding from Vocational Rehabilitation Services and the U.S. Department of Education. Standards for canes were developed and certification standards for O&M specialists were established. As the profession of O&M emerged, professional organizations in the blindness field organized divisions for O&M specialists and gave awards to their members. The inception of an itinerant model for O&M services for children began and instruction was expanded to people who were blind with additional disabilities. To spread the word about O&M, newsletters documenting important events and accomplishments in the field were published (Wiener & Siffermann, 2010).

During the 1970s, regional and state O&M conferences were held, O&M certification requirements changed, and the O&M code of ethics was adopted. Innovative practices emerged, such as the use of paraprofessionals, low vision device and visual efficiency training, and generic O&M instructional programs for people with disabilities other than blindness. In 1976, the first O&M techniques book, *Orientation and Mobility Techniques: A Guide for the Practitioner* by Everett Hill and Purvis Ponder, was published. Certification for O&M specialists also changed, with visual criteria modified from a specific visual acuity and field to more general functional visual requirements (e.g., ability of the O&M specialist to monitor a student from 375 feet) (Wiener & Siffermann, 2010).

The 1970s and 1980s brought about the feminization of the field of O&M. Initially, all foot orientors and O&M specialists were men. However, when O&M instruction became available for children who were blind in public schools, women started entering the field of O&M. Over the subsequent years, the majority of O&M specialists have been women, and the trend continues today (Uslan, Hill, & Peck, 1989).

From 1980 to 2000, the field of O&M published more textbooks (*Foundations of Orientation and Mobility*) and conducted research focused on O&M that was funded by the government (National Institutes of Health, National Institute on Disability and Rehabilitation Research) as well as other funding sources (universities). The O&M Archives opened at Maryland School for the Blind. O&M services for infants, toddlers, and preschoolers emerged. In 2000, the O&M certification board moved from the Association for Education and Rehabilitation of the Blind and Visually Impaired (AER) to the Academy for Certification of Vision Rehabilitation and Education Professionals (ACVREP), a national independent certifying body that now certifies O&M specialists, vision rehabilitation therapists, low vision therapists, and assistive technology instructional specialists. AER also offered an approval process for university O&M personnel preparation programs to ensure high instructional standards in the field (Wiener & Siffermann, 2010).

From 2001 to the present, the field of O&M has seen the emergence of certification for O&M instructors who are blind and the establishment of a university training program at Louisiana Tech University to teach individuals nonvisual

techniques using a philosophy called Structured Discovery Cane Travel. These O&M instructors are certified under the national orientation and mobility certification (NOMC) by the National Blindness Professional Certification Board (NBPCB). A plethora of position papers on O&M topics—the use of occlusion in O&M instruction, the roles of O&M specialists in public schools, programs for O&M assistants, O&M for individuals without visual impairment—have been published by the O&M Division of AER. Third-party reimbursement and licensure of O&M specialists have also been issues actively pursued during this period (Wiener & Siffermann, 2010).

The Office of Special Education Programs of the U.S. Department of Education stresses the importance of all educators implementing evidence-based instructional practices with children with special needs (Horner et al., 2005). In various areas of special education research, such as in the education of children with autism, studies using single-subject design methodology have contributed to evidence-based instructional strategies for special education professionals to use with children with disabilities (Kratochwill et al., 2013). However, in the field of O&M, the number of studies using single-subject design is limited. O&M specialists need to conduct intervention studies with students with visual impairments to conceive and add to already established evidence-based practices (Banda, Okungu, Griffin-Shirley, Meeks, & Landa-Vialard, 2015). Finding the time, funding, and knowledge concerning this methodology to engage in this research presents challenges for practitioners and university faculty. (See Appendix A at the back of this book for further discussion of data-collection methods and single-subject designs.)

The field of O&M in the United States has gone through many changes. Some of the concerns and issues that emerged during the early years of the field, such as use of paraeducators, certification of O&M specialists and their roles when serving different populations of individuals with vision loss, licensure, and funding, are still relevant today. Current issues facing the field of O&M are discussed in the last section of this chapter.

Roles and Responsibilities in O&M Service Delivery

Role of the O&M Specialist

O&M services are usually provided by O&M specialists who have university training in this field and are certified by ACVREP or NBPCB. O&M specialists certified by ACVREP are known as certified orientation and mobility specialists (COMSs), while individuals certified by NBPCB are NOMCs (Jacobson, 2013; Wiener & Siffermann, 2010). State departments of education may recognize one or both certifications in deciding who will provide O&M services to children with visual impairments living in their states; some states may have their own O&M certifications or credentials.

O&M specialists teach concept development, sensory training, mobility skills, orientation systems, solicitation of assistance, use of community resources and public transportation, safety issues, decision-making skills, and assistive technology (Fazzi, 2014). They are the only professionals responsible for instructional outcomes related to O&M (Griffin-Shirley & Trusty, 2017; Griffin-Shirley et al., 2000). O&M specialists may provide one-on-one instruction, small-group instruction, collaborative consultation with other team members, emotional support to students and family members, and in-service training to schools, agencies, and the community.

O&M specialists provide instruction that allows students with visual impairments to develop the needed travel skills at the same level as their sighted peers. For example, a first grader who is blind should be able to take a note from the teacher to the principal's office. For young children with visual impairments and additional disabilities, the goal of O&M services is to reduce dependency within a familiar routine.

Role of the Teacher of Students with Visual Impairments

Teachers of students with visual impairments play a valuable role in the provision of O&M services. Their role includes:

- Referring all students with visual impairments for an O&M evaluation
- Coordinating with the O&M specialist in meeting the travel needs of children with visual impairments at home, at school, and in the community, thus meeting the identified educational goals and needs across the ECC
- Conducting joint functional vision evaluations with O&M specialists
- Teaching and reinforcing guide techniques and basic O&M skills such as trailing, protective techniques, room *familiarization*
- Using current O&M language and terms when talking to students and other educational team members
- Promoting the development of concepts and motor skills in children with visual impairments

- Being a second voice on the educational team who understands O&M and the potential of children with visual impairments to develop age-appropriate travel skills
- Orienting students to new classrooms and schools; solving problems in daily routines; reinforcing O&M skills related to travel in daily routes; and supporting students using school buses and other forms of transportation
- Monitoring the safety of students when they are using their O&M skills
- Collaborating with family members and other team members to facilitate, promote, and reinforce travel skills
- Collaborating with the O&M specialist and other team members to make appropriate environmental modifications that enhance safe and independent movement for students with visual impairments
- Co-teaching motor skills, independent living skills, social skills, recreation and leisure skills, and self-determination

Other responsibilities may include co-teaching the use of orientation aids (e.g., tactile maps), optical devices (e.g., telescopes, magnifiers), and sensory training (e.g., auditory training) (Fazzi, 2014; Griffin-Shirley & Trusty, 2017). However, teaching the use of the long cane, adaptive mobility devices, and electronic travel aids, along with complex travel in the community, is the sole responsibility of the O&M specialist.

Roles of Other Professionals

Professionals who are dually certified as teachers of students with visual impairments and

O&M specialists tend to spend more time serving as a teacher rather than acting as an O&M specialist (Griffin-Shirley, McGregor, & Jacobson, 1999). This focus on academic and other specialized needs may result in children with vision loss not receiving the appropriate amount of O&M services that they require. Working with their administrators, dual-certified professionals can advocate for the essential time needed for O&M instruction (Griffin-Shirley, Pogrund, Smith, & Duemer, 2009). Fazzi (2014) recommends that "dually-certified professionals need to be creative in designing programs that are complementary to one another" (p. 270). For example, when teaching a child who is blind to read a tactile map, the dual-certified professional can be working on braille, spatial concepts, and geography simultaneously.

Gabriella Davis

Figure 1.1 Receiving early intervention services can help teach parents how to motivate their child to move.

From infancy to high school graduation, children with visual impairments also receive O&M instruction and support from many other professionals who assist them with their travel (Jacobson, 2013). For example, children with visual impairments who have additional disabilities may receive assistance from physical therapists to learn how to walk and from occupational therapists to improve fine motor coordination. Early intervention services from early childhood specialists can teach parents how to motivate their child to move (see Figure 1.1). Prescription of, and basic instruction in, the use of optical devices is provided by optometrists or ophthalmologists who specialize in low vision (Jacobson, 2013), but O&M specialists expand instruction in the use of such devices into the real world (see Figure 1.2). The roles and responsibilities of these professionals often overlap (see Chapter 11 for information on collaboration). It is important for all these professionals to collaborate with one another as well as with the families to provide children with visual impairments with high-quality instruction and positive outcomes.

Provision of O&M Services

O&M services are provided by an itinerant O&M specialist within the home, school, or community, or at a special-purpose school, such as a residential school, for students who are blind or visually impaired. If transition-age young adults with visual impairments are attending a center-based rehabilitation training program offering vocational training to people who are blind or visually impaired, then

Gabriella Davis

Figure 1.2 Instruction in the use of optical devices, such as using a monocular to read a menu or sign, is important in the acquisition of O&M skills.

O&M instruction is typically provided on-site at the center. Similarly, for adults with visual impairments, O&M services are provided using either an itinerant model (in their home areas) or a center-based model (in a rehabilitation facility).

Models of Instruction

O&M services are largely provided using an itinerant or center-based model (Bina, Naimy, Fazzi, & Crouse, 2010). Each model has advantages and disadvantages (see Sidebar 1.3). In the itinerant model, an O&M specialist travels to students with visual impairments to deliver O&M instruction, usually at their homes or

Advantages and Disadvantages of Models of Instruction

Itinerant Model

Advantages

- O&M training is provided in locations that students frequent; therefore, instruction can be more generalized.
- Educational team members (e.g., family members, general and special education teachers, physical and occupational therapists, speech-language pathologists, nurses) can observe the O&M training provided to students. The O&M specialist is on hand to answer their questions and concerns about the travel abilities and needs of the students.
- Students are in their neighborhood schools, interacting with their nondisabled peers in educational, social, and recreational settings (Swenson, 1995). O&M skills can be practiced and reinforced in all these settings.
- Caseloads can be diverse, encouraging O&M specialists to constantly learn about new syndromes, teaching techniques for students with additional disabilities, strategies to use with infants, and so on. This diversity keeps the job interesting and allows for creative and innovative practices.

Disadvantages

- In many cases, O&M services tend to be minimal (e.g., 60 minutes twice a month), making progress toward meeting student outcomes slow.
- It may be difficult to provide transportation to lesson locations. Each school district has its own policy for transporting students off campus. To get to the mall for a lesson, arrangements may need to be made to use a school bus, taxi, school vehicle, or other form of transportation.

- O&M specialists spend many hours traveling to different locations to meet the students they teach (Griffin-Shirley et al., 1999). For example, in an eight-hour day, the O&M specialist may be involved in only four hours of direct instruction since he or she may spend the other four hours on the road traveling from school to school, covering as much as a 250-mile area.
- It can be difficult to find time to collaborate with students' educational or rehabilitation team members (Griffin-Shirley et al., 2009). Many of these team members are also itinerant service providers, making it difficult to schedule time to formally meet and discuss the progress and concerns of their mutual students.
- The vehicle used by the itinerant O&M specialist becomes an office, holding all student files and equipment. If a specialist does not have a piece of O&M equipment a student needs, the student may have to wait until the next lesson to receive it, which could take several weeks or longer, depending on the specialist's schedule.
- O&M specialists may work with students of all ages, possibly from birth to 22 years. Consequently, the specialist must be knowledgeable about teaching children of all ages with varying eye conditions, intellectual functioning levels, and physical abilities (Griffin-Shirley et al., 2009). Such diversity can be challenging for some O&M specialists who prefer using a more structured curriculum.
- Public relations are a large part of the job. Itinerant professionals have to establish a positive rapport with school-based educational personnel. Building this rapport takes a lot of time and finesse. Interpersonal skills are paramount

SIDEBAR 1.3

when working in an itinerant model with various personnel.

- O&M specialists may feel isolated if they are the only professional serving an entire district or region.

Center-Based Model
Advantages

- All educational team members are located in one place, such as a residential school or private agency, making collaboration easy. Since they are all specialists who work with students who are visually impaired, they have similar educational backgrounds, knowledge, and experiences.
- The residential staff is well versed in O&M techniques students should be using and can reinforce these skills with students after school hours on a daily basis.
- Locations for O&M training are well established within the community. Local store owners are already familiar with students visiting their establishments on lessons to ask for information or purchase items; therefore, interactions between owners and students tend to be very positive.

- Since students typically live on-site, there is no travel time involved for O&M specialists to meet their students.
- O&M training can occur more frequently (e.g., 45 minutes three times a week).
- The demographics at some residential schools are very similar; today the population is primarily children who are blind or visually impaired with additional disabilities. It may be common to see many children with CVI, intellectual disabilities, autism, or cerebral palsy.
- Usually, there are two or more O&M specialists employed at a center. They can share knowledge and work together to address difficult student situations.

Disadvantages

- Generally, O&M instruction is not provided in students' homes and communities. Students have to be able to generalize skills learned at the center and apply them to their home environments, unless the O&M specialist provides follow-up training in their home areas, which does not always happen.
- Family support may be more difficult to obtain if the family lives in a different city or state than where the residential facility is located.

schools. In this model, the itinerant O&M specialist travels from school to school providing O&M services and equipment to students with visual impairments and consulting with educational professionals (Correa-Torres & Howell, 2004; Knott, 2002). In the center-based model, training is provided within a facility (e.g., a special-purpose school for students who are blind or visually impaired) and its surrounding areas (LaGrow & Weessies, 1994). In this model, the center-based O&M professional

provides O&M instruction on-site and does not travel to multiple schools or homes.

Populations Who Receive O&M Services

Individuals who receive O&M services are children and adults who are blind or who have low vision and students with visual and multiple impairments such as deafblindness, physical disabilities, intellectual disabilities, learning disabilities, autism, and health impairments, among others (Geruschat & Smith, 2010; LaGrow & Long, 2011). These individuals may be born with a visual impairment (i.e., congenitally blind or visually impaired) or acquire their visual impairment later in life (i.e., adventitiously blind or visually impaired) from an accident, a degenerative eye condition, tumor, or other cause or trauma, and can range in age from infancy through adulthood (Jacobson, 2013). O&M lessons may involve an infant learning how to reach for a talking stuffed bear, a toddler being taught how to use a cane, or a teenager being instructed in how to call a bus company to obtain the local bus schedule. Individuals are unique; therefore, O&M instruction is designed to meet each person's age-appropriate needs and desires at any given time (LaGrow & Long, 2011).

Legislation Governing O&M Training and Services

Many significant pieces of federal and state legislation have been passed in the last few decades that govern the provision of O&M services for students and adults with visual impairments as well as their safety. The current iteration of the Individuals with Disabilities Education Improvement Act states that O&M services are "provided to blind or visually impaired children by qualified personnel to enable those students to attain systematic orientation to and safe movement within their environments in school, home, and community" (IDEA, 2004, 34 C.F.R. § 300.34[c][7][i]). The following are descriptions of important pieces of legislation as well as examples of how each law affects the provision of

O&M services and the safety of students and travelers.

Individuals with Disabilities Education Act

Originally passed as the Education for all Handicapped Children Act in 1975, the second reauthorization of the law in 1990 changed the name to the Individuals with Disabilities Education Act (IDEA). The main provisions of the 1990 law dealt with transition planning for life after school for students with visual impairments 16 years of age or older, the inclusion of assistive technology devices in the Individualized Education Program (IEP), and requirements that children with disabilities be educated alongside their typically developing peers in the least restrictive environment. In addition, the term "handicapped" was changed to "disabled," person-first language was emphasized (e.g., a student who is blind, not a blind student), and traumatic brain injury and autism were included as new categories under the law (Yell, Rogers, & Rogers, 2012).

The 1997 amendments included the addition of O&M as a related service (supportive services required for a student with a disability to benefit from special education) and Part B, which governs the Assistance to States for the Education of Children with Disabilities program. They also offered mediation to parents prior to due process hearings.

The 2004 reauthorization renamed the law as the Individuals with Disabilities Education Improvement Act (although it is still commonly referred to as IDEA). This reauthorization included some changes in IEP procedures, further clarification regarding least restrictive environment, and a definition of highly qualified teachers who should be providing special education and related services, such as O&M specialists (Spungin & Huebner, 2017).

The response-to-intervention approach was also introduced through IDEA. This approach addresses the diagnosis of a learning disability based on a student's response to a scientifically based intervention rather than a discrepancy model (Yell et al., 2012). A student's educational planning team can then refer the student for an O&M evaluation conducted by an O&M specialist to determine if the student needs O&M instruction.

————

Jake, a 7-year-old with CVI, appears to be missing the curbs in front of his school and the stairs inside the school building. Therefore, Jake's special education teacher is referring him for an O&M evaluation during Jake's next IEP meeting.

Americans with Disabilities Act

The Americans with Disabilities Act (ADA), passed in 1990, was the most far-reaching civil rights legislation ever enacted in the history of disability policy in the United States (Spungin & Huebner, 2017). The ADA prohibited discrimination against individuals with disabilities in the areas of public accommodations, employment, transportation, state and local government services, and telecommunications. The law also stated that accommodations must be barrier-free and accessible for individuals with disabilities. Professionals and educators who work with students with disabilities need to ensure that as students enter the workforce and focus on self-advocacy, they are aware of their rights under the ADA (Yell et al., 2012).

————

Susan, a high school student who is blind, is ready to graduate and is interested in getting a dog guide. She is learning about accommodations in the workplace and what adaptations or modifications she needs to request when applying for jobs. According to the ADA, once she receives her dog guide, Susan can bring her dog guide to her workplace.

Elementary and Secondary Education Act

The Elementary and Secondary Education Act (ESEA) was the first federal law to authorize government spending on programs to support K–12 education. For the first time, this act funded pilot programs for students with disabilities (Yell et al., 2012). Originally passed in 1965 and reauthorized in 2001 as the No Child Left Behind and in 2015 as the Every Student Succeeds Act, it increased educational opportunities for all students, created scholarships for low-income college students, and provided federal grants to state educational agencies to improve the quality of elementary and secondary education with a focus on accountability in achievement gaps among underserved and vulnerable students. States were now held accountable for the achievement of children with and without disabilities.

————

Tena is Hispanic and resides in low-income housing in New York City. When she was in high school, Tena and her guidance counselor discussed her going to college to become an elementary school teacher. However, she did not have sufficient funding to attend school. Her guidance counselor suggested that she apply for federal grant funding for low-income students. She applied and received funding to attend Columbia University.

When Tena was in third grade, a guest speaker named Joe had come to her class with his dog guide, Fred. Joe discussed how Fred was trained and the assistance Fred provided to him when he travelled. Because of her experience with Joe and Fred, Tena decided she wanted to become a reader for students who are blind or visually impaired. During her four years at Columbia, Tena read to several students with visual impairments and loved every minute of it.

Tena graduated from Columbia and became a public-school teacher in New York City for 3 years. During this time, she had children with visual impairments in her classroom who reminded her of Joe and Fred and the college students to whom she read. Tena decided to apply to a university program to train as an O&M specialist. She was accepted and is currently on her way to becoming a vision professional.

Rehabilitation Act

The Rehabilitation Act of 1973 was the first piece of civil rights legislation for children and adults with disabilities that prohibited discrimination on the basis of disability in programs that are run by or that receive funding from the federal government. Under this law, children with disabilities who are at least 16 years old can receive work evaluations, job training, and assistance for locating a job. Supported employment is also available for individuals who are severely disabled and who need ongoing job support in order to succeed in a work setting (Turnbull, Turnbull, Wehmeyer, & Shogren, 2013).

Section 504 of the Rehabilitation Act defines the rights of individuals with disabilities to participate in, and have access to, program benefits and services as well as appropriate accommodations.

―――――

Employment opportunities for teenagers who are blind or visually impaired are offered through a summer program funded by their state vocational rehabilitation agency. Mr. Lacey, an O&M specialist, is teaching Jessica, a 16-year-old student who has retinopathy of prematurity, how to travel from her dormitory to her job at the local senior center.

Assistive Technology Act

The Technology-Related Assistance for Individuals with Disabilities Act, passed in 1988 and reauthorized in 1994, 1998, and in 2004 as the Assistive Technology Act, provides funding to develop statewide information and training programs and direct aid to meet the assistive technology needs of individuals with disabilities of all ages (Bina et al., 2010; Turnbull et al., 2013). Specifically, it requires schools to provide the necessary technology to assist students who are transitioning from one program to another and offer information to students when they are applying for assistive technology loans (Turnbull et al., 2013). Assistive technology can include low- and high-tech devices and can range from items such as canes and wheelchairs to video magnifiers and screen-reading programs.

―――――

Melina, a child with cerebral palsy and CVI, receives a new wheelchair to use because she has outgrown her old one. Mr. Lopez, her O&M specialist, is eager to instruct Melina in how to use a long cane with her wheelchair in her school building, in collaboration with Melina's physical therapist.

Pedestrian Safety Enhancement Act

The Pedestrian Safety Enhancement Act of 2010 mandated that all vehicles on the road, including hybrid and electric cars, must make some noise, although the type and volume of the noise were not specified in the law. The deadline given by the National Highway Traffic Safety Administration for automakers to equip all new hybrid and electric vehicles with sounds that meet the federally determined standard is September 1, 2019. This requirement has significant safety implications not only for the traveler who is blind, but for all pedestrians.

━━━━

Sherry is learning to cross the street at a busy lighted intersection. Her O&M specialist has taught her how to use traffic sounds to align herself before crossing and to cross with the parallel traffic next to her. However, with increasing numbers of quiet hybrid and electric cars on the roads, Sherry is finding it ever more challenging to confidently use the skills she learned in her O&M lessons to safely cross the street.

O&M Evaluation Bill

In Texas, the O&M Evaluation Bill passed in 2013 requires that all students with visual impairments have an O&M evaluation by an O&M specialist for eligibility upon initial referral for special education, and that the O&M specialist be part of the educational team and be involved in the decision of whether a student needs an O&M evaluation at each three-year reevaluation. It is no longer up to the teacher of students with visual impairments or other team members to make a referral for an O&M evaluation in Texas. Other states have similar legislation, but it would be in the best interest of children with visual impairments if all states adopted this legislation.

━━━━

Lily has visual and multiple impairments and has not previously received an O&M evaluation by an O&M specialist since no one on her educational team thought she could benefit from O&M services because of her significant intellectual disability. Once Lily was evaluated by an O&M specialist, however, it was determined that she could learn to use a cane to independently travel around her school.

Evaluation, Program Planning, and Implementation of O&M

Evaluation

All children who are visually impaired or who are suspected of having a visual condition, irrespective of age or other disabilities, should have an O&M evaluation completed by an O&M specialist. Goal 6 of *The National Agenda for the Education of Children and Youths with Visual Impairments, Including Those with Multiple Disabilities* (Huebner, Merk-Adam, Stryker, & Wolffe, 2004) calls for "careful and comprehensive assessments of students with visual impairments" (p. 12) as being essential to instructional planning. Additionally, Goal 8 states, "All educational goals and instruction will address the academic and expanded core curricula based on the assessed needs of each student with visual impairments" (p. 13). As the professional responsible for conducting O&M evaluations for children with visual impairments, O&M specialists determine the type and amount of services needed (Griffin-Shirley, Kelley, & Smith, 2006; Huebner et al., 2004).

The main purposes of an O&M evaluation are to determine eligibility for O&M services for students with visual impairments and to identify students' strengths and needs. During the evaluation, O&M specialists focus on determining a student's current skill level, progress concerning educational goals related to O&M, and the efficacy of an O&M instructional program (Bina et al., 2010). An important part of the evaluation process is the rapport that develops between the O&M specialist and the student (LaGrow & Long, 2011). The student's skill levels are assessed using evaluation tools, observation of the student in a variety of familiar and unfamiliar age-appropriate environments, and interviews with family members, other educational team members, and the student him- or herself, if appropriate. For students who have some functional vision, evaluations should also occur in a variety of lighting conditions and at night. Based on the evaluation results, educational goals and objectives are determined, followed by the development of an instructional program in O&M (LaGrow & Long, 2011).

According to IDEA (2004), evaluations must be administered in the child's native language by trained personnel and be valid, reliable, and standardized. Validity represents the test's ability to assess the construct or skill it claims to measure. Reliability is the consistency of the test over time. For the test to be standardized, the following demographic data of the sample must be taken into account: gender, race, socio-economic status, geographic distribution, and urban or rural residence. It is important that the sample reflect the demographics of the population from which it was drawn.

Many O&M specialists have developed their own checklists or use already developed evaluation tools (Pogrund et al., 2012) or a combination of tools to identify the O&M needs of the students they serve (Bina et al., 2010). See Sidebar 1.4 for a list of O&M evaluation tools. These tools, most of which are criterion-referenced, can be easily downloaded or purchased for record keeping, reporting, and planning. These evaluation tools and strategies assist the O&M specialist in identifying the specific strengths and areas of need concerning the O&M skills of their students with visual impairments. There are currently no validated O&M evaluation tools available. The small population size and extreme heterogeneity of the students who receive O&M services make the development of valid and reliable evaluation tools a challenge for the field.

According to Bina et al. (2010), the O&M evaluation should include "relevant background information, mobility skills proficiency, orientation skill application, conceptual understanding, visual functioning, auditory functioning, . . . communication skills, independent living skills, and social skills and behaviors" (p. 416). Other specific areas concerning background information may include an environmental assessment, psychological and intellectual functioning, the student's cultural background, and family concerns and issues related to independent travel (Bina et al., 2010; Knott, 2002; LaGrow & Long, 2011).

Each evaluation domain has different components. For example, the domain of mobility skills may include prior O&M instruction;

SIDEBAR 1.4

O&M Evaluation Tools

- *Birth-to-6 Orientation and Mobility Inventory* (Maner, Martinez-Cargo, & Anderson, 2016): Evaluates six domains with a numerical score to assess O&M functioning in infants, toddlers, and preschoolers.
- *Comprehensive Initial and Ongoing Evaluation* (Pogrund et al., 2012): Evaluates the level of functioning in O&M of students aged 3–21. Includes orientation skills, mobility skills, and concept development in five environments.
- *CVI Range* (Roman-Lantzy, 2018): Provides an assessment instrument to be used by both teachers of students with visual impairments and O&M specialists to identify the visual characteristics of students with CVI.
- *Developmentally Appropriate Orientation and Mobility* (Anthony, Lowry, Brown, & Hatton, 2004): Is used to complete a family-centered O&M assessment that is then utilized to write a report.
- *INSITE Developmental Checklist* (Morgan & Watkins, 1989): Evaluates many domains of development, including motor skills.
- *Inventory of Purposeful Movement Behaviors* (Anthony, 1992): Evaluates preschoolers, incor-

porating a variety of skills from existing early childhood instruments.

- *The Oregon Project for Preschool Children Who Are Blind or Visually Impaired* (Anderson, Boigon, Davis, & DeWaard, 2007): Evaluates developmental levels of children with visual impairments (primarily those without additional disabilities) in eight areas (cognitive, language, socialization, vision, compensatory skills, self-help, fine motor skills, and gross motor skills), guides the selection of educational goals, and documents the acquisition of skills.
- *Orientation & Mobility Inventory* (NMSBVI, 2012): Evaluates all O&M domains for school-age children who are blind.
- *Preschool Orientation and Mobility Screening* (Dodson-Burk & Lantzy, 2012): Evaluates the O&M skills of children with visual impairments from birth to age 5, with or without additional disabilities.
- *Texas Two-Steps: Successfully Teaching Early Purposeful Skills* (Brown et al., 2018): Early childhood O&M evaluation and curriculum for children with visual impairments from birth to age 5.

Source: Adapted from Griffin-Shirley, N., & Trusty, S. (2017). Orientation and mobility. In M. C. Holbrook, C. Kamei-Hannan, & T. McCarthy (Eds.), *Foundations of education: Vol. II. Instructional strategies for teaching children and youths with visual impairments* (3rd ed., pp. 654–698). New York, NY: AFB Press.

---

movement ability, including a student's integration of reflexes, gait, posture, balance, stamina, and pace; techniques such as guide techniques, basic skills (e.g., trailing, protective techniques) and cane skills; and the areas in which the student uses his or her mobility skills (Bina et al., 2010). Often the evaluation occurs in the child's natural environment (e.g., home, classroom,

school, neighborhood). Upon completion of a thorough O&M evaluation, the O&M specialist writes up a report to share the results with the IEP team. Based on these outcomes, appropriate goals and objectives are recommended, along with the type and amount of service to be provided. (See Appendix B at the back of this book for a sample O&M evaluation report.)

Program Planning

There are several tools O&M specialists can use to recommend intensity of service: the *Orientation & Mobility Visual Impairment Scale of Service Intensity of Texas* (*O&M VISSIT*; Texas Action Committee, 2015) and the *Orientation & Mobility Severity Rating Scale* (O&MSRS) or the *Orientation & Mobility Severity Rating Scale Plus* (O&MSRS+; Michigan Department of Education, 2017a, 2017b). *The O&M VISSIT* is designed to determine the amount and type of O&M service needed based on individual student needs identified from evaluation results. This tool can be used for all students of any age, with any degree of visual impairment, or with any additional disabilities. The Michigan rating scales are two separate scales for determining the need for O&M services, one for students with visual impairments and one for students with visual and multiple impairments. These scales take into consideration a variety of categories including the student's level of vision, use and proficiency of travel tools, and spatial and environmental conceptual understanding, among others.

Goals and objectives related to O&M skills are developed by a collaborative team of professionals, including an O&M specialist, who works with children and their families to meet their specific needs (see Chapter 11 for further information on teams and collaboration). Subsequently, the O&M specialist develops and implements O&M instructional programs to carry out the stated goals and objectives. There are several O&M curricula available that provide a framework for planning and teaching O&M skills to students with visual impairments. The most comprehensive O&M curriculum for students ages 3–21 is *TAPS—Teaching Age-Appropriate Purposeful Skills: An Orientation and Mobility Curriculum for Students with Visual Impairments* (Pogrund et al., 2012). This curriculum provides a wide range of goals and objectives in several environmental domains: home or living, school or campus, residential, and commercial and public transportation. Each objective is accompanied by suggested teaching strategies to serve as a guide for O&M instructional practices. In addition, there are many supplementary ideas and resources in the *TAPS* appendices to enhance specific areas of instruction. There are also other curricula that can be used with younger children that include components of O&M. These include *The Oregon Project for Preschool Children Who Are Blind or Visually Impaired* (Anderson et al., 2007), which includes curricula on gross and fine motor skills as well as concept development, and *Texas Two-Steps: Successfully Teaching Early Purposeful Skills* (Brown et al., 2018), which has a similar format of goals, objectives, and strategies as *TAPS*, but with a focus on working with children from birth through age 5. (See the Resources section in the online AFB Learning Center for more information on the tools mentioned in this chapter.) Ongoing evaluation of instructional programs is imperative to ensure students with visual impairments are making progress (Bina et al., 2010; Pogrund et al., 2012).

Implementation

Single-subject research design has provided educators with systematic data collection and evaluation of an intervention that can contribute to evidence-based practices in the field of O&M (Horner et al., 2005). Data collection can be used to evaluate the effectiveness of O&M instructional programs and to monitor the progress of the O&M skills of children with visual impairments. (See Appendix A at the back of this book for more information on data collection using single-subject design methodology.)

There are a variety of data-collection methods that can be used by O&M specialists to track student progress. They include prompt data sheets, progress data sheets, spreadsheets for behavioral interventions that may be needed for the student to focus on O&M skills, counting simple tallies with a clicker, timing how long a skill takes using a timer, and frequency data sheets, among others. The data collected is then used to modify the O&M instructional program. Modifications in the instructional program may include a change in goals, reinforcers, assistive technology, teaching techniques, delivery method, and teaching environments (Bina et al., 2010). In this age of accountability, it is imperative that O&M specialists and the professionals who work with them keep thorough data on their students' progress throughout O&M instruction.

Jolene, a student who is blind and who has additional disabilities, was not focusing her attention during O&M lessons. It was obvious the correct reinforcer (e.g., praise, a toy, five minutes of play time) for Jolene was not identified by Mr. Gates, her O&M specialist. Prior to working with Jolene, Mr. Gates did not complete a preference assessment. If Mr. Gates had completed the preference assessment, Jolene's primary reinforcer would have been identified prior to starting the lesson and then used during the lesson to keep her attention on the task at hand.

(See Appendix A at the back of this book for information about preference assessments and their importance in O&M instruction.)

Current Issues in the Field of O&M

There are a number of current issues affecting the field of O&M, some related to philosophies and teaching approaches that the field has been struggling with for some time and others that are an outgrowth of changing times outside of the O&M field (see Sidebar 1.5 for a list of current issues affecting the field of O&M). One of the issues includes licensure of O&M specialists, state certification, and reimbursement for O&M services. While O&M services have long been recognized and funded for students within schools as required by special education law, the same cannot be said for adult service providers. Without licensure for O&M specialists, it will be difficult to obtain third-party (e.g., Medicare, Medicaid, private insurance) reimbursement for O&M services for adults with visual impairments. Licensure is typically done state by state, and with the small number of O&M specialists in each state, it can be hard to justify the expense of a licensing administration in each state such as those that exist for other professionals like physical and occupational therapists and speech-language pathologists.

The complex built environment in which we live today (e.g., channelized turn lanes, roundabouts, quiet hybrid and self-driving cars) also presents many challenges for O&M professionals, specifically regarding the impact it has on their students who are blind. For example, a self-driving car may bring up many questions, such as, When will it be available for people who are blind to drive? Will the car accurately recognize a person who is blind crossing a street with a cane? What laws will be developed regarding this type of car? Additionally,

SIDEBAR 1.5

Current Issues Affecting the Field of O&M

- Updating the O&M Code of Ethics to make it current with practice
- Passing state licensure and state certification for O&M specialists
- Obtaining third-party, Medicaid, and Medicare reimbursement for O&M services
- Hiring O&M assistants in public schools
- Using the conventional O&M approach and structured discovery model of O&M instruction
- Determining when to use occlusion during lessons
- Teaching O&M to students who have disabilities but do not have a visual impairment
- Supporting people with disabilities providing O&M instruction
- Advocating for financial support of university personnel preparation programs
- Conducting research on evidence-based practices for the practitioner

- Measuring efficacy of O&M instruction; need for valid and reliable evaluation tools that are precise enough to measure O&M skills
- Determining when to use individual versus group lessons
- Recognizing the effect of complex built environment features (e.g., roundabouts) and quiet electric and hybrid vehicles on O&M instruction
- Acknowledging the need for environmental modifications, yet recognizing when they may not be needed
- Valuing the importance of early intervention O&M instruction
- Understanding how to teach veterans blinded by IEDs, which can result in traumatic brain injury
- Supporting passage of legislation by all states to provide O&M evaluations and services to all children who are visually impaired from birth to age 22

practitioners are still grappling with ongoing professional issues, such as hiring O&M assistants, determining whether to use occlusion during lessons, advocating for financial support of university personnel preparation programs, conducting and publishing evidence-based research that informs the practitioner how to teach O&M skills, deciding when to use individual versus group lessons, supporting individuals with disabilities becoming O&M specialists, and updating the O&M Code of Ethics (Wiener & Siffermann, 2010).

A relatively new challenge facing adult service providers in the VA is how to teach O&M skills to blinded veterans who have returned home from wars in the Middle East and Afghanistan and who were injured by improvised explosive devices (IEDs). These veterans often have additional problems related to traumatic brain injuries that can affect their memory, spatial awareness, and emotional stability, so traditional O&M strategies used in VA rehabilitation centers may not always work with this population (Tanielian & Jaycox, 2008).

Legislation to provide O&M evaluations and services to all children who are visually impaired from birth to age 21 (or 22 if the student turns 22 while in the last year of an educational program) should be passed by all states. There are far too many infants, toddlers, preschoolers, students with low vision, and students with a wide range of multiple impairments who have not had an O&M evaluation to assess their O&M needs, and a far larger number of students who have never received any O&M services because there is an assumption that they do not need them. The reality is that many of these students could benefit greatly from O&M instruction at various points throughout their educational experience, and they have the right to be evaluated by a qualified O&M specialist for this determination to be made. To provide an effective assessment, valid and reliable O&M assessment tools need to be developed that can effectively measure O&M skills.

There are ongoing differences of opinion regarding the best instructional approach to take when teaching O&M skills. Most university training programs teach conventional O&M techniques including the use of functional vision to enhance travel, which does not emphasize discovery learning. In the structured-discovery approach, attitude is believed to be the most important part of effective travel. Rather than focusing on teaching techniques in a sequential manner, as proposed in more traditional models of O&M instruction, the instructor's role is to encourage the student to discover methods that will solve orientation problems. The instructor encourages learning through self-discovery and emphasizes self correction of errors (Pogrund et al., 2012). Use of full occlusion by wearing a blindfold during training is supported in this model as a way to build confidence and learn nonvisual skills first. Both models have merit and, in most cases, a combination of the two models, based on individual student needs, is the best instructional approach.

Early intervention O&M instruction is a growing area of interest and importance for young children with visual impairments. In the early years of the field, no consideration was given to O&M being of value to infants, toddlers, and preschoolers. But in recent years, O&M services have been provided on a more regular basis for these young children (Anthony et al., 2002; Dewald et al., 2015). During the first year of life, the development of purposeful or intentional movement is a central focus. The O&M specialist has an important role in supporting infants with visual impairments and their families by providing encouragement in movement and in acquiring information. The O&M specialist also provides support to families about the needs of their children with visual impairments as well as modifications to traditional O&M techniques to meet the unique needs of these children.

While the introduction of canes to toddlers and preschoolers who are blind or visually impaired is commonplace now, it was groundbreaking in the late 1980s (Pogrund & Rosen, 1989) when the first open dialogue about the positive benefits of O&M instruction and cane usage for young children began. Having the expertise of an O&M specialist on any early intervention team is of significant value for a young child with a visual impairment, as more evidence-based practices, evaluation tools, and curricula address the O&M needs of this population (see Figure 1.3).

The ongoing personnel shortage in the field of O&M is another critical issue as the number of children with visual impairments, as well as the number of older adults with visual impairments, continues to grow. At the same time, many vision professionals are nearing retirement age, and it is hard for personnel

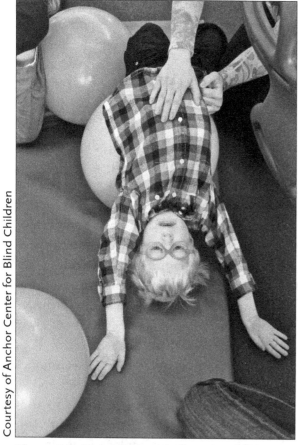

Courtesy of Anchor Center for Blind Children

Figure 1.3 The O&M specialist provides support to families about the needs of their children with visual impairments as well as modifications to traditional O&M techniques to meet the unique needs of these children.

Jenelle Racher

Figure 1.4 Accessible pedestrian signals, which include pushbuttons and audible information, alert travelers with visual impairments when it is time to cross an intersection.

preparation programs to keep up with the demand of hiring O&M specialists (DeMario & Heinze, 2001). "Personnel shortages are due to increasing demand, inadequate supply, and high attrition rates" (Ludlow, Conner, & Schechter, 2005, p. 15). Funding at the federal level for O&M programs varies from year to year, and over the past fifty years, O&M programs have come and gone once they no longer had the support of federal grant funding (Silberman, Ambrose-Zaken, Corn, & Trief, 2004). Some states have advocated for state funds to be earmarked

for personnel preparation of vision professionals. This strategy has increased the capacity of O&M specialists to meet personnel shortage needs in those states.

Another controversial issue in the field of O&M is whether environmental modifications should be made or if travelers who are blind or visually impaired should learn to adjust to environmental features and architectural barriers without any modifications. One of the classic areas of disagreement concerns whether *accessible pedestrian signals* (APSs; see Figure 1.4) should be installed at intersections to alert the traveler with a visual impairment (either through audible or vibrotactile means) that it is time to cross the street. Many O&M specialists and some consumers who are blind support the installation of such devices at most major intersections while others feel they are not necessary and that the traveler should just adapt to the traffic sounds at intersections. Similar arguments are made for and against the development of currency that can be distinguished tactilely.

Summary

The field of O&M has a long history; however, it is a fairly new field in the United States, where it has strong ties to the U.S. Department of Veterans Affairs. Once use of the long cane by adults who were blind or visually impaired had been well established, professionals teaching children with visual impairments began instructing their students in its use. Today, O&M services are provided to both children and adults with visual impairments. Teams of professionals are integral in teaching and supporting these individuals to travel independently. Legislation concerning O&M instruction and services has been passed, and research is being conducted in many areas of O&M, including the efficacy of O&M instruction and ways to evaluate and track student progress.

References

Americans with Disabilities Act of 1990, Pub. L. No. 101-336 (1990).

Anderson, S., Boigon, S., Davis, K., & DeWaard, C. (2007). *The Oregon Project for Preschool Children Who Are Blind or Visually Impaired* (6th ed.). Medford: Southern Oregon Education Service District.

Anthony, T. L. (1992). *Inventory of purposeful movement behaviors.* Denver: Colorado Department of Education, Special Education Services Unit.

Anthony, T. L., Bleier, H., Fazzi, D. L., Kish, D., & Pogrund, R. L. (2002). Mobility focus: Developing early skills for orientation and mobility. In R. L. Pogrund & D. L. Fazzi (Eds.), *Early focus: Working with young children who are blind or visually impaired and their families* (2nd ed., pp. 326–404). New York, NY: AFB Press.

Anthony, T. L., Lowry, S. S., Brown, C. J., & Hatton, D. D. (Eds.). (2004). *Developmentally appropriate orientation and mobility.* OSEP Grant Project H325B00003. Chapel Hill: University of North Carolina at Chapel Hill, FPG Child Development Institute, Early Intervention Training Center for Infants and Toddlers with Visual Impairments.

Assistive Technology Act of 2004, Pub. L. No. 108-364 (2004).

Banda, D. R., Okungu, P. A., Griffin-Shirley, N., Meeks, M. K., & Landa-Vialard, O. (2015). Teaching orientation and mobility skills for students with autism and visual impairments in public schools: A data-based study. *International Journal of Orientation and Mobility, 7,* 34–43.

Bart, O., Katz, N., Weiss, P. L., & Josman, N. (2008). Street crossing by typically developed children in real and virtual environments. *OTJR: Occupation, Participation and Health, 28*(2), 1–8.

Bina, M. J., Naimy, B. J., Fazzi, D. L., & Crouse, R. J. (2010). Administration, assessment, and program planning for orientation and mobility services. In W. R. Wiener, R. L. Welsh, & B. B. Blasch (Eds.), *Foundations of orientation and mobility: Vol. I. History and theory* (3rd ed., pp. 389–433). New York, NY: AFB Press.

Bledsoe, C. W. (2010). The originators of orientation and mobility training. In W. R. Wiener, R. L. Welsh, & B. B. Blasch (Eds.), *Foundations of orientation and mobility: Vol. I. History and theory* (3rd ed., pp. 434–485). New York, NY: AFB Press.

Brown, J., Hallak, T., Garrett, M., Nelson, G., Sewell, D., Uriegas, O., . . . Wood, M. (2018). *Texas two-steps: Successfully teaching early purposeful skills.* Austin: Texas School for the Blind and Visually Impaired.

Cmar, J. L. (2015). Orientation and mobility skills and outcome expectations as predictors of employment for young adults with visual impairments. *Journal of Visual Impairment & Blindness, 109*(2), 95–106.

Correa-Torres, S. M., & Howell, J. J. (2004). Facing the challenges of itinerant teaching: Perspectives and challenges from the field. *Journal of Visual Impairment & Blindness, 98*(7), 420–433.

DeMario, N. C., & Heinze, T. (2001). The status of distance education in personnel preparation programs in visual impairment. *Journal of Visual Impairment & Blindness, 95*(9), 525–532.

Dewald, H. P., Faris, C., Borg, K. S., Maner, J., Martinez-Cargo, L., & Carter, M. (2015). Expanding the frontiers of orientation and mobility for infants and toddlers in New Mexico and Utah. *Journal of Visual Impairment & Blindness, 109*(6), 502–507.

Dodson-Burk, B., & Lantzy, C. (2012). *Preschool orientation and mobility screening* (2nd ed.). Alexandria, VA: Association for Education and Rehabilitation of the Blind and Visually Impaired.

Education for All Handicapped Children Act, Pub. L. No. 94-142 (1975).

Elementary and Secondary Education Act, Pub. L. No. 89-10 (1965).

Elementary and Secondary Education Act (No Child Left Behind), Pub. L. No. 107-110 (2001).

Every Student Succeeds Act, Pub. L. No. 114-95 (2015).

Fazzi, D. L. (2014). Orientation and mobility. In C. B. Allman & S. Lewis (Eds.), *ECC essentials: Teaching the expanded core curriculum to students with visual impairments* (pp. 248–282). New York, NY: AFB Press.

Franck, L., Haneline, R., Brooks, A., & Whitstock, R. (2010). Dog guides for orientation and mobility. In W. R. Wiener, R. L. Welsh, & B. B. Blasch (Eds.), *Foundations of orientation and mobility: Vol. I. History and theory* (3rd ed., pp. 277–295). New York, NY: AFB Press.

Geruschat, D. R., & Smith, A. J. (2010). Low vision for orientation and mobility. In W. R. Wiener, R. L. Welsh, & B. B. Blasch (Eds.), *Foundations of orientation and mobility: Vol. I. History and theory* (3rd ed., pp. 63–83). New York, NY: AFB Press.

Goodman, W. (1989). *Mobility training for people with disabilities: Children and adults with physical, mental, visual, and hearing impairments can learn to travel.* Springfield, IL: Charles C Thomas.

Griffin-Shirley, N., Kelley, P., & Smith, D. (2006). *The development of an orientation and mobility evaluation (DOME) for children and adults with blindness and visual impairment.* Unpublished manuscript.

Griffin-Shirley, N., McGregor, D., & Jacobson, W. H. (1999). Survey of dual-certified orientation and mobility instructors. *Journal of Visual Impairment & Blindness, 93*(3), 133–139.

Griffin-Shirley, N., Pogrund, R. L., Smith, D. W., & Duemer, L. (2009). A three-phase qualitative study of dual-certified vision education professionals in the Southwest United States. *Journal of Visual Impairment & Blindness, 103*(6), 354–366.

Griffin-Shirley, N., & Trusty, S. (2017). Orientation and mobility. In M. C. Holbrook, C. Kamei-Hannan, & T. McCarthy (Eds.), *Foundations of education: Vol. II. Instructional strategies for teaching children and youths with visual impairments* (3rd ed., pp. 654–698). New York, NY: AFB Press.

Griffin-Shirley, N., Trusty, S., & Rickard, R. (2000). Orientation and mobility. In A. J. Koenig & M. C. Holbrook (Eds.), *Foundations of education: Vol. II. Instructional strategies for teaching children and youths with visual impairments* (2nd ed., pp. 529–568). New York, NY: AFB Press.

Hill, E., & Ponder, P. (1976). *Orientation and mobility techniques: A guide for the practitioner.* New York, NY: American Foundation for the Blind.

Hill, E. W. (1986). Orientation and mobility. In G. T. Scholl (Ed.), *Foundations of education for blind and visually handicapped children and youth* (pp. 315–340). New York, NY: American Foundation for the Blind.

Horner, R. H., Carr, E. G., Halle, J., McGee, G., Odom, S., & Wolery, M. (2005). The use of single-subject research to identify evidence-based practice in special education. *Exceptional Children, 71*(2), 165–179.

Huebner, K. M., Merk-Adam, B., Stryker, D., & Wolffe, K. (2004). *The national agenda for the education of children and youths with visual impairments, including those with multiple disabilities* (Rev. ed.). New York, NY: AFB Press.

Individuals with Disabilities Education Act (IDEA), Pub. L. No. 101-467 (1990).

Individuals with Disabilities Education Act Amendments of 1997, Pub. L. No. 105-17 (1997).

Individuals with Disabilities Education Improvement Act (IDEA), 20 U.S.C. § 1400 (2004).

Jacobson, W. H. (2013). *The art and science of teaching orientation and mobility to persons with visual impairments* (2nd ed.). New York, NY: AFB Press.

Johnson, L. B. (1965). *Public papers of the president of the United States: Lyndon B. Johnson, 1963–1964.* Washington, DC: Office of the Federal Register.

Knott, N. I. (2002). *Teaching orientation and mobility in the schools: An instructor's companion.* New York, NY: AFB Press.

Kratochwill, T. R., Hitchcock, J. H., Horner, R. H., Levin, J. R., Odom, S. L., Rindskopf, D. M., & Shadish, W. R. (2013). Single-case intervention research design standards. *Remedial and Special Education, 34*(1), 26–38.

LaGrow, S. J., & Long, R. G. (2011). *Orientation and mobility: Techniques for independence* (2nd ed.). Alexandria, VA: Association for Education and Rehabilitation of the Blind and Visually Impaired.

LaGrow, S. J., & Weessies, M. (1994). *Orientation and mobility: Techniques for independence.* Palmerston, New Zealand: Dunmore Publishing.

Ludlow, B. L., Conner, D., & Schechter, J. (2005). Low incidence disabilities and personnel preparation for rural areas: Current status and future trends. *Rural Special Education Quarterly, 24*(3), 15–24.

Maner, J., Martinez-Cargo, L., & Anderson, D. L. (2016). *Birth-to-6 Orientation and Mobility Inventory.* Alamogordo: New Mexico School for the Blind and Visually Impaired.

Michigan Department of Education, Low Incidence Outreach. (2017a). *Orientation & Mobility Severity Rating Scale (O&MSRS).* Lansing, MI: Author. Retrieved from https://mdelio.org/blind-visually-impaired/severity-rating-scales

Michigan Department of Education, Low Incidence Outreach. (2017b). *Orientation & Mobility Severity Rating Scale Plus (O&MSRS+).* Lansing, MI: Author. Retrieved from https://mdelio.org/blind-visually-impaired/severity-rating-scales

Morgan, E., & Watkins, S. (1989). *INSITE developmental checklist: Assessment of developmental skills for young multihandicapped sensory impaired children.* North Logan, UT: Hope Publishing.

New Mexico School for the Blind and Visually Impaired (NMSBVI). (2012). *Orientation & Mobility Inventory.* Alamogordo, NM: Author. Retrieved from www.nmsbvi.k12.nm.us/WEB/O&M_INVENTORY/O&M_Inventory.htm

O&M Evaluation Bill, Texas Education Code C § 30.002, Education for Children with Visual Impairments H.B. 590 (2013).

Pedestrian Safety Enhancement Act of 2010, Pub. L. No. 111-373 (2010).

Pogrund, R., Sewell, D., Anderson, H., Calaci, L., Cowart, M. F., Gonzalez, C. M., . . . Roberson-Smith, B. (2012). *TAPS—Teaching age-appropriate purposeful skills: An orientation and mobility curriculum for students with visual impairments* (3rd ed.). Austin: Texas School for the Blind and Visually Impaired.

Pogrund, R. L., & Rosen, S. J. (1989). The preschool blind child can be a cane user. *Journal of Visual Impairment & Blindness, 83*(9), 431–439.

Rehabilitation Act of 1973, 29 U.S.C. § 701 (1973).

Roman-Lantzy, C. (2018). *Cortical visual impairment: An approach to assessment and intervention* (2nd ed.). New York, NY: AFB Press.

Sapp, W., & Hatlen, P. (2010). The expanded core curriculum: Where we have been, where we are going, and how we can get there. *Journal of Visual Impairment & Blindness, 104*(6), 338–348.

Silberman, R. K., Ambrose-Zaken, G., Corn, A. L., & Trief, E. (2004). Profile of personnel preparation programs in visual impairments and their faculty: A status report. *Journal of Visual Impairment & Blindness, 98*(12), 741–756.

Spungin, S. J., & Huebner, K. M. (2017). Historical perspectives. In M. C. Holbrook, T. McCarthy, & C. Kamei-Hannan (Eds.), *Foundations of education: Vol. I. History and theory of teaching children and youths with visual impairments* (3rd ed., pp. 3–49). New York, NY: AFB Press.

Swenson, A. M. (1995). Itinerant teaching: An insider's view. *RE:view, 27*(3), 113–116.

Tanielian, T., & Jaycox, L. H. (Eds.). (2008). *Invisible wounds of war: Psychological and cognitive injuries, their consequences, and services to assist recovery.* Santa Monica, CA: RAND Corporation.

Texas Action Committee for the Education of Students with Visual Impairments, Service Intensity Subcommittee. (2015). *O&M VISSIT: Orientation & Mobility Visual Impairment Scale of Service Intensity of Texas.* Austin, TX: Author. Retrieved from http://www.tsbvi.edu/o-m-vissit

Turnbull, A., Turnbull, R., Wehmeyer, M. L., & Shogren, K. A. (2013). *Exceptional lives: Special education in today's schools* (7th ed.). Upper Saddle River, NJ: Pearson Education.

Tuttle, D. W., & Tuttle, N. R. (2004). *Self-esteem and adjusting with blindness: The process of responding to life's demands* (3rd ed.). Springfield, IL: Charles C Thomas.

Uslan, M., Hill, E., & Peck, A. (1989). *The profession of orientation and mobility in the 1980s: The AFB competency study.* New York, NY: AFB Press.

Wiener, W. R., & Siffermann, E. (2010). The history and progression of the profession of orientation and mobility. In W. R. Wiener, R. L. Welsh, & B. B. Blasch (Eds.), *Foundations of orientation and mobility: Vol. I. History and theory* (3rd ed., pp. 486–532). New York, NY: AFB Press.

Wolffe, K., & Kelly, S. M. (2011). Instruction in areas of the expanded core curriculum linked to transition outcomes for students with visual impairments. *Journal of Visual Impairment & Blindness, 105*(6), 340–349.

Yell, M. L., Rogers, D., & Rogers, E. L. (2012). The history of the law and children with disabilities. In M. L. Yell (Ed.), *The law and special education* (3rd ed., pp. 45–62). Upper Saddle River, NJ: Pearson Education.

2

Concept Development

Wendy Sapp

Questions to Guide Your Reading of This Chapter

➤ What are the five types of orientation and mobility (O&M) concepts that students with visual impairments need to learn?

➤ Why is concept development important for children with visual impairments?

➤ What unique roles do O&M specialists play in concept development for students with visual impairments?

➤ What are the advantages of partners collaborating to support the concept development needed for O&M?

Learning to direct one's own mental processes with the aid of words or signs is an integral part of the process of concept formation. (Vygotsky, 1986, p. 108)

Concepts serve as the building blocks of more complex tasks and skills. Concepts are the mental representations that allow people to identify, organize, make inferences about, and build connections between experiences, including people, places, things, events, and actions. A clear and complete understanding of concepts is critical for students to be successful in orientation and mobility (O&M). This chapter explores how age and developmental level affect concept development and discusses the categories of concepts most important for O&M, tools for evaluating O&M concepts, and instructional and collaborative strategies for teaching O&M concepts.

Development and the Effect of Visual Impairment

Human development is a remarkable, unfolding process that continues throughout the life span. The development of children is a continuous process consisting of stages at which specific skills and concepts are typically mastered. For children with typical vision, concept development usually follows a regular and predictable pattern, with vision serving as a unifying sense to help children understand their world. When children experience visual impairment or blindness, however, they must be provided with alternative methods for accessing their world and developing their cognitive abilities.

Urie Bronfenbrenner developed an *ecological systems theory* that proposes that a child's characteristics as well as his or her social and physical environments interact to promote or hinder the child's development (Bronfenbrenner, 1979;

SIDEBAR 2.1
Key Terms

Body concepts Understanding one's body parts, body movements, and body functions.

Cognitive constructivism Educational theory that suggests individuals cannot be given knowledge but rather must construct their understanding from interactions with the world.

Concepts Mental representations that allow people to identify, organize, make inferences about, and build connections between experiences, including people, places, things, events, and actions.

Developmental stage theory Idea proposed by Piaget that states that cognitive development occurs from the interaction of biological maturation and environmental experience.

Ecological systems theory Model proposed by Bronfenbrenner that states that a child's characteristics and social and physical environments interact to influence development.

Environmental concepts Awareness and understanding of one's surroundings that enhance the ability to travel safely and independently.

Spatial concepts Awareness and understanding of the space around an individual, including cardinal directions and notions of laterality and directionality.

---

see Sidebar 2.1 for definitions of key terms). According to Bronfenbrenner's theory, human development is influenced by both internal and external factors. The development of children with visual impairments is shaped by internal characteristics that educators cannot control, such as degree of visual impairment and presence or absence of additional disabilities. How-

ever, development is also affected by factors that can be influenced, such as the physical environment a child experiences, the expectations of important adults such as parents, caregivers, and teachers, and opportunities to interact with other people and with their environment in meaningful ways. If the physical and social environments are appropriate, a child with a visual impairment and no additional disabilities is expected to develop at a rate and in a sequence similar to that of typically sighted children, though some skills may be acquired in a different order (Warren & Hatton, 2003).

Looking more specifically at developmental sequence, Jean Piaget developed one of the most commonly accepted theories of cognitive development in children, often referred to as *developmental stage theory* (Piaget & Inhelder, 1969; Wadsworth, 2003). Piaget proposed that cognitive development occurs from the interaction of biological maturation and environmental experience. He divided human development into four main stages: sensorimotor, preoperational, concrete operational, and formal operational.

Piaget's Stages of Cognitive Development

Sensorimotor Stage

The sensorimotor stage begins at birth and continues until a child develops language. In the sensorimotor stage, children learn about their world by coordinating their sensory input, such as vision and hearing, with motor experiences, such as grasping and sucking. During this stage, a child moves from reflexive to intentional movements to interact with the environment (see Chapter 3 for more information on reflexes and purposeful movement). For children with visual impairments, cognitive development is shaped by the absence of visual input or the limited visual input that the child receives. Without consistent, meaningful visual information, children with visual impairments rely on other senses to help them understand and interact with their world, resulting in a need for different experiences to encourage development. Piaget stated that the most important milestone in the sensorimotor stage is the development of object permanence, an understanding that objects continue to exist even when the child cannot see or hear them. Object permanence is an especially important O&M concept for infants and toddlers with visual impairments. Mastering object permanence allows children with visual impairments to begin to understand that the world exists beyond their reach and enables them to develop a mental representation of reality. Children who are born blind are typically delayed in the development of object permanence (around 15 months versus 6 months for a child with typical vision), and they often have an atypical sequence of development of this cognitive skill.

Preoperational Stage

The preoperational stage lasts from the emergence of language, at around 2 years of age, until approximately 7 years of age. Children in this stage can think in images and symbols, as indicated by the use of language, and they can engage in symbolic and imaginative play, but they cannot yet use formal logic. In this stage, children begin to ask many questions and try to understand why things are the way they are, a process that serves as a stepping stone to developing formal logic. Several characteristics are common in children of this age. Egocentrism is exhibited from 2 to 4 years of age and involves an inability to consider perspectives (physical or mental) other than the child's own. Centration, which is typically present throughout the preoperational stage, occurs when a child focuses on one characteristic of a situation rather than noticing multiple characteristics at once. Children in the preoperational stage typically do not demonstrate the understanding of conservation, the recognition that a substance can remain the same in different formats, such as the fact that a given amount of liquid remains the same even when poured into differently shaped containers.

Children with visual impairments benefit from support in moving through the preoperational stage of development. Visual impairment reduces the amount of information children receive about the world around them, especially the world beyond what they can touch. Because children with visual impairments receive less information about the world that is distant from them than children with typical sight, the sensory input they receive about themselves, as opposed to about the world around them, is greater than that received by children with typical sight. Children who are blind or visually impaired sometimes remain in the preoperational stage longer than children with typical sight, thus demonstrating egocentrism longer. Children with visual impairments need extensive, repeated interactions with the world around them to help them move beyond an egocentric understanding of their environment. Repeated interactions with the world around them are also necessary for children with visual impairments to develop in other aspects during this stage, such as moving beyond centration and developing an understanding of conservation. Since children with visual impairments can rarely learn through watching the world around them, they need to interact with concrete materials to explore and develop these concepts (Luckner, Bruce, & Ferrell, 2016).

Concrete Operational Stage

The concrete operational stage lasts from ages 7 to 11. In this stage, children begin to use formal logic, but to make sense of the logic, they typically require concrete examples rather than abstract tasks. Children with visual impairments need concrete interactive experiences to gain the specific cognitive skills and use of logic that develop during this stage. Reverse thinking begins in this stage and refers to the ability to reverse an action or thought process. For example, reverse thinking allows a child who knows a simple route from the front of the school to the classroom (walk to the first hallway, turn right, classroom is second door on right) to reverse this route to return to the front of the school (turn left out of the classroom, walk to the first hallway, turn left and end at the school entrance). At this stage, children are able to understand conservation and realize that the same amount of fluid exists in a short, wide glass as a tall, narrow glass when both are measured and poured in the same way, or that the same quantity of material can be formed into different shapes without losing the original amount.

Formal Operational Stage

The formal operational stage takes place from age 11 to the mid- to late teens. In this stage, children are capable of abstract thought, metacognition (thinking about thinking), and advanced problem solving. If children with visual impairments have had sufficient experiences and interactions during the earlier stages of development, they usually develop skills in the formal operational stage easily, though specific gaps in knowledge and understanding may become apparent as the adolescent applies previous knowledge to new situations.

It is critical that teachers and other service providers tailor instruction to a child's appropriate developmental level and that children with visual impairments be provided with extensive, hands-on experiences at all stages to allow them to develop skills and knowledge. When children have additional disabilities, they may progress through these stages more slowly, so a child's cognitive developmental stage should be determined through evaluation rather than assumed based on the child's age. On the other hand, it is also important to use age-appropriate materials and activities within the child's developmental level.

Concept Development in O&M

This chapter focuses on the development of concepts necessary for O&M, specifically body concepts, spatial concepts, environmental concepts, time and distance concepts, and concepts to minimize risk. The development of accurate and complete concepts is critical for children with visual impairments to be successful as independent travelers. Concepts allow children to know where they are in space, understand there is a place they want to go, and develop a plan to travel safely from one location to the next.

To develop concepts, children must have real-world experiences. *Cognitive constructivism* is the educational philosophy that individuals cannot be given knowledge but rather must construct their own understanding of the world through learning. According to cognitive constructivism, learning must have two components: learning should actively engage learners with other people and with their own environment and learning should be whole and authentic rather than consisting of isolated skills. As described by Smith (2012), when learning a symbol (word, object, action), the child must experience the real "thing" together with the symbol in a meaningful way. O&M instruction is most effective when it actively engages the child in real-world learning.

Though all of the concepts discussed in the following sections are important, they are not prerequisites for learning O&M skills. For example, a child does not need to be able to point to or name his or her hand to be able to hold a cane or an adaptive mobility device in that hand, nor does a child need to be able to follow directions about putting objects in front of each other to be able to hold the cane in front of his or her body. Depending on the situation, students may learn concepts first, then skills, or students may learn skills and concepts concurrently as they construct their understanding of the world around them.

Body Concepts

Shortly after birth, children begin to develop *body concepts*, including understanding their body parts, how their bodies move, and what they can do with their bodies. Although infants with typical sight may enjoy gazing at their hands and examining how they move and touch, children who are blind or visually impaired can feel, smell, and taste their hands but they cannot see them, and children who have low vision may not be able to see their hands clearly or see all parts of their hands at one time. Beginning at birth, it is critical for children with visual impairments to have experiences to help them learn about their bodies through the senses they have available to them. In general, children proceed from identifying major body

parts (e.g., head, arms, legs) to smaller body parts (e.g., toes, belly button, ears) to less-defined body parts (e.g., waist, ankle). Along with learning their own body parts, children also learn that other people have similar body parts. Understanding body parts is critical for children with visual impairments to be able to follow O&M instructions.

As children with visual impairments learn that they have distinct body parts, they begin to learn how those body parts move. They discover that elbows bend, fingers curl, and wrists rotate. When typically sighted children see objects or people that interest them, they are encouraged to reach for them or move toward them, thus prompting an understanding of how their bodies move. Without that consistent, clear visual input, children with visual impairments often move less than children with vision, resulting in fewer opportunities for developing motor skills and concepts about their bodies. Knowledge of body movements is critical for efficient, graceful mobility, including walking and using devices such as canes. Sidebar 2.2 lists some of the body concepts that children who are visually impaired need to learn.

Spatial Concepts

As children with visual impairments develop an awareness that their bodies are separate from the world around them, they begin to understand concepts of space (see Figure 2.1). Spatial awareness involves laterality, directionality, and cardinal directions. Laterality refers to identifying the right or left side of one's body or of a structure, such as a child's left hand or the right side of a table. Laterality is the location of the left and right side from the child's own perspective. This includes an awareness of turning right and left to reach a destination.

SIDEBAR 2.2

Body Concepts

The following is a partial list of body concepts that children who are blind or visually impaired need to learn. (For a complete listing of body concepts, refer to the assessments provided in Table 2.1.)

Major Body Parts

- Arms
- Legs
- Head
- Trunk

Smaller Body Parts

- Ears
- Toes
- Fingers
- Belly button

Less-Defined Body Parts

- Wrists
- Ankles
- Elbows
- Knees
- Waist

Functions of Body Parts

- Hear with ears
- See with eyes
- Smell with nose
- Taste with tongue
- Feel with hands

Movement of Body Parts

- Ankles and wrists rotate in a circular motion
- Knees and elbows bend in one direction

Directionality refers to understanding the location of objects in space in relation to one another, such as a toy is in the box, the cup is on the table, or the door is to the right of the chair. Directionality also includes understanding the left and right side of others, such as recognizing that when you face someone, that person's right hand is in front of your left side. Cardinal directions, the main points on a compass (north, east, south, west), provide an important way to improve spatial awareness for many people with visual impairments when applied to the real world rather than if used only with a map. Children typically learn to apply spatial concepts in relation to their own bodies first (for example, understanding a toy is behind them or identifying their right hand). Later they can apply the concept to another object or person, such as placing a toy behind a box or recognizing another person's left and right side. Sidebar 2.3 provides a list of the *spatial concepts* children need to learn to move and travel safely and independently.

Students then begin to learn what cardinal directions are and how to use them as an orientation aid when moving through space. Although sighted children typically do not fully grasp the concept of cardinal directions until around ages 8–10 (Clipson-Boyles, 2000), many children with visual impairments learn these concepts earlier (after understanding degree turns such as 90- and 180-degree turns) because they are useful for orientation purposes and are used more frequently in their O&M instruction. Teaching cardinal directions can be an abstract concept for many students, yet it is an important one to learn as early as possible. Students with visual impairments first need to understand that there is nothing visible in geographic directions and that they do not leave

SIDEBAR 2.3

Spatial Concepts

The following is a list of spatial concepts that children who are blind or visually impaired need to learn to travel safely and independently.

Laterality (Left and Right)

- Of self
- Of objects
- Of other people

Directionality

- Right and left from the perspective of other people
- Positional concepts (e.g., in, on, under, beside, behind, etc.)
  - Relation to self (e.g., put your hand on top of your head)
  - Self-to-object relationship (e.g., stand beside the door)
  - Object-to-object relationship (e.g., put the paper under the book)

Cardinal Directions

- North
- East
- South
- West

Wendy Sapp

Figure 2.1 A child who is deafblind stretches a tube above her head as she explores the concepts of up and down.

"north" behind once they walk away from it. The concept of cardinal directions being a constant reference point because they are always in the same place needs to be learned. Tactile maps, tactile compasses, or the face of a clock can be used initially to teach these concepts. Using teaching mnemonics such as "Never Eat Sour Watermelons" or "Never Eat Soggy Waffles" may help some students remember the order and relationship of cardinal directions. When teaching cardinal directions, it is best to start with small objects as a reference tool, then move to a familiar room (e.g., bedroom or classroom), then to hallways at school, then to unfamiliar indoor environments, and finally to unfamiliar outdoor environments. Generalization of the use of cardinal directions can be taught with more advanced concepts such as the movement of people along a sidewalk or traffic along a street, the location of a sidewalk, corner names (e.g., the northeast corner of an intersection or the southwest corner of a block), and the direction of the sun at varying times of the day. Formulating routes, crossing intersections, and planning and executing bus routes all require the use of cardinal directions.

Spatial awareness provides essential information for O&M development and brings structure to the environment, helping children with visual impairments develop an orientation to their surroundings. Maintaining orientation encourages children to explore and makes those explorations meaningful and purposeful. Spatial awareness also provides the basis for understanding directions such as "Your book is behind you" and O&M instructions such as "Stand beside me" or "Hold the cane in front of you" (Skellenger & Sapp, 2010).

Environmental Concepts

Environmental concepts refer to an awareness about one's surroundings that enhance the ability to travel safely and independently (Fazzi & Petersmeyer, 2001; see Figure 2.2). There are numerous environmental concepts that are important for O&M. They include concepts about the natural world, such as the position of the sun; concepts about indoor environments, such as shapes of rooms and arrangements of floors within a building; concepts about outdoor environments, including traffic patterns and neighborhood block layouts; and interpreting information from sounds. Environmental awareness helps a traveler who is blind or visually impaired maintain orientation, regain orientation when lost, and make safe decisions about when and where to travel (i.e., when it is safe to cross a street). Sidebar 2.4 provides a few examples of environmental concepts that children with visual impairments need to learn.

Time and Distance Concepts

Understanding time and distance concepts is critical for independent travel. Students with visual impairments need to learn distance concepts using a variety of formal (e.g., feet, miles) and informal (e.g., blocks, steps) measurement systems. They also need to have a sense of

Wendy Sapp

Figure 2.2 A student who is blind improves her understanding of the concept of "opening," a critical environmental concept for independent travel.

minutes and hours and how much time has passed to understand if they have walked too far or not far enough to reach a destination. Time-distance systems refer to combining the concepts of time and distance to understand how long it should take to reach a destination based on how far away it is. For example, understanding time-distance concepts helps students realize that it takes more than 2 minutes to walk a route that includes six blocks, and that it should not take them 15 minutes to reach the end of one block. Time-distance concepts can assist students with visual impairments in

---

SIDEBAR 2.4

Environmental Concepts

The following is a partial list of environmental concepts that children who are blind or visually impaired need to learn. (For a complete listing of environmental concepts, refer to the assessments provided in Table 2.1.)

Nature Concepts

- Passive sound clues (available while traveler is quiet)
- Active sound clues (echoes from clapping, clicking, or whistling)
- Sun clues
- Olfactory clues
- Wind clues

Indoor Concepts

- Shape of rooms
- Layout of furniture and appliances in rooms
- Arrangement of floors in a building
- Standard layout of hallways

Outdoor Concepts

- Residential/business blocks (e.g., shapes, relation between blocks)
- Street features (e.g., lampposts, mailboxes, crosswalk buttons)
- Natural features (e.g., grass, trees, dirt)
- Human-made features (e.g., houses, buildings, sidewalks)
- Traffic patterns
- Traffic control systems
- Parking lots

SIDEBAR 2.5

Time and Distance Concepts

The following is a list of time and distance concepts that children who are blind or visually impaired need to learn to help them reach their desired destinations.

- Hours
- Minutes
- Seconds
- English units (e.g., feet, yards, miles)
- Metric units (e.g., meters, kilometers)
- Informal measurements (e.g., length of a city block, number of steps, length of a residential block)

---

realizing when they are close to reaching a destination so they can begin to look for landmarks and determine if they have traveled beyond their desired destination. Examples of time and distance concepts are listed in Sidebar 2.5.

Concepts to Minimize Risk

O&M instruction does not guarantee that students with visual impairments will always be safe, but it does provide skills and concepts so students can minimize the risks of traveling. Students with visual impairments receiving O&M instruction learn numerous skills to minimize risk as they travel, but they also need to learn concepts that help minimize risk, starting with being responsible for one's own safety and responding to safety commands (e.g., "Stop") from others. Additional concepts include sources of danger (e.g., moving cars) and emergency drills (e.g., fire and

SIDEBAR 2.6

Concepts to Minimize Risk

The following is a list of concepts to minimize risk that children who are blind or visually impaired need to learn to travel safely and independently.

- Safety commands
  - "Stop"
  - "No"
  - "Wait"
- Environmental dangers (e.g., cars, drop-offs)
- Societal dangers (e.g., safe versus unsafe strangers)
- Maintaining control of one's own travel (e.g., knowing where you are when traveling with a guide)
- Body language that does not communicate being a "victim" (e.g., posture, stride)
- Knowing when one's vision may not be reliable and recognizing the need to use alternative and safer travel methods in conjunction with functional vision

tornado drills). One critical concept related to minimizing risk for students with low vision is to recognize when they cannot rely on vision to provide enough information to travel with acceptable risk or provide accurate enough information for orientation, either as a result of low acuity, restricted visual fields, glare, lighting levels, fatigue, or other factors. These students not only need to learn alternative sensory skills to gain information to reduce their risk, but they also need to learn when to rely on specific sensory information. Sidebar 2.6 lists concepts to reduce risk needed for independent travel.

Evaluation of Concepts

A complete O&M evaluation includes a thorough assessment of concepts. Though states and districts have different guidelines for referring students for an O&M evaluation, all children with visual impairments need to receive at least a periodic evaluation from an O&M specialist. Parents and teachers should not assume that a child with a visual impairment has sufficient knowledge of concepts to travel safely; O&M evaluations often find lack of knowledge of concepts that the rest of the child's educational team did not anticipate.

For example, a young child with a visual impairment often travels well in familiar environments, showing an ability to stay oriented and move purposefully, but may have difficulty in new environments. The child's education teams may think that since the child does not travel independently in new environments, the child would not benefit from O&M instruction. However, an O&M evaluation may find problems in areas such as spatial awareness that make it difficult for the child to learn new environments (e.g., a new classroom) or that prevent the child from demonstrating age-appropriate independence. The earlier an evaluation is conducted and the earlier these types of issues are recognized, the easier it is to remedy them.

If older students appear to travel well, it may not be immediately apparent that they are experiencing complications in their understanding of concepts. For example, a student who has low vision may determine when it is safe to cross a signal-controlled intersection based on the nearest traffic light the student can see. This method may work often enough that no one recognizes the student has a problem. However,

Figure 2.3 An adolescent must have a more highly developed concept of cardinal directions to use a GPS system to independently hike a nature trail than to travel in a residential neighborhood.

the light the student is using may only control traffic in one direction for the cross street and may not provide information about traffic traveling in the other direction or turning traffic, both of which can affect the student's line of travel. In this situation, the student lacks knowledge of concepts about traffic patterns and signal-controlled intersections that are necessary for safe travel. Older students also travel in more complex environments, requiring a deeper understanding of spatial and environmental concepts to travel safely and independently than was needed when they were younger (see Figure 2.3).

To evaluate concepts, the O&M specialist follows a similar process to other evaluations of students with visual impairments. The O&M specialist begins by reviewing the student's

records. Interviews with the student, teachers, and family members are important to identify concepts in which a student is demonstrating difficulty and to address concerns team members may have. While gathering information through reviews of records and interviews is important, the evaluator must also observe the student. Observations of the student in a variety of environments provides information about how the student demonstrates use of concepts in daily life, including when a concept may be partially mastered but not fully integrated into the student's life. Finally, direct evaluation of concepts provides the remaining essential information regarding a student's understanding and application of concepts.

As part of the evaluation, the O&M specialist examines concepts that are important for the student's current environments as well as concepts that are necessary in future environments. Students with visual impairments may have the concepts necessary for current environments but need to develop additional concepts to be successful in unfamiliar environments they will be entering in the near future. Changing environments may mean that students are expected to travel in more complex environments or travel more independently, both of which could require them to demonstrate more advanced concepts to be successful. For example, a student who travels independently on campus but who has not traveled in the community without a guide may not be aware of the relationship of the sidewalk to the grass line, street, or driveways. Further concept development would be needed before that student could travel alone in a more complex residential environment.

There are a variety of tools that contain sections on addressing O&M concepts, but there is no single tool that adequately addresses all

O&M concepts that all children need to learn. Table 2.1 lists many of the evaluation tools that are available, along with the types of concepts assessed and the age or developmental level for which each tool is appropriate. Given that many concepts are unique to a student's environment (e.g., rural versus urban travel), O&M specialists need to use their professional knowledge to determine concepts to assess that may not be included on formal evaluation tools.

Regardless of the formal and informal evaluation tools used, the O&M specialist must determine the level at which a student understands a concept. Children are often able to verbalize information that they do not fully understand. As appropriate to the concept being evaluated, the assessment requires the child to verbalize the definition of a concept (if the child has verbal skills), demonstrate or locate the concept, and apply the concept. For certain concepts, a child also needs to know the function and features of the object, such as understanding the function of a traffic control signal. For example, when assessing the spatial concept "beside," the O&M specialist can ask the child what it means for an object to be "beside" the child; to place an object "beside" another object; or when walking a route, give the child instructions to follow directions that include the term "beside," such as locating the door beside a water fountain. Often a child is able to demonstrate a concept in a controlled environment or answer questions about a concept, but cannot apply that knowledge to travel situations. The O&M specialist must carry out a thorough evaluation to determine whether a child partially or fully understands a concept.

A final consideration in evaluating concepts is to adjust the assessment to the unique needs of the student's environment. Though students of the same developmental level will likely demonstrate similar skills in terms of body concepts, spatial concepts, time and distance concepts, and concepts to minimize risk, they may have very different needs with regard to environmental concepts. An 11-year-old student who is totally blind and lives in a large metropolitan area may be expected to independently cross streets and take the subway to school, which requires concept development related to urban street features, public transportation, traffic patterns, and more. An 11-year-old student who is totally blind and lives on a farm in a small rural community may need to learn how to safely maneuver on a large farm, which requires concept development related to uneven terrain, electric fences, and the use of wind, olfactory, and sun clues. A thorough O&M evaluation requires that the O&M specialist take into consideration all of the student's environments.

Instructional Methods

Once an O&M specialist has determined that the student with a visual impairment may be struggling in understanding O&M concepts or will need to learn certain concepts to function in a new environment, the student must receive instruction in those concepts. There are four basic methods by which concepts can be taught by the O&M specialist and reinforced by other educational team members, including the family (for more information on teams, see Chapter 11). Concepts can be taught through direct instruction, in daily routines, within O&M skills instruction, and embedded in instruction of other content areas. Though a variety of educational team members may be involved in instruction of concepts, the O&M specialist is a key member of the team. The O&M specialist

TABLE 2.1

Evaluation Tools for Concept Development

Tool	Age/ Developmental Age	Concepts Assessed				
		Body	Spatial	Environmental	Time-Distance	Safety
Birth-to-6 O&M Inventory (Maner, Martinez-Cargo, & Anderson, 2016)	Birth–6 years	X	X	X	X	X
Body-Image of Blind Children (Cratty & Sams, 1968)	5–16 years	X	X			
Boehm Test of Basic Concepts (Boehm-3) (Boehm, 2001a)	K–2nd grade		X	X		
Boehm-3 Preschool (Boehm, 2001b)	3–5 years		X	X		
Boehm-3 Preschool Tactile Edition (Ferrell, Smyth, Henderson, & Boehm, 2014)	3–5 years		X	X		
Hill Performance Test of Selected Positional Concepts (Hill, 1981)	6–10 years	X	X	X		X
INSITE Developmental Checklist (Morgan, 1989)	Birth–6 years	X	X	X		X
Inventory of Purposeful Movement Behaviors (Anthony, 2004a)	Birth–5 years		X			X
O&M Assessment: Early Years (Anthony, 2004b)	Birth–3 years	X	X			X
O&M Inventory (NMSBVI, 2012)	K–12th grade	X	X	X	X	X
Oregon Project for Preschool Children (Anderson, Boigon, Davis, & DeWaard, 2007)	Birth–6 years	X	X	X		X
Preschool O&M Screening (Dodson-Burk & Lantzy, 2012)	3–6 years	X	X	X	X	X

(continued on next page)

TABLE 2.1 (*continued*)

Tool	Age/ Developmental Age	Concepts Assessed				
		Body	Spatial	Environmental	Time-Distance	Safety
TAPS: Teaching Age-Appropriate Purposeful Skills (Pogrund et al., 2012)	Preschool–High School	X	X	X	X	X
Texas Two-Steps: Successfully Teaching Early Purposeful Skills (Brown et al., 2018)	Birth–5 years	X	X	X		

See the References at the end of this chapter for bibliographic information concerning these evaluation tools.

provides direct instruction to the student with a visual impairment to ensure that concepts are taught completely and accurately so the student can apply them in safe, independent travel.

Regardless of the instructional method used, most young children with visual impairments and many older learners absorb information best through part-to-whole learning. Part-to-whole learning is based on the principle that learners must learn the components of large, complex tasks and concepts prior to understanding the entire task or concept. Children with visual impairments may lack an overarching understanding of many concepts, especially those involving large spaces and environments. Therefore, they need to have numerous hands-on experiences to learn "parts" before they can put them together as a "whole." For example, a child with a visual impairment starting preschool for the first time will need to experience many aspects or "parts" of the classroom, such as the feel of the carpet, the location of objects throughout the room, the warmth of the sun through the windows, and the sound of other children playing before putting together a "whole" concept of the classroom.

Some students, especially older children and adolescents, may benefit from whole-part-whole learning in which the "whole" concept is introduced first, followed by detailed instruction in each part, and finishing with a review of the "whole" concept. For example, a student who is learning about bus travel may benefit from an introduction to concepts around bus travel such as the why, what, when, and where. The student can then learn the "parts" or details related to each concept, such as reading a timetable, locating a bus stop, and identifying the correct stop for exiting the bus. Finally, the student puts all the components back together to demonstrate an understanding of the concepts involved in bus travel.

The following sections provide information about the four basic methods of O&M instruction. For more detailed information and extensive examples of providing instruction, refer to *Imagining the Possibilities: Creative Approaches to Orientation and Mobility Instruction for Persons Who Are Visually Impaired* (Fazzi & Petersmeyer,

2001), *Early Focus: Working with Young Children Who Are Blind or Visually Impaired and Their Families* (Pogrund & Fazzi, 2002), and both volumes of the third edition of *Foundations of Orientation and Mobility* (Wiener, Welsh, & Blasch, 2010).

Direct Instruction

Many concepts require direct instruction to be fully understood. Direct instruction introduces the concept and teaches the student with a visual impairment how to demonstrate the concept, often incorporating fun activities such as games, songs, and mnemonics. Direct instruction allows the O&M specialist to introduce concepts incrementally while documenting each component the student has mastered before moving to a more complex aspect of the concept. For example, many students who are blind or visually impaired require direct instruction in the layout of streets and blocks. Though this information can be included in travel lessons such as walking around a block, most students benefit from initial instruction detailing the shapes and sizes of blocks and how blocks connect to one another. For example, a student can use wooden blocks or other materials to create a tactile map of residential blocks, sidewalks, and streets (see Figure 2.4). The student can then practice tracing routes on the tactile map to complete walking "around a block" or "walking three blocks," concepts that can be confusing when first encountered.

Daily Routines

Embedding instruction about concepts into daily routines is an excellent strategy to help children with visual impairments gain experi-

Tiffany Paschal

Figure 2.4 A child with a visual impairment receives direct instruction using a tactile map to develop a concept of the layout of five hallways that branch off from a central room in her school.

ence with concepts. Short, frequent, low-stress exposure can help children fully master concepts and begin to apply them to new situations. For example, young children can practice identifying body parts, body movements, and laterality through songs (e.g., "The Hokey Pokey," "Head, Shoulders, Knees, and Toes") that are often incorporated into early childhood

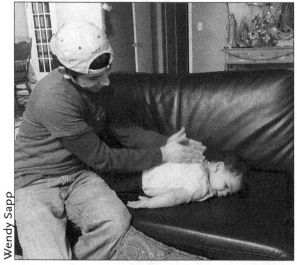

Wendy Sapp

Figure 2.5 A 13-month-old who is blind learns about body parts as his father discusses the names of body parts while touching each body part during a daily massage.

activities in the classroom and at home. These same concepts can be incorporated into daily routines (see Figure 2.5) such as dressing and bathing by naming body parts (e.g., "I'm washing your left arm") and, as the child begins to gain a better understanding of the concept, the child can be asked to participate using instructions involving specific body parts (e.g., "Give me your right foot and I'll tie your shoe").

Instruction in O&M Skills

O&M concepts and instruction in O&M skills are often intertwined. As students practice O&M skills, they are asked to apply concepts. Verbal directions that appear relatively simple can require extensive understanding of concepts. For example, the direction for correctly positioning the hand for guide technique can be stated as: "Grip the guide's upper arm just above the elbow, with your thumb on the outside of the guide's arm and your fingers on the inside of the guide's arm." Following these instruc-

tions to get into this basic O&M position includes concepts in body parts (arm, upper arm, elbow, thumb, and fingers), spatial concepts (above), and spatial concepts in relation to another person (inside and outside in reference to the guide's body). Though some students, such as those with adventitious blindness, master all of these concepts before learning guide technique, other students, such as very young children or students with significant intellectual disabilities, need to use guide technique before they are able to demonstrate each concept in isolation. Students do not need to master all these concepts prior to beginning instruction in guide technique; the concepts and the skill can be taught concurrently.

Some concepts, however, should be fully mastered before they are applied to certain O&M skills. For example, considering the physical risks involved in stepping out into a street, a student should understand the danger that cars pose and the meaning of a "stop" command before learning to independently cross streets. For other concepts, students may make more progress if they begin to develop a concept and then further refine their understanding of the concept through instruction in O&M skills. A student may initially receive extensive direct instruction in locating cardinal directions on a map as well as turning to face the desired direction. The student can then deepen that understanding by applying the concept of cardinal directions to complete a route. For other students, teaching a concept alongside the skill in which it is applied is a more effective method for teaching both skills and concepts. For example, the concept of a fire hydrant may be best learned by students if it is taught while traveling a route in a residential neighborhood. O&M specialists need to carefully evaluate the concepts to be learned and the learning styles of students to determine the most effective approach and must plan and present the concepts in a systematic way to provide a learning path for students.

Instruction in Other Content Areas

Many concepts required for O&M overlap with concepts needed for other areas of instruction, including areas of the general education curriculum and the expanded core curriculum (ECC). The general education curriculum requires students to master several concepts that are part of O&M instruction, such as right or left, parallel or perpendicular, and cardinal directions in subjects such as math, geography, and science. Students with visual impairments, however, often need more extensive instruction to grasp the concept of the right and left side of a person facing them (directionality) because they lack the visual experiences that come from another person's perspective. Students with visual impairments are expected to apply concepts of parallel and perpendicular and cardinal directions at a more sophisticated level (e.g., using them to follow a route, cross streets, and locate a destination) than their typically sighted peers, who usually only have to answer paper-and-pencil questions about these concepts. Therefore, O&M specialists play an important role in instruction in order to ensure the students learn concepts at the level required to meet their travel needs.

O&M concepts are related to all areas of the ECC. Examples have already been provided of O&M concepts incorporated into academics and independent living skills. O&M concepts are also closely tied to career skills, recreation and leisure skills, social skills, self-determination skills, sensory efficiency skills, and assistive technology skills. Children will not experience success in future careers if they do not possess the O&M concepts necessary for safe and independent travel. Many recreation and leisure opportunities, including sports such as beep baseball, Tae Kwon Do, and rock climbing, demand knowledge of O&M concepts such as understanding body parts and spatial concepts to participate. Social skills such as facing the person to whom you are speaking and self-determination skills such as requesting or refusing assistance are integral to traveling independently. Understanding when to apply these skills is an important concept that can be taught within O&M lessons as students ask for directions, solicit assistance, and refuse unwanted assistance.

For students with low vision, O&M provides an important opportunity to learn the concept of what information they can gain from their senses, when to rely on information from which senses, and how to use optical devices. Often, through O&M instruction, students learn to use senses they may not typically use in academic instruction. For example, students with low vision who are braille readers may use visual input as a source of information for O&M while students with low vision and sufficient vision to read print may rely on auditory information for street crossings under certain lighting and environmental conditions. O&M instruction is essential in helping students learn when to rely on other senses (Geruschat & Smith, 2010). Many technology skills can also be useful for O&M travel, including the use of apps and other devices for wayfinding and cardinal directions. Through careful planning and communication, the O&M specialist and the teacher of students with visual impairments can coordinate evaluation and instruction to efficiently teach and reinforce concepts across all areas of the ECC.

(See Chapter 9 for more information on how to integrate O&M skills into other ECC areas.)

Collaborating with Partners

As discussed in the previous section, many O&M concepts overlap with concepts typically taught by parents, general education teachers, and teachers of students with visual impairments. All partners involved in a student's education play a role in concept development. Regardless of who is providing or reinforcing instruction, the instruction must be accurate. Unfortunately, other disciplines often do not require that students master concepts at an accuracy level adequate for O&M. For example, many general education social studies curricula recommend having students learn cardinal directions by pointing overhead for north, to their right for east, down for south, and to the left for west. Though this strategy may be effective in teaching students to remember the directions on a traditional compass rose on a map, it is not effective in teaching children how to apply cardinal directions in the real world. In the real world, north is not overhead but is instead a direction to the front, back, or side of the student. Teaching strategies commonly used by O&M specialists, such as turning to face each cardinal direction while standing in a cardboard box and touching the correct side or using mnemonics to remember the order of cardinal directions (e.g., Never Eat Sour Worms), are more appropriate instructional strategies to help prepare students to use cardinal directions while traveling. All partners working with students with visual impairments must ensure that concepts are taught in an accurate and meaningful way so that students truly understand the concepts and can apply them

appropriately. (See Chapter 11 for more information on collaboration and working with partners.)

In many collaborative models, the O&M specialist takes the primary lead in teaching concepts, and other partners reinforce the concepts once the basics are mastered. Depending on the needs of the student and the structure of the student's educational team, all or some team members may work together to teach concepts. For instance, a general education mathematics teacher, a teacher of students with visual impairments, and an O&M specialist can work together to provide instruction on parallel and perpendicular directions that overlap with the instruction provided by each professional. A parent, physical therapist, occupational therapist, and O&M specialist can collaborate to prioritize body concepts and spatial concepts that everyone addresses concurrently. In some cases, for children with severe multiple impairments, teams may jointly plan a unit or routine focusing on a related concept that all partners address. In these situations, some concepts will be related to O&M, and all partners will teach those concepts during that unit or routine. Team teaching, at least for an initial lesson, offers a way to ensure that team members provide consistent instruction, reducing any potential confusion on the part of the student. It is also important for the O&M specialist to continue monitoring the instruction provided by other team members to ensure consistency and mastery of the concept by the student.

Whatever approach the educational team takes in providing instruction in O&M concepts, good communication among all partners is essential (Slatoff, 2014). Communication can be maintained through a variety of methods including regularly scheduled team meetings for planning and progress review, a written or online communication log to document progress on skills and concepts, and e-mails, texts, and phone calls for periodic updates and to share important information between meetings. Communication can also include links to video clips on teaching concepts, online lesson plans, or other resources that assist partners in providing concept instruction.

Regardless of the collaborative model used and communication system in place, the O&M specialist serves as the central provider of instruction in O&M concepts. The involvement of other partners enhances instruction but does not take the place of instruction by an O&M specialist. Given the critical importance of mastering O&M concepts for a student's safe and independent travel, the O&M specialist must take the lead role in ensuring that appropriate concepts are taught, evaluated, and mastered. With appropriate concept development, students with visual impairments have a strong foundation to become successful and independent travelers.

Summary

Beginning in infancy, students continue to refine their understanding of concepts throughout their lives. The use of rich language and real-life experiences and the willingness of all educational team members to share in the responsibility of teaching is key to strong concept development. Even when every effort is made to develop concepts, gaps may still be discovered. Applying a broad-minded approach will make it easier for students with visual impairments to continue to gather new information that will allow them to develop new concepts as lifelong learners.

References

Anderson, S., Boigon, S., Davis, K., & DeWaard, C. (2007). *The Oregon Project for Preschool Children Who Are Blind or Visually Impaired* (6th ed.). Medford: Southern Oregon Education Service District.

Anthony, T. L. (2004a). Inventory of purposeful movement behaviors. In T. L. Anthony, S. S. Lowry, C. J. Brown, & D. D. Hatton (Eds.), *Developmentally appropriate orientation and mobility*. Chapel Hill: University of North Carolina at Chapel Hill, FPG Child Development Institute, Early Intervention Training Center for Infants and Toddlers with Visual Impairments.

Anthony, T. L. (2004b). *O&M assessment: Early years of birth through three years*. In T. L. Anthony, S. S. Lowry, C. J. Brown, & D. D. Hatton (Eds.), *Developmentally appropriate orientation and mobility*. Chapel Hill: University of North Carolina at Chapel Hill, FPG Child Development Institute, Early Intervention Training Center for Infants and Toddlers with Visual Impairments.

Boehm, A. E. (2001a). *Boehm test of basic concepts (Boehm-3)* (3rd ed.). San Antonio, TX: Psychological Corporation.

Boehm, A. E. (2001b). *Boehm test of basic concepts (Boehm-3) preschool* (3rd ed.). San Antonio, TX: Psychological Corporation.

Bronfenbrenner, U. (1979). *The ecology of human development: Experiments by nature and design*. Cambridge, MA: Harvard University Press.

Brown, J., Hallak, T., Garrett, M., Nelson, G., Sewell, D., Uriegas, O., . . . Wood, M. (2018). *Texas two-steps: Successfully teaching early purposeful skills*. Austin: Texas School for the Blind and Visually Impaired.

Clipson-Boyles, S. (Ed.). (2000). *Putting research into practice in primary teaching and learning*. New York, NY: Routledge.

Cratty, B. J., & Sams, T. A. (1968). *The body-image of blind children*. New York, NY: American Foundation for the Blind.

Dodson-Burk, B., & Lantzy, C. (2012). *Preschool orientation and mobility screening* (2nd ed.). Alexandria, VA: Association for Education and Rehabilitation of the Blind and Visually Impaired.

Fazzi, D. L., & Petersmeyer, B. A. (2001). *Imagining the possibilities: Creative approaches to orientation and mobility instruction for persons who are visually impaired.* New York, NY: AFB Press.

Ferrell, K. A., Smyth, C. A., Henderson, B., & Boehm, A. (2014). *Boehm test of basic concepts (Boehm-3) preschool* (Tactile ed.). Louisville, KY: American Printing House for the Blind.

Geruschat, D. R., & Smith, A. J. (2010). Improving the use of low vision for orientation and mobility. In W. R. Wiener, R. L. Welsh, & B. B. Blasch (Eds.), *Foundations of orientation and mobility: Vol. II. Instructional strategies and practical applications* (3rd ed., pp. 54–90). New York, NY: AFB Press.

Hill, E. W. (1981). *The Hill performance test of selected positional concepts.* Chicago, IL: Stoelting.

Luckner, J. L., Bruce, S. M., & Ferrell, K. A. (2016). A summary of the communication and literacy evidence-based practices for students who are deaf or hard of hearing, visually impaired, and deafblind. *Communication Disorders Quarterly, 37*(4), 225–241.

Maner, J., Martinez-Cargo, L., & Anderson, D. L. (2016). *Birth-to-6 Orientation and Mobility Inventory.* Alamogordo: New Mexico School for the Blind and Visually Impaired.

Morgan, E. C. (1989). *INSITE developmental checklist: A comprehensive developmental checklist for multihandicapped sensory impaired infants and young children: Short version, ages 0–2.* Logan, UT: SKI-HI Institute.

New Mexico School for the Blind and Visually Impaired (NMSBVI). (2012). *Orientation & Mobility Inventory.* Alamogordo, NM: Author. Retrieved from www.nmsbvi.k12.nm.us/WEB/O&M_INVENTORY/O&M_Inventory.htm

Piaget, J., & Inhelder, B. (1969). *The psychology of the child.* New York, NY: Basic Books.

Pogrund, R. L., & Fazzi, D. L. (Eds.). (2002). *Early focus: Working with young children who are blind or visually impaired and their families* (2nd ed.). New York, NY: AFB Press.

Pogrund, R., Sewell, D., Anderson, H., Calaci, L., Cowart, M. F., Gonzalez, C. M., . . . Roberson-Smith, B. (2012). *TAPS—Teaching age-appropriate purposeful skills: An orientation and mobility curriculum for students with visual impairments* (3rd ed.). Austin: Texas School for the Blind and Visually Impaired.

Skellenger, A. C., & Sapp, W. K. (2010). Teaching orientation and mobility for the early childhood years. In W. R. Wiener, R. L. Welsh, & B. B. Blasch (Eds.), *Foundations of orientation and mobility: Vol. II. Instructional strategies and practical applications* (3rd ed., pp. 163–207). New York, NY: AFB Press.

Slatoff, A. (2014). *Communication: The key to collaboration between special and general education teachers* (Master's thesis). Retrieved from Dominican Scholar (Paper 154), http://scholar.dominican.edu/masters-theses/154

Smith, M. (2012). *SAM: Symbols and Meaning.* Louisville, KY: American Printing House for the Blind.

Vygotsky, L. S. (1986). *Thought and language.* Cambridge, MA: MIT Press.

Wadsworth, B. J. (2003). *Piaget's theory of cognitive and affective development* (5th ed.). New York, NY: Pearson.

Warren, D. H., & Hatton, D. D. (2003). Cognitive development of children with visual impairments. In F. Boller & J. Grafman (Series Eds.) & S. J. Segalowitz & I. Rapin (Vol. Eds.), *Handbook of neuropsychology: Vol. 8, Part II. Child neuropsychology, part II* (2nd ed., pp. 439–458). New York, NY: Elsevier.

Wiener, W. R., Welsh, R. L., & Blasch, B. B. (Eds.). (2010). *Foundations of orientation and mobility* (3rd ed., Vols. I–II). New York, NY: AFB Press.

3

Motor Development

Sandra J. Rosen and Rona L. Pogrund

> **Questions to Guide Your Reading of This Chapter**
>
> ➤ Why is the integration of primitive reflexes so important for the acquisition of future mobility skills?
> ➤ What are some of the motor differences seen in children with visual impairments as compared to their peers with vision?
> ➤ How are the three major sensory systems—visual, proprioceptive, and vestibular—interconnected, and how do they relate to motor development in young children?

Watching a child makes it obvious that the development of his mind comes about through his movements. (Montessori, 1949)

Much of what young children learn comes through visual imitation. Children with visual impairments, however, often miss opportunities for imitative learning. For these children, information gained from other senses and through active movement play a vital role in many developmental areas. The importance of movement cannot be overstated. Exploring the environment through movement is a critical component for positive developmental out-

comes in every child (Adolph & Joh, 2007; Bunker, 1991). Movement facilitates cognition, social skills, communication, and self-help skills in addition to motor development (Diamond, 2000, 2007).

At its most basic level, movement is the result of two interrelated physical functions: sensory input and motor output. Sensory input includes visual, auditory, and tactile functions. Motor output consists of muscle tone and a complex array of motor reflexes (primitive, involuntary responses) and *reactions* (mature motor responses) to environmental stimuli (see Sidebar 3.1 for definitions of key terms). Operating as a feedback mechanism (see Figure 3.1), this interaction between the two functions is observed when people perform any motor skill, even one as simple as picking up a pen from a table. To pick up the pen, an individual uses visual feedback to identify the location of the pen, motor coordination to bring the hand to the pen, and proprioception (awareness of the position of one's body parts) to verify that the hand is moving through space as desired.

The *integration* of these functions (known collectively as sensorimotor functions) determines the physical efficiency with which people perform not only everyday tasks but everything they do. Integration begins at birth and occurs every time infants or toddlers move

Key Terms

Applied behavior analysis Process of providing systematic interventions to improve behavior and demonstrating that the interventions are responsible for the behavior change.

Cephalocaudal From head to toe.

Crawling Moving through the environment by pulling oneself on one's stomach. Also called "belly crawling" or "army crawling."

Creeping Moving through the environment on the hands and knees.

Cruising Walking sideways along furniture, a wall, or other surface using both hands for support on the surface.

Distal Point on the body located further from the trunk than another point on the body.

Equilibrium reactions Balance reactions; automatic movements of the body to restore and maintain the center of gravity over the base of support.

Extensor muscles Muscles of the body that straighten or extend joints.

Facilitation activities Actions to promote optimum functioning of the sensory system, motor system, or both.

Fine motor skills Using small muscles, such as those in the hands and fingers, toes, and tongue, to aid in coordinated movement.

Gait pattern Manner or style of walking.

Gross motor skills Movement of the large muscles of the body, including arms and legs.

High guard Extending the arms up with bent elbows, such that the hands are raised to the level of the shoulders. Often used by toddlers for balance as they begin to walk.

Hypertonia High muscle tone.

Hypotonia Low muscle tone.

Integration Different body systems working together to promote optimal functioning.

Isolating motions Separation of motions; allowing movement at one joint while restricting movement at a nearby joint.

Low guard Holding the arms down at the side in a stationary position while walking rather than swinging them.

Neurodevelopmental Relating to the growth and development of the brain or central nervous system.

Prehension Picking up, grasping, or taking hold of an object.

Prone Position of lying face down.

Proprioception Awareness of the relative position of the parts of the body to one another in space.

Proximal Point on the body located closer to the trunk than another point on the body.

Quadriceps Large four-muscle group located on the front of the thigh that is responsible for extending the knee joint.

Quadruped Position of being on all fours.

Reactions Mature motor responses that provide the ability to adjust to movement and to maintain an upright posture against gravity.

SIDEBAR 3.1

Reciprocal arm swing Normal forward and backward movement of the arms (concurrent with the movement of the opposite leg) when walking.

Sensory integration Process by which a person receives information through the senses, organizes the information, and uses it in everyday activities.

Shoulder girdle Set of structures that connect the arms to the trunk; consists of the clavicle (collarbone), scapula (shoulder blade), and coracoid process (protrusion on the scapula to which ligaments and tendons attach).

Stabilizing joints Restricting motion in selected joint(s) to provide a stable foundation for support or to facilitate precise motion at nearby joint(s); holding firm.

Supine Position of lying on the back, facing upward.

Tactile avoidance Evading contact with novel textures or tactile sensations due to a tendency to be overwhelmed by and fearful of them; commonly a result of sensory integration problems. Previously referred to as tactile defensiveness and tactile hypersensitivity.

Tactile selectiveness Aversion to contacting certain textures or tactile sensations while experiencing no issues contacting other textures. Not related to sensory integration problems.

Vestibular system Sensory system located in the inner ear and brain that helps to control balance.

---

in response to sensory stimulation. It continues as children grow and interact with their environment. Most children make significant changes in the way they move during the first few years of life as they increase their ability to control both the large and small muscles of their bodies. Both children's *gross motor skill* development and their *fine motor skill* development have direct ties to their mobility skills. Through neurological development of the sensory and motor systems, children acquire an erect posture and a mature *gait pattern* (manner of walking) that, in turn, lead to the ability to run, hop, skip, walk a straight line, and perform a variety of coordinated and efficient movements. This chapter will present a brief overview of the neurological building blocks of sensorimotor functions and how the development of children born without functional vision differs from that of their sighted peers.

Building Blocks of Sensorimotor Development

Building Block 1: Neurological Reflexes and Reactions

There are several types of reflexes involved in daily motor functioning. At a neurological level, the development of coordinated movement begins in infancy with primitive reflexes, which are automatic, stereotypical movements directed by a primitive part of the brain, the brain stem. These reflexes are executed without the involvement of higher levels of brain function such as the cerebral cortex. The reflexes of newborns dominate movement, allow for survival, and set the stage for early primitive learning. Reflexes play a vital role in the development of muscle tone and coordinated movement later in life. Some neurological reflexes are retained

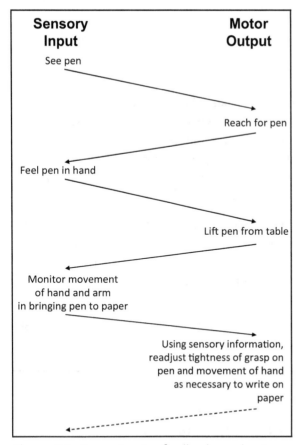

Figure 3.1 Sensorimotor feedback mechanism.

Source: Adapted from Rosen, S. (2010). Kinesiology and sensorimotor functioning for students with vision loss. In W. R. Wiener, R. L. Welsh, & B. B. Blasch (Eds.), *Foundations of orientation and mobility: Vol. I. History and theory* (3rd ed., p. 144). New York, NY: AFB Press.

coordinated movement throughout the life span.

Many variables can impede this natural developmental progression. A genetic predisposition or inherited characteristics, stressors during pregnancy, birth trauma, and environmental deprivation can all interfere with normal neurological development (Nelson, 2017). For example, in some countries, children in orphanages are left to lie in cribs with no movement or stimulation for long periods of time and may exhibit certain reflexes long past the typical stage when they should have integrated.

It is also commonly recognized that when people are under stress, these primitive reflexes can momentarily reappear, even in individuals who have experienced normal integration of reflexes. Retained primitive reflexes can impede later behavior, motor control, sensory perception, eye-hand coordination, and cognition (Callcott, 2012; Ferrell, 2011). Certain combinations of retained reflexes may also reveal themselves in ways that affect emotional and social well-being and academic progress. Some manifestations of *neurodevelopmental* delay (a delay in the growth and development of the brain or central nervous system) that may be observed later in life include dyslexia, learning disabilities, poor handwriting, poor sequencing, attention problems, poor organizational skills, poor posture, awkward gait, poor gross and fine motor skills, confusion between left and right, and reversals of letters in print or braille (Blythe, 2010; Rogers, Hepburn, & Wehner, 2003). If primitive reflexes are present beyond their normal developmental period, they can sometimes be considered atypical and evidence of an immature central nervous system, thus resulting in neurodevelopmental delay. Primitive reflexes

throughout life, such as swallowing, gagging, yawning, and even the knee-jerk reflex that doctors test by tapping a small hammer-like instrument against the knee.

As infants gain experience in movement, these primitive reflexes coalesce into a higher level of central nervous system control at the cerebral-cortex level and give way to mature, automatic reactions beginning at about 3–4 months of age. These reactions continue to develop during the first year of life and support are often retained in the presence of some forms of cerebral palsy, in which case activities to integrate reflexes and facilitate reactions should only be done in consultation with a physical therapist or an occupational therapist. See Table 3.1 for reflexes commonly observed in infants.

Effect of Asymmetrical Tonic Neck Reflex on O&M

Of the primitive reflexes, the one that most notably affects the sensorimotor skills of children with visual impairments is the asymmetrical tonic neck reflex (ATNR; see Table 3.1), or "fencing reflex." This reflex occurs when infants are placed on their backs and their heads turn to the side, causing the arm and leg on the side to which the head is turned to extend and the opposite arm and leg to bend.

The ATNR is normally present only within the first few months of life and is typically fully integrated by around 6 months of age (Anthony, Lowry, Brown, & Hatton, 2004; Blythe, 2002). This reflex is a precursor to the development of eye-hand coordination in infants. If infants contact an object when they extend their arms, they will not only experience proprioceptive input from reaching, they will also receive tactile input from any objects that they touch, as well as visual feedback, if available. By reproducing this experience, infants are able to reach and touch an object over and over (Colangelo, 1999).

It has been suggested that some of the coordination difficulties experienced by children who are born with visual impairments relate directly to the poor sensorimotor integration of primitive reflexes such as the ATNR (Rosen, 2010). For example, children who are visually impaired generally achieve the ability to cross the midline (median line of the body) with their hands later than sighted children do (Griffin,

1981; Sleeuwenhoek, Boter, & Vermeer, 1995; Zanandrea, 1998).

If the ATNR persists and does not integrate, it can interfere with

- grasping and hand-to-mouth activities such as feeding;
- reaching across the body's midline;
- developing eye-hand coordination as a result of the head continually turning to one side;
- tracking visually, such as difficulty holding something at mid-range for reading;
- rolling and the development of crawling;
- sitting or lying symmetrically;
- engaging in symmetrical activities and positions and midline activities such as bilateral hand usage;
- using symmetrical body alignment and the ability to walk in a straight line of travel (resulting in veering), which is critical in street crossings; and
- centering of the cane hand, which affects cane usage and increases the tendency to veer as the opposite shoulder is pulled backward.

Activities to help integrate the ATNR include those that involve using both hands together at midline. Midline play should be encouraged in children with visual impairments because it facilitates the integration of any remaining traces of the ATNR and leads to more purposeful movement. Examples of activities that help integrate ATNR are provided in Sidebar 3.2.

In addition, practicing activities that involve crossing the midline of the body helps children integrate the left and right sides of the body and increases overall functioning and mobility skills. Such purposeful play also facilitates

TABLE 3.1

Common Reflexes in Infants

Reflex	Approximate Age of Development	Description of Reflex	Illustration of Reflex
Stepping Reflex	Birth–3 months	When the soles of the feet touch a flat surface while the infant is supported at trunk, feet appear to attempt to walk by placing one foot in front of the other (even though infants this young cannot support their own weight).	
Tonic Labyrinthine Reflex (TLR)	Birth–3 months	When the infant is in a supine position (lying on the back), there is an increase in muscle tone in the extensor muscles of the body. When the child is in a prone position (lying on the stomach), there is an increase in muscle tone in the flexor muscles of the body.	
Moro Reflex	Birth–4 months	Elicited by raising the head slightly and allowing it to drop. A normal response consists of extension, followed by flexion of the arms and legs, and usually a brief cry.	
Startle Reflex	Observed in typical newborns but usually suppressed by 3–4 months of age	A sudden jerking of the body or sudden flexion, extension, and repeated flexion of the extremities. While similar to the Moro in appearance, it is elicited by a sudden loud noise or movement or a light or cold stimulus.	
Palmar Grasp Reflex	Birth–5 months	Occurs when the palm of the hand is stimulated and the infant closes his hand around the stimulus.	

TABLE 3.1

Reflex	Approximate Age of Development	Description of Reflex	Illustration of Reflex
Asymmetrical Tonic Neck Reflex (ATNR)	Birth–6 months	"Fencing reflex" that occurs when an infant is placed on his back and his head turns to the side. The arm and leg on the side to which his head is turned extend, and the opposite arm and leg bend.	
Plantar Reflex	Birth–8 months	Occurs when pressure is placed on the ball of the foot and the toes curl.	
Symmetrical Tonic Neck Reflex (STNR)	2–12 months	When the infant's neck flexes, the arms flex and the legs extend; when the neck extends, the arms extend and the legs flex. This is not a true primitive reflex, but rather a transitional reflex that assists the infant to transition from a lying position to readiness to be able to crawl and creep. To truly crawl or creep, however, this reflex must integrate to undo the automatic linking of the head and extremities.	

Illustrations of reflexes provided by Robert Nailon.

the integration of information that is gained through the senses.

Postural Reactions

Automatic postural reactions consist of movements that occur in response to, or in anticipation of, changes in the body's position relative to gravity. Reactions provide the foundation for an individual's ability to adjust to movement and maintain an upright posture against gravity (Alexander, Boehme, & Cupps, 1993; Zafeiriou, 2004). Unlike reflexes, reactions are considered mature neurological responses, which are retained throughout life and serve to

---

SIDEBAR 3.2

Sample Activities to Integrate ATNR

Activities for Young Children

Any activity that provides a reason for infants who are blind or visually impaired to put their hands together facilitates midline experiences:

• Holding a bottle
• Playing "Pat-a-Cake"
• Using both hands to explore a new toy

Activities for Older Children

• Placing one hand at midline while performing search patterns or reading a map
• Holding the wrist of the cane hand to keep it centered when first learning the touch technique
• Using both hands to explore an object held at midline

---

support higher-level movement, balance, and coordination (Rosen, 2010). Reactions appear during the first year of life as neurological reflexes fade. See Table 3.2 for common postural reactions in infants and young children.

There are two major types of postural reactions that play a critical role in mobility: protective extension reactions and equilibrium reactions.

Protective Extension Reactions. Protective extension reactions stimulate the arms and legs to extend in reaching out to break a fall. They serve to protect the body from injury in response to a fall or sudden loss of balance. Protective extension reactions are stimulated by vestibular input (balance system in the inner ear) signaling a sudden change in the head's position relative to gravity. They allow people to use their arms and legs for support when moving in and out of positions (e.g., into and out of a sitting position) and to break a fall. When protective extension reactions are not well developed, children tend not to reach out in response to a fall and may be at a higher risk for injury. In young children, protective extension reactions typically begin to develop at the following ages (Mulligan, 2003):

• Downward: 4–5 months
• Sideways: 6–7 months
• Forward: 7–8 months
• Backward (sitting): 9–10 months

Equilibrium Reactions. *Equilibrium reactions* are integrated responses that help maintain balance when a child's center of gravity is disturbed by an external force. They are an integral part of maintaining balance while walking. Equilibrium reactions are facilitated largely by the proprioceptive system and work to maintain balance against moderated (not sudden) changes in an individual's center of gravity. These reactions can be invisible changes in muscle tone or fully visible movements of the neck, shoulders, trunk, pelvis, arms, and legs counteracting the direction of any change to balance. Once children develop equilibrium reactions, they no longer need to use their hands and arms for support, thus freeing their upper extremities to develop fine motor skills and perform protective techniques as they move through the environment. Equilibrium reactions typically begin to develop between 5–12 months of age and continue to be refined until about 4–5 years of age (Mulligan, 2003):

TABLE 3.2

Common Automatic Postural Reactions

Reaction	Approximate Age of Development	Description of Reaction	Illustration of Reaction
Labyrinthine Righting	Birth–2 months	When the trunk is tilted laterally away from the vertical position, the head adjusts position to remain upright. This reaction is mediated by the vestibular system.	
Head on Body Righting	4–5 months	When the head is turned to the right or left (e.g., when rolling), the shoulders follow. This reaction is the beginning of learning to roll over.	
Body on Body Righting	4–5 months	When the pelvis is turned to the right or left (e.g., when rolling), the shoulders follow; when the shoulders are turned, the pelvis follows. This reaction is also part of learning to roll over.	
Protective Extension	"Parachute reaction" in children; emerges at different levels between 4–10 months • Downward (4–5 months) • Sideways (6–7 months) • Forward (7–8 months) • Backward (9–10 months)	In response to a fall or sudden loss of balance, legs and arms extend in the direction of the fall as if to break the fall.	

(continued on next page)

TABLE 3.2 (*continued*)

Reaction	Approximate Age of Development	Description of Reaction	Illustration of Reaction
Landau	6–7 months	When a child is lifted under the trunk, there is an increase in muscle tone in the extensor muscles of the body, and the head, arms, and legs lift up in extension.	
Equilibrium	Emerges at different levels between 5–21 months • Prone (5–6 months) • Supine (7–8 months) • Sitting (7–10 months) • Quadruped (9–12 months) • Kneeling (10–15 months) • Standing (12–21 months)	The reactions appear and continue to develop as the infant transitions from a horizontal position to sitting, standing, and walking.	

Illustrations of reactions provided by Robert Nailon.

- *Prone* (on one's stomach): 5–6 months
- *Supine* (on one's back): 7–8 months
- Long-sitting: 7–10 months
- *Quadruped* (on all fours): 9–12 months
- Kneeling: 10–15 months
- Standing: 12–21 months

Building Block 2: Muscle Tone

The development of muscle tone is a recognized problem for children born without functional vision (Boehme, 1990; Ferrell, 2011; Jan, Freeman, & Scott, 1977; Jan, Robinson, Scott, & Kinnis, 1975; Rosen, 1997; Sonksen, Levitt, & Kitsinger, 1984). Normally, the brain sends a continuous flow of neurological impulses to the muscles to keep them in a state of readiness for movement. In a condition known as *hypotonia* (low muscle tone)—commonly observed in children born without functional vision—the flow of neural impulses from the brain to the muscles is insufficient to maintain a state of readiness. Therefore, when the muscles need to move, the brain must first send a higher level of neural impulses to bring the muscles to a state of readiness and then send additional impulses to stimulate movement. As a result, movements may seem slow or weak. Children who have low muscle tone may have trouble maintaining an erect posture against gravity and may exhibit clumsiness when moving, their heads may drop forward or may sway or move nonpurposefully if they are bored, and their arm and hand muscles may be weak.

A study of children who are blind in Canada (Jan et al., 1975) found that hypotonia was linked to the age of onset of visual impairment (children born blind had a higher incidence). Another study of children who are blind found that hypotonia was connected to the delayed development of motor skills (Illingworth, Nair, & Russell, 2013). The presence of a visual impairment limits opportunities for visual feedback of motor skills during infancy, making it difficult for children to practice proprioceptive awareness and develop related muscle tone (Rosen, 2010). The best way to improve muscle tone is through activity and movement, especially activities that involve weight-bearing movement (e.g., creeping, wheelbarrow games where children walk on their arms while an adult holds their feet off the ground) and movement against resistance (e.g., lifting weights, pulling or pushing objects).

In contrast to hypotonia, children who have certain types of brain injuries have high postural tone, or *hypertonia*, meaning that their muscles have an abnormal increase in tension and a resistance to stretching. It may be hard for these children to relax their muscles, especially when under stress or when excited. As a result, their limbs have a tendency to remain stiff and either bent or extended, interfering with voluntary movement. Collaborating with a physical or an occupational therapist is essential when working with children who have hypertonia.

Building Block 3: Sensory Systems

Proprioception is the awareness of the position of the body and its parts in space. Sensors in the body, called proprioceptors, are primarily embedded in an individual's joints, muscles, and tendons. These sensors are activated by movement as well as by bearing and shifting weight.

"Proprioception helps a child know how to move by supplying sensory information about the position of the limbs in space and influencing judgment on how fast and how far to move in order to reach a target" (Strickling & Pogrund, 2002, p. 293). Infants typically receive proprioceptive stimulation throughout the day as they interact with family members or caregivers. When infants voluntarily move their extremities and trunk, this action stimulates the proprioceptive sensory endings. Sighted infants use vision to observe each body movement with interest, fine-tuning their proprioceptive awareness through visual feedback (e.g., watching their hands and feet move as they play with them). When proprioceptive awareness is not fine-tuned, children usually demonstrate an immature gait pattern, impaired balance, and poor fine-motor coordination.

Decreased proprioception is often associated with hypotonia, so the same resistance activities that help to improve muscle tone will also stimulate the proprioceptive sense. Additionally, if a child is suspected of having poor proprioceptive awareness, a physical therapist can suggest child-specific *facilitation activities* to promote optimum functioning of the sensory and motor systems.

The *vestibular system* originates from receptors in the inner ear and provides information about acceleration and deceleration of the body. This system is related to movement of the head and the pull of gravity. Proper vestibular function leads to spatial orientation, balance, and equilibrium (Goldberg et al., 2012). Vestibular function further interacts with visual and proprioceptive information, allowing a child to move efficiently (Marendaz, Stivalet, Barraclough, & Walkowiac, 1993). If a vestibular problem is suspected, educational team members are encouraged to talk with an occupational therapist, who can work with the child on activities to help improve vestibular function.

Visual impairment is not just the loss of one sensory system; it can involve the disruption of vestibular and proprioceptive processing. Therefore, having one sensory system that is not fully functioning can result in other systems also being compromised. It is not uncommon for children with visual impairments to also have sensory problems involving their vestibular or proprioceptive systems because these systems are interwoven with effective motor development and function.

Mannerisms

Mannerisms (sometimes called stereotypies) are repetitive or self-stimulatory behaviors that are evident in some children, including children with visual impairments. As an expression of an unmet physiological or psychological need, some mannerisms reflect a need for increased stimulation of a specific sensory system (Ellis, 2015). For example, rocking and head swaying provide vestibular stimulation; finger flicking and hand flapping stimulate the proprioceptive system; eye poking stimulates the visual system and can therefore be rewarding to a child who is blind. At times, stereotypies can signify concentration, or even boredom (often these mannerisms will be performed with slow repetitions); stereotypies may also signify overload or stress (fast repetitions of mannerisms are sometimes used by a child to "tune out").

Even though these behaviors may be meeting a need for the child, they can be detrimental to social interactions with others (Pring & Tadic, 2010). Many children who are blind or visually impaired do not realize the impact of these movements on other people because they cannot see how people who are sighted usually hold their heads and bodies during conversations. Sometimes, stereotypies can even be physically injurious to the child. For example, excessive eye poking may cause retinal damage (even if the "starbursts" being "seen" are reinforcing to the child with minimal or no vision).

Identifying the need being met by a mannerism may help to determine alternative activities that may be more socially appropriate or safer that can take the place of the undesired behavior. For example, the need for more vestibular stimulation results in rocking, swaying, or repetitive head movements, so providing more time for age-appropriate activities such as swinging, swaying in a rocking chair, or being transported in a carrier on a parent's body may reduce the need for these self-stimulatory movements. Similarly, keeping a child's hands busy with engaging, enjoyable activities may reduce the amount of eye poking that occurs. Keeping children active and involved in meaningful activities that stimulate their sensory systems and increase their motor competence early on is a positive way to address such mannerisms before they become routine. Although children who are blind or visually impaired may be unaware of the social implications of their mannerisms (e.g., that constant rocking is a distraction to others), some children may have the cognitive ability to understand such a concept. For these children, reminding them of the effect their mannerisms have on others, by providing a gentle touch on the shoulder as a predetermined cue that a child is rocking, can help them increase awareness of their actions.

Over time, mannerisms can become ingrained habits that can be difficult to eliminate. If this is the case, or if the child does not have the cognitive ability to understand the implications of mannerisms or the desire to control them, one option is to introduce an applied behavior analysis approach (Alberto & Troutman, 2012; DeMario & Crowley, 1994). *Applied behavior analysis* is a scientifically validated approach to responding to behavior and understanding how behavior is affected by the environment. It focuses on explaining how learning takes place using principles such as positive reinforcement. Applied behavior analysis uses specific behavioral strategies to bring about meaningful behavioral change.

Sensory Integration

Sensory integration is "the neurological process that organizes sensation from one's own body and from the environment and makes it possible to use the body effectively within the environment. The spatial and temporal aspects of inputs from sensory modalities are interpreted, associated, and unified" (Ayres, 1989, p. 11; see also Bundy & Murray, 2002). In other words, sensory integration is the process by which sensory information is received through the body's sense organs and systems (i.e., eyes, ears, nose, skin, tongue, as well as muscles and joints), relayed through the central nervous system, then "integrated" into action, perception, and other experiences. It is believed that optimal cognitive and motor development depends on the functioning of the basic sensory systems (Bundy & Murray, 2002). Some occupational therapists are specially trained in sensory integration therapy and should be consulted if a child is demonstrating problems with sensory integration.

Ayres (1989) identified a pattern of behaviors that she called sensory integration dysfunction, now called sensory processing disorder (Bundy & Murray, 2002), which is characterized by difficulty processing auditory and tactile information and a tendency to be over- or understimulated by the sensory experiences of life. Signs of sensory processing disorder can include dyspraxia (problems with motor planning), clumsiness, inability to filter out background stimuli from primary stimuli, and excessive resistance to certain tastes or smells or to auditory or tactile input.

Sensory integration therapy proposes that sensory input can be provided systematically and thus can force the central nervous system to process it (Bundy & Murray, 2002). Sensory integration therapy is based on the theory that the more processing carried out by the central nervous system, the more efficient it becomes, resulting in more effective motor output. Sensory integration therapy has been used successfully with children who have neurological disorders as well as with some children with visual impairments. Because of the need for highly developed tactile systems, a child who is blind may receive tactile input from sensory integration therapy through organized bombardment of the central nervous system, which can help the child interpret touch correctly (Ricketts, 2008).

Some children who are blind or visually impaired exhibit *tactile selectiveness*, an aversion to contacting certain textures or sensations, or *tactile avoidance* (previously referred to as tactile defensiveness or tactile hypersensitivity), an unwillingness to make tactile contact with novel objects and a tendency not to explore tactilely (Downing & Chen, 2003). Tactile sensations that others may not even notice can cause extreme irritation and discomfort for children with tactile selectiveness, to the point that even a light touch can be unpleasant for them. These children may also dislike others touching them, getting their hair washed or cut, being bathed, changing clothes, getting their hands dirty, wearing clothes with tags, or being too close to others.

For children with tactile sensitivity, it is important to forewarn them before touching them or handing them objects, touch them with a firmer rather than a lighter touch, and avoid touch by using other sensory systems whenever possible. Sometimes, children with sensory integration difficulties may also have auditory hypersensitivity (e.g., aversion to loud noises), oral hypersensitivity (e.g., avoiding foods with a certain texture, dislike of brushing teeth), or visual hypersensitivity (e.g., aversion to bright lights, discomfort in outdoor lighting) (Wilbarger & Wilbarger, 2002). The occupational therapist with training in sensory integration therapy can help children integrate tactile and other sensory systems at a neurological level so they can tolerate and use sensory information more effectively.

Guiding Principles of Sensorimotor Development

For anyone working with young children who are blind or visually impaired, it is important to first understand typical motor development in children with vision. Without this baseline knowledge, it can be hard to recognize when a child with a visual impairment is experiencing motor difficulties or challenges.

Motor development typically progresses in a specific order, and this order influences the acquisition of movement. The direction in which motor development proceeds can be categorized as follows (Cech & Martin, 2002):

- *Cephalocaudal*: Muscular development, which proceeds from head to toe (from head and neck to trunk, then to arms and hands, and finally to legs and feet). (The one exception to this rule is in the development of standing posture, which will be discussed later in this chapter.)
- *Proximal* to *distal*: Control of muscles, starting closest to the midline and then expanding out into the extremities (from trunk and head, to arms and legs, to hands and feet).
- *Gross to fine* and *general to specific*: Motor skills that progress from the use of large muscles (leg and arm movements) to small muscles (discrete hand movements).

It is true that both gross and fine motor skills follow a typical developmental pattern, with one skill building upon the next. Table 3.3 shows the stages of gross motor skill development for children with typical vision and Table 3.4 shows the stages of gross motor skill development for children with visual impairments. It is important to remember that children develop at their own pace and that such developmental charts should be used only as a guideline (Adolph & Joh, 2007). It is not unusual for children both with and without vision to develop outside of these typical parameters. Families and teachers should not be alarmed if a child does not reach a motor milestone exactly on target. However, if significant delays occur, it would be wise to seek out the opinion of a pediatrician, physical therapist, or occupational therapist.

The consequence of significant delays in motor skill development is that undeveloped skills

TABLE 3.3

Sequence of Gross Motor Skill Acquisition for Sighted Children

Age of Onset of Skill	Gross Motor Skill or Activity Observed
Birth–4 weeks	Initial physiological flexion, asymmetrical posturing (due to primitive reflex involvement); visual response to faces, light, some shapes
1–2 months	Movements into extension through spine, arms and legs move out into space, begins to lift head against gravity while prone (prone-on-elbows position); visual interest in objects and actions of people in the environment
3–5 months	More symmetry in movement, visual development assists with dissociation of head movement from upper-body movement; visually directed reaching, first with two hands, then one hand; head control improves; independent rolling
6–8 months	Sits independently after being propped, using one or both hands for support; grasps, releases, and transfers toys and other small objects; begins moving in and out of sitting position; primitive reflexes are integrated; crawling and creeping emerge as a way to access people or objects (purposeful movement through space)
9–11 months	Pulls to stand with minimal assistance, manages all transitional movements independently (such as sit-to-stand and stand-to-floor); goal-directed movement through space continues; stands alone momentarily, begins walking
12–14 months	Walks with one hand held or begins walking independently; chooses between walking and creeping depending on the task; moves onto and off of low furniture
15–18 months	Walks well independently on level surfaces; begins to negotiate inclines and declines; needs help with steps
21–24 months	Manages stairs with minimal assistance and a handrail; running begins; accesses rocking toys, uses push and pull toys; spinal posture is usually established by this time
36 months	Runs, kicks, balances briefly on one foot, jumps in place, alternates feet when climbing stairs

Source: Reprinted from Strickling, C. A., & Pogrund, R. L. (2002). Table 9.1: Sequence of gross motor skills acquisition for sighted children. In R. L. Pogrund & D. L. Fazzi (Eds.), *Early focus: Working with young children who are blind or visually impaired and their families* (2nd ed., p. 291). New York, NY: AFB Press.

do not provide the foundation needed for the development of new or more advanced motor skills. For example, if an infant cannot bear weight on his or her forearms while on the stomach, the result is poor development of *shoulder girdle* stability, neck and trunk *extensor muscles*, and, in turn, poor control of the head, neck, arms, and hands.

Motor Differences in Children with Visual Impairments

For purposeful movement to occur, three major sensory systems need to work together: proprioceptive, vestibular, and visual. It is vision,

TABLE 3.4

Sequence of Gross Motor Skill Acquisition for Children with Visual Impairments

Age of Onset of Skill	Gross Motor Skill or Activity Observed
Birth–4 weeks	Initial physiological flexion (a bending movement), asymmetrical posturing (due to primitive reflex involvement); touch, movement, and sound are the primary stimuli
1–2 months	Movements into extension through spine (arms and legs move out into space), prone-on-elbows positioning remains difficult; interested in play on the body, attends to rhythms and physical handling
3–5 months	More symmetry in movement, tendency to avoid prone positioning; head control emerges in supported sitting, likes supine (on back) position; hands remain lightly fisted
6–8 months	Sits independently after being propped, using one or both hands for support; briefly holds objects placed into the hand, sometimes mouthing them, sometimes simply releasing them; moves from sitting to supine position and pivots in a circle; limited crawling in pursuit of objects or people
9–11 months	Pulls to stand with minimal assistance; may be up on toes for several months; manages all transitional movements independently (such as sit-to-stand and stand-to-floor); may begin goal-directed movement through space, if encouraged
12–14 months	Walks indoors with one hand held, sometimes with two; creeping continues, though some completely skip creeping as a means of locomotion; may cruise on furniture
15–18 months	Walks independently on level surfaces; begins to negotiate indoor inclines and declines with physical assistance from an adult; may move down declines using a crouched position and searching with hands; limited exploration of outdoor or unfamiliar environments
21–24 months	Manages stairs with moderate assistance and a handrail and/or adult assistance; walks independently in familiar surroundings; begins learning simple routes for daily activities and how to use landmarks in ambulation
36 months	Travels indoors independently in familiar settings; development of dynamic balance; age-appropriate motor skills like running, jumping, and kicking balls usually are not yet established

Source: Reprinted from Strickling, C. A., & Pogrund, R. L. (2002). Table 9.2: Sequence of gross motor skill acquisition for children with visual impairment. In R. L. Pogrund & D. L. Fazzi (Eds.), *Early focus: Working with young children who are blind or visually impaired and their families* (2nd ed., p. 297). New York, NY: AFB Press.

together with the vestibular and proprioceptive systems, that provides the feedback mechanism by which children develop a sensorimotor foundation, increase their knowledge of spatial relations, and develop body awareness and balance (Strickling & Pogrund, 2002). As a result of the interactions between visual, vestibular, and proprioceptive sensory inputs in the central nervous system, when vision is impaired, the proprioceptive and vestibular systems may also experience delays in development or may not develop fully (Rosen, 2010). Sensorimotor development in children with visual impairments is also at risk due to a lack of opportunities for imitative learning, in which children mimic the actions of others whom they observe. Children who have visual impairments may also have limited opportunities for movement, further compounding the problem because it is active movement, including weight-bearing activities, that develops joint stability and muscle tone.

In general, children with visual impairments develop static or stable sensorimotor skills (e.g., sitting, standing) at the same age as their sighted peers. However, gross motor skills that are dynamic or mobile, involving movement in the environment (e.g., creeping, walking), can be delayed in children with visual impairments (Bouchard & Tetreault, 2000; Maida & McCune, 1996; Norris, Spaulding, & Brodie, 1957; Wagner, Haibach, & Lieberman, 2013). The following sections discuss some of the motor milestones with the most significant impact on future O&M skills for children with visual impairments.

Prone on Elbows

One of the key motor milestones is prone on elbows (supporting weight on the forearms while lying on the stomach). This prone-on-elbows position allows children to see people and objects nearby and provides for free head movement in all directions. It is visual stimuli that typically motivate children to raise and turn the head in this prone position (Ferrell, 2011; Strickling & Pogrund, 2002). This position also helps develop upper-body strength and encourages important independent head and neck movements that, in turn,

are essential to the development of coordination later on.

The American Academy of Pediatrics (AAP) has, since 1992, recommended that infants not be placed in the prone position for sleeping and that supine is the safest position for sleeping to reduce the risk of sudden infant death syndrome (SIDS). In a 2011 policy statement on infant sleeping, the AAP updated its safe infant sleeping recommendations, which continued to advise placing babies on their backs for sleep, but which also included the need for daily supervised "tummy time" to facilitate motor development and minimize the risk of flat head syndrome (a flattening of the normal curvature on the back of the skull thought to be caused by excessive time lying on the back). Additional sleeping safety guidelines were also included to reduce the risk of SIDS (American Academy of Pediatrics, 2011). Without enough time in the prone position, infants are at risk for additional motor delays. Therefore, promoting tummy time while children are awake is even more important because it empowers children to begin to raise their heads and push up with their arms.

It is commonly observed that infants who are visually impaired dislike being in the prone position (Ferrell, 2011; Strickling & Pogrund, 2002) and are not as motivated as sighted infants to maintain the prone position to observe people or objects. Infants who are blind typically prefer to lie on their backs because this position provides security and a solid reference point, and infants can also hear better in this position than in the prone position. The prone position requires more effort on the part of the infant to breathe since it is difficult for the infant to lift the head as a result of hypotonia. The prone position also makes it more difficult for the infant to interact with others. Until they begin to crawl, however, it is important to encourage

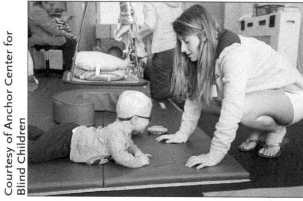

Courtesy of Anchor Center for Blind Children

Figure 3.2 It is important to encourage infants to perform activities, such as playing with toys or interacting with an adult, in the prone-on-elbows position to promote weight bearing and reaching.

infants who are blind or visually impaired to spend time doing activities in the prone position. Playing with toys or interacting with an adult while in the prone position should emphasize weight-bearing and reaching (see Figure 3.2). Placing the infant on a knee or on a wedge, or placing a rolled towel under the chest can help to elevate the upper chest, making it easier for the infant to breathe while on the stomach and placing the arms in a position to bear weight or to reach. The prone position allows for the development of the shoulder girdle and the head and neck muscles and is critical for posture and future gross and fine motor skill development. While the prone-on-elbows position may be static, the movement of elevating on the arms while in the prone position is dynamic and therefore may not develop in a child with a visual impairment until 6–8 months, in contrast to 2–3 months for a child who is sighted.

Reaching

Another significant motor milestone is reaching. Sighted children learn to reach around

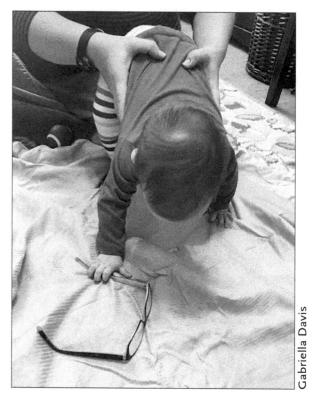

Gabriella Davis

Figure 3.3 Reaching is a significant motor milestone for children with visual impairments.

3–6 months of age; children who are blind learn to reach around 9–12 months of age (see Figure 3.3). Reaching does not involve movement in the environment, so why does its development appear delayed? While visually mediated reaching develops at around 3–6 months of age, reaching toward a sound or toward objects hidden from view in both infants who are sighted and infants who are blind develops at around 9–12 months of age (Fazzi et al., 2002; Ihsen, Troster, & Brambring, 2010). Thus, what appears as a delay is actually quite typical. However, lack of reaching until a later age does limit a child's interaction with the environment and can cause delays in a child's concept development and motivation to move.

Sitting

Sitting typically develops in sighted children and children with visual impairments at around 6–9 months of age. For sighted children, it introduces a new visual perspective, so it is often a motivating position. The concept of "visual verticality" is learned while a child maintains vertical alignment of the spine and stabilizes the trunk in space. Visual verticality allows infants to begin to learn to judge and predict where they are in space and frees their upper limbs from the need to maintain balance in an erect posture; thus, by staying vertical, infants can use their arms for reaching (Rochat & Bullinger, 1994). Most infants can go from sitting to prone and back to sitting by around 9 months of age, after they have learned to sit without support. Being able to sit without support allows infants to use their hands and arms for exploration rather than for balance (see Figure 3.4). Since sitting is a relatively stable and consistent milestone, children who are blind typically sit within about a month of sighted children (Brambring, 2006), but getting into and out of sitting, which is a more fluctuating milestone, typically takes a little longer for a child with a visual impairment (Bayley, 2005). Reaching and moving to and from the sitting position are considered to be among the most critical precursors to creeping (Maida & McCune, 1996) which, as discussed next, is a critically important skill.

Crawling and Creeping

Once a child starts to move purposefully, the typical sequence is *crawling* (on the belly) then *creeping* (on all fours) at 6–8 months, standing at 6–9 months, and walking at 9–18 months. In order to creep, infants need to be able to reach

Michael Rosen

Figure 3.4 Being able to sit without support allows infants to use their hands and arms for exploration rather than for balance.

for an object and move from a sitting to a creeping position.

Many children who are born with visual impairments either show delays in creeping or completely skip that stage of independent movement (Strickling & Pogrund, 2002; Troster, Hecker, & Brambring, 1994). For some children, it might be due to a lack of visual modeling combined with low muscle tone and resulting instability at the shoulder girdle that make creeping difficult. In place of creeping, some children prefer to scoot along the floor on their bottoms to protect their head from bumping into objects in the environment, and some infants who are blind creep backward to reduce the risk of

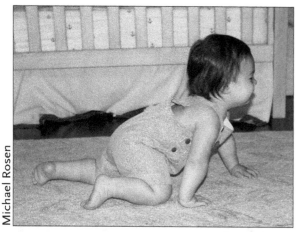

Michael Rosen

Figure 3.5 Creeping may help develop upper-body strength and hand dexterity important for future braille and O&M skills.

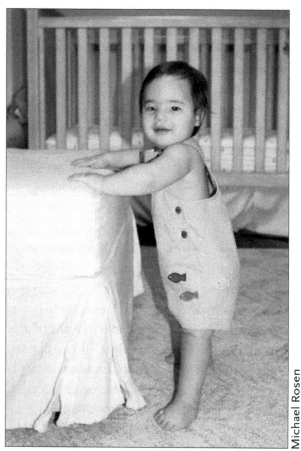

Michael Rosen

Figure 3.6 By 9 months of age, most children can pull up and hold on to furniture for support.

hitting their head. The consequences of not creeping include decreased upper-body strength, decreased trunk rotation, and decreased joint stability in the shoulder girdle (Rosen, 2010). Some early interventionists believe that creeping (see Figure 3.5) may establish a foundation of upper-body strength and hand dexterity important for future braille and O&M skills as well as provide greater tactile tolerance of different surfaces (Ferrell, 2011).

Standing and Cruising

By 9 months of age, most children, whether blind or sighted, can pull up and hold onto furniture for support (see Figure 3.6). Again, the primary incentive to stand is visual (e.g., the child sees the remote control on the coffee table and figures out how to get it). Some children, when first learning to stand, will stand on their toes in an effort to increase sensory feedback. If this position persists, intervention by a physical therapist may be beneficial. As children move from crawling and creeping to unsupported walking, they often engage in an intermediate activity called *cruising*. Cruising refers to the act of walking sideways along furniture, a wall, or kitchen cabinets, using both hands to support oneself on the surface. Cruising serves many functional purposes (Anthony et al., 2004; Lowry & Hatton, 2002) including:

- Providing repeated experience with common objects, landmarks, and surfaces. This experience may help to develop broader environmental concepts, an understanding of object permanence, and goal-directed movement.

- Providing initial opportunities to develop a mental map of an area. This experience, in turn, may lead to greater confidence and incentives for movement as independent walking emerges.

- Preparing the child for trailing at a later point in time.

Walking

Walking follows cruising, and most children are motivated to walk by seeing or hearing something they want to reach. Walking generally begins with two hands held by an adult, then moving to one hand as balance improves. Independent walking typically depends on factors such as muscle tone, proprioception, balance reactions, motivation, and environmental stimulation.

Many children, regardless of their visual ability and to help maintain balance when learning to walk, initially hold their hands and arms up with their elbows bent, a position referred to as *high guard* (Strickling & Pogrund, 2002; see Figure 3.7). Walking without support is often delayed in children with visual impairments. The median age of walking for a full-term infant who is blind is 18 months (Ferrell, 1998).

A word of caution regarding the use of devices such as infant walkers should be noted here. Walkers are extremely dangerous and their use should be kept to a minimum or avoided altogether. In the past, over 25,000 young children have been sent to emergency rooms each year due to walker accidents (AAP, 2001). Most accidents result from rolling down stairs or drop-offs or from terrain changes. Infant walkers are especially dangerous and require constant adult supervision when in use. The AAP (2001) recommends that infant walk-

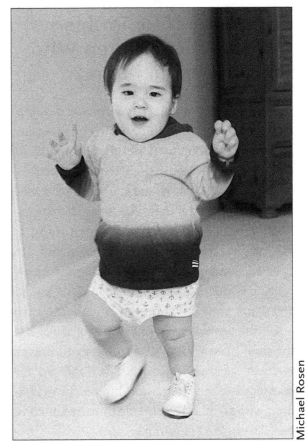

Figure 3.7 A high guard position initially helps a child maintain balance when learning to walk.

ers not be sold in the United States and that they be replaced with saucers, play tables, or swings that are less mobile. Most pediatricians and physical therapists also feel that infant walkers may inhibit development of normal motor patterns and balance and may decrease opportunities for crawling and creeping (Anthony, Bleier, Fazzi, Kish, & Pogrund, 2002; Siegel & Burton, 1999).

The potential consequences of motor development differences observed in children with visual impairments and their long-term effect on O&M skills are discussed in the next section.

Common Motor Problems Observed in Children Who Are Congenitally Blind

As noted earlier in the chapter, motor development is sequential, and a visual impairment can affect the development of most motor skills (Brambring, 2006; Samalot-Rivera, Lieberman, & Haibach, 2015). Low muscle tone, decreased proprioceptive awareness, the presence of primitive reflexes, and incomplete fine-tuning of neurological reactions, such as those involved in balance, combine to also cause difficulty in stabilizing joints and isolating motions, and lead to awkward transitional movements that in turn affect the development of fine motor skills and the skills most associated with successful travel: posture, gait, and balance. See Table 3.5 for commonly observed motor differences in children who are blind or visually impaired as compared to sighted children.

Joint Stability and Isolating Joint Motions

The development of some motions, such as wrist rotation, are primarily visually motivated and reinforced. For example, a young sighted child uses wrist rotation to obtain different visual perspectives of an object without having to change the grip on the object. Without vision to facilitate learning of specific motions, it becomes necessary to rely on proprioception and joint stability. For truly coordinated movement to take place, motion at some joints must be isolated from motion at other joints. Since body parts are moved by the most proximal joint, joints and body segments nearest to the target joint and body part must be stabilized

first. For example, to efficiently rotate the wrist to turn a doorknob (a motion that occurs at the elbow), the shoulder and upper arm must be stable. Otherwise the entire arm moves, rather than just the elbow and forearm, and results in motion that is far less efficient and graceful. Similarly, to bend and straighten just the wrist when performing the touch technique with the long cane, it is necessary to hold the elbow and forearm, and the shoulder and upper arm, stable.

As a result of low muscle tone and inadequate proprioceptive development, some children who are congenitally blind have difficulty *stabilizing joints* (restricting motion in selected joints to provide a stable foundation for precise motion at nearby joints) and *isolating motions* (allowing movement at one joint while restricting movement at a nearby joint). To compensate for the lack of stability, children with visual impairments will often use certain positions that provide physical stability to perform a movement (e.g., elevating the shoulders; see Figure 3.8) to raise the arm. This motion stabilizes the shoulder girdle against the neck structures and is sometimes called "stacking." Children may also assume a "W" position when sitting on the ground (see Figure 3.9a) to provide physical stability at the pelvis rather than using trunk muscles to maintain an upright posture. The "W" position, however, should be discouraged as it may contribute to hip displacement and knee injury. Physical therapists generally recommend tailor sitting (legs crossed in front; see Figure 3.9b) or side sitting (alternating sides periodically) as preferred ways to sit that do not harm the body.

Age-appropriate activities to increase muscle tone and proprioceptive awareness such as weight-bearing activities (e.g., wheelbarrow

TABLE 3.5

Difference in Gross Motor Development between Sighted Children and Children Who Are Blind

Sighted	Congenitally Blind
Muscle Tone	
Typical	Hypotonia
Reflex and Reaction Integration	
ATNR: Fully integrated	ATNR: May not be fully integrated
Protective extension: Well developed	Protective extension: Weak or absent
Equilibrium: Well developed for child's age (i.e., mature gait pattern)	Equilibrium: Not well developed for child's age (i.e., immature gait pattern)
Coordination	
Easily isolates joint motions	Difficulty isolating joint motions
Natural transitional movements (e.g., standing up from the ground)	Awkward transitional movements
Posture	
Head erect	Head down (neck flexion)
Shoulders erect	Shoulders rounded
Trunk: backward lean; lordosis (sway back) may be present	Trunk erect
Hips extended	Hips flexed
Knees straight	Knees hyperextended or flexed
Feet point forward	Feet turned out
Gait	
Narrow stride width (distance between the feet in a plane perpendicular to the line of travel)	Wide stride width
Normal step length	Short step length
Feet point forward	Feet turned out
Reciprocal arm swing	Lack of reciprocal arm swing

games, creeping through an obstacle course) and joint compression (e.g., jumping, marching) can be effective in helping children with visual impairments develop joint stability and improve their ability to isolate motions at joints.

Fine Motor Skills

Prehension skills are the hand movements used to pick up, grasp, and hold objects. After the palmar grasp reflex—the primitive reflex that causes the hand to stay closed in a fist if

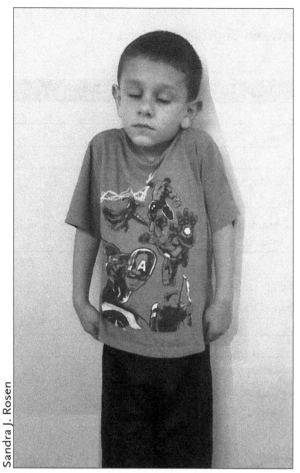

Sandra J. Rosen

Figure 3.8 A position such as elevating the shoulders provides a child with a visual impairment with the stability to perform a movement.

something touches the palm—integrates between 0–5 months of age, the child begins to voluntarily use the hands more and more over the next two years. Fine motor skills—those used to coordinate finger movement—become more precise as the child learns to pick up smaller and smaller objects and to purposefully isolate finger motions.

By being able to observe his or her hands, a child who is sighted develops the proprioceptive awareness to form a strong foundation for fine motor skills. However, for a child who is blind or visually impaired and who does not have the ability to benefit from this visual feedback, proprioception does not always develop fully, thereby interfering with the acquisition of fine motor skills. Furthermore, visual impairment reduces the child's incentive to bring the hands together within visual range.

Poor fine motor skills can affect different aspects of O&M and functioning in the classroom. Being able to grasp and manipulate an adaptive mobility device or a long cane is connected to upper-extremity strength and prehension skills. Using scissors, reading braille, tactilely identifying landmarks, trailing, using protective techniques, reading tactile maps, performing independent living skills, and using systematic search patterns are all related to fine motor skill development.

Understanding that hands are a part of the body is one of the first stages of body awareness for a child with a visual impairment, followed by understanding that hands can be useful. Intervention is needed to facilitate finding the hands for infants who are blind, playing with the hands at midline (see Figure 3.10), and developing grasp and wrist rotation. A list of the general stages of grasp development, demonstrating fine motor skill refinement, are provided in Table 3.6. Creative activities and games that require the use of developmentally appropriate types of grasp help children increase their awareness and practice of fine motor skills. See Table 3.7 for ideas of functional activities that can help develop fine motor skills in young children at different ages. An occupational therapist can also suggest specific activities for each stage of fine motor development.

Sandra J. Rosen

Figure 3.9 Sitting in a "W" position (A) may contribute to hip displacement and knee injury, while tailor sitting (B) provides a safe and stable position for maintaining an upright posture.

Courtesy of Anchor Center for Blind Children

Figure 3.10 Playing with the hands at midline helps a child with a visual impairment build an understanding that hands are a part of the body and that they are useful.

Posture

The low muscle tone experienced by many children with visual impairments can result in a number of postural problems. One of the most common postural problems is a head that is rotated to the side, held forward of the neck, or even hanging down instead of being held erect and facing forward (Rosen, 2010). It is important to determine why an atypical head position is occurring. Is it due to low muscle tone? Is it due to scoliosis (a sideways curvature of the spine)? Is it due to visual function? Children who

TABLE 3.6

General Development of Grasp

Grasp	Approximate Age of Development	Description of Grasp	Illustration of Grasp
Crude Palmar Grasp	4–5 months	Child grasps an object in the ulnar (little finger) side of the palm. The thumb is not used.	
Palmar Grasp	5–6 months	Child holds an object in the center of the palm. Again, the thumb is not used.	
Radial Palmar Grasp	6–7 months	Child holds an object in the radial (thumb) side of the palm. The ulnar-side fingers are used for stability and the thumb begins to oppose (move toward the pads of the fingers) and actively help press the object into the palm.	
Raking Grasp	7–8 months	Child picks up objects by bending the radial (thumb-side) fingers to "rake" objects into the palm.	
Radial Digital Grasp	8–9 months	Child holds the object by using the thumb and radial fingers to help secure the object, while flexing the ulnar fingers for stability.	
Inferior Pincer Grasp	8–9 months	Child adducts the thumb (moving it across the palm instead of leaving it on the side of the palm) and secures the object against the extended index finger.	

TABLE 3.6

Grasp	Approximate Age of Development	Description of Grasp	Illustration of Grasp
Pincer Grasp	10–12 months	Child holds the object between the thumb and index finger. The thumb and index finger are held in a full opposition position, in which the pads of each face one another and are used to secure the object. (Note: This is different from the neat pincer grasp, in which the child secures an object using the tip of the index finger instead of the pad.)	

Illustrations of grasps provided by Sandra J. Rosen.

Source: Adapted from Columbia University Medical Center, Community Pediatrics. (2009). Developmental progression of the grasp. New York, NY: Author. Retrieved from http://www.columbia.edu/itc/hs/medical/residency/peds/new_compeds _site/grasp.doc

have low vision may need to turn their head to find the best viewing position, and children with scoliosis may not be able to maintain good alignment of the head and trunk because of physical limitations. Also, children who have low vision tend to hold their head forward while trying to improve visual functioning for near tasks. The rounded shoulders commonly observed as a result of low muscle tone in the trunk cause children to hold their heads down. It is important to indicate to children the social implications of this type of head position and how to selectively correct it, if possible, when desired (e.g., during a conversation with someone sighted to show interest). It is not uncommon for children who are blind to turn an ear toward the speaker or hold their heads down to listen better, but they should be taught the social implications of such head positions if they are capable of understanding.

If the child is young, or highly motivated, some postural problems can be corrected. For example, in addition to verbal feedback about posture, a physical therapist might recommend some exercises to improve posture or have the child wear a weighted vest to provide resistance to hypotonic trunk muscles that, in turn, can facilitate improved muscle tone in the trunk and possibly improved head position and tendency to round the shoulders. When considering whether to try and correct a child's head position, a team approach to intervention is needed. A physical therapist can analyze body positioning while a teacher of students with visual impairments or O&M specialist can analyze the effect of the visual impairment.

Gait

Common gait patterns observed in individuals born without functional vision include using a wide base of support, out-toeing (pointing the feet outward rather than forward), lack of *reciprocal arm swing*, and short steps. These are not

TABLE 3.7

Functional Activities for Development of Grasp and Fine Motor Skills

As children who are sighted and children who have visual impairments develop grasp and fine motor skills, their development can be observed and promoted by practicing the following functional activities.

Approximate Age	Development of Grasp and Fine Motor Skills	Suggested Activities
2–4 months	The palmar grasp reflex remains strong. The child begins to reach for objects—albeit with poor motor control—but is not yet able to grasp them.	None
4–8 months	The palmar grasp reflex weakens and the child is able to reach for objects easily. The child begins to hold larger objects using both hands and transfers objects from one had to the other, although not easily.	• Play with squeeze toys • Squeeze clay or Play-Doh • Take objects out of containers • Play with sand
8–12 months	The child transfers objects from one hand to the other and uses both hands to hold larger objects. The child is able to release objects voluntarily, although perhaps not in a well-controlled manner. The child is not yet able to manipulate objects in the hand.	• Sing songs and clap hands at midline • Stack cans, rings, blocks, or nesting cups • Turn pages in a book • Roll ball • Put shapes into a shape sorter
1–2 years	The child uses the pincer grasp to hold very tiny objects and the radial palmar grasp to pick up slightly larger ones. The child is able to release objects in a controlled manner and begins to develop the ability to move objects from the fingers into the palms. The child stabilizes with one hand while manipulating an object with the other hand and can point with an isolated index finger.	• Build a tower with 1-inch blocks • Scribble or color with crayons • Do large puzzles • Place pegs in a pegboard • Make fingerprints in clay or Play-Doh • Put coins in a slot
2–3 years	The child begins to develop the ability to move objects from the palm into the fingers. The child can now use both hands together.	• Open simple containers with lids • Play with wind-up toys • String large beads • Play with finger puppets • Pour from one container into another • Stabilize a bowl while stirring

TABLE 3.7

Approximate Age	Development of Grasp and Fine Motor Skills	Suggested Activities
3–4 years	The child can manipulate large buttons and is able to use the hands well to dress and undress. The child is able to grasp a pencil in a mature tripod grasp (with the thumb, index, and middle fingers working together to grasp the pencil).	• Color with pencils, crayons, and markers • Button, zip, and snap • Paint with a paintbrush or finger paint • String smaller beads
4–6 years	The child now has refined motor skills and can use one hand consistently for fine motor activities. The child can dress with limited support and can spread and cut soft foods.	• Tie shoes • Use fork and knife for cutting • Manage a mouse and keyboard on a computer • Manipulate Lego pieces • Use office tools and supplies: stapler, hole puncher, glue, scissors

abnormalities of gait, but rather compensations for the poor fine-tuning of equilibrium reactions. These characteristics also resemble the gait patterns of sighted toddlers (Haibach, Wagner, & Lieberman, 2014). In other words, the gait of individuals with congenital blindness is not abnormal, but the development of a normal gait pattern stops prematurely due to the lack of balance to support its development. Small steps limit the time spent on the support of one foot before the child has both feet touching the ground again. This pattern leads to the appearance of a "shuffling" gait in which there is a notable lack of heel strike followed by the toe pushing off with each step. A wide gait and out-toeing compensate for poor balance by providing a broader base of support. Out-toeing also positions the ligaments in the joints to provide more stability at the knee joint, reducing the demand on the hypotonic *quadriceps*, which stabilize the knee

during weight-bearing. Pointing the feet outward also limits the flexibility of the hips to support larger steps. The tendency of children who are blind to hold their arms at their side, a position called *low guard*, keeps the arms near the body's center of gravity and limits any challenge to balance that can occur as the arms swing.

An immature gait pattern can cause significant mobility problems. For example, short step lengths and out-toeing tend to decrease walking speed. This, in turn, not only limits efficiency of travel, but also leads to an increased tendency to veer during street crossings (Rosen, 1988). Anecdotal evidence suggests that immature gait patterns are also associated with decreased endurance while traveling.

Several methods exist that can help children practice walking with more mature gait patterns. While research has not yet validated these approaches, there are some indications that they may be helpful. For example, using weighted push toys, adaptive mobility devices, or a long cane can help a young child move more confidently and freely in the environment, thereby exercising balance skills as the child walks, with the potential to improve gait and posture if practiced during the preschool years (before gait patterns stabilize). For example, introducing a cane to a toddler who has good balance may reduce fear of movement as the toddler explores his or her surroundings and may result in improved posture and gait (Bronwen, 2010; Pogrund & Rosen, 1989).

Gait patterns tend to stabilize around 6–7 years of age (Rosen, 2010; Sutherland, Olshen, Cooper, & Woo, 1980), so the optimum time to begin activities designed to facilitate the development of a mature gait pattern is during the preschool years. If immature gait patterns are observed in a child who is preschool age or older, it is important to seek the consultation of a physical therapist to try to correct such immature gait patterns and prevent problems as the child grows older.

Teaming to Develop Motor Skills

It has been established that most children who grow up without functional vision progress through the same stages of motor development as children who have vision, however, they do acquire some skills later, the development of some skills may stop at a premature stage, and the quality of their movement is often compromised (Brambring, 2006; Haibach et al., 2014; Rosen, 2010; Strickling & Pogrund, 2002). While children who have low vision and even some without functional vision develop motor skills with little or no intervention, many

children will need help learning basic motor skills to participate in activities alongside their sighted peers. It is often early intervention provided by professionals who are knowledgeable about the effect of vision loss on development that makes the difference in motor outcomes for these children. The promotion of motor development leads to a higher likelihood of success in mobility skills, social skills, recreational skills, daily living skills, and health and fitness (Adolph & Berger, 2005; Diamond, 2007).

When working with young children with multiple disabilities, it is important that the O&M specialist, teacher of students with visual impairments, physical therapist, occupational therapist, early interventionist, special education teacher, and any other educational team members communicate regularly with one another and work on shared goals for the child's optimal motor development. It is essential to include family members in supporting motor development objectives so that appropriate strategies are used on a daily basis at home as well as in school.

The O&M specialist is a critical member of a child's educational team whenever motor development skills are being addressed. The O&M specialist possesses a wealth of knowledge about the effect of vision loss on development and learning as well as an understanding of the implications for future O&M skills if motor development is not addressed effectively in the early years. Other team members can turn to the O&M specialist for expertise on purposeful movement within an O&M context. The O&M specialist can teach other team members, such as occupational and physical therapists, early interventionists, and family members, basic O&M skills (see Chapter 6) that these team members can reinforce with the child. The O&M specialist can also teach the importance of supporting motor skills and milestones, such as prone on elbows or purposeful reaching, that will ultimately lead to safer and more efficient movement for the child.

Collaboration by all members of the educational team is critically important in promoting the development and generalization of motor skills. Adults who spend the most time with the child each week (typically a family member, caregiver, paraeducator, or classroom teacher) are vital members of this team since they are the ones who need to reinforce and support motor skills throughout the day. A collaborative approach to intervention among all team members is important to ensure the best motor outcomes for children who are blind or visually impaired. (See Chapter 11 for more information on collaboration.)

Summary

For individuals with visual impairments, quality is as important as function. There may be times when the need for function outweighs the need for quality in performing a task. For example, a child may need to learn a route or how to perform an independent living skill immediately, whether or not it is done with the highest level of grace or coordination. However, when it comes to sensorimotor development and functioning, quality cannot always be ignored in a rush for function. Because the acquisition of higher-level motor skills relies heavily on the development of lower-level skills and abilities, it is important to weigh any immediate need against the long-term benefit of emphasizing quality in movement.

When it comes to O&M, one of the most notable examples deals with the consequences of not addressing an immature gait pattern early on. Immature gait patterns can lead to veering during street crossings later. Rather than dealing with the frustration and stress experienced by both the child and the O&M specialist when trying to correct the tendency to veer during street crossings, it may be more effective to address proprioceptive, muscle tone, and balance needs while the child is young in order to develop mature, efficient gait patterns. These mature gait patterns, in turn, facilitate the ability to travel in a straight line later (Rosen, 2010).

For children with visual impairments, the significance of motor skill development and movement in general cannot be overemphasized. It is safe, graceful, and efficient movement that facilitates success in O&M, social skills, recreation and leisure, future vocational goals, and independent living skills. All areas of the expanded core curriculum are affected by a limited ability to move, so a solid foundation in sensorimotor skills has a long-term impact on overall growth and development for a child who is blind or visually impaired.

References

Adolph, K. E., & Berger, S. E. (2005). Physical and motor development. In M. H. Bornstein & M. E. Lamb (Eds.), *Developmental science: An advanced textbook* (5th ed., pp. 223–281). New York, NY: Psychology Press.

Adolph, K. E., & Joh, A. S. (2007). Motor development: How infants get into the act. In A. Slater & M. Lewis (Eds.), *An introduction to infant development* (2nd ed., pp. 63–80). New York, NY: Oxford University Press.

Alberto, P. A., & Troutman, A. C. (2012). *Applied behavior analysis for teachers* (9th ed.). Upper Saddle River, NJ: Pearson Education.

Alexander, R., Boehme, R., & Cupps, B. (1993). *Normal development of functional motor skills: The first year of life.* Tucson, AZ: Therapy Skill Builders.

American Academy of Pediatrics, Committee on Injury and Poison Prevention. (2001). Injuries associated with infant walkers. *Pediatrics, 108*(3), 790–792.

American Academy of Pediatrics, Task Force on Sudden Infant Death Syndrome. (2011). SIDS and other sleep-related infant deaths: Expansion of recommendations for a safe infant sleeping environment. *Pediatrics, 128*(5), 1030–1039. Retrieved from http://pediatrics.aappublications.org/content/pediatrics/early/2011/10/12/peds.2011-2284.full.pdf

Anthony, T. L., Bleier, H., Fazzi, D. L., Kish, D., & Pogrund, R. L. (2002). Mobility focus: Developing early skills for orientation and mobility. In R. L. Pogrund & D. L. Fazzi (Eds.), *Early focus: Working with young children who are blind or visually impaired and their families* (2nd ed., pp. 326–404). New York, NY: AFB Press.

Anthony, T. L., Lowry, S. S., Brown, C. J., & Hatton, D. D. (2004). Foundations of developmentally appropriate mobility. In T. L. Anthony, S. S. Lowry, C. J. Brown, & D. D. Hatton (Eds.), *Developmentally appropriate orientation and mobility*. Chapel Hill: University of North Carolina at Chapel Hill, FPG Child Development Institute, Early Intervention Training Center for Infants and Toddlers with Visual Impairments.

Ayres, A. J. (1989). *Sensory integration and praxis tests*. Torrance, CA: Western Psychological Services.

Bayley, N. (2005). *Bayley Scales of Infant and Toddler Development (Bayley-III): Motor scale kit* (3rd ed.). San Antonio, TX: Psychological Corporation.

Blythe, P. (2002). The role of the primitive asymmetrical tonic neck reflex (ATNR) in balance, co-ordination problems and specific learning difficulties, including dyslexia [Monograph]. Chester, England: INPP.

Blythe, S. G. (2010, April). *Neuro-motor maturity as an indicator of developmental readiness for education*. Paper presented at the Institute for Neuro-Physiological Psychology Conference, Miami, FL.

Boehme, R. (1990). *The hypotonic child: Treatment for postural control, endurance, strength, and sensory organization* (Rev. ed.). Tucson, AZ: Therapy Skill Builders.

Bouchard, D., & Tetreault, S. (2000). The motor development of sighted children and children with moderate low vision aged 8–13. *Journal of Visual Impairment & Blindness, 94*(9), 564–573.

Brambring, M. (2006). Divergent development of gross motor skills in children who are blind or sighted. *Journal of Visual Impairment & Blindness, 100*(10), 620–634.

Bronwen, S. (2010). Early long cane use: A case study. *AER Journal: Research and Practice in Visual Impairment and Blindness, 3*(1), 26–29.

Bundy, A. C., & Murray, E. A. (2002). Sensory integration: A. Jean Ayres' theory revisited. In A. C. Bundy, S. J. Lane, & E. A. Murray (Eds.), *Sensory integration: Theory and practice* (2nd ed., pp. 3–33). Philadelphia, PA: F.A. Davis.

Bunker, L. K. (1991). The role of play and motor skill development in building children's self-confidence and self-esteem. *The Elementary School Journal, 91*(5), 467–471.

Callcott, D. (2012). Retained primary reflexes in pre-primary-aged indigenous children: The effect on movement ability and school readiness. *Australasian Journal of Early Childhood, 37*(2), 132–140.

Cech, D. J., & Martin, S. (2002). *Functional movement development: Across the lifespan* (2nd ed.). Philadelphia, PA: Elsevier Saunders.

Colangelo, C. A. (1999). Biomechanical frame of reference. In P. K. Kramer & J. Hinojosa (Eds.), *Frames of reference for pediatric occupational therapy* (2nd ed., pp. 257–322). Philadelphia, PA: Lippincott Williams & Wilkins.

DeMario, N. C., & Crowley, E. P. (1994). Using applied behavior analysis procedures to change the behavior of students with visual disabilities: A research review. *Journal of Visual Impairment & Blindness, 88*(6), 532–543.

Diamond, A. (2000). Close interrelation of motor development and cognitive development and of the cerebellum and prefrontal cortex. *Child Development, 71*(1), 44–56.

Diamond, A. (2007). Interrelated and interdependent. *Developmental Science, 10*(1), 152–158.

Downing, J. E., & Chen, D. (2003). Using tactile strategies with students who are blind and have severe disabilities. *Teaching Exceptional Children, 36*(2), 56–60.

Ellis, C. R. (2015, December 4). Childhood habit behaviors and stereotypic movement disorder. *Medscape.* Retrieved from http://emedicine.medscape.com/article/914071-overview#showall

Fazzi, E., Lanners, J., Ferrari-Ginevra, O., Achille, C., Luparia, A., Signorini, S., & Lanzi, G. (2002). Gross motor development and reach on sound as critical tools for the development of the blind child. *Brain and Development, 24*(5), 269–275.

Ferrell, K. A. (1998). *Project PRISM: A longitudinal study of developmental patterns of children who are visually impaired: Executive summary* (CFDA 84.0203C—Field-initiated research H023C10188). Greeley: University of Northern Colorado.

Ferrell, K. A. (2011). *Reach out and teach: Helping your child who is visually impaired learn and grow* (2nd ed.). New York, NY: AFB Press.

Goldberg, J. M., Wilson, V. J., Cullen, K. E., Angelaki, D. E., Broussard, D. M., Buttner-Ennever, J. A., . . . Minor, L. B. (2012). *The vestibular system: A sixth sense.* New York, NY: Oxford University Press.

Griffin, H. C. (1981). Motor development in congenitally blind children. *Education of the Visually Handicapped, 12*(4), 106–111.

Haibach, P. S., Wagner, M. O., & Lieberman, L. J. (2014). Determinants of gross motor skill performance in children with visual impairments. *Research in Developmental Disabilities, 35*(10), 2577–2584.

Ihsen, E., Troster, H., & Brambring, M. (2010). The role of sound in encouraging infants with congenital blindness to reach for objects. *Journal of Visual Impairment & Blindness, 104*(8), 478 488.

Illingworth, R. S., Nair, M. K. C., & Russell, P. (2013). *Illingworth's the development of the infant and the young child: Normal and abnormal* (10th ed.). New Delhi, India: Elsevier Health Sciences.

Jan, J. E., Freeman, R. D., & Scott, E. P. (1977). Visual impairment in children and adolescents. New York, NY: Grune & Stratton.

Jan, J. E., Robinson, G. C., Scott, E., & Kinnis, C. (1975). Hypotonia in the blind child. *Developmental Medicine & Child Neurology, 17*(1), 35–40.

Lowry, S. S., & Hatton, D. D. (2002). Facilitating walking by young children with visual impairments. *RE:view, 34*(3),125–133.

Maida, S. O., & McCune, L. (1996). A dynamic systems approach to the development of crawling by blind and sighted infants. *RE:view, 28*(3), 119–134.

Marendaz, C., Stivalet, P., Barraclough, L., & Walkowiac, P. (1993). Effect of gravitational cues on visual search for orientation. *Journal of Experimental Psychology: Human Perception and Performance, 19*(6), 1266–1277.

Montessori, M. (1949). *The absorbent mind.* Adyar, India: The Theosophical Publishing House.

Mulligan, S. (2003). *Occupational therapy evaluation for children: A pocket guide.* Philadelphia: Lippincott Williams & Wilkins.

Nelson, S. L. (2017, December 7). Developmental coordination disorder. *Medscape.* Retrieved from http://emedicine.medscape.com/article/915251-overview#a4

Norris, M., Spaulding, P. J., & Brodie, F. H. (1957). *Blindness in children.* Chicago, IL: University of Chicago Press.

Pogrund, R. L., & Rosen, S. J. (1989). The preschool blind child can be a cane user. *Journal of Visual Impairment & Blindness, 83*(9), 431–439.

Pring, L., & Tadic, V. (2010). The behavioral and cognitive manifestations of blindness in children. In R. D. Nass & Y. Frank (Eds.), *Cognitive and behavioral abnormalities of pediatric diseases* (pp. 531–543). New York, NY: Oxford University Press.

Ricketts, L. (2008). Occupational therapy and sensory integration for visual impairment. *Texas Sense-Abilities, 2*(4), 16–24.

Rochat, P., & Bullinger, A. (1994). Posture and functional action in infancy. In A. Vyt, H. Bloch, & M. Bornstein (Eds.), *Francophone perspectives on structure and process in mental development* (pp. 15–34). Hillsdale, NJ: Lawrence Erlbaum.

Rogers, S. J., Hepburn, S., & Wehner, E. (2003). Parent reports of sensory symptoms in toddlers with autism and those with other developmental disorders. *Journal of Autism and Developmental Disorders, 33*(6), 631–642.

Rosen, S. J. (1988). [Correlation between gait patterns and veering tendency in travelers who are congenitally blind.] Unpublished raw data.

Rosen, S. J. (1997). Kinesiology and sensorimotor function. In B. B. Blasch, W. R. Wiener, & R. L. Welsh (Eds.), *Foundations of orientation and mobility* (2nd ed., pp. 170–199). New York, NY: AFB Press.

Rosen, S. J. (2010). Kinesiology and sensorimotor functioning for students with vision loss. In W. R. Wiener, R. L. Welsh, & B. B. Blasch (Eds.), *Foundations of orientation and mobility: Vol. I. History and theory* (3rd ed., pp. 138–172). New York, NY: AFB Press.

Samalot-Rivera, A., Lieberman, L. J., & Haibach, P. (2015). Teaching two critical locomotor skills to children who are blind or have low vision. *Journal of Visual Impairment & Blindness, 109*(2), 148–153.

Siegel, A. C., & Burton, R. V. (1999). Effects of baby walkers on motor and mental development in human infants. *Journal of Developmental & Behavioral Pediatrics, 20*(5), 355–361.

Sleeuwenhoek, H. C., Boter, R. D., & Vermeer, A. (1995). Perceptual-motor performance and the social development of visually impaired children. *Journal of Visual Impairment & Blindness, 89*(4), 359–367.

Sonksen, P. M., Levitt, S., & Kitsinger, M. (1984). Identification of constraints acting on motor development in young visually disabled children and principles of remediation. *Child: Care, Health and Development,10*(5), 273–286.

Strickling, C. A., & Pogrund, R. L. (2002). Motor focus: Promoting movement experiences and motor development. In R. L. Pogrund & D. L. Fazzi (Eds.), *Early focus: Working with young children who are blind or visually impaired and their families* (2nd ed., pp. 287–325). New York, NY: AFB Press.

Sutherland, D. H., Olshen, R., Cooper, L., & Woo, S. L. (1980). The development of mature gait. *The Journal of Bone & Joint Surgery, 62*(3), 336–353.

Troster, H., Hecker, W., & Brambring, M. (1994). Longitudinal study of gross-motor development in blind infants and preschoolers. *Early Child Development and Care, 104,* 61–78.

Wagner, M. O., Haibach, P. S., & Lieberman, L. J. (2013). Gross motor skill performance in children with and without visual impairments—Research to practice. *Research in Developmental Disabilities, 34*(10), 3246–3252.

Wilbarger, J., & Wilbarger, P. (2002). Wilbarger approach to treating sensory defensiveness and clinical application of the sensory diet. Sections in alternative and complementary programs for intervention. In A. C. Bundy, S. J. Lane, & E. A. Murray (Eds.), *Sensory integration: Theory and practice* (2nd ed., pp. 335–338). Philadelphia, PA: F. A. Davis.

Zafeiriou, D. I. (2004). Primitive reflexes and postural reactions in the neurodevelopmental examination. *Journal of Pediatric Neurology, 31*(1), 1–8.

Zanandrea, M. (1998). Play, social interaction, and motor development: Practical activities for preschoolers with visual impairments. *Journal of Visual Impairments & Blindness, 92*(3), 176–188.

4

Brain Research and Implications for Orientation and Mobility

Melanie Kalene Meeks and Nora Griffin-Shirley

> ## Questions to Guide Your Reading of This Chapter
>
> ➤ What are the different parts and functions of the brain?
> ➤ How does neuroplasticity affect the functionality of individuals with visual impairments?
> ➤ What are the implications of brain research for orientation and mobility?
> ➤ What does brain research tell us about vision therapy?

The human brain is a most unusual instrument of elegant and as yet unknown capacity. (Stuart Seaton, as cited in Harrison, 2013)

In recent years the collective understanding of the brain has changed so dramatically, and the long-held beliefs about how the brain works have shifted so much that this period should be called the era of the brain. This chapter will briefly review some pertinent underlying principles about the brain and then delve more in-depth into the exciting and ever-expanding world of brain science and how it affects the practice of orientation and mobility (O&M).

Brain Basics

The *neuron*, also known as the nerve cell, is arguably the building block of the brain and certainly the most widely studied component (see Sidebar 4.1 for definitions of key terms). This type of cell comprises most of our understanding of how the nervous system carries information and communicates with the body. Dr. Santiago Ramón y Cajal first described the neuron in 1888 (López-Muñoz, Boya, & Alamo, 2006). Since that time, neuroscience, as the name suggests, has been almost single-mindedly focused on the neuron. Although recent research has shifted away from this neuronal bias, the neuron is still an appropriate starting place (Rasband, 2016).

The nervous system has long been compared to an electrical circuit. The nervous system includes the nerves of the brain as well as the rest of the body. The central nervous system is composed of the nerves of the brain and spinal cord while the rest of the body is innervated

Key Terms

Cerebral visual impairment (CVI) Visual dysfunction associated with neurological history. A broader term than cortical visual impairment (although commonly used synonymously) that encompasses visual impairment that stems from areas anatomically outside of the cortical region of the brain.

Cortical visual impairment (CVI) Visual dysfunction associated with brain injury, insult, or developmental anomaly; not explained by an eye exam, which is often normal.

Evidence-based practice Interdisciplinary term referring to professional practices backed by acceptable research evidence.

Glia Connective tissue of the nervous system that consists of several different types of cells that play different roles in the body.

Neuromodulation Process by which a given neuron regulates a group of neurons; or control of brain activity by internal physiological processes or externally applied controls.

Neuron Cell that carries electrical impulses; basic unit of the nervous system that consists of a cell body, an axon, and dendrites.

Neuroplasticity Ability of the brain to repair itself by reorganizing synaptic connections, especially following an injury or in response to intervention and learning; ability of the brain to change throughout the lifespan.

Post trauma vision syndrome (PTVS) Cluster of visual symptoms or symptoms related to visual dysfunction following a traumatic brain injury.

Randomized controlled trial (RCT) Accepted gold standard for research designed to provide unbiased, empirical evidence, which requires randomly assigning participants to treatment or control groups for a predetermined amount of time and ending at a predetermined end point.

Triune brain model Theoretical concept consisting of three brain layers—reptilian, paleomammalian, and neomammalian—which represent the brain in the context of evolutionary development.

Vision rehabilitation Teaching or rehabilitation practices that include various interventions aimed at improving visual functioning and abilities.

Vision therapy Eye exercises designed to correct or improve dysfunctions of the visual system, such as oculomotor and binocular vision problems, administered by an optometrist specializing in this treatment.

Visual efficiency training Training students with low vision to use their vision as effectively as possible to interpret visual information and for functional tasks.

Visual stimulation (or visual training) Using visual materials as training tools to stimulate vision, with the intent of improving visual function in a behaviorally measurable way.

Neuron

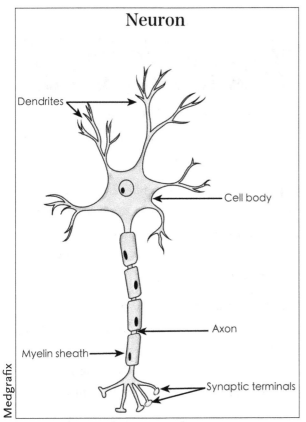

Dendrites

Cell body

Axon

Myelin sheath

Synaptic terminals

Medgrafix

Figure 4.1 The basic units of the nervous system, neurons are composed of a cell body, axons, and dendrites.

Tripartite Synapse

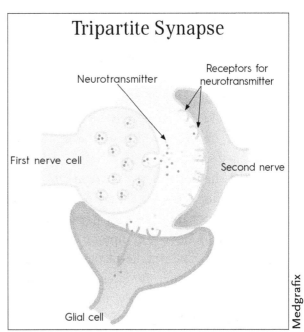

Neurotransmitter

Receptors for neurotransmitter

First nerve cell

Second nerve

Glial cell

Medgrafix

Figure 4.2 The synapse is the communication point between two neurons.

by peripheral nerves. The peripheral nerves that innervate the body include autonomic nerves, which are responsible for the involuntary control of internal organs, and somatic nerves, which include both motor nerves that control voluntary movement and sensory nerves that transmit information from the senses.

Neurons are the basic units of the nervous system and consist of a cell body, axons, and dendrites (see Figure 4.1). Dendrites can be thought of as input channels that "listen to" or receive impulses from other neurons. Likewise, the axon can be thought of as a conduit for electrical transmission, or sending "wire," used to

send information to the dendrites of adjacent neurons. The point where two neurons communicate is called the synapse (see Figure 4.2). The synapse is a tiny gap where two neurons come very close but do not actually touch. In this synaptic gap, the neurons communicate with each other by sending out messengers called neurotransmitters.

Neurotransmitters are chemicals that serve as messengers between neurons. Neurotransmitter communication occurs when the neuron before the synapse, called the presynaptic neuron, releases a neurotransmitter into the synaptic gap. This neurotransmitter then diffuses across the tiny synaptic gap where the neuron after the synapse, the postsynaptic neuron, receives the neurotransmitter into special receptors that are unique to the type of neurotransmitter. The receptors on the postsynaptic neuron can be excitatory or inhibitory, conveying the action message from the neurotransmitter, and making the neuron more or less likely to "fire" or discharge the message to other connected neurons. Excitatory action potentials increase the activity of the postsynaptic neuron and make it more likely to signal other connected neurons while inhibitory action potentials decrease activity after the synapse and make the postsynaptic neuron less likely to signal other neurons (Nunez & Srinivasan, 2006). This signaling process usually occurs very quickly, followed by uptake of the neurotransmitter. The uptake of neurotransmitters may recycle them for later use or dispose of them. More importantly, uptake removes the neurotransmitter from the synaptic gap so that the signal stops. Figure 4.2 shows only a single synapse, but it is important to keep in mind that neurons are highly interconnected through many synapses. The glial cell that appears to be overseeing synaptic transmission will be discussed later in this chapter.

Many neurotransmitters are created in the cell body of the neuron, but some are produced elsewhere. Around 90 percent of serotonin, for example, is produced in the digestive tract and in blood platelets (Berger, Gray, & Roth, 2009). Neurotransmitters signal mood, memory, sexual desire, appetite, aggression, and much more. The primary roles of some common neurotransmitters are described in Sidebar 4.2.

Neurotransmitters also serve to modulate the activity of interconnected neurons, a function not unlike the conductor of an orchestra. The availability of neurotransmitters in the synaptic gap affects the speed and character—coordination with neural groups so that end function is smooth and of desirable amplitude—of the communication. Drugs used to treat psychological and neurological illnesses

SIDEBAR 4.2

Major Neurotransmitters and Their Functions

Dopamine Controls reward and pleasure centers and can be excitatory or inhibitory. Many addictive drugs cause the release of dopamine.

Epinephrine Also called adrenaline, this stress transmitter controls the fight-or-flight response, raises heart rate, slows digestion, increases sugar in the bloodstream, enlarges pupils, and causes faster blood clotting.

GABA (gamma-aminobutyric acid) The major inhibitory neurotransmitter, it works on many parts of the brain to slow down or inhibit the activity of neurons to which it attaches. Low levels of it are present in seizures, intoxication, and anxiety.

Glutamate This excitatory, most abundant neurotransmitter is involved in memory and learning.

Norepinephrine Also called noradrenaline, this excitatory neurotransmitter raises blood pressure by constricting vessels.

Serotonin Called the "feel-good hormone," it affects mood, hunger, arousal, aggression, impulse control, sexual desire, sleep, some social behaviors, heart function, muscle function, and endocrine (hormone) function. Individuals with depression usually exhibit decreased levels.

Substance P Located in many parts of the body and affecting a wide variety of neuron types, it is involved in pain perception, mood regulation, and anxiety.

often target neurotransmitter availability. Shortage of a neurotransmitter may cause a weakened signal. For example, a shortage of serotonin, the "feel good" neurotransmitter, is linked to depression. Conversely, the antidepressant Prozac inhibits serotonin uptake, allowing more serotonin to be available for a longer period of time in the synaptic gap, which relieves the symptoms of depression. In another example, cocaine inhibits the uptake of the neurotransmitter dopamine, which controls reward and pleasure centers, making it available for a longer period of time in the synaptic gap, and causing the postsynaptic neuron to be repeatedly bombarded with a pleasurable signal.

The small electrical changes caused by these communications allow scientists to "listen" to neuronal activity with very sensitive electronic devices. Many advances in the understanding of the brain have come as a result of improved sensitivity of these devices, which today are able to pinpoint electrical activity down to a single synapse (Nunez & Srinivasan, 2006).

Neuromodulation

Communication in the brain involves highly interconnected groups of neurons. This collection makes up neural messages that form brain waves, which, in turn, form a type of neuronal symphony. At any given time, some neurons stimulate this symphony while others serve to slow down or down-regulate this communication (Gazzaniga, 2015).

Just as neurotransmitters serve to modulate individual neurons, neural areas also require a more global regulation. This neural regulation is called *neuromodulation* and is necessary to maintain a harmonious and functional balance in brain function. Neurons in certain brain areas serve to modulate the function of other areas of the brain. As a result, a dysfunction attributed to one brain area may be the result of dysfunction in another area and its subsequent neuromodulation malfunction. One example can be observed in people with an injury to their frontal lobe, which modulates functions of the limbic system, the emotional center of the brain. People with frontal-lobe injury often exhibit some emotional instability. This sign of limbic dysfunction is caused by the inability of the frontal lobe to provide its normal neuromodulation to the limbic center of the brain. Neuromodulation will be revisited later in the chapter in the context of brain injury.

Glia

Another type of cell of great importance is the neuroglia, also called *glia* or glial cell. Neuroglia have always made up more of the brain than neurons, yet occupied a minuscule space in brain literature until recently. The word glia was derived from a Greek word meaning "glue," which reflects the role that early science assigned to its function. Glia were thought to exist mainly to hold neurons together. However, more recent research has revealed that their importance may have been sorely underestimated. The data collected from Einstein's brain after his death hints at the importance of glia. The brain that powered his amazing intelligence was rich in neuroglia yet, surprisingly, only had an average number of neurons (Fields, 2009).

Glia include several different types of cells with important roles, such as astrocytes, which play a role in regulating the blood flow and external chemical environment of neurons, and oligodendrocytes, which form the myelin sheath that surrounds the axons of neurons (Torres et al., 2012). This myelin sheath (see Figure 4.1) is made of a fatty substance that serves to insulate neuronal axons. Without this substance, the axons would leak electrical impulses, a condition observed in degenerative diseases like multiple sclerosis and Alzheimer's disease. Glial cells are also associated with almost every form of brain cancer (Fields, 2009).

During embryonic growth, another type of glia, called radial glia, are responsible for the earliest framework, or scaffolding, of the brain. This glial scaffolding is used to guide neurons into place during embryonic brain formation. These radial glia retract and seem to disappear after the brain is formed. However, they are available to return in the case of neural damage or disease (Anthony, Klein, Fishell, & Heintz, 2004; Fields, 2009; Kriegstein & Alvarez-Buylla, 2009). Incredibly, in the last decade, researchers have observed these glial cells giving birth to neurons in the adult brain (Fields, 2009; Merkle, Tramontin, García-Verdugo, & Alvarez-Buylla, 2004). This research is groundbreaking both because it was historically believed that new neurons could not form in the adult brain and because neurons were not conceptualized as cellular descendants of lowly glial cells.

Glial cells do not send and receive direct electrical impulses the same way neurons do, so their communication has been overlooked for decades by equipment primarily designed to measure neuronal activity. Glial cells appear to broadcast their communication in a more scattered manner instead of passing information in a linear, cell-to-cell fashion as in classic neuronal communication (Fields, 2009). Their role in neuromodulation has not been identified until recently. Glial cells monitor the activity of neurons at the synapse. This new synaptic model,

called the tripartite synapse, reflects the new understanding of the role of glia (Haydon, 2001; see Figure 4.2). It was also recently discovered that glia are involved in directing the formation of new synapses, modulating neuronal blood supply, and responding to neuronal crisis (Fields, 2009; Pfrieger, 2009). These are revolutionary findings for a cell class that was presumed to be strictly support for the more important neuron.

Glia made another astonishing appearance on recent findings related to functional magnetic resonance imaging (fMRI) scans. These scans are used to map brain areas that are active when a person is performing a certain task. They have been used extensively since the 1990s to pinpoint where different functional activities are controlled in the brain. Researchers using fMRI in this way can display impressive images of the brain, with lighted areas presumed to be indicators of increased neuronal activity. However, due to a recently improved fMRI technique, researchers have determined that the areas that light up on an fMRI image are, in fact, the result of glial activity (Fields, Woo, & Basser, 2015). This single finding may rewrite much of our current understanding of the brain.

The science of neuroglia promises new strategies for treating neurodegenerative disorders, brain cancer, and traumatic brain injury, as well as challenges long-held beliefs about how the nervous system learns and communicates. Much information about brain science has been written based on an erroneous interpretation of fMRI images attributed to neuronal activity. Glial science is truly in its infancy as scientists seek to answer basic questions about how these cells function and communicate. The emerging science of neuroglia holds great promise for the future.

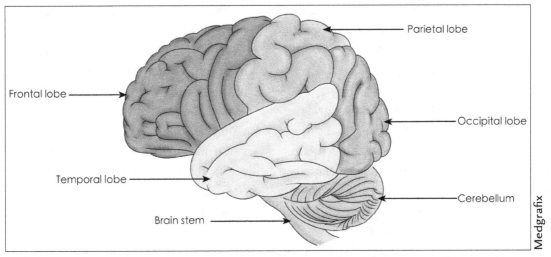

Figure 4.3 Each hemisphere of the brain is divided into four lobes: occipital, parietal, temporal, and frontal.

Structure of the Brain

The brain is divided into two hemispheres. Each hemisphere is divided into four lobes: occipital, parietal, temporal, and frontal (see Figure 4.3). The functions generally performed by each lobe are listed in Sidebar 4.3.

SIDEBAR 4.3

Primary Functions of the Four Lobes of the Brain

Occipital	Vision, visual association
Parietal	Spatial relationships, taste, somatosensory (sensory) association
Temporal	Hearing, smell, auditory association, memory
Frontal	Intellectual thought, language acquisition, behavior, emotional control, motor movement, impulse control

Localization

In neuroscience, localization is the attempt to pinpoint where activities or behaviors are controlled in the brain. Although it is now clear that the brain can reassign functions and do so almost in real time (Doidge, 2015). Researchers have found it interesting and instructive to think about how tasks are generally assigned to specific areas of the brain. Pierre Paul Broca (1861/2011), a French neurosurgeon, was the first to demonstrate localized function of the brain. By studying people who were aphasic or unable to speak, Broca identified a key area in the brain needed for speech (Broca, 1861/2011; LaPointe, 2012). This area of the brain, called Broca's area, and its function gained more clarity with the advent of specialized brain imaging techniques. During the 1990s, Broca's area was shown to be active in producing musical syntax, auditory hallucinations in schizophrenics, and even internal speech (Hinke et al., 1993; McGuire, Murray, & Shah, 1993). The latest research indicates this area might be used to coordinate the input of information from many areas of the brain prior to, but not during, the production of speech (Flinker et al., 2015).

Triune Brain Model

In 1952, Dr. Paul MacLean, a physician and neuroscientist, developed the *triune brain model* (MacLean, 1985). This model, which is theoretical rather than anatomical, has been criticized for being overly simplistic, but it still permeates much of the information exchange about the brain. The model consists of three layers he named the reptilian brain, mammalian brain, and primate brain or neocortex, which he conceptualized to represent the three stages of evolutionary development.

In this model, the reptilian, or lower, brain is comprised of the brain stem and cerebellum (see Figure 4.3) and is very instinct-driven. The reptilian brain runs automatically, without conscious control, and is responsible for basic survival functions like respiration, heart rate, and body temperature. It also initiates primal instincts like aggression, dominance, sex, greed, and obsession (Kean, 2014). The cerebellum, which helps to coordinate movement, is known as the "little brain" because it looks like a miniature version of the brain, with two hemispheres and folded indentations. This brain structure is seen in reptiles, while the higher-level neocortex is not, leading to the nickname "reptilian brain." The brain stem controls arousal as well as automatic functions of the heart, lungs, digestive tract, and other organs. Following a traumatic injury that might render a person unconscious, only the brain stem remains "awake" to preserve vital functions. Similarly, the brain stem is responsible for the hair standing up on the back of the neck when a person experiences a sudden scare because it signals the release of fight-or-flight chemicals.

The middle layer, called the paleomammalian brain, contains the limbic system. This area of the brain is composed of the hippocampus, amygdala, and hypothalamus (Bowden & Dubach, 2003). It is responsible for emotions and value judgments and is involved in relaying sensory input and storing strong memories, especially when they relate to an emotional experience (Kean, 2014). The olfactory system, or sense of smell, is connected almost directly to the limbic system. This connection is why the scent of something from a person's past can invoke a vivid memory of a certain place and time with unusual clarity.

Finally, neomammalian or primate brain, called the neocortex or just cortex, is the outer layer of the brain and represents the higher-order thinking that makes us uniquely human. It encompasses consciousness, language, abstraction, planning, and perception (Kean, 2014). This layer is the reasonable part of the brain that makes decisions based on logic. Much human behavior, however, is driven by the innate lower-brain areas, which are predominantly emotional or instinctual. Situations in which a person feels stressed or threatened cause a reduced level of function. For instance, road rage is triggered in some people when they feel a threat to their safety on the highway. In this state of mind, the heart and respiratory rates are elevated and behavior tends to be aggressive. In another example, doctors are usually discouraged from treating their own family members because their higher-level neocortical function is reduced to a limbic response because of the emotional connection to the patient. The same could be said of O&M specialists teaching O&M skills to their spouse or child who is visually impaired. Based on the terminology of the triune brain model, this natural response on the part of providers makes reaching logical and objective clinical decisions very difficult because it brings the person's neocortical function down to a more primitive, reptilian response.

While much training and preparation is based on logical, sequential, neocortical presentations, both the reptilian and limbic influences on behavior and learning are significant. People who are visually impaired may be in a persistent state of threat, and some finesse by the O&M specialist may be required to build trust and a sense of safety before learning can occur. Even after students no longer feel threatened or unsafe, a period of emotional adjustment to their visual impairment may be required before O&M lessons are productive (Tuttle & Tuttle, 2004).

Neuroplasticity

As late as the 1990s, mainstream neuroscience supported the idea that the adult brain was unable to change or repair itself after injury, an ability known as *neuroplasticity*. Historically, neuroplasticity was only thought to occur during fetal development and maybe briefly during the first few years of life. Toward the end of the 1990s, however, mainstream science eventually came to accept research that had been evolving over time and gathering evidence in support of lifelong neuroplasticity (Grafman, 2000; Grafman & Litvan, 1999). Much of that once-discounted research clearly demonstrated neuroplasticity in the laboratory, but it had been dismissed as not being representative of the potential for change in the adult brain (Doidge, 2007).

On the heels of this paradigm shift came a series of events that generated interest and funding for traumatic brain injury (TBI). The wars in Iraq and Afghanistan produced an estimated 360,000 American combat veterans who received traumatic brain injuries, largely as a result of encounters with improvised explosive devices (IEDs) (Weinick et al., 2011). Around the same time, the U.S. National Football League launched a brain injury research initiative because of the large number of concussions and head injuries occurring in the sport. In addition, a multitude of institutions and individual researchers joined in the collaborative pursuit to increase the wealth of knowledge about neuroplasticity through the study of brain injury. This knowledge produced a sea change in the understanding of the way the brain functions.

Some critics of neuroplasticity credit Dr. Norman Doidge and his bestselling *The Brain That Changes Itself* (2007) with popularizing neuroplasticity in mainstream culture. Doidge has brought brain science to life for millions of people using his own style. Long before his book was published, however, "pioneer neuroplasticians," as Dr. Doidge calls them, spent years in the laboratory developing the experimental evidence that had already entered the mainstream. Critics argue that the word *neuroplasticity* is not a new concept and has, in fact, been around since the 1960s. To be clear, this mainstream regard for neuroplasticity does not refer to the fetal or infantile changes in the brain, which have been accepted for many years, but rather to confronting the basic tenet that the mature, adult brain is unable to change itself, a hypothesis taught to most professionals prior to the 1990s. As a result of this fundamental belief, many medical professionals struggle against this original principle when suggesting patients try therapies aimed at neuroplastic change. For instance, while a psychiatrist might suggest that a student try biofeedback to treat attention deficit hyperactivity disorder (ADHD), the psychiatrist would also warn that although this approach may treat the underlying symptoms, it is not a cure. Given the traditional mindset of professionals regarding neuroplasticity, the question remains whether any observable changes are the result of changes in the student's brain function. As discussed in the example of Daniel Kish later in this chapter, neuroplasticity research using biofeedback will demonstrate that neuroplastic change is, in fact, a lasting cure in many situations (Thaler, Arnott, & Goodale, 2011).

Types of Plasticity

One of the major turning points in the understanding of the ever-changing brain came in 1999 when Jordan Grafman published a framework for how neuroplasticity might occur. This framework was the result of years of observation of patients and their life trajectories following penetrating brain injuries—traumatic injuries that penetrate the skull and cause physical damage to the brain. Grafman was one of the original authors of a longitudinal study of Vietnam War veterans with penetrating brain injuries that ultimately produced over 200 papers (Pogoda, Levy, Helmick, & Pugh, 2017). Grafman's (2000) paper was one of the major turning points in the widespread acceptance of neuroplasticity because it bridged the gap between research and practice and provided a conceptual framework for how neuroplasticity occurs (Grafman, 2000). Sidebar 4.4 describes the functional types of neuroplasticity that Grafman proposed, and which are still accepted today.

SIDEBAR 4.4
Functional Types of Neuroplasticity

- **Crossmodal reassignment:** Reassignment of a sensory processing area in the brain to another sense, usually after the loss of the original sense (Grafman, 2000). Daniel Kish, who is blind, is the most famous example of this type of neuroplasticity. Daniel navigates using auditory clicks, which were shown to be processed in his occipital lobe, a brain area typically known for processing vision (Thaler et al., 2011).
- **Homologous area adaptation:** Reassignment of a cognitive task to a homologous brain area, an area similar in position but located in the opposite hemisphere (Grafman, 2000). This type of neuroplasticity usually occurs early in life and has been shown to be effective when a person is missing an entire hemisphere (Doidge, 2007).
- **Compensatory masquerade:** A unique application of a cognitive process to perform a certain task that previously relied on a now impaired cognitive function. This type of neuroplasticity can be a subtle change. For instance, if spatial orientation is impaired after a brain injury, a person might use verbal labeling and memorization of landmarks for wayfinding on a route.
- **Map expansion:** Expansion of a brain area triggered by use. Neuroplasticity is competitive, so the skills that are used will expand their neural real estate while unused ones will shrink their brain map (Grafman, 2000). For example, London taxi drivers take a lengthy and detailed test that requires up to five years of preparation. Researchers studied the candidates and found that those who were successful had an increase in volume of their hippocampus, an area active in memory storage (Doidge, 2007).

While new synapses undoubtedly form in everyday learning, significant and lasting neuroplastic changes occur—especially in the adult—during ardent, intentional, mindful learning. See Sidebar 4.5 for information on rehabilitation that promotes neuroplastic change, based on recommendations from several scientists noted for their contribu-

tions to the understanding of neuroplasticity, and Sidebar 4.6 for tips on promoting neuroplastic learning.

Neuroplasticity in Action

The science of neuroplasticity has gained much credence from the study of people with sensory

---

SIDEBAR 4.5
Neuroplasticity Changes Everything

Development and Developmental Delay

Children with developmental delays have previously been offered compensatory mechanisms, or ways to "catch up" to their neurotypical counterparts. Common knowledge today indicates that neuroplastic mechanisms drive development that takes a different path but arrives at the same destination. In other words, children with developmental delays may be able to harness neuroplasticity to develop neuronal circuits that may perform at the same level in some or all of the functions of their neurotypical peers. Examples include increases in fluid intelligence after training nonverbal reasoning (Bergman Nutley et al., 2011), brain reorganization following intervention in children with congenital hemiplegia (Inguaggiato, Sgandurra, Perazza, Guzzetta, & Cioni, 2013), and brain reorganization following movement therapy in children with cerebral palsy (Sutcliffe, Gaetz, Logan, Cheyne, & Fehlings, 2007).

Rehabilitation

Acceptance of neuroplasticity means that rehabilitation, which has historically focused on compensatory mechanisms, can now share focus in a restorative role. Rehabilitation professionals have probably observed more evidence of the brain's

ability to repair itself than most other specialists. In many places around the world, it is common to offer visual stimulation in both acquired vision loss (Diamond, 2001; Grüner & Terhaag, 2000; Schmid & Keliris, 2014; Zhu et al., 2009) and developmental visual impairment (Kiarie, 2004). These rehabilitation professionals have included visual stimulation because they have observed that it works.

Aging and Neurodegeneration

In some ways, you can say today's elderly population is part of an experiment. It is not fully known how long the average person can delay, or perhaps even prevent, the cognitive decline associated with aging by intentionally pursuing neuroplastic exercises. An appreciation of the brain's neuroplastic ability to improve cognitive function has prompted several companies to release programs aimed at exactly this purpose. However, the extent to which these cognitive-training programs are able to thwart the cognitive effects of aging has recently come under scrutiny. While the possibility of neuroplasticity as a treatment option remains promising, the future of such programs remains unclear and more research will be needed to determine their effectiveness.

SIDEBAR 4.6
Helping the Brain Change: Tips for Promoting Neuroplastic Learning

- **Control training time**: Practice activities that promote significant neuroplastic change (such as O&M skills) for 20 minutes at a time, once a day, but with no more than 5–7 minutes devoted to each individual activity. (Training sessions can occur more than once per day if there is time for rest in between sessions.)
- **Pair thoughts and actions**: Neurons that "fire together wire together," so pairing thoughts and movements creates stronger connections. This strategy can be accomplished by pairing mental practice with physical practice when learning a new technique. First, talk about the technique with the student, and then walk through the technique again during physical practice.
- **Control intensity**: The mental intensity of an activity must be at a high level for the student in order to promote neuroplastic change. An activity's level of difficulty should be adjusted to be slightly above the student's comfort level, but not so high that the student feels it is out of reach. The ideal intensity for an activity should be difficult enough that it can be sustained for no more than 5–7 minutes before the student feels significant mental fatigue, which may be indicated by a decreased ability to perform the task.
- **Promote engagement**: Activities should be meaningful to the student. The more engaged the student is and the more the brain is stimulated, the more changes will be observed. Neuroplastic change is not a passive process; it is directly related to the student's level of engagement.
- **Provide feedback**: Feedback can be automatic, like the auditory information provided by a cane, or delivered artificially, such as through verbal feedback from the instructor. Ideally, feedback should occur immediately following the action and should be constructive.

---

loss. Likewise, people with brain damage and sensory loss have much to gain from the study and application of recent research on the brain. This moment in history is as much the era of rehabilitation as it is the era of the brain. The field of rehabilitation has an intimate understanding and intuitive sense of the power of neuroplasticity. Examples abound of human performance outpacing what is thought to be theoretically possible. For example, while scientists speculated whether localized brain functions could be performed in different parts of the brain, people born with a missing brain hemisphere and those who have had hemispheres removed became reasonably functional in skills previously attributed to the lobe they were missing (Gazzaniga, 2015). While scientists debated whether opportunities for change were closed after brain injury, stroke victims who had lost the use of limbs for over twenty years learned to use their inoperative limbs by restricting the preferred limbs and forcing the brain to rewire the function of the lost limb (Doidge, 2007). While scientists theorized about what happened to areas of the brain associated with sensory processing after that sense was lost, individuals who were blind taught us that sensory processing areas in the brain do not go unused, as illustrated in the example of Daniel Kish.

In a famous case, Daniel Kish, who is blind, learned remarkable functional navigation using echolocation—the ability to detect objects in the environment by using echoes from those objects—by actively creating sounds such as tongue clicks that would bounce off other objects and inform him how far away they were (Thaler et al., 2011). He later participated in an fMRI study that played back his tongue clicks while recording functional images of his brain waves. This study clearly demonstrated neuroplastic change because the fMRI showed that he was processing the auditory clicks in the occipital lobe, where vision is normally processed (Thaler et al., 2011). Similarly, reading braille has also been shown to coincide with activity in the occipital lobe in individuals who are blind (Amedi, Merabet, Bermpohl, & Pascual-Leone, 2005; Hamilton & Pascual-Leone, 1998), and children who are blind have been observed as having an occipital lobe response to sound and spoken language (Bedny, Richardson, & Saxe, 2015). Much of the established information about the potential for change in the human brain has been acquired by studying individuals who have overcome injuries or disabilities.

Aberrant Neuromodulation

The term neuromodulation refers to how a neuron might use neurotransmitters to exert control over a group of neurons. The term also applies to the modulation, or control, of brain activity by internal physiological processes (e.g., behavioral controls, neural controls, glial controls) or externally applied controls (e.g.,

electrical signals, implanted drug-delivery systems) (Levy, 2014). The term neuromodulation might still be considered a slight misnomer since it does not account for glial involvement and, in some cases, may be more accurately described as glialmodulation. Nevertheless, in terms of the natural physiological process, a dysfunction in a person's neuromodulation results in an impaired rhythm of brain function, perhaps only in one area of the brain. Doidge (2007) described this dysfunction as one instrument in a symphony being out of tune. This, he said, creates a noisy brain, which will have difficulty performing correctly. Others have used the term disorganized to describe these types of aberrant brain-wave patterns (Hayashi-Kurahashi et al., 2012). While these descriptions are superficial, they serve as a starting point for deeper discussions on how brain injuries or abnormalities affect function.

Aberrant neuromodulation can be the result of a developmental disorder or acquired brain injury, which is a brain injury experienced after birth either from trauma (e.g., blow to the head, shaken baby syndrome) or some other insult (e.g., oxygen deprivation, toxin exposure, stroke). Brain injuries and insults, and the ensuing problems with neuromodulation, often result in visual dysfunction. But there are also times when the symptoms and syndromes caused by aberrant neuromodulation are not directly associated with visual symptoms. Epilepsy, for example, is a failure in neuromodulation. Specifically, it results from the failure to down-regulate neural activity and has been likened to an electrical storm in the brain. Additionally, ADHD is caused by problems with neuromodulation that result from inadequate amounts of one focused type of brain wave (Vernon, Frick, & Gruzelier, 2004).

Even though these are not visual syndromes, they often are associated with symptoms of visual dysfunction and, likewise, benefit from treatment approaches that improve overall neuromodulation.

Biofeedback

If it is accepted that neuroplasticity is a possibility and that aberrant neuromodulation shows up as impaired physiological functioning, then there should be a way to use neuroplasticity to help improve neural function. Biofeedback is a technique that uses electronic sensors to send feedback to a person to teach the person to control bodily functions that are normally automatic. Biofeedback is being used to treat numerous disorders by training people to control their neural activity to improve the symptoms of aberrant neuromodulation. This treatment typically works by starting with an initial evaluation from a neuropsychiatrist who performs a quantitative electroencephalogram (qEEG), a type of electrical mapping of brain activity that gives a quantitative measure of specific types of brain waves. This data is used to define the target brain waves and program the biofeedback device. The patient wears a special headpiece with electrical sensors that monitor brain-wave activity during biofeedback. This headpiece is more like a hat and less like the cumbersome, multiwired electrodes used in traditional EEGs, though it is equipped with electrodes. In one commercially available device, the patient watches a movie or game on a screen while the brain waves are monitored. If the target waves drop too low, the movie image will begin to fade and will eventually go dark unless the patient brings them back into range. The patient must focus, by quieting the mind or centering thoughts, to bring his or her brain waves into the range of focus preset on the instrument. Initially, the level of difficulty is set very low until the person learns how to control the target waves. As proficiency increases, the level of difficulty increases. In this way, the person is taught by the biofeedback device how to modulate brain activity voluntarily in real time (Vernon et al., 2004). Months of cognitive therapy is often required to obtain the same results gained in a short period of time with biofeedback. The efficacy of this treatment has been compared to the typical intervention for ADHD using medication. Many studies have demonstrated equal or greater benefit of biofeedback in improving behavioral symptoms or increasing intelligence test scores and academic achievement compared to medication intervention for ADHD (see, for example, Fuchs, Birbaumer, Lutzenberger, Gruzelier, & Kaiser, 2003; Masterpasqua & Healey, 2003). Biofeedback has also been used to treat chronic pain (Gildenberg, 2006), autism spectrum disorders (Coben, Sherlin, Hudspeth, McKeon, & Ricca, 2014; Friedrich et al., 2015), learning disabilities (Hurt, Arnold, & Lofthouse, 2014), age-related macular degeneration (Pacella et al., 2012), and many other conditions.

The benefits of biofeedback training have been shown to be durable. Strehl et al. (2006) demonstrated that people with ADHD who were trained in biofeedback continued their improvement beyond the training period. They had better measures at 6 months after treatment ended, and those measures became stable at 2 years after training ended (Strehl et al., 2006). In contrast, benefits quickly fade and symptoms return after medication or typical behavioral interventions (Brown et al., 2006). In addition, the negative side effects of medication, including depression, anxiety, sleep disturbance, and stomachache, can continue even after the medication is stopped (Brown et al., 2006).

The promise for the future of biofeedback appears great, but the caveat is that expertise is limited, expensive, and not usually covered by health insurance. Additionally, physicians who perform qEEG testing, a required component of initial biofeedback setup, may or may not offer biofeedback as a therapy technique. Biofeedback offers some important benefits, which is a good starting place for discussing the manipulation of neuroplasticity. Not only does biofeedback work, its effects on neural function are documented, and it has been demonstrated to cause lasting change. Biofeedback provides an immediate, real-time signal (i.e., the feedback) to bring unconscious processes under conscious control, using an individual's cognitive control to activate change. The next section will explain how these techniques can be applied to teaching students with visual impairments.

Incorporating Brain Research into Vision Education and Rehabilitation

Neuroplasticity after infancy is real, and it is possible to influence it. As this idea is introduced into the vision field, it is important to take a moment to understand its history and current acceptance in the field.

In the 1960s, research conducted with children who have low vision demonstrated the possibility of improving visual function through targeted teaching practice aimed at stimulating vision to increase visual efficiency (Barraga,

1964, 1965). Barraga's ideas shifted the paradigm from the prevailing theory at the time: "sight saving" for young children with low vision (Vervloed, Janssen, & Knoors, 2006). This philosophy discouraged the use of low vision because of the belief that using limited or low vision might further impair it.

However, in the 1990s, Barraga's ideas came under scrutiny by Ferrell and Muir (1996), who cited a lack of research evidence as a reason to abandon the practice. Furthermore, it became a contentious issue as a teaching practice when it was suggested that it devalued people who were blind and promoted false hopes and inappropriate expectations (Ferrell & Muir, 1996). The authors also argued that behavioral interpretations of improvements in visual efficiency did not take into consideration other factors such as maturity, expectations, and diminished fear.

It is interesting to compare this timing to the acceptance of neuroplasticity. In 1996, neuroplasticity was starting to make its assent into the mainstream scientific community and garnering acceptance by the public. In 2006, Vervloed et al. undertook another serious review of the evidence. They attempted to standardize the terminology around the field of *vision rehabilitation*, in which they included various interventions aimed at improving visual functioning and abilities. In their review of the evidence for using vision rehabilitation in young children, the authors noted that terms used in the field included vision stimulation, visual stimulation, and visual training, but that these terms are used inconsistently in the literature (Vervloed et al., 2006).

Inconsistent terminology is one reason that evidence for vision rehabilitation has been difficult to collect. Another reason is what is accepted as evidence. The scientific community still relies heavily on *randomized controlled trials* (RCTs), the accepted gold standard for research designed to provide unbiased, empirical evidence. RCTs randomly assign participants to treatment or control (no treatment) groups for a predetermined amount of time and ending at a predetermined end point. While this design is intended to reduce bias, practitioners have complained that it does not lend itself well to complex, highly individualized cases. It is important to keep in mind that the RCT was not always considered a necessity; case reports and observations were how much of the early knowledge about the brain was documented. However, this changed in 1961 when an alarming number of stillbirths and birth defects were linked to a drug called thalidomide. In response, the U.S. Congress passed legislation in 1962 that required that all new drugs receive "adequate and well-controlled investigations" (Bothwell, Greene, Podolsky, & Jones, 2016). The Food and Drug Administration (FDA) interpreted this to mean that new drugs be tested using RCT and, thus, the era of the RCT began and RCT was adopted by various fields as a required standard. And the idea of *evidence-based practice*, or professional practice backed by RCT research, became an interdisciplinary term.

Vision therapy demonstrates how profoundly the acceptance of neuroplasticity affects professional practice and how slowly this acceptance occurs. Vision therapy consists of eye exercises designed to correct oculomotor and binocular vision problems, which are administered by optometrists specifically trained in this intervention. These exercises transform how vision is processed, not by changing the eye but by changing the processing in the brain. While

optometrists offer hundreds of research documents to support the use of vision therapy, they have been unable to garner support from the medical community (i.e., ophthalmologists, medical doctors, pediatricians). Similarly, optometry trials are often discounted based on research design, but the medical community has been uninterested in conducting their own trials. This resistance may be due to thinking that acceptance of vision therapy would violate the long-held theoretical principle that neuroplasticity is absent once the infant and toddler years have passed. However, a research trial conducted by the Mayo Clinic declared vision therapy to be effective in improving oculomotor and binocular vision problems, which is a significant departure from this long-held viewpoint (Leong et al., 2014).

As a teaching practice, *visual stimulation or training*, which uses visual materials to stimulate vision as a means of improving visual function, still garners both support and dissent. Visual stimulation is the practice of presenting passive light stimulation (e.g., lights, videos, colored cards) with the intended purpose of improving visual function. In other parts of the world, offering visual stimulation to children and adults with both developmental and acquired visual loss is standard practice (Kiarie, 2004; Trauzettel-Klosinski, 2011). This approach is not part of the current standard practice in the United States, and visual stimulation is a term rarely used in the field of visual impairment in the U.S. It would be imprudent to offer visual stimulation to a person who is blind without accepting neuroplasticity. Research that embraces neuroplasticity is emerging. Examples include a project in which the optic nerve in a rat with acquired blindness was damaged, and sight was successfully restored through stimulation of the recently injured nerve (Lim et al., 2016). Another project demonstrated improved visual acuity through use of a computer-assisted visual-stimulation program in children with low vision (Tsai, Hsu, Wu, Chen, & Su, 2016). However, it is also becoming clear that the potential for the application of neuroplasticity in the field of visual impairment has yet to be reached.

O&M specialists and teachers of students with visual impairments have recognized the need for *visual efficiency training* (i.e., visual training aimed at improving specific skills like scanning, tracking, and tracing that are used in functional tasks), especially for students with low vision (Geruschat & Smith, 2010). Early intervention specialists, low vision specialists, and visual impairment educators can provide intervention strategies for children with low vision to help them learn to use their vision optimally during everyday activities (Ferrell, 2010).

In the context of historical understanding, in which the mature brain is unable to change, vision rehabilitation is strictly a matter of compensatory skills education. However, if operating with the understanding that it is possible to change visual function by changing neural function and that neuroplasticity is possible in children and adults, then the focus shifts to supporting and encouraging the underlying mechanisms of neuroplasticity, with vision rehabilitation comprising compensatory skills training, visual efficiency training, and visual stimulation as part of routine practice. Additionally, vision professionals should seek the highest levels of evidence for changes in practice but understand that RCTs may inherently miss the complexity and variation of individuals in vision rehabilitation. It is likely that future projects will demonstrate the benefits of visual stimulation in both research and practice.

Getting the Brain in the Mood to Learn

Avoiding Stress

In teaching students with visual impairments, it is hard to ignore the influence of what MacLean called the lower, or reptilian, brain. Physical and psychological stress activates the reptilian fight-or-flight response, which is designed to keep a person safe in times of danger. The body turns off nonessential functions, including digestion, immune function, reproduction, and learning, during this stress response. The brain then prepares the body to either fight or flee by increasing blood flow, respiration, and pupil size. Unfortunately, people can get stuck in this state because of constant anxiety. Individuals with vision loss may come to O&M lessons experiencing a heightened sense of threat to their safety and perhaps even a fight-or-flight response that is stuck in the "on" position. It is the job of the O&M specialist to bring the person out of this threat position so that robust learning can take place. This does not mean that a person under stress cannot learn. However, a person who is under stress will not learn or retain information as well as a person who is relaxed and in a positive state of mind when learning begins. A high level of stress is not conducive to meaningful learning because it can constrict blood vessels, thus reducing blood flow to the brain, increasing breathing and heart rates, and causing muscles to tense. Ensuring that a student is calm and positive prior to starting an O&M lesson increases the chances that the student will be able to problem solve, concentrate, pay attention, and learn (Goleman, 1995; Tennant, 2005).

Relaxed Exploration

The accomplishments a child makes by the age of 4, including controlling all body parts, walking, talking, and running, are all mostly achieved without deliberate instruction. These early learning experiences model how neuroplasticity is best accomplished: in relaxed and nurtured states of exploration. Children often learn to sit up while trying to reach their feet. Other lessons throughout life can be learned in the same efficient and integrated way. This process involves immersing a person in a pleasurable and relaxed exploration that proceeds from one inquiry to the next, as directed by the learner, such as a child exploring a playground. The intensity of an exercise that encourages neuroplasticity must be sufficiently difficult to challenge the child to perform past his or her comfort level. Due to this intensity, the duration of specific activities should only last 5–7 minutes. A good gauge of the intensity is if the individual is unable to continue or becomes frustrated after this short period of time.

O&M 'Dance'

Recent research has uncovered data about motor skill learning that athletes and musicians have long understood. In 2015, Bassett, Yang, Wymbs, and Grafton studied people learning motor skill tasks and took a series of brain images during the process. The students who learned the fastest were the ones who could let go of the higher-level visual processing and reasoning part of the brain and use areas devoted solely to motor control, similar to how a dancer might abandon thought and reason and just embrace the dance. It seems motor skills may be learned faster when allowed to strengthen and unite free of executive interference (Bassett et al., 2015).

This reasoning can also be applied to students receiving O&M instruction. For example, a student spends time holding the cane and practicing the arc repetitively while seated or standing (but not traveling), until the cane begins to feel like an extension of the student's sensory and tactile self. During this time, the student learns the appropriate angle, reasoning, and purpose of the cane and listens to the sound of an arcing cane in a familiar room without the additional sensory input of forward motion or the environment. In other words, the student uses this time to focus on establishing the initial intellectual information and isolated motor skills for cane use. When the student has honed the motion of the cane arc into an automatic and comfortable motor movement, the student is ready to move forward. The O&M specialist gives the student instructions to move forward and feel the rhythm of the cane movement, but not think about the details (e.g., whether the arc is centered, if the angle is sufficient, if the cane tip height is appropriate). At this point, the student can "dance," so to speak, by letting go of higher-level processing and reasoning concerning what the cane should be doing in that moment and allowing the brain the opportunity to integrate the skill. When compared to learning a new sport or playing an instrument, it seems reasonable to assume that the intellectual and interpretive part of the brain will be active in the early learning stages, but, as athletes and musicians are aware, overthinking an accomplished motor skill is sure to ruin their game and may, in fact, hinder higher-level accomplishment.

Immediate Feedback

One of the most powerful and often overlooked tenets of neuroplastic change is the concept of immediate feedback. Immediate feedback is vital for learning skills that are highly integrated and cognitively diverse—such as learning to navigate without vision or with low vision—because it moves complex neural processing, in tiny increments, closer and closer to a target goal. Just like the biofeedback mechanisms used to improve neuromodulation, the cane can be used to provide immediate feedback to O&M students. In this scenario, biofeedback does not refer to an electronic device but to natural feedback provided by the environment. O&M instruction can benefit from the knowledge that the brain learns best when it receives immediate feedback by recognizing that this feedback guides skill acquisition. The O&M specialist should take into consideration the feedback the environment is offering and devise how best to position the student to learn from it.

Visual skills are highly integrated (closely related to attention, perception, vestibular function) and cognitively diverse, in that a single glance can convey form, shape, color, depth, lighting, and dimension, as well as abstract concepts like loneliness, deception, and excitement. Similarly, the skills required for O&M training are also highly integrated and cognitively diverse. Feedback provided by the cane is natural, immediate, and can serve as a neuroplastic guide. However, many O&M special-

ists have a tendency to intervene during times most likely to produce neuroplastic change. This may include times when a student is disoriented or when a collision with an object is imminent. O&M specialists must allow students to experience natural feedback even if it results in an unexpected collision. Instructors must always take safety into account, but, wherever possible, they should allow students to receive immediate feedback from the cane, even when it may be negative. In these scenarios, the cane should be viewed as a feedback device for integrating highly interconnected and cognitively diverse tasks, such as those of O&M skills.

Student Interest and Motivation

Value systems affect the ability of the student to retain information. Children place intrinsic value in play, so activities that are fun and playful are meaningful for children. Adults, however, may not find value in an activity simply because it is fun and may instead disregard the activity as frivolous and irrelevant. Neuroplastic change is difficult, if not impossible, when the person does not value the activity or expected outcome. Therefore, it is essential to introduce each new activity or skill by stating the intended purpose and likely benefit in terms that are relevant to that individual.

Curiosity is a strong driver of motivation. While O&M lessons should be structured and the goals directed, students should also be provided with an opportunity to explore their own questions fully, within the learning framework. Moreover, the O&M specialist should focus his or her queries and attention on incidental items in the environment that the student may have missed. This focus is where O&M becomes so important, because it is necessary to let the student engage in active exploration while interjecting guiding questions as needed. The structured discovery model of O&M that encourages exploration and independent problem solving motivates this curiosity, as long as the student's level of stress is taken into account during the process.

Application of Brain Research for Practitioners Working with Children

Developmental Neuroplasticity

Neuroplasticity is present throughout life but is more effortless in young children. The brains of young children are metabolically primed to acquire new information while the brains of adults must overcome established networks or neural pathways in order to learn a new skill. The periods of greatest learning potential during infancy and early childhood—before age 3—were considered critical prior to the acceptance of lifelong neuroplasticity. It was understood that during these periods of rapid brain development, skills such as language were easier to acquire. Moreover, it was believed, until recently, that any brain injury that occurred after these critical periods resulted in irreparable loss of function. Vision was believed to be particularly vulnerable to deprivation of stimulation during these critical periods of development. In the 1960s, researchers demonstrated that kittens deprived of light during early development would be functionally blind as adults (Hubel & Wiesel, 1962; Wiesel & Hubel, 1965). Therefore, vision, in particular, was thought to have a strict critical period after which it would

not develop. This belief may have been self-fulfilling since the neuroplastic ability of the adult brain may require a more focused effort to train visual ability. However, later related work with kittens reared in the dark demonstrated that both cellular and functional vision could be recouped substantially, although with some visual deficits (Kaye, Mitchell, & Cynader, 1981; Mower, Berry, Burchfiel, & Duffy, 1981; van Hof-Van Duin, 1976).

Today, with the growing understanding of lifelong neuroplasticity, rehabilitation and educational efforts, including O&M, can focus on harnessing its power with confidence. The acquisition and training of visual skills, as well as the ability to navigate without vision, are highly dependent on neuroplasticity. O&M instruction with young students should take into consideration a student's age and the ease of harnessing neuroplastic change. O&M instruction with older children and adults must overcome established neural pathways and, therefore, will likely follow a less fluid learning path. Thus, O&M specialists should always consider the impact of their students' neuroplastic age when designing an O&M instructional program.

Promoting Useful Vision

An important consideration in teaching children with visual impairments is focusing on developing any useful vision they may have. Visual development, like language development, occurs more freely in young children, when neuroplasticity is a fluid process and young brains are primed to acquire knowledge and skills.

In the past, the critical period of visual development was thought to be absolute, but recent research has revealed some plasticity. Pawan Sinha, a neuroscientist at the Massachusetts Institute of Technology, launched Project Prakash (Sanskrit for light) in 2003 to help children who were blind in India. A young man named SK became one of the first beneficiaries of the humanitarian program. SK was born with a rare condition called aphakia, an absence of the lens of the eye. He grew up in poverty and did not have access to eyeglasses until he was 29 years old. At that time, he was given a pair of eyeglasses, but based on the enduring idea of a critical period for visual development, he was not expected to develop vision. After about 18 months, he began to gradually identify two-dimensional objects, and later, three-dimensional objects. Sinha reasoned that SK surpassed expectations because the principle of a critical period of visual development was applied too broadly. It was assumed that since his vision would not improve, his ability to interpret visual images would also not improve (Mandavilli, 2006). Instead, Sinha suggested the possibility that different visual skills, such as motion detection, color interpretation, stereovision (which allows for three-dimensional interpretation), and visual integration have different critical periods (Mandavilli, 2006).

Amblyopia, commonly known as lazy eye, provides another example of the neuroplastic potential of vision. Amblyopia is a condition in which vision in one of the eyes is reduced because the eye and brain are not working together properly. Amblyopia causes several functional vision problems including dysfunctions in spatial vision. Until the late 1990s, amblyopia was thought to be untreatable after the critical period of visual development. Several studies since that time have shown improvement in adult amblyopia using vision therapy (Sagi, 2011). More recently, the use of transcranial stimulation paired with perceptual learning vi-

sion therapy has shown improved speed in the perceptual learning required to improve functional vision in adults (Campana, Camilleri, Pavan, Veronese, & Giudice, 2014).

Even though recent findings have expanded the bounds of the critical period of visual development, early stimulation and intervention is still important. Jackson (1983) warned against the use of optical devices in children with low vision because using high magnification in medium to near tasks limits the use of peripheral vision, causing children not to learn to use their existing peripheral vision. It is known today that neuroplasticity follows the "use it or lose it" principle, so any peripheral retinal areas that are not stimulated will not wire correctly to their target areas in the brain. O&M specialists who work with young children should take advantage of the increased potential for neuroplasticity and try to balance near and peripheral training in children with low vision.

Although neuroplasticity can occur throughout a person's life, it is still an easier process to wire children's brains in positive, functional ways. Vision develops most freely in early childhood and is guided by central and peripheral vision, so interventions for visual efficiency should be practiced for both central and peripheral vision. Therefore, O&M specialists and other members of the educational team should encourage the use of existing functional vision both in and out of the classroom.

Brain-Related Visual Impairment

Visual processing involves at least 30 different areas of the brain and 8 of the 12 cranial nerves, so it is not surprising that visual impairment is closely associated with brain dysfunction (Ciuffreda, Ludlam, Thiagarajan, Yadav, & Capo-Aponte, 2014). The close relationship between visual impairment and brain dysfunction goes beyond merely function and proximity. The retina is formed as part of the brain during development, and both the eyes and the brain are responsible for vision throughout life. Anything that affects the brain has the potential to affect vision. A confusing and overlapping set of terms is used to describe visual dysfunctions that stem from neurological foundations. Different professions tend to use different terms to describe the visual consequences of brain injury or insult (see Table 4.1 for a comparison of these terms).

Terminology

Cortical visual impairment (CVI), also referred to as *cerebral visual impairment,* is a condition in which visual disorders or visual perception issues result from damage to the visual pathways or centers of the brain (Lueck & Dutton, 2015). This neurological visual disorder is typically indicated when there is a normal or close to normal eye examination that does not explain visual performance, a medical history that typically includes neurological problems, and the presence of unique visual or behavioral characteristics. Although the terms are sometimes used interchangeably, cerebral visual impairment is generally considered to be broader in scope and encompasses cortical visual impairment. However, the definition of CVI continues to evolve as more is learned about the brain and sensory processing (Soto, 2017). Some causes of CVI include premature birth, neurological disorders, stroke, acquired brain injury, hydrocephalus (increased pressure in the brain), and metabolic disorders.

CVI is the term most commonly used in educational settings to refer to visual impairment caused by brain injury or dysfunction. Even a mild traumatic brain injury such as a concussion can result in visual impairment. Though not an explicit part of the definition, CVI generally refers to people with a severity of symptoms greater than those observed in mild cases of brain injury. However, greater incidence of CVI and improved recognition has recently resulted in better identification of more subtle cases (Dutton et al., 2004). Most children with CVI have some degree of vision with a prognosis of continued improvement in visual recovery (Groenveld, Jan, & Leader, 1990; Roman-Lantzy, 2018).

Post trauma vision syndrome (PTVS) is a term used mostly by eye care professionals to describe a range of visually related symptoms that can result from brain injury, including poor balance, headaches, poor concentration, inability to tolerate crowded or busy places, disorientation, delayed visual memory, and fatigue (Suter & Harvey, 2011). The characteristics of PTVS are observed in varying degrees in mild, moderate, and severe brain injury. Vision professionals developed this term mainly to address symptoms in adults, so it may not be as useful in the assessment of children. The fact that PTVS does not directly address children is not an indication that it does not exist in children; it is just a different term used by professionals. And interest in studying children with visual symptoms related to traumatic brain injury continues to grow.

While the terms CVI and PTVS are not equivalent, there is significant overlap in both conditions and the literature addressing them. The functional result of a brain injury, insult, or developmental anomaly can manifest itself as a

TABLE 4.1

Comparison of Common Visual Terminology

Post Trauma Vision Syndrome (PTVS)	Cortical Visual Impairment (CVI)	Cerebral Visual Impairment (CVI)
Definition		
Cluster of visual symptoms or symptoms related to visual dysfunction following traumatic brain injury. Similar symptoms may be seen following a stroke.	Visual dysfunction associated with brain injury, insult, or developmental anomaly; not explained by an eye exam, which is often normal. Sometimes used synonymously with cerebral visual impairment.	Visual dysfunction associated with neurological history; a broader term than cortical visual impairment (although commonly used synonymously) that encompasses visual impairment that stems from areas anatomically outside of the cortical region of the brain.
Use		
Used most often in medical fields, optometry, and ophthalmology.	Used most often in the educational community.	Used primarily in educational and interdisciplinary circles.
Common Characteristics		
• Headache • Disorientation • Fatigue • Poor concentration • Poor coordination • Ocular motor deficits • Difficulty with attention and organization • Balance deficit • Visual-spatial distortions with associated neuromotor affects • Blurred or double vision • Convergence insufficiency • Accommodative dysfunction • Low blink rate • Veering during mobility • Inability to concentrate for near tasks	• Strong color preference, often for red or yellow • Movement needed to attract and sustain visual attention • Visual latency • Visual field preferences and/or visual field loss • Difficulties with cluttered visual fields • Light gazing • Difficulty with distance viewing • Aberrant or absent visual reflexes • Difficulty with visual novelty; preference for familiar items • Absence of visually guided reach • Hemianopia or other visual field loss	Cortical visual impairment is a subset of cerebral visual impairment, so symptoms observed in cortical visual impairment can also be seen in cerebral visual impairment. • Impaired perception of movement • Impaired recognition of people, shapes, objects • Orientation problems • Impaired coordination of limb movement

(continued on next page)

107

TABLE 4.1 (*continued*)

Post Trauma Vision Syndrome (PTVS)	Cortical Visual Impairment (CVI)	Cerebral Visual Impairment (CVI)
• Inability to tolerate visually crowded or busy places • Difficulty reading that may or may not be related to blurred vision • Visual memory deficits • Anomalous egocentric orientation • Poor color and contrast sensitivity • Spatial neglect		

Sources: Adapted from Dutton, G. N. (2013). The spectrum of cerebral visual impairment as a sequel to premature birth: An overview. *Documenta Ophthalmologica, 127*(1), 69–78; Lueck, A. H., & Dutton, G. N. (Eds.). (2015). *Vision and the brain: Understanding cerebral visual impairment in children.* New York, NY: AFB Press; Roman-Lantzy, C. (2018). *Cortical visual impairment: An approach to assessment and intervention* (2nd ed.). New York, NY: AFB Press; Suter, P. S., & Harvey, L. H. (Eds.). (2011). *Vision rehabilitation: Multidisciplinary care of the patient following brain injury.* Boca Raton, FL: CRC Press.

singular visual functional impairment, such as the inability to distinguish colors or loss of depth perception, or in syndromes that include a cluster of visual symptoms, conditions such as CVI or PTVS. The functional result of brain injury might be more evident as epilepsy, autism spectrum disorders, attention disorders, cerebral palsy, perceptual disorders, psychological syndromes, or motor impairments. It is important to note that disabilities arising from brain dysfunctions can manifest themselves as different impairments (i.e., visual, auditory, cognitive, mental, physical) that are inherently associated with each other. The tendency to separate people with disabilities into exclusive categories and the inaccuracy of that assumption has repeatedly been revealed in research. Some examples include increased incidence of visual impairment in children with autism (Gense & Gense, 1994) as well as autistic-like features in children who are congenitally blind (Brown, Hobson, Lee, & Stevenson, 1997), cognitive visual problems observed in children with hydrocephalus (Houliston, Taguri, Dutton, Hajivassiliou, & Young, 1999), CVI in children with cerebral palsy (Dutton et al., 2004; Lueck & Dutton, 2015), and visual impairment in children who were born prematurely (Dutton, 2013).

As stated earlier, anything that affects the brain has the potential to affect vision. For children who have a neurological history (e.g., premature birth, cerebral palsy, ADHD, autism), visual impairment should be suspected until it can be ruled out. It is also a mistake to assume that if no visual impairment is listed in a child's records that the child has been screened for a visual impairment. Children who have any neurological history should have a thorough vision screening that includes a functional vision evaluation in addition to a standard eye exam that measures visual acuity (near and distant), peripheral fields, and ocular health.

O&M for Children with CVI

CVI is the leading cause of visual impairment in children in first-world countries (Roman-Lantzy, 2018). Visual abilities in children with CVI vary, but in general, characteristics observed in children with CVI include color preferences, attraction to movement (especially shiny objects), visual latency (delayed response in reacting to an object), visual field preferences, difficulties with visual complexity, attraction to light, difficulty with distance viewing, absent or delayed blink reflex to a perceived threat, preference for familiar objects, and not looking and reaching simultaneously (Roman-Lantzy, 2010, 2018). Children with CVI are often not able to use their vision consistently, and significant variability in visual function may be observed from day to day (Roman-Lantzy, 2010). The more severe the CVI, the greater the presence and degree of visual characteristics associated with CVI. The characteristics of CVI may improve over time and with intervention, but recovery may take years, and full recovery may not be possible.

To assess students with CVI, O&M specialists and teachers of students with visual impairments can use the CVI Range (Roman-Lantzy, 2010, 2018). The CVI Range can be completed by one or more members of an educational team and provides information on the effects of CVI at increasing levels of visual functioning. Once the assessment is completed, specific strategies can be implemented to improve the visual function-

ing of children with CVI, which, in turn, assists with their O&M skills (see Sidebar 4.7). For example, if a student with CVI can locate visual targets, these targets can be placed in a school to assist the student with following a route. Additional O&M strategies that can be used with students with CVI can be found in *TAPS—Teaching Age-Appropriate Purposeful Skills: An Orientation and Mobility Curriculum for Students with Visual Impairments* (Pogrund et al., 2012) and in the CVI chapter of *Foundations of Orientation and Mobility* (Roman-Lantzy, 2010).

Summary

This chapter has encouraged consideration of ideas and concepts traditionally thought to be outside the realm of the field of O&M. Many other areas of brain research can also prove relevant both personally and professionally, including the emerging fields of epigenetics, which studies how biological mechanisms switch genes on and off, and psychoneuroimmunology, which studies the interaction between the brain and the immune system. It is important for O&M specialists and other collaborative partners on the O&M team to be well informed about the latest findings and exciting discoveries that are happening in brain research so that they can apply them in their O&M instruction when working with students with visual impairments.

The research emerging from different scientific fields can have a great impact on the rate of implementation due to the widespread availability of this information. Now more than ever, it falls to professionals serving on the educational or rehabilitation team of a student who is blind or visually impaired to keep current on the

---

SIDEBAR 4.7

O&M Strategies for Working with Students with CVI

Roman-Lantzy (2010, 2018) suggests that teaching strategies and modifications used when working with students with CVI should be individualized, based on the student's CVI characteristics as well as O&M principles. The following are a few strategies and modifications that can be used by the O&M specialist as well as other members of the educational team.

- Present objects in a student's preferred visual field.
- Draw attention to non-preferred visual fields with movement or use of a preferred color.
- Increase visual attention to visual fields at a distance that are not preferred.
- Use lights, Mylar pom-poms, or other reflective materials with light shining on an object to motivate reaching behavior or movement.
- Present target objects against a contrasting color background.
- Use familiar objects.
- Use single-colored objects presented against contrasting solid backgrounds.
- Attach a familiar object to a novel object you want the student to view to make it easier to initially view the novel object.

- Accommodate visual latency by allowing extra time to view objects.
- To make a student's desk highly visible, place a yellow ink blotter on the desk and use clear contact paper to keep it in place.
- Use a chair that is a different color from the color of the student's desk.
- Use reflective tape or paint to mark stairs and other elevation changes.
- Travel in brightly lit corridors.
- Use a brightly colored rug or other material to label a landmark; remove it once the student becomes familiar with the landmark.
- Use verbal prompts such as "slow," "look," and "check."
- Make the student aware that visual field preferences may create potential hazards during O&M instruction. Practice increasing the use of other fields.
- Start with a simple, controlled environment. Be aware of impediments and complications as the student's travel environment becomes more visually complex or contains high levels of sensory complexity (e.g., noisy downtown area).

---

latest discoveries and become lifelong learners. Staying up-to-date on brain research not only enhances professional practice in working on O&M skills with students with visual impairments, but it is also good for the brain!

References

Amedi, A., Merabet, L. B., Bermpohl, F., & Pascual-Leone, A. (2005). The occipital cortex in the blind: Lessons about plasticity and vision. *Current Directions in Psychological Science, 14*(6), 306–311.

Anthony, T. E., Klein, C., Fishell, G., & Heintz, N. (2004). Radial glia serve as neuronal progenitors in all regions of the central nervous system. *Neuron, 41*(6), 881–890.

Barraga, N. C. (1964). *Increased visual behavior in low vision children.* New York, NY: American Foundation for the Blind.

Barraga, N. C. (1965). Effects of experimental teaching on the visual behavior of children with low vision. *American Journal of Optometry and Archives of American Academy of Optometry, 42*(9), 557–561.

Bassett, D. S., Yang, M., Wymbs, N. F., & Grafton, S. T. (2015). Learning-induced autonomy of sensorimotor systems. *Nature Neuroscience, 18*(5), 744–751.

Bedny, M., Richardson, H., & Saxe, R. (2015). "Visual" cortex responds to spoken language in blind children. *The Journal of Neuroscience, 35*(33), 11674–11681.

Berger, M., Gray, J. A., & Roth, B. L. (2009). The expanded biology of serotonin. *Annual Review of Medicine, 60*, 355–366.

Bergman Nutley, S., Söderqvist, S., Bryde, S., Thorell, L. B., Humphreys, K., & Klingberg, T. (2011). Gains in fluid intelligence after training non-verbal reasoning in 4-year-old children: A controlled, randomized study. *Developmental Science, 14*(3), 591–601.

Bothwell, L. E., Greene, J. A., Podolsky, S. H., & Jones, D. S. (2016). Assessing the gold standard—Lessons from the history of RCTs. *The New England Journal of Medicine, 374*(22), 2175–2181.

Bowden, D. M., & Dubach, M. (2003). BrainInfo: An online interactive brain atlas and nomenclature. In R. Kötter (Ed.), *Neuroscience databases: A practical guide* (pp. 259–273). Dordrecht, The Netherlands: Kluwer Academic Publishers.

Broca, P. (2011). Remarks on the seat of spoken language, followed by a case of aphasia. *Neuropsychology Review, 21*(3), 227–229. (Original work published 1861)

Brown, R. T., Antonuccio, D., DuPaul, G. J., Fristad, M., King, C. A., Leslie, L. K., . . . Vitiello, B. (2006). *Report of the working group on psychotropic medications for children and adolescents: Psychopharmacological, psychosocial, and combined interventions for childhood disorders: Evidence base, contextual factors, and future directions.* Washington, DC: American Psychological Association.

Brown, R., Hobson, R. P., Lee, A., & Stevenson, J. (1997). Are there "autistic-like" features in congenitally blind children? *Journal of Child Psychology and Psychiatry, 38*(6), 693–703.

Campana, G., Camilleri, R., Pavan, A., Veronese, A., & Lo Giudice, G. (2014). Improving visual functions in adult amblyopia with combined perceptual training and transcranial random noise stimulation (tRNS): A pilot study. *Frontiers in Psychology, 5*, 1402.

Ciuffreda, K. J., Ludlam, D. P., Thiagarajan, P., Yadav, N. K., & Capo-Aponte, J. (2014). Proposed objective visual system biomarkers for mild traumatic brain injury. *Military Medicine, 179*(11), 1212–1217.

Coben, R., Sherlin, L., Hudspeth, W. J., McKeon, K., & Ricca, R. (2014). Connectivity-guided EEG biofeedback for autism spectrum disorder: Evidence of neurophysiological changes. *NeuroRegulation, 1*(2), 109–130.

Diamond, P. T. (2001). Rehabilitative management of post-stroke visuospatial inattention. *Disability and Rehabilitation, 23*(10), 407–412.

Doidge, N. (2007). *The brain that changes itself: Stories of personal triumph from the frontiers of brain science.* New York, NY: Penguin Books.

Doidge, N. (2015). *The brain's way of healing: Remarkable discoveries and recoveries from the frontiers of neuroplasticity.* New York, NY: Penguin Books.

Dutton, G. N. (2013). The spectrum of cerebral visual impairment as a sequel to premature birth: An overview. *Documenta Ophthalmologica, 127*(1), 69–78.

Dutton, G. N., Saaed, A., Fahad, B., Fraser, R., McDaid, G., McDade, J., . . . Spowart, K. (2004). Association of binocular lower visual field impairment, impaired simultaneous perception, disordered visually guided motion and inaccurate saccades in children with cerebral visual dysfunction—A retrospective observational study. *Eye, 18*(1), 27–34.

Ferrell, K. A. (2010). Visual development. In A. L. Corn & J. N. Erin (Eds.), *Foundations of low vision: Clinical and functional perspectives* (2nd ed., pp. 299–338). New York, NY: AFB Press.

Ferrell, K. A., & Muir, D. W. (1996). A call to end vision stimulation training [Comment]. *Journal of Visual Impairment & Blindness, 90*(5), 364–366.

Fields, R. D. (2009). *The other brain: From dementia to schizophrenia, how new discoveries about the brain are revolutionizing medicine and science.* New York, NY: Simon & Schuster.

Fields, R. D., Woo, D. H., & Basser, P. J. (2015). Glial regulation of the neuronal connectome through local and long-distant communication. *Neuron, 86*(2), 374–386.

Flinker, A., Korzeniewska, A., Shestyuk, A. Y., Franaszczuk, P. J., Dronkers, N. F., Knight, R. T., & Crone, N. E. (2015). Redefining the role of Broca's area in speech. *Proceedings of the National Academy of Sciences of the United States of America, 112*(9), 2871–2875.

Friedrich, E. V., Sivanathan, A., Lim, T., Suttie, N., Louchart, S., Pillen, S., & Pineda, J. A. (2015). An effective neurofeedback intervention to improve social interactions in children with autism spectrum disorder. *Journal of Autism and Developmental Disorders, 45*(12), 4084–4100.

Fuchs, T., Birbaumer, N., Lutzenberger, W., Gruzelier, J. H., & Kaiser, J. (2003). Neurofeedback treatment for attention-deficit/hyperactivity disorder in children: A comparison with methylphenidate. *Applied Psychophysiology and Biofeedback, 28*(1), 1–12.

Gazzaniga, M. S. (2015). *Tales from both sides of the brain: A life in neuroscience.* New York, NY: Harper Collins.

Gense, M. H., & Gense, D. J. (1994). Identifying autism in children with blindness and visual impairments. *RE:view, 26*(2), 55–62.

Geruschat, D. R., & Smith, A. J. (2010). Improving the use of low vision for orientation and mobility. In W. R. Wiener, R. L. Welsh, & B. B. Blasch (Eds.), *Foundations of orientation and mobility: Vol. II. Instructional strategies and practical applications* (3rd ed., pp. 54–90). New York, NY: AFB Press.

Gildenberg, P. L. (2006). History of electrical neuromodulation for chronic pain. *Pain Medicine, 7*(1), S7–S13.

Goleman, D. (1995). *Emotional intelligence: Why it can matter more than IQ.* New York, NY: Bantam Books.

Grafman, J. (2000). Conceptualizing functional neuroplasticity. *Journal of Communication Disorders, 33*(4), 345–356.

Grafman, J., & Litvan, I. (1999). Evidence for four forms of neuroplasticity. In J. Grafman & Y. Christen (Eds.), *Neuronal plasticity: Building a bridge from the laboratory to the clinic* (pp. 131–140). Berlin, Germany: Springer-Verlag.

Groenveld, M., Jan, J. E., & Leader, P. (1990). Observations on the habilitation of children with cortical visual impairment. *Journal of Visual Impairment & Blindness, 84*(1), 11–15.

Grüner, M. L., & Terhaag, D. (2000). Multimodal early onset stimulation (MEOS) in rehabilitation after brain injury. *Brain Injury, 14*(6), 585–594.

Hamilton, R. H., & Pascual-Leone, A. (1998). Cortical plasticity associated with braille learning. *Trends in Cognitive Sciences, 2*(5), 168–174.

Harrison, C. S. (2013). *My child: "The quick fix?" One day at a time.* Houston, TX: CSR Publishing.

Hayashi-Kurahashi, N., Kidokoro, H., Kubota, T., Maruyama, K., Kato, Y., Kato, T., . . . Okumura, A. (2012). EEG for predicting early neurodevelopment in preterm infants: An observational cohort study. *Pediatrics, 130*(4), e891–e897.

Haydon, P. G. (2001). Glia: Listening and talking to the synapse. *Nature Reviews Neuroscience, 2*(3), 185–193.

Hinke, R. M., Hu, X., Stillman, A. E., Kim, S. G., Merkle, H., Salmi, R., & Ugurbil, K. (1993). Functional magnetic resonance imaging of Broca's area during internal speech. *Neuroreport, 4*(6), 675–678.

Houliston, M. J., Taguri, A. H., Dutton, G. N., Hajivassiliou, C., & Young, D. G. (1999). Evidence of cognitive visual problems in children with hydrocephalus: A structured clinical history-taking strategy. *Developmental Medicine & Child Neurology, 41*(5), 298–306.

Hubel, D. H., & Wiesel, T. N. (1962). Receptive fields, binocular interaction and functional architecture in the cat's visual cortex. *The Journal of Physiology, 160*(1), 106–154.

Hurt, E., Arnold, L. E., & Lofthouse, N. (2014). Quantitative EEG neurofeedback for the treatment of pediatric attention-deficit/hyperactivity disorder, autism spectrum disorders, learning disorders, and epilepsy. *Child and Adolescent Psychiatric Clinics of North America, 23*(3), 465–486.

Inguaggiato, E., Sgandurra, G., Perazza, S., Guzzetta, A., & Cioni, G. (2013). Brain reorganization following intervention in children with congenital hemiplegia: A systematic review. *Neural Plasticity*, ePUB.

Jackson, R. M. (1983). Early educational use of optical aids: A cautionary note. *Education of the Visually Handicapped, 15*(1), 20–29.

Kaye, M., Mitchell, D. E., & Cynader, M. (1981). Depth perception, eye alignment and cortical ocular dominance of dark-reared cats. *Developmental Brain Research, 2*(1), 37–54

Kean, S. (2014). *The tale of the dueling neurosurgeons: And other true stories of trauma, madness, affliction, and recovery that reveal the surprising history of the human brain.* New York, NY: Little, Brown and Company.

Kiarie, M. W. (2004). Education of students with visual impairments in Kenya: Trends and issues. *International Journal of Special Education, 19*(2), 16–22.

Kriegstein, A., & Alvarez-Buylla, A. (2009). The glial nature of embryonic and adult neural stem cells. *Annual Review of Neuroscience, 32*, 149–184.

LaPointe, L. L. (2012). *Paul Broca and the origins of language in the brain.* San Diego, CA: Plural Publishing.

Leong, D. F., Master, C. L., Messner, L. V., Pang, Y., Smith, C., & Starling, A. J. (2014). The effect of saccadic training on early reading fluency. *Clinical Pediatrics, 53*(9), 858–864.

Levy, R. M. (2014). The evolving definition of neuromodulation. *Neuromodulation: Technology at the Neural Interface, 17*(3), 207–210.

Lim, J.-H. A., Stafford, B. K., Nguyen, P. L., Lien, B. V., Wang, C., Zukor, K., . . . Huberman, A. D. (2016). Neural activity promotes long-distance, target-specific regeneration of adult retinal axons. *Nature Neuroscience, 19*(8), 1073–1084.

López-Muñoz, F., Boya, J., & Alamo, C. (2006). Neuron theory, the cornerstone of neuroscience, on the centenary of the Nobel Prize award to Santiago Ramón y Cajal. *Brain Research Bulletin, 70*(4–6), 391–405.

Lueck, A. H., & Dutton, G. N. (Eds.). (2015). *Vision and the brain: Understanding cerebral visual impairment in children.* New York, NY: AFB Press.

MacLean, P. D. (1985). Brain evolution relating to family, play, and the separation call. *Archives of General Psychiatry, 42*(4), 405–417.

Mandavilli, A. (2006). Visual neuroscience: Look and learn. *Nature, 441*(7091), 271–272.

Masterpasqua, F., & Healey, K. N. (2003). Neurofeedback in psychological practice. *Professional Psychology: Research and Practice, 34*(6), 652–656.

McGuire, P. K., Murray, R. M., & Shah, G. M. S. (1993). Increased blood flow in Broca's area during auditory hallucinations in schizophrenia. *The Lancet, 342*(8873), 703–706.

Merkle, F. T., Tramontin, A. D., García-Verdugo, J. M., & Alvarez-Buylla, A. (2004). Radial glia give rise to adult neural stem cells in the subventricular zone. *Proceedings of the National Academy of Sciences of the United States of America, 101*(50), 17528–17532.

Mower, G. D., Berry, D., Burchfiel, J. L., & Duffy, F. H. (1981). Comparison of the effects of dark rearing and binocular suture on development and plasticity of cat visual cortex. *Brain Research, 220*(2), 255–267.

Nunez, P. L., & Srinivasan, R. (2006). *Electric fields of the brain: The neurophysics of EEG* (2nd ed.). New York, NY: Oxford University Press.

Pacella, E., Pacella, F., Mazzeo, F., Turchetti, P., Carlesimo, S. C., Cerutti, F., . . . Giorgi, D. (2012). Effectiveness of vision rehabilitation treatment through MP-1 microperimeter in patients with visual loss due to macular disease. *Clinical Therapeutics, 163*(6), e423–e428.

Pfrieger, F. W. (2009). Roles of glial cells in synapse development. *Cellular and Molecular Life Sciences, 66*(13), 2037–2047.

Pogoda, T. K., Levy, C. E., Helmick, K., & Pugh, M. J. (2017). Health services and rehabilitation for active duty service members and veterans with mild TBI. *Brain Injury, 31*(9), 1220–1234.

Pogrund, R., Sewell, D., Anderson, H., Calaci, L., Cowart, M. F., Gonzalez, C. M., . . . Roberson-Smith, B. (2012). *TAPS—Teaching age-appropriate purposeful skills: An orientation and mobility curriculum for students with visual impairments* (3rd ed.). Austin: Texas School for the Blind and Visually Impaired.

Rasband, M. N. (2016). Glial contributions to neural function and disease. *Molecular & Cellular Proteomics, 15*(2), 355–361.

Roman-Lantzy, C. (2010). Teaching orientation and mobility to students with cortical visual impairment. In W. R. Wiener, R. L. Welsh, & B. B. Blasch (Eds.), *Foundations of orientation and mobility: Vol. II. Instructional strategies and practical applications* (3rd ed., pp. 667–711). New York, NY: AFB Press.

Roman-Lantzy, C. (2018). *Cortical visual impairment: An approach to assessment and intervention* (2nd ed.). New York, NY: AFB Press.

Sagi, D. (2011). Perceptual learning in vision research. *Vision Research, 51*(13), 1552–1566.

Schmid, M. C., & Keliris, G. A. (2014). Filling-in versus filling-out: Patterns of cortical short-term plasticity. *Trends in Cognitive Sciences, 18*(7), 342–344.

Soto, D. (2017). Glossary. In M. C. Holbrook, T. McCarthy, & C. Kamei-Hannan (Eds.), *Foundations of education: Vol. I. History and theory of teaching children and youths with visual impairments* (3rd ed., pp. 489–508). New York, NY: AFB Press.

Strehl, U., Leins, U., Goth, G., Klinger, C., Hinterberger, T., & Birbaumer, N. (2006). Self-regulation of slow cortical potentials: A new treatment for children with attention-deficit/hyperactivity disorder. *Pediatrics, 118*(5), 1530–1540.

Sutcliffe, T. L., Gaetz, W. C., Logan, W. J., Cheyne, D. O., & Fehlings, D. L. (2007). Cortical reorganization after modified constraint-induced movement therapy in pediatric hemiplegic cerebral palsy. *Journal of Child Neurology, 22*(11), 1281–1287.

Suter, P. S., & Harvey, L. H. (Eds.). (2011). *Vision rehabilitation: Multidisciplinary care of the patient following brain injury.* Boca Raton, FL: CRC Press.

Tennant, V. (2005, September). The powerful impact of stress. Baltimore, MD: Johns Hopkins University, School of Education, New Horizons for Learning. Retrieved from http://archive.education.jhu.edu/PD/newhorizons/strategies/topics/Keeping%20Fit%20for%20Learning/stress.html

Thaler, L., Arnott, S. R., & Goodale, M. A. (2011). Neural correlates of natural human echolocation in early and late blind echolocation experts. *PLoS ONE, 6*(5), e20162.

Torres, A., Wang, F., Xu, Q., Fujita, T., Dobrowolski, R., Willecke, K., . . . Nedergaard, M. (2012). Extracellular Ca^{2+} acts as a mediator of communication from neurons to glia. *Science Signaling, 5*(208), ra8.

Trauzettel-Klosinski, S. (2011). Current methods of visual rehabilitation. *Deutsches Ärzteblatt International, 108*(51–52), 871–878.

Tsai, L. T., Hsu, J. L., Wu, C. T., Chen, C. C., & Su, Y. C. (2016). A new visual stimulation program for improving visual acuity in children with visual impairment: A pilot study. *Frontiers in Human Neuroscience, 10*, 157.

Tuttle, D. W., & Tuttle, N. R. (2004). *Self-esteem and adjusting with blindness: The process of responding to life's demands* (3rd ed.). Springfield, IL: Charles C Thomas.

van Hof-Van Duin, J. (1976). Development of visuomotor behavior in normal and dark-reared cats. *Brain Research, 104*(2), 233–241.

Vernon, D., Frick, A., & Gruzelier, J. (2004). Neurofeedback as a treatment for ADHD: A methodological review with implications for future research. *Journal of Neurotherapy, 8*(2), 53–82.

Vervloed, M. P., Janssen, N., & Knoors, H. (2006). Visual rehabilitation of children with visual impairments. *Journal of Developmental & Behavioral Pediatrics, 27*(6), 493–506.

Weinick, R. M., Beckjord, E. B., Farmer, C. M., Martin, L. T., Gillen, E. M., Acosta, J. D., . . . Scharf, D. M. (2011). *Programs addressing psychological health and traumatic brain injury among U.S. military servicemembers and their families.* Santa Monica, CA: RAND Corporation, Center for Military Health Policy Research. Retrieved from https://www.rand.org/content/dam/rand/pubs/technical_reports/2011/RAND_TR950.pdf

Wiesel, T. N., & Hubel, D. H. (1965). Comparison of the effects of unilateral and bilateral eye closure on cortical unit responses in kittens. *Journal of Neurophysiology, 28*(6), 1029–1040.

Zhu, J., Wu, X., Gao, L., Mao, Y., Zhong, P., Tang, W., & Zhou, L. (2009). Cortical activity after emotional visual stimulation in minimally conscious state patients. *Journal of Neurotrauma, 26*(5), 677–688.

5

Spatial Orientation and Secondary Senses

Laura Bozeman

Movement is the key to learning. It's our body's senses that feed the brain environmental information with which to form an understanding of the world and from which to draw when creating new possibilities. (Hannaford, 2005, p. 15)

Orientation is using sensory information to know where you are and where you are going in relation to significant objects in the environment. Mobility is moving from one point to another safely, effectively, and as independently as possible. Together, orientation and mobility (O&M) represent the fusion of sensory information, concepts, spatial awareness, and safe and efficient travel that opens the door for the student to be able to understand the environment and move safely within it (Bozeman & McCulley, 2010).

For the child with vision, most learning is incidental, and movement occurs out of visual interest. For the young child with a visual impairment, however, movement may not occur naturally and must be intentionally supported (Anthony, Bleier, Fazzi, Kish, & Pogrund, 2002). In order to understand the multiple facets of orientation, the child must be able to interpret and integrate sensory information, understand spatial concepts, and possess spatial awareness.

Wayfinding refers to guided action and planning to reach a goal (Darken & Peterson, 2002; see Sidebar 5.1 for definitions of key terms). Purposeful movement is known to be an important tool for learning (Hannaford, 2005) and key to understanding the environment for a student with a visual impairment (Long & Giudice, 2010; Skellenger & Sapp, 2010). This chapter will review how students with visual impairments organize space and how orientation is regained after a student becomes disoriented. The use of other senses and how they are incorporated into overall spatial orientation will also be explored. Lastly, the role of partners in developing and supporting sensory development and spatial awareness will be presented.

How Children with Visual Impairments Organize Space

The belief that all children can learn if guided and given appropriate supports fosters high expectations for each student (Fazzi & Naimy, 2010). To be able to organize their surroundings, children with visual impairments must possess basic abilities as a foundation on which to build future organizational skills. Skellenger and Sapp (2010) use the term O&M development to describe the competencies necessary to build future O&M skills. These skills include body awareness, body-part relationships, body-to-object relationships, and relationships between objects in the environment (Anthony et al., 2002; Bozeman & McCulley, 2010). Young children are constantly growing and integrating physical aspects of their bodies with their cognitive abilities. The child with a visual impairment must develop mental representations of what things are supposed to be. This understanding of spatial concepts is a continuous process, intrinsically linked to development in the young child.

Spatial Concepts

Concept development begins at birth. Typically developing children gather information visu-

---

SIDEBAR 5.1

Key Terms

Allocentric frame of reference Understanding the relationship between objects and locations as related to one another, independent of the student's current position.

Descriptive mediation Clear and specific language used to describe the environment and relate those characteristics to the interest of the student.

Echolocation Using reflected sound to gather information and detect the presence of objects in the surrounding environment.

Egocentric frame of reference Understanding the location of objects in the environment as related to the student's body position.

Incidental learning Observation of other people and activities.

Laterality Understanding that the body has a right and a left side from one's own perspective.

Object permanence Recognition that objects continue to exist even though they cannot be observed, heard, or touched.

Parallel talk Approach in which the O&M specialist verbalizes the movements and actions of the student as the student travels through the environment.

Self-talk Approach in which the student verbalizes what he or she is thinking as the student analyzes and travels through the environment.

Sound shadow Break or partial break in sound created when an object is located between the sound source and the traveler.

Wayfinding Planning and strategy that guide action, movement, and the ability to reach a destination while traveling through the environment.

ally, and for them, *incidental learning* (learning by observing people or activities) plays a huge role in concept development. For children with visual impairments, the development of spatial concepts requires purposeful guidance that builds on a simple to complex, concrete to abstract process. This approach to learning builds a foundation of simple and concrete concepts that are then expanded to more complex and abstract ideas (Bozeman & McCulley, 2010; Ferrell, 1997; Mangold, 2003). Children with visual impairments may not reach for objects or people or initiate movement until they have a conceptual understanding of the presence of objects and people in the environment (Anthony, Lowry, Brown, & Hatton, 2004). For children with visual impairments, the environment requires thoughtful description. *Descriptive mediation* refers to the process of using clear, precise language to describe aspects of the environment and link those characteristics to the interests of the child (Chen, 2014).

First, the child with a visual impairment needs to understand *object permanence* and recognize that objects continue to exist even when they cannot be observed, heard, or touched. The next step is for the child to name objects and understand the characteristics of objects and that they have size, shape, texture, and mass (i.e., big, round, rough). Spatial concepts (e.g., top, bottom, inside) would come next, and following that, abstract concepts (e.g., compass directions and characteristics such as the height of a tall building) that cannot be experienced through the student's remaining senses) (Bozeman & McCulley, 2010). Reinforcement of these concepts can be incorporated into normal daily routines. (For more on concept development, see Chapter 2.)

Spatial Awareness

Spatial awareness is intrinsically linked to concept development and follows the same sequence of simple to complex and concrete to abstract. Fundamental concepts include four main categories of spatial awareness: body awareness, body-to-body (body-part) relationships, body-to-object relationships, and object-to-object relationships (Bozeman & McCulley, 2010).

Body Awareness

For all children, body awareness is the understanding that the body has parts and the parts have names. Body awareness begins with the newborn and is the foundation for other, more complex spatial concepts (Bozeman & McCulley, 2010). Body awareness begins with learning the major body parts (e.g., head, eyes, hands, feet) that are typically referred to more frequently by family members, caregivers, and early interventionists when teaching young children. Smaller or less-defined body parts (e.g., elbow, wrist, calf, chin, shin) are usually learned later in the developmental process.

Often, a child learns about the body through normal daily routines. Typical routines include bathing, dressing, and other self-care skills. Routines can be used to develop and reinforce an understanding of body awareness (see Sidebar 5.2). For example, while bathing a child, the parent can wash and verbally name body parts by saying, "Let's wash your arm" or "Let's wash your leg" (see Figure 5.1).

Games and songs are also wonderful strategies for teaching body awareness and spatial abilities (Fazzi & Naimy, 2010; Sapp, 2011). Games that promote body awareness for young children include "This Little Piggy," "Pat-a-

SIDEBAR 5.2

Routines to Support Body Awareness

Routines are a great way to integrate and support concepts and learning. Spatial concepts are best taught with tangible objects at appropriate times. These routines also include the natural actions of the teacher and the student (Chen, 2014). An example of a functional routine approach can include teaching a student the route to the office in school because the student takes the attendance sheets to the office for the teacher each day.

Predictable routines and activities that have a clear beginning, middle, and end help support the rhythm of the day and the purpose of the activity. The O&M specialist can also use this approach to teach routes to the student. Predictability leads to familiarity and the desired result of spatial awareness and orientation to an area.

Body awareness can be developed during bath time when a parent, family member, or caregiver washes and verbally labels the child's feet, arms, and other parts of the body. The routine of dressing is another opportunity to reinforce body awareness. As the caregiver helps the child put his or her arm through the sleeve or pull up his or her pants to the waist, a verbal description of the routine and the body parts involved helps the child understand the concepts as he or she moves through each step. Learning can also occur during mealtime. For example, as the child is eating, the caregiver can verbalize the actions, such as saying, "Let me wipe your mouth" or "Let me wipe your hands."

Progress occurs as the child is able to do more on his or her own and can follow simple instructions such as washing the face and hands when requested. Learning body parts as part of daily routines and activities is the best way to reinforce this learning in a functional context. Rather than saying, "Show me your nose," it is better to teach the child about this body part by saying, "Use the tissue to wipe your nose."

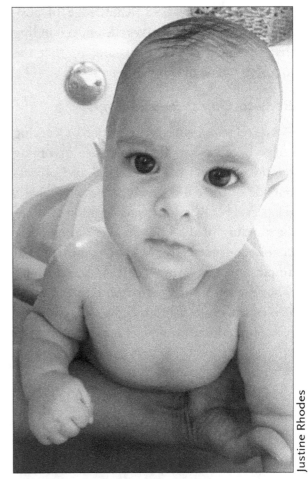

Justine Rhodes

Figure 5.1 Daily routines such as bathing can help develop and reinforce an understanding of body awareness.

Cake," and "Head, Shoulders, Knees, and Toes" (Bozeman & McCulley, 2010).

Body-to-Body (Body-Part) Relationships

The next level of spatial awareness is the relationship of the child's body parts to each other. This includes the understanding that the body has a right and a left side (i.e., *laterality*). A simple example of body-part relationships might be the child clapping two hands together, while a more complex understanding would involve the child being able to put the right hand on the left knee or cover the left eye with the right hand when asked. Knowledge of positional concepts also involves the understanding that the knee is above the foot or that the mouth is below the nose.

Body-to-Object Relationships

This level requires a large transition or learning curve because it is the first phase involving relationships between the child and objects outside of the child's body. A body-to-object relationship takes into consideration the understanding of the body in relation to other people and objects in the environment. Examples include asking a child to stand by another person in line or to come to the other side of the desk. A more complex application of this relationship might include asking the child to stand in front of Sue, but behind Molly (see Figure 5.2).

Positional concepts are used throughout O&M. Foundational knowledge of body-to-object relationships is crucial for the student to understand how to position his or her back against the wall in order to square off or align his or her right or left side to trail the wall and locate an intersecting hallway or door opening. To be able to use a tactile model of the environment to move around an area, the student must have working knowledge of body-to-object relationships. A great mapping strategy that emphasizes body-to-object understanding is using the student's back as a mapping surface (Bozeman & McCulley, 2010). The O&M specialist takes the student to a home base, for

Figure 5.2 Spatial relationships include concepts of sitting "next to" another student or "on top of" a foam block.

Courtesy of Anchor Center for Blind Children

Figure 5.3 Body-to-object relationships are important concepts to help students understand how to position themselves and move around an area.

example, the door to a classroom, and "draws" the locations of landmarks and key clues to understand the room and where things are located in relation to the student's body position. These relationships and positional concepts are essential to a more advanced understanding of the relationships between objects from an allocentric (outside of the student's body) frame of reference (Long & Giudice, 2010; see Figure 5.3).

Object-to-Object Relationships

Understanding object-to-object relationships is the next more abstract and complex level of spatial awareness. To develop this understanding, the O&M specialist may choose three objects within a familiar environment that are important to the student with a visual impair-

ment and that are logically related. For example, within the classroom, the objects can be the teacher's desk, the student's desk, and the door to the classroom. Helping the student understand the relationships between these objects and that the locations of the objects do not change is essential to moving to more complex relationships. A more complex example within a school might include choosing the door to the bathroom, the door to the principal's office, and the entrance to the school. The bathroom is across from the office door, which is located on the right after entering the building. In addition, understanding object-to-object relationships can be strengthened by tactile maps and models. These tools can help the student apply environmental relationships and ultimately create a mental map that is vital to reaching the next level of spatial orientation (Bozeman & McCulley, 2010).

Understanding the relationships between objects is necessary to gain proficiency in more complex aspects of spatial orientation. The process begins with simple, concrete concepts and builds in complexity to encompass not only relationships between the student's body and other objects, but associations between objects in the larger environment. Teaching this progression of concepts requires an organized approach in order for the student to successfully integrate all aspects of spatial orientation.

Spatial Orientation

The theory of spatial orientation involves asking three questions:

1. Where am I? (The student should know his or her present position in space.)
2. Where is my objective? (Answering this question requires knowledge of the spatial

layout to know the relative position of different objects or places.)

3. How do I get there? (The answer to this question requires using spatial concepts such as landmarks, clues, compass directions, and numbering systems.)

Two fundamental principles are critical to spatial orientation: spatial updating and frame of reference. As with spatial concepts, these principles also range from simple to complex and concrete to abstract.

Spatial Updating

Spatial updating is a dynamic process that refers to the ability of the student to keep track of the changing relationships between him- or herself and objects in the environment as the student travels through the environment. This skill requires the student to alter his or her cognitive representation or mental map of the area as well as understand the changing relationships that occur as the student moves through the space (Long & Giudice, 2010). As the student moves through the space, he or she integrates spatial concepts and recognizes the location of key objects in the environment.

———

Paula is standing at the door to her classroom. Her teacher's desk is at the other end of the room, on the right, at 1 o'clock (if using the clock face for positional reference). If she walks into the classroom and across to the other end of the room, the teacher's desk will now be at Paula's 3 o'clock position since the relationship of the teacher's desk to Paula has changed. If Paula turns around to exit the classroom, the teacher's desk will now be located at her 9 o'clock position.

Frame of Reference

Two frames of reference are related to spatial mapping and movement. In an *egocentric frame of reference,* the student uses his or her body as a reference point to the location of other objects in the area. For example, "The restroom door is on my right." An *allocentric frame of reference* allows the student to conceptualize the environment from a global perspective, understanding how objects relate to one another. For example, "The attendance office is next to the front entrance door." The relationships between the objects remain unchanged as the student moves through an area (Bozeman & McCulley, 2010). The associations among objects outside of the student's body require an understanding of remote objects that are beyond the reach of the student (Long & Giudice, 2010). An allocentric frame of reference allows a student to orient from different positions and to more easily create alternate routes and pathways since the frame of reference is not connected to the position of the student's body. The perception of space does not change as the student's body moves through it, allowing for more sophisticated mental mapping (Thinus-Blanc & Gaunet, 1997). Information obtained through the student's senses provides the foundation for gathering pieces of the mental map.

Use of Senses in O&M

Children receive sensory input from birth, and how they process and integrate that information is critical to their orientation in space. Ideally, the senses of hearing, touch, smell, and sight (vision) work together to provide a "picture" of the world and information to orient the student (Anthony et al., 2002; Bozeman &

McCulley, 2010). (Although taste is one of the five main senses, it is used less frequently than the other senses when gathering information from the environment, so it will not be addressed in this chapter.) Sight and hearing provide quality information beyond arm's reach and are known as distance senses. For a student with reduced visual abilities, hearing becomes the primary distance sense (Guth, Rieser, & Ashmead, 2010). An important difference between vision and hearing as a distance sense is that while vision is continuous, hearing is not (e.g., a car goes by and then is out of hearing range, dogs bark and then stop, an air conditioner turns on and off). Hearing also does not provide the same confirmation as vision about the existence of an object in the early months of life (Smith, 2012).

Vision also plays an important role in incidental learning. A typically sighted child will use a whole-to-part approach to learning, first understanding the characteristics of an object as a whole, then discovering how the different parts make up that whole. For a child with a significant visual impairment that occurred before the development of visual memory, learning may be more of a part-to-whole approach. The child with a visual impairment may explore an object with the hands, first absorbing information about the parts of the object. For example, the child may touch the legs of a chair but have difficulty putting the parts together to form the whole concept of a chair, a piece of furniture on which to sit. Furthermore, the part-to-whole approach is fragmented and may cause problems in generalizing the concept to include all types of sitting options, including dining chairs, bar stools, rocking chairs, and benches. Using and integrating sensory input are key to understanding concepts

and helping the child with a visual impairment organize his or her world.

Hearing

For the child with a visual impairment who cannot make use of visual information, hearing becomes the primary sense for gathering distance information. Hearing can provide information about the location of people or objects and pinpoint the direction of the sound, which is critical for orientation. Together with auditory input, the student uses the other senses to gather and integrate information and verify cognitive representations. Sound acquires meaning only after sustained integration (paired tactile, motor, and auditory interaction) to develop the concept. Furthermore, a sound needs meaning before it can provide any useful information about its source, cause, or location.

Sound is usually categorized by intensity, perceived as loudness that is measured in decibels and frequency or pitch that is measured in Hertz. There are two main categories of hearing loss. Conductive hearing loss is the result of a problem with the transmission of the sound; for example, an obstruction in the outer ear canal or fluid in the middle ear from an infection would impede transmission of the sound. While most conductive hearing loss is temporary, the muffled sounds that result can negatively affect the student's orientation. A sensorineural hearing loss is caused by damage to the inner ear or beyond and is usually permanent. Sensorineural hearing loss can occur when the hair cells in the cochlea are damaged due to loud noises, infection, certain medications, or tumors on the auditory nerve (Bozeman & Bozeman, 2016). For a student with hearing loss, hearing aids may be an option. Recent developments in hearing aid technology allow for better localization, which can be beneficial for the student with vision and hearing loss. Significant losses in hearing (in addition to vision loss) may require the use of specific communication intervention strategies in order for the student to request information or receive assistance while traveling (Bourquin & Moon, 2008).

As with any skill, the use of sound in orientation can be developed and improved over time. The process follows the simple to complex theory where the student must first be aware of a sound, then turn toward the sound, identify the sound, and finally progress to the more difficult concept of walking parallel to the sound.

Echolocation is another important auditory skill. *Echolocation* refers to the use of reflected sound to detect the presence of objects in the environment. An example of echolocation is the difference in the sound produced by a cane tip striking the floor of a hallway versus a stairwell (Lawson & Wiener, 2010). Echolocation can be used to avoid obstacles, locate openings, trail a wall or other surface, and detect corners and make turns without contacting a wall. Echolocation is a skill some students may naturally possess while others may need to learn to enhance this skill. Some students create their own sound signals to facilitate echolocation using cane taps, hand clickers, whistling, clapping, or tongue clicks. The social implications of such sounds should be discussed with students so they are aware of them, but use of these sounds to aid in echolocation is a beneficial orientation skill for many students (Anthony et al., 2002).

Another use of sound for orientation includes auditory triangulation, using both ears to pinpoint a sound source. The left ear is one point of the triangle, the right ear is the second point, and the sound source is the third point. Sounds arrive at the two ears at different times, with the ear closest to the sound source receiving a more intense signal than the farther ear. This technique is useful in identifying traffic sounds and can help with alignment during street crossings. A student who is blind will need to use auditory skills for alignment with parallel traffic to know when it is safe to cross the street (see Figure 5.4).

Another use of sound for orientation purposes is understanding the concept of a *sound shadow*. A sound shadow is a break in sound created when an object is located between the sound source and the traveler and blocks the sound. For example, when walking down a sidewalk following parallel traffic on the street, a cane user who is blind might encounter a sound shadow when there are diminished traffic sounds because of a large van parked along the curb. O&M specialists should be careful to position themselves behind the student at an intersection instead of at the corner between the traffic and the student listening for traffic sounds to avoid inadvertently becoming a sound shadow for the student.

O&M specialists should have a thorough understanding of how hearing works and the information provided by this sense. Consideration of how the student with a visual impairment uses sound and how it can be enhanced are keys to improving orientation for the student (Lawson & Wiener, 2010). Any student with a visual impairment should be referred to an audiologist and evaluated for potential hearing problems to determine if hearing aids or other assistive listening devices may be needed (Anthony et al., 2002). For any students with hearing aids or cochlear implants, working in conjunction with an audiologist is essential for

Figure 5.4 Auditory skills can aid in identifying traffic sounds to assist with alignment during street crossings.

Touch

The sense of touch conveys information about pressure, temperature, and pain. The student can acquire information about the characteristics of an object through touch if the object is within arm's reach. The student should be provided with opportunities to explore and use touch to develop the sense and to integrate concepts (see Figure 5.5).

While orienting to the environment, a student may feel the temperature difference on the skin when walking under the shade of a tree, indicating that there is an object above that is blocking the sun. Using a cane extends the stu-

successful O&M instruction since adjustments to these devices often need to be made when traveling in the natural environment.

dent's tactile reach, allowing the student to feel the difference in textures beneath the cane (vibrotactilely through the hand) and through the feet when walking on the sidewalk or on the grass, providing information about the student's location and clues to help with orientation (Guth et al., 2010). Touch must be paired with cognition to serve as a meaningful orientation aid. Touch must also involve movement across a surface to stimulate nerve endings and provide information about the texture of the object or surface. Tactile contact without movement only provides information about the existence, temperature, and firmness (e.g., hard or soft) of an object. The sense of touch is also used in orientation to locate the position of the sun (e.g., feeling warmth on the face or back of the neck), figure out direction based on prevailing winds, and use tactile maps to plan routes and

Heather Gmur

Figure 5.5 The sense of touch is important in acquiring information about the characteristics and textures of objects within a child's reach.

familiarize oneself with the environment (see Figure 5.6).

Smell

The olfactory system, or sense of smell, is often used as a clue in orientation. The smell of dinner cooking can offer clues about the location of the kitchen, or the smell of fresh bread may indicate the presence of a bakery when traveling an outdoor route. The smell of an object or location may not be considered a landmark, though, since it may or may not always be present, and the wind can carry odors, making it difficult to locate the source (Anthony et al., 2002; Koutsoklenis & Papadopoulos, 2011).

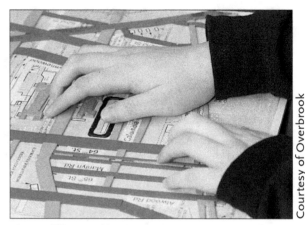

Courtesy of Overbrook School for the Blind

Figure 5.6 Students can use tactile maps for orientation to plan routes and familiarize themselves with the environment.

Sight

Sight, or the use of vision, is a distance sense that provides both quantity (a large amount) and quality (detail) of information. Encouraging the use of any functional vision a student may have (see Figure 5.7) provides the student with knowledge about the environment and the ability to remain oriented within it. Information about form, color, light direction, and the presence of objects can be used in the student's O&M lessons. For example, the student may be able to see light on his or her right side to note an open door while traveling down a hallway or be able to read the room number on a door. The ability to see color can also help to discern a particular landmark or article of clothing the teacher may be wearing.

A thorough assessment of how the student uses information from all the senses can help guide the O&M specialist's instruction (Anthony et al., 2002). Using and integrating available senses is critical to orientation.

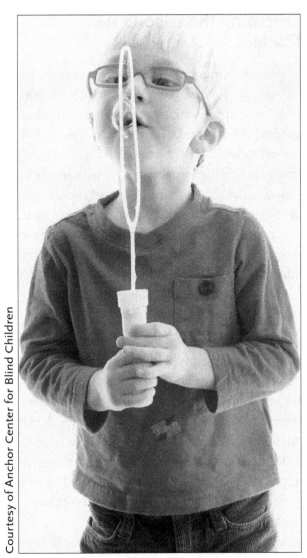

Courtesy of Anchor Center for Blind Children

Figure 5.7 Visually tracking bubbles is one way to improve visual efficiency and encourage use of functional vision.

Cognitive Process for Orientation

Hill and Ponder (1976) presented a cognitive process for orientation that is ongoing and that uses the influx of continuous sensory information to shape and refine the mental map as the student moves through the environment (Fazzi & Barlow, 2017; Hill & Ponder, 1976; see Figure 5.8).

1. While the student is stationary, gather all sensory information.
2. Analyze and organize the sensory information.
3. Select the information that is relevant to the task.
4. Establish a hypothesis based on the information gathered and create a plan.
5. Execute the plan.

This process is continuous. As the student moves to execute the plan, ongoing sensory

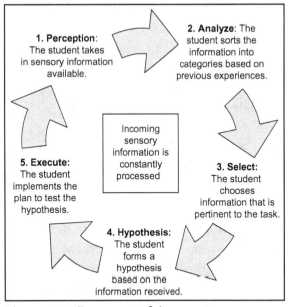

Figure 5.8 Illustration of the cognitive process.

Source: Reprinted from Bozeman, L., & McCulley, R. M. (2010). Figure 2.1: The cognitive process. In W. R. Wiener, R. L. Welsh, & B. B. Blasch (Eds.), *Foundations of orientation and mobility: Vol. II. Instructional strategies and practical applications* (3rd ed., p. 36). New York, NY: AFB Press.

information is received, analyzed, and filtered for relevance to the task, continually updating the information (Bozeman & McCulley, 2010). This continuous updating provides information to the student that he or she is on track, confirming the student's location as well as information needed for recovery if the student becomes disoriented.

Teaching Routes

As with other learning, mobility skills begin in infancy with intentional reaching, rolling, crawling, or creeping toward an object or sound. As the child develops and as his or her abilities allow, these skills may include walking and more advanced movements.

A child may use a toy as a mobility device (e.g., grocery cart, lawn mower, or Corn Popper) to provide advanced warning of objects in his or her path. An adaptive mobility device may be prescribed that provides more body-width protection as the child moves through the environment. Finally, a long cane may be introduced, which requires more coordination and conceptual integration to obtain information about the environment.

The child with a visual impairment usually begins learning routes in the home that follow the routines and patterns of the day. Routes from the bedroom to the bathroom or kitchen grow into routes in other indoor environments, such as within the school, and eventually expand to routes in outdoor environments, such as going to the mailbox or next door to visit a friend. Each subsequent stage builds on the former and broadens the child's world.

Orienting the Disoriented Student

There are numerous strategies to support reorientation for the student who has become lost. Most approaches involve supporting and guiding the steps noted in the cognitive process for orientation. If the student is disoriented, problem solving is necessary. There are four stages to problem solving: (1) understand that a problem exists; (2) find alternative strategies to solve the problem; (3) formulate a hypothesis from the available options; and (4) evaluate the effectiveness of the hypothesis (Bozeman & McCulley, 2010; see Sidebar 5.3).

Self-Talk and Parallel Talk

In the cognitive process, the student is using perceptual information that is available within the environment. Once that information is recognized and labeled (concepts), a plan is developed. It is beneficial for the O&M specialist to follow that process and support learning to better understand the mental map in the student's mind. These strategies also assist in reorientation.

A good tool to help the O&M specialist understand the student's mental map is *self-talk* or inner speech, based on the work of Vygotsky (1987). In self-talk, the O&M specialist asks the student to verbalize what he or she is thinking as the student analyzes and travels through the environment. Not only does self-talk help the O&M specialist understand what the student is thinking, but it also helps to promote the student's memory (Schickedanz, Schickedanz, Forsyth, & Forsyth, 1998; Vygotsky, 1987).

A related strategy is *parallel talk*. In this approach, the O&M specialist verbalizes the

Problem Solving in Orientation

A traveler using a long cane lives in a city neighborhood that is mostly residential but is adjacent to a small-business area and has access to bus transportation. The 11-square-block area is represented by Figure 5.9.

Walnut Street forms the north border of the area. It is a commercial street with many shops and restaurants. Going south from Walnut, the parallel east-west streets are Virginia Street, Kentucky Street, Tennessee Street, and Fifth Avenue (a busy four-lane street with fast-moving traffic). The block from Tennessee Street to Fifth Avenue is uphill going toward Fifth.

The north-south streets in the area, starting from the easternmost and going toward the west, are Negley Avenue, Ivy Avenue, Maple Avenue, Oak Avenue, Locust Avenue, and Aiken Avenue. Negley and Aiken are busy two-lane streets that also carry bus traffic.

Except for the perimeter streets, all the streets within the area are quiet and tree-lined. They usually carry modest amounts of vehicle and pedestrian traffic.

Mike, who travels with a long cane, lives on the west side of Oak Avenue between Kentucky and Tennessee streets. His destination this morning is the coffee shop on the south side of Walnut Street between Oak and Maple avenues. He routinely enjoys coffee and boards a bus at the shelter that is just west of the coffee shop.

This morning, Mike had a lot on his mind. As he traveled north on Oak Avenue and approached Kentucky Street, his cane stuck briefly in a crack just before he got to the curb and affected his line of

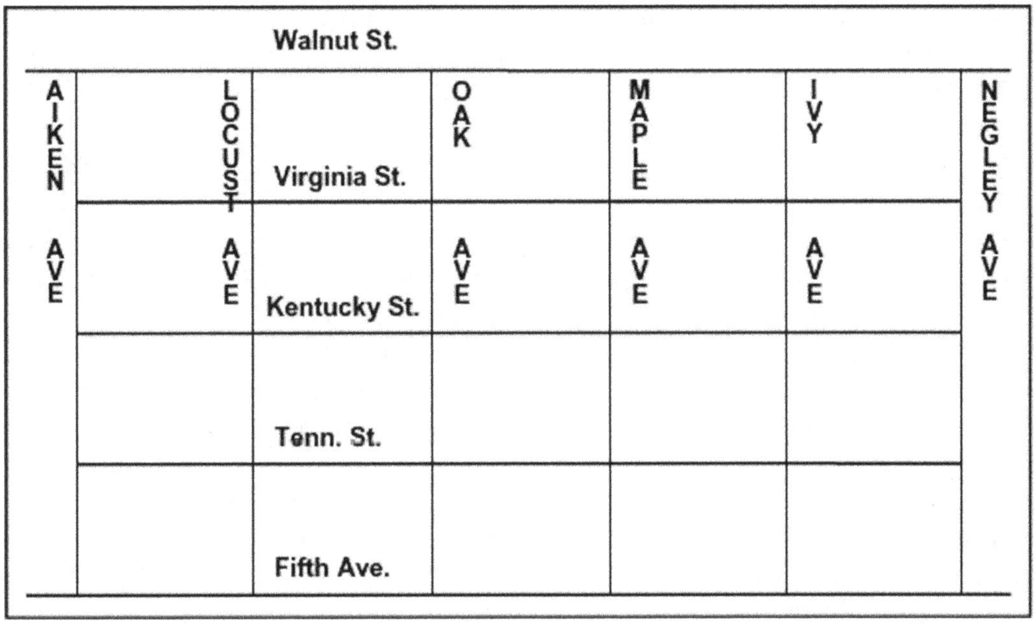

Figure 5.9 Map grid for problem-solving example.

(continued on next page)

direction. Since there was not much traffic along these two streets to verify his line of direction, he trusted that he was okay and inadvertently made a diagonal crossing. As he stepped up on the curb, a car passed and Mike adjusted his line of travel to have the traffic on his right and continued. As a result of the diagonal crossing, Mike was now heading east along Kentucky Street instead of north along Oak Avenue.

Just before coming to the end of the block, Mike noticed a large shrub covering part of the sidewalk. In all his trips along Oak Avenue, he had never noticed this shrub before. It also seemed to him that the block was slightly longer than the block along Oak Avenue between Kentucky and Virginia streets. Now he began to worry about that last crossing he made. He did seem to be out in the street a little longer than usual.

When he arrived at Maple Avenue, he could not tell for sure whether he was at the southwest corner of Oak and Virginia (location A) as planned or whether he had made a diagonal crossing and was now at the northwest corner of Kentucky and Maple (location B). The combination of the protruding shrub and the slightly longer block suggested to Mike that he might not be at the intended corner. But the sound of this intersection was no different from the sound of the intersection he was intending to reach. Had the sun been shining that morning, its location relative to his facing position could have confirmed to him that he was facing east instead of north. But it was a cloudy day. He suspected that he had an orientation problem.

As Mike considered his options, he concluded that he could go one of four ways. (1) He could turn around and retrace his steps. Regardless of whether he was at the corner of Oak and Virginia or at the corner of Kentucky and Maple, if he retraced his steps he would arrive at a quiet intersection. Neither of these would provide any distinctive information to verify his location. (2) He could turn right, cross the street that was on his right, and walk a block in that direction. Once again, this choice, whether he was at location A or location B, would bring him to a quiet intersection that would not solve the problem. (3) Mike could turn left and walk another block. Once again, in neither case would he come to an intersection that would give him information to solve his location and facing problems. (4) He could cross the street in front of him and walk another block. If he was at location A, facing north at Oak and Virginia, one more block north would bring him to Walnut and Oak. He would recognize the sound of pedestrian and vehicle traffic. This would confirm that he had not made a mistake and he could continue to his destination. If, however, he was facing east at location B, another block in that direction would bring him to another quiet intersection. In this case, he could then conclude that he was at the corner of Kentucky and Ivy facing east. Once his location and facing direction had been confirmed, he could then plan his new route to the coffee shop.

Faced with these options, Mike decided to select option 4, cross the street in front of him and proceed in the direction he was facing. After walking one block, he came to a quiet intersection and concluded that he was now at the corner of Kentucky and Ivy facing east. With this confirmation, Mike decided that he would turn left and walk two blocks to get to Walnut Street. Hearing the pedestrian and commercial traffic along Walnut confirmed that his decision was correct. At that point, he turned west, walked along Walnut Street, came to and crossed Maple Avenue, and then located the coffee shop.

Mike also had realized that the process of finding the coffee shop would have to change a

SIDEBAR 5.3

little. Normally, as he walked east along Walnut, he would notice the bus shelter on his left, and the door to the coffee shop would be the next door on his right. Coming from the east, Mike had to walk to the point where he heard the bus shelter on his right. Then he traced his steps backward to the first door to find the coffee shop. Arriving at the coffee shop was the ultimate verification that his problem-solving process had been effective.

Source: Adapted from Bozeman, L., & McCulley, R. M. (2010). Sidebar 2.2: Problem solving in orientation. In W. R. Wiener, R. L. Welsh, & B. B. Blasch (Eds.), *Foundations of orientation and mobility: Vol. II. Instructional strategies and practical applications* (3rd ed., pp. 37–39). New York, NY: AFB Press.

movements and actions of the student as the student travels through the environment. This may help make the student more aware of his or her movements, turns, and other actions that affect the student's travel (Bozeman & McCulley, 2010).

Reorienting Students with Vision Loss and Spatial Orientation Problems

As discussed throughout this chapter, learning strategies for spatial orientation progress from simple to complex and concrete to abstract. Fazzi (2014) stated that understanding the environment may not come naturally to the student with a visual impairment and additional disabilities. Using strategies that take advantage of naturally occurring opportunities and routines can be beneficial (Bozeman & McCulley, 2010).

Students with visual impairments and cognitive challenges may require modifications in the teaching approach when frequent disorientation occurs and traditional strategies do not work. The thoughtful choice of initial routes can promote success and support learning. Any naturally occurring routes (e.g., to the bathroom, to the kitchen) should be taught first since they can be practiced and supported numerous times throughout the day.

Choosing clear, concrete landmarks that are located in a linear pattern may also be helpful. For example, using a rote route approach, such as traveling from landmark A, to B, then to C, is simpler than more abstract travel from landmark A to C, bypassing landmark B.

If existing clues in the environment are subtle, the instructor may use artificial clues such as a radio playing at the location where the student must turn to find the kitchen. This artificially generated clue functions as a sound source that is easily recognized and serves as a beacon for the student when traveling. A similar approach can be to use tactile labels along the route, placing them in locations where the student will easily contact the labels when trailing a wall. Moving from simple to complex, these clues can be tapered off gradually once the clue is associated with critical features of the route in the mind of the student.

Task analysis can be used to break down the route into smaller, more easily mastered parts that are practiced until these parts can be linked together to create the entire route. A related strategy is backward chaining. This technique teaches the final section of a route first and then works backward through the steps of the route until the whole route has been completed. For example, the student will first need to locate the grocery store door, then the part of the route consisting of crossing of the street closest to the store, then the portion of the route from the student's home up to that street crossing, and so on. Finally, after practicing and putting the sections of the route together, the student can travel from home to the grocery store in one lesson.

There are many different types of maps. Some maps are tangible while others require a more advanced level of spatial and conceptual understanding. A student may not be able to use an abstract tactile map that requires an understanding of object-to-object relationships, but may be able to use a serial map that requires an understanding of body-to-object relationships. One example is an auditory serial map. This serial map can consist of recorded directions that denote each step of a route. Examples of recorded directions can include: "Walk out of the front door of your home; travel straight on the sidewalk until you reach the grass"; the next step would be to "turn right and walk one block to Main Street." The student can listen to each step of the route, stop the recording, travel that portion of the route, and turn on the recording to travel the next portion of the route. Each step of the route requires the student to use body-to-object relationships of spatial awareness. Using smartphone or GPS technology with auditory routes is another helpful tool for the student experiencing orientation problems. (See Chapter 7 for more information about GPS.)

Students who consistently get disoriented may need to redefine independence as requesting assistance from others when needed. These students need to be taught and need to understand how to make use of a guide for orientation purposes by asking open-ended questions to gather information (e.g., What is the name of this street in front of me?) and giving clear directions (e.g., Can you please take me to the front door of the library?). These strategies are often referred to as interdependence and can successfully allow a student to reach a goal or destination.

An alternative to traveling on foot may include teaching students who have problems with orientation to schedule and use paratransit services, taxis or ride-sharing services, or hire personal drivers. Again, students should learn to clearly communicate where they are and where they want to go. Understanding exactly where the van, taxi, or driver will arrive and where they will drop the student off at the desired destination is critical.

Role of Partners in Sensory Development and Spatial Awareness

Service-delivery models include a team of family members and professionals who collectively support the student. When all team members are aware of the student's goals and objectives in the areas of spatial awareness and the use of sensory systems, they can support those goals within daily routines. If everyone on the team knows what strategies to reinforce, the chances of generalizing orientation skills increase. If all team members use the same language and the same prompts throughout the school day and at home, spatial awareness skills are learned more quickly. It is important for the O&M specialist to suggest strategies that other team members can use in daily activities and routines with the student. For example, if the student is working on body-to-body relationships and laterality, then the teacher of students with visual impairments can use the terms "left" and "right" throughout a braille reading lesson, the physical therapist can have the student put the left side of his or her body against the wall, the classroom teacher can ask the student to raise the right hand when he or she wants to be called upon in class, and parents can use the terms "left" and "right" during bath time. (See Chapter 11 for more information on collaboration.)

As with any team process, communication is key to success (Correa, Fazzi, & Pogrund, 2002). The various team members not only work on the goals of their own areas of focus, but find ways to support expectations and strategies of the other team members. This approach reinforces continuity for the student throughout the natural routines of the day. If a student uses a natural landmark, such as a fire extinguisher on the wall, as a signal about when to square off to cross the hall to get to the restroom, all team members at school should know about that landmark and how the student should place his or her back against it to square off and reinforce these skills on a daily basis.

Summary

For the child with a visual impairment, supporting sensory awareness and spatial concept development begins at birth. Since incidental learning may be difficult, purposeful description and the careful use of natural routines are critical to develop the foundations for spatial awareness and the cognitive processes used in orientation and purposeful movement. Including the family and the entire educational team in supporting sensory awareness and spatial orientation enhances student learning.

References

Anthony, T. L., Bleier, H., Fazzi, D. L., Kish, D., & Pogrund, R. L. (2002). Mobility focus: Developing early skills for orientation and mobility. In R. L. Pogrund & D. L. Fazzi (Eds.), *Early focus: Working with young children who are blind or visually impaired and their families* (2nd ed., pp. 326–404). New York, NY: AFB Press.

Anthony, T. L., Lowry, S. S., Brown, C. J., & Hatton, D. D. (Eds.). (2004). *Developmentally appropriate orientation and mobility*. OSEP Grant Project H325B00003. Chapel Hill: University of North Carolina at Chapel Hill, FPG Child Development Institute, Early Intervention Training Center for Infants and Toddlers with Visual Impairments.

Bourquin, E., & Moon, J. (2008). Studies on obtaining assistance by travelers who are deaf-blind. *Journal of Visual Impairment & Blindness, 102*(6), 352–361.

Bozeman, L., & Bozeman, K. (2016). Sensory changes with age: Assessment strategies for older adults with visual impairment. In N. Griffin-Shirley & L. Bozeman (Eds.), *O&M for independent living: Strategies for teaching orientation and mobility to older adults* (pp. 21–43). New York, NY: AFB Press.

Bozeman, L., & McCulley, R. M. (2010). Improving orientation for students with vision loss. In W. R. Wiener, R. L. Welsh, & B. B. Blasch (Eds.), *Foundations of orientation and mobility: Vol. II. Instructional strategies and practical applications* (3rd ed., pp. 27–53). New York, NY: AFB Press.

Chen, D. (Ed.). (2014). *Essential elements in early intervention: Visual impairment and multiple disabilities* (2nd ed.). New York, NY: AFB Press.

Correa, V. I., Fazzi, D. L., & Pogrund, R. L. (2002). Team focus: Current trends, service delivery, and advocacy. In R. L. Pogrund & D. L. Fazzi (Eds.), *Early focus: Working with young children who are blind or visually impaired and their families* (2nd ed., pp. 405–442). New York, NY: AFB Press.

Darken, R. P., & Peterson, B. (2002). Spatial orientation, wayfinding, and representation. In K. M. Stanney (Ed.), *Handbook of virtual environments: Design, implementation, and applications* (pp. 493–518). Mahwah, NJ: Lawrence Erlbaum.

Fazzi, D. L. (2014). Orientation and mobility. In C. B. Allman & S. Lewis (Eds.), *ECC essentials: Teaching the expanded core curriculum to students with visual impairments* (pp. 248–282). New York, NY: AFB Press.

Fazzi, D. L., & Barlow, J. M. (2017). *Orientation and mobility techniques: A guide for the practitioner* (2nd ed.). New York, NY: AFB Press.

Fazzi, D. L., & Naimy, B. J. (2010). Teaching orientation and mobility to school-age children. In W. R. Wiener, R. L. Welsh, & B. B. Blasch (Eds.), *Foundations of orientation and mobility: Vol. II. Instructional strategies and practical applications* (3rd ed., pp. 208–262). New York, NY: AFB Press.

Ferrell, K. A. (1997). What is it that is different about a child with blindness or visual impairment? In P. Crane, D. Cuthbertson, K. A. Ferrell, & H. Scherb (Eds.), *Equals in partnership: Basic rights for families of children with blindness or visual impairment* (pp. v–vii). Watertown, MA: Perkins School for the Blind and the National Association for Parents of Children with Visual Impairments.

Guth, D. A., Rieser, J. J., & Ashmead, D. H. (2010). Perceiving to move and moving to perceive: Control of locomotion by students with vision loss. In W. R. Wiener, R. L. Welsh, & B. B. Blasch (Eds.), *Foundations of orientation and mobility: Vol. I. History and theory* (3rd ed., pp. 3–44). New York, NY: AFB Press.

Hannaford, C. (2005). *Smart moves: Why learning is not all in your head* (2nd ed.). Salt Lake City, UT: Great River Books.

Hill, E., & Ponder, P. (1976). *Orientation and mobility techniques: A guide for the practitioner.* New York, NY: American Foundation for the Blind.

Koutsoklenis, A., & Papadopoulos, K. (2011). Olfactory cues used for wayfinding in urban environments by individuals with visual impairments. *Journal of Visual Impairment & Blindness, 105*(10), 692–702.

Lawson, G. D., & Wiener, W. R. (2010). Audition for students with vision loss. In W. R. Wiener, R. L. Welsh, & B. B. Blasch (Eds.), *Foundations of orientation and mobility: Vol. I. History and theory* (3rd ed., pp. 84–137). New York, NY: AFB Press.

Long, R. G., & Giudice, N. A. (2010). Establishing and maintaining orientation for mobility. In W. R. Wiener, R. L. Welsh, & B. B. Blasch (Eds.), *Foundations of orientation and mobility: Vol. I. History and theory* (3rd ed., pp. 45–62). New York, NY: AFB Press.

Mangold, S. S. (2003). Speech-assisted learning provides unique braille instruction [Practice report]. *Journal of Visual Impairment & Blindness, 97*(10), 656–660.

Sapp, W. (2011). Somebody's jumping on the floor: Incorporating music into orientation and mobility for preschoolers with visual impairments [Practice report]. *Journal of Visual Impairment & Blindness, 105*(10), 715–719.

Schickedanz, J. A., Schickedanz, D. I., Forsyth, P. D., & Forsyth, G. A. (1998). *Understanding children and adolescents* (3rd ed.). Boston, MA: Allyn & Bacon.

Skellenger, A. C., & Sapp, W. K. (2010). Teaching orientation and mobility for the early childhood years. In W. R. Wiener, R. L. Welsh, & B. B. Blasch (Eds.), *Foundations of orientation and mobility: Vol. II. Instructional strategies and practical applications* (3rd ed., pp. 163–207). New York, NY: AFB Press.

Smith, M. (2012). *SAM: Symbols and meaning: Guidebook, assessment and games book.* Louisville, KY: American Printing House for the Blind.

Thinus-Blanc, C., & Gaunet, F. (1997). Representation of space in blind persons: Vision as a spatial sense? *Psychological Bulletin, 121*(1), 20–42.

Vygotsky, L. S. (1987). Thinking and speech (N. Minick, Trans.). In R. W. Rieber & A. S. Carton (Eds.), *The collected works of L. S. Vygotsky: Vol. I. Problems of general psychology* (pp. 39–288). New York, NY: Plenum Press.

6

Basic Orientation and Mobility Skills

Christopher Tabb and Amy Van der Veer

Questions to Guide Your Reading of This Chapter

➤ How can basic orientation and mobility techniques promote independence for the student?

➤ What are the roles of the guide and the student when using guide technique while traveling?

➤ How can the type of vehicle affect familiarization and seating?

➤ Where would students apply protective techniques, and why would they elect to use them?

Its [mobility training] scope begins with teaching basic movement within a room and extends, through a series of small steps, to the complexities of long-distance travel. For every rung of the mobility ladder, there is a corresponding one on the ladder of mobility training. (Goodman, 1989, p. 34)

This chapter focuses on the basic skills needed by individuals who are blind or who have low vision to travel in familiar and unfamiliar areas. Most of the skills in this chapter will be used primarily with students who are functionally blind (those who rely mainly on tactile and auditory information for learning), but there may

be occasions when a student who has low vision may also need to use some of these skills selectively (e.g., at night or in an area with low lighting). At other times, the student with functional vision may be able to rely on his or her visual skills, but knowing how to use guide technique or protective techniques, if needed, can be valuable as well. Procedures concerning the execution of these basic skills, as well as adaptations, are provided in this chapter. Detailed information about instruction in the use of the long cane and travel in more complex environments is not included because orientation and mobility (O&M) specialists are the only professionals who should recommend, issue, and teach the use of long canes, other mobility devices, or complex travel skills to children with visual impairments. (For further information on teaching O&M skills and techniques, see Fazzi & Barlow, 2017; Jacobson, 2013; LaGrow & Long, 2011; and Wiener, Welsh, & Blasch, 2010.) Using basic guide technique, protective techniques, and techniques for alignment; learning room familiarization; knowing how to properly store a cane; and understanding how to search for dropped objects are just some of the O&M techniques addressed in this chapter. These are basic O&M skills that the teacher of students with visual impairments can teach and support and that other educational team members can also support. In this chapter, the student refers to either a child or an adult with a visual impairment.

Guide Techniques

Basic Guide Technique

Basic *guide technique* provides a safe and efficient travel option when additional support from another individual is needed or desired by a student with a visual impairment (see Sidebar 6.1 for definitions of key terms). When another person is guiding a student who is blind, that person is using guide technique. (This technique may sometimes be referred to as sighted guide or human guide technique, although guide technique is now the widely accepted term.) The advantages of using guide technique include the availability of any person generally being able to act as a guide, it is easy to teach to someone, and it allows for the opportunity to socialize in unfamiliar or crowded environments, where orientation can often be challenging. The disadvantages include the student becoming dependent on others, overuse of the technique discouraging a student's feeling of independence and self-worth, and walking with an untrained guide causing the student to be fearful of possible injury (La-Grow & Long, 2011).

Even though guide technique is a dependent method of travel, using this technique does provide some level of control for students who are blind or visually impaired because it gives them the ability to end the physical connection whenever they feel the need to do so just by letting go. Uninformed guides may grab a student's

---

SIDEBAR 6.1
Key Terms

Alignment techniques Methods that assist individuals who are blind or visually impaired with positioning for travel in a straight line.

Direction taking Alignment technique in which an individual uses a surface such as a wall to gain a straight line of travel from a parallel surface by projecting a travel path forward.

Guide technique Method for providing appropriate assistance to an individual with a visual impairment to travel safely and efficiently with a guide.

Hines break Technique used to accept, correct, or refuse assistance from an individual trying to provide help as a guide.

Protective techniques Strategies for keeping the body safe while traveling by positioning the hand to provide protection to the upper and lower body to avoid contact with objects or obstacles. Can be used with or without a cane.

Room familiarization Organized process of exploring a room and determining its general layout as well as the relative positions of its contents and features using systematic strategies.

Search patterns Systematic approaches for locating or retrieving objects through exploration of an area.

Squaring off Alignment technique in which an individual uses a surface such as a wall to position the body and establish a line of travel, usually perpendicular to the surface.

Trailing Technique used to maintain orientation and a line of travel or locate landmarks by contacting and following a surface with the hand. Can be used in conjunction with a cane.

arm and pull the student to the desired destination, creating an unsafe situation.

Some general rules of etiquette when using guide technique:

- Always identify yourself when approaching someone who is blind.
- Always ask if the person would like assistance and honor his or her response.
- When leaving the person you are guiding, make sure you let the person know you are leaving and always place the person's hand on an anchor (e.g., a chair, a doorway) rather than leaving the person out in open space.
- Once you are comfortable using guide technique with a person who is blind or visually impaired, it is fine to talk and socialize as you walk together, as long as you continue to pay attention to when you need to give cues for safety or efficiency to the person you are guiding.

Procedure

1. If the student requests assistance, the guide may give the student a verbal cue such as, "Would you like to take my arm?" or the guide may touch the back of the student's hand with the back of her hand.
2. The student grasps the guide's arm with his hand in a *C* shape, similar to holding a soda can (see Figure 6.1).
   a. The student holds the guide's right arm just above the elbow with his left hand if located on the guide's right side (or with the right hand if on the guide's left side) and is positioned a half-step behind the guide, facing in the same direction.
   b. The student's left shoulder should be aligned behind the guide's right shoulder

or vice versa. Together, the guide and the student should take up the space of one and a half people.
   c. The guide needs to make sure the student is holding onto her arm with a secure grip, but not too tight, so that the student will not lose his grip if someone bumps into him or if the student loses his balance.
3. The guide should keep her guiding arm relaxed down by her side rather than bent. A relaxed arm will relay more of the guide's natural body movements to prepare the student for the next action (e.g., turning, reaching for a door handle, starting to ascend stairs).
4. The student should maintain his guiding arm close to his body, forming a 90-degree angle with his elbow. The student's wrist should be in a neutral position, neither flexed nor extended, while the forearm is positioned straight.
   a. The 90-degree angle at the elbow provides the student with tactile information in an up or down direction that might indicate elevation changes such as steps or curbs.
   b. The difference in the height between the student and the guide will determine the exact angle and where the student positions his arm, but it should approximate a 90-degree angle.
5. The guide is responsible for making sure the student does not walk into obstacles.
6. The pace of walking is determined by the slower of the two individuals. For example, if the student has an orthopedic problem and walks slowly, then he will set the pace of travel. However, if the guide has a

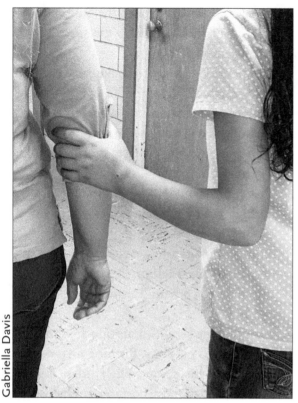

Gabriella Davis

Figure 6.1 Correct position for guide technique.

need to travel slowly, then she will set the pace.

7. Occasionally, while walking, the guide should check the alignment of the student and make sure the student maintains a half-step position behind the guide.

Adaptations

A number of alternative grasps can also be used if the student is a small child or if he has poor balance:

- A student who is much shorter in height than the guide, such as a small child, can make contact with the guide and grasp the guide's wrist or her index and middle fin-

gers, maintaining an approximate 90-degree angle with the elbow (Sapp, 2004a).

- A student with balance issues or weakness may need to link his arm through the guide's arm and hold onto the guide's forearm. This position decreases the space between the guide and the student while providing additional support.

- If a child is likely to run away, then it is best to bring the guide's opposite arm across her body and place it on top of the student's arm, enveloping the student's arm between the guide's forearms to prevent the child from leaving the guide without warning or getting into a dangerous situation.

- In some cases, although not the desired position, if the guide is significantly shorter than the student, it may be necessary for the student to hold onto the shoulder of the guide while traveling since the student may not be able to reach the guide's arm near the elbow without bending over, which creates an awkward posture. This shoulder position, however, does not provide the same types of body cues as the correct guide technique position.

- If the student uses a long cane, the student has options for holding the cane while being guided.
  - If the cane folds, the student can fold up the cane and carry it in a holster, purse, or backpack.
  - The student can hold the cane in his non-guiding hand, making sure not to contact or trip the guide when positioning the cane.
  - If relying solely on the guide, the student can hold the cane vertically, or in a diag-

onal position out to the side of his body, away from the guide, if he feels he needs additional protection.

Reversing Direction with a Guide

This technique allows the student and guide to change the direction of travel 180 degrees. This technique may be used if the guide and student need to reverse direction when a student has forgotten something and needs to go back and get it, or when a student and guide enter an elevator and need to turn around to exit the elevator doors.

Procedure

1. The guide can verbally indicate or tactilely cue the student that they need to change direction and then stop and turn toward the student in order to change direction.
2. The student releases his grip and turns 90 degrees toward the guide. The guide also turns 90 degrees toward the student. Contact is maintained throughout the turn to prevent disorientation and provide a point of reference. Once the guide and student face each other, the guide initiates contact with the back of her free hand for the student to grasp the free arm, then releases the original grasp (Jacobson, 2013).
3. The student and guide both turn another 90 degrees away from each other to face the opposite direction of travel, completing a full 180-degree turn.
4. Once facing the opposite direction, the student resumes his grasp above the elbow and the student and guide reestablish basic guide position.

Adaptation

If there is enough space to make a turn in the opposite direction (e.g., a wide opening in a hallway), the guide can lead the student in a circular motion to turn in the opposite direction. It is important for the guide to lead the turn and not make the student move in any awkward or backward motions (i.e., do not turn in toward the student to turn around and change direction).

Changing Sides with a Guide

This technique allows the student to change sides from one arm of the guide to the other. It may sometimes be necessary to change sides with a guide to reduce contact with others or with an obstacle, to avoid a drop-off, to hold onto a handrail (see Negotiating Stairs with a Guide), when going through doorways (see Negotiating Doors with a Guide), or in crowded corridors (see Narrow Passageway Technique with a Guide).

Procedure

1. While the student and guide continue walking forward, the student grasps the guide's arm with his free hand just above his current grip (see Figure 6.2a).
   a. If the student needs to change sides while stopped, the guide should make sure that wherever they pause to change sides will not cause a disruption in the flow of pedestrian traffic.
2. The student releases the initial grip and moves that hand toward the guide's other arm (see Figure 6.2b). Some people find it helpful to lightly trail their fingers along

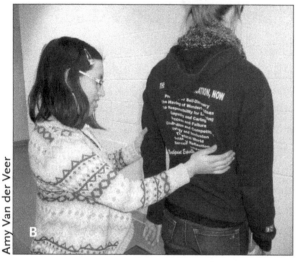

Amy Van der Veer

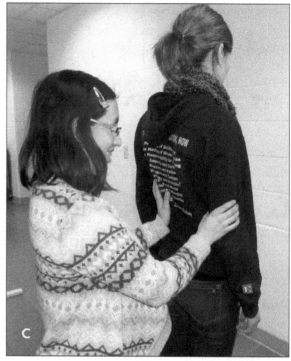

Figure 6.2 Changing sides with a guide: The student grasps the guide's arm with the free hand just above the current grip (A), releases the initial grip and moves that hand toward the guide's other arm (B), and releases the grip on the original side and trails that hand to the guide's opposite arm (C).

the guide's back until the opposite arm is reached.

3. The student's grip on the side from which he is transferring is released, and his hand trails to the opposite arm (see Figure 6.2c). The student then assumes the proper grip just above the elbow on the other side of the guide's body.

4. The grip is resumed on the other side of the guide. It is important to note that the student should not release his grip on the guide's original arm until his hand placement on the guide's other arm is in the proper position and the new grip is secure.

Narrow Passageway Technique with a Guide

This technique enables the student and guide to navigate safely through a narrow space or a crowded pedestrian area by reducing the width of the guide and the student.

Procedure

1. When traveling through narrow spaces such as doorways, hallways, between furniture, or on a crowded sidewalk, the guide will move her guiding arm behind and toward the small of her back.

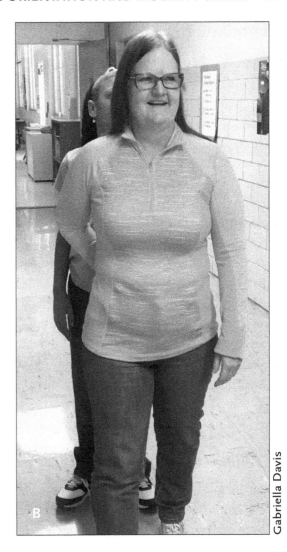

Gabriella Davis

Figure 6.3 Narrow passageway technique: The student slides the grip down the guide's arm to the guide's wrist (A) while stepping behind the guide (B).

2. With the guide's arm in this position, the student slides his hand down the guide's arm to the guide's wrist while stepping behind the guide and extending his arm (see Figures 6.3a and 6.3b).

   a. The student should be walking one full step behind the guide. The student's arm should be extended enough to avoid stepping on the guide's heels.

3. The student may want to place his free hand on the guide's other shoulder to confirm single-file alignment.

4. After clearing the narrow passageway, the guide returns her arm to her side and the student moves back to his original position.

Adaptation

Some students may need a more deliberate prompt and possibly physical guidance with moving their hand to and from the wrist of the guide as the team goes into and out of the narrow passageway technique. For example, the guide may need to assist the student in moving his hand down to the proper position on the wrist and aligning himself behind the guide.

Negotiating Doors with a Guide

The purpose of this technique is for the student and guide to move through doorways in a safe, efficient, and graceful manner. Doors are frequently encountered during travel. The guide needs to prompt the student a step or two prior to approaching the door, using a verbal cue such as, "We are approaching a door." The student's free hand should always be on the same side as the door's hinges and the direction in which the door opens. The guide provides the student with two pieces of information about the door by saying, "Hinges on the right (or left)" and "Door opens to the right (or left)." It may be necessary for the student to change sides when traveling through a door or release the hand needed to hold the door. The student should also be informed whether the door pushes or pulls open to assist in holding the door open as the guide and student pass through the doorway.

Procedure

1. As the guide and student approach the door, the guide notifies the student where the door hinges are (or whether the door opens to the right or left) and whether it is a push (opening away from them) or pull (opening toward them) door.
2. The guide moves her arm behind her back and this cues the student to bring his grip down to the guide's wrist and position himself behind the guide as they move through the doorway (unless the doorway is wide enough to accommodate the width of two people walking side by side).
   a. The student may need to cue the guide if he needs the guide to stop while changing sides. For example, if the hinges are on the right, the door pushes open, and

the student is holding onto the guide with his right hand (so he is on the guide's left side), the student will need to change sides to the right either while walking (a dynamic change) or after the guide has stopped (a static change) in order to assist with holding the door open (see procedure for Changing Sides with a Guide).
   b. A static side change may be necessary if the student is small, inexperienced, has poor balance, or is carrying a bag and needs a moment to reorganize.
3. The guide should not turn around to hold the door open, but rather pause, if needed, to make sure the student has control of the door with his free hand when passing through.
4. Once the student is provided with information about the door (i.e., push or pull, in which direction it opens), the student will sweep, or move his arm away from the guide with his palm facing out until he contacts the door, and will continue to hold the door open until both the guide and the student have cleared the door (see Figure 6.4). To avoid injury, it is important to make sure that when the student is reaching for the door to push or pull it, he does not place his fingers in the door crack near the hinges.
5. If the door is not self-closing, the guide will need to verbally request that the student close the door behind him after they are both safely on the other side.

Adaptations

- Students who are in the early stages of conceptual development may need different cues when going through a doorway. For example, they may not have a working memory or knowledge of where door hinges are

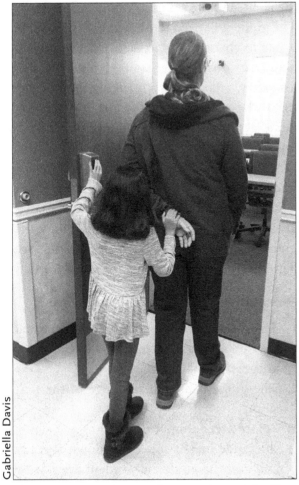

Figure 6.4 Negotiating doors with a guide: The student holds the door open while being guided through the doorway.

Gabriella Davis

and how they relate to the direction a door opens. In this case, the guide may want to use the words such as "toward" and "away" along with the direction in which the door is opening (e.g., "The door opens toward us and to your left" or "The door opens away and to the right").

- More experienced students may not need to change sides when going through a doorway, they may only need to switch the hand that is holding their guide to free up the opposite hand to catch or push the door as they

go through it. Then, after passing through the doorway, they resume their previous guide technique position.

- If a student has balance or physical problems and cannot assist with holding the door, an alternative can be for the guide to walk through the door backward while holding both of the student's arms for support. They can resume guide technique after clearing the door.

Hines Break or Cross-Body Technique

The purpose of this technique is to interrupt an unsolicited attempt by someone trying to provide assistance as a guide. Imagine a scenario in which you are blind and standing at a corner when someone unexpectedly grabs you by the wrist and starts pulling you across the street, all the while saying, "I'll help you, here you go." Before you know it, you are in the middle of the street, but which street? Though well intentioned, this type of unsolicited aid is often not welcomed by an individual who is blind and can be very disorienting to that individual. To handle this situation politely yet assertively, a person who is blind can use the *Hines break*, also referred to as the cross-body technique, to accept or decline the aid.

Procedure

1. The student keeps his feet shoulder-width apart or slightly wider to have a stable base of support.
2. The student brings the wrist or arm that is being grabbed across his body toward the opposite shoulder.
3. With his free hand, the student grasps the person's wrist.

4. The student pulls the person's wrist away from his arm until the person loses grip of the arm. This movement is done quickly, firmly, and politely. The student needs to remember that even though the person does not know how to assist someone who is blind, she is trying to be helpful.

5. If the student wishes to accept the aid, he can grasp the person's elbow just after freeing himself from the initial contact and add, "Thank you. It is much easier for me to be guided if I take your elbow and follow you."

6. If the student does not wish to accept the aid, the student releases the person's grasp and politely declines the offer. The student can also suggest to the person that the next time she would like to help, she should first ask the person who is blind if he would like assistance and then offer her elbow to be grasped.

Negotiating Stairs with a Guide

This technique enables the student and guide to ascend (see Figure 6.5a) or descend (see Figure 6.5b) stairs safely. As the student and guide approach a flight of stairs, it is important for the guide to inform the student that they will be negotiating stairs and whether the stairs are ascending or descending. It is typically best to work on going up stairs first due to the potential fear that some people have about falling down stairs. Once the student is comfortable going up, going down stairs with a guide may be less intimidating. Usually, a student should hold on to the guide with his left hand so that his right hand is free to hold the handrail if he needs it for support (see Figure 6.5b). (In some countries, the flow of pedestrian traffic may be on the left rather than

the right, and the position would be reversed.) The guide will need to be aware if the student wants to change sides so he can have his right hand free to grip the handrail. At times, whether for safety, efficiency, or orienting to new settings, the student using a cane may request guide assistance when ascending or descending stairs. In this case, the student can hold the cane vertically in his free hand or, if using his free hand to hold the handrail, the student can hold the cane vertically in the hand that is gripping the guide's arm by placing the cane under the thumb of the gripping hand (see Figure 6.5c).

Procedure

1. The guide verbally notifies the student that they are approaching stairs and whether they are going up or down.

2. The guide pauses at the edge of the first step.

3. Before ascending or descending the stairs, the guide makes sure the student is ready and that the guide and student are side by side and facing the first step.

   a. It is important to align perpendicularly against the stairs so both the guide and the student square off in front of the first step, with their feet facing forward toward the stairs and not positioned at an angle.

4. The guide takes the first step.

5. The student follows one step behind the guide.

6. The guide pauses by drawing her guide arm forward, at a landing or at the completion of the stairs, to alert the student that he has one more step left before he reaches the landing. The leveling off of some handrails may serve as another clue that the landing has been reached.

Gabriella Davis

Figure 6.5 Negotiating stairs with a guide: The student follows one step behind the guide as they ascend and descend stairs (A). The student may hold a handrail for support (B). If using a cane, the student can hold the cane vertically in the hand gripping the guide's arm (C).

7. At the landing, the guide and student resume their normal guide position, walking pace, and intended direction of travel.

Seating with a Guide

This technique allows a guide to safely and gracefully assist a student who is blind to locate a seat and lower himself into the seat. Students may need the help of a guide to find seats at concerts, school assemblies, and lectures. These occasions may require a process for auditorium seating. Banquets, shopping, and visiting someone's home warrant another approach, while guiding someone to a desk chair, couch, or bench requires a slightly different approach. It is important for the student to clear his seat prior to sitting in case an object has been left on it. When attending a banquet or other event with a presenter, the guide should inform the student where the presenter is located in relation to where the student is sitting so that the student can orient his attention in the appropriate direction.

Procedure for General Seating with a Guide

1. The guide approaches the desired chair from the front or the side.
2. The guide tells the student where he is in relation to the chair and slowly guides him up to the chair.
3. The guide places her hand on the back or the side of the chair and the student slides his hand down the guide's arm to contact the chair.
4. The student should use the back of his hand to do a quick sweep of the seat prior to sitting.
5. It is important to allow the student to orient himself to the chair and then seat himself.

The chair should not be moved unless requested by the student. If the chair is moved, the guide will need to reorient the student to the chair.

a. If the student is going to sit on a couch, bench, or large chair that is up against a wall, the seat will need to be approached from the front. The guide will walk the student up to the front of the seat until the student's knees or shins are touching the seat. The guide will tell the student what kind of seat it is. The student will explore the seat and seat himself, clearing first by sweeping his hand across the seat to make sure it is clear of objects. It is important to have the student approach the seat using upper-body protective technique (see the following section) as he is leaning over to explore in order to protect his head from any hazards above the seat.

6. The guide should tell the student if there is a table nearby and the position of the table in relation to the student.
7. When the student is ready to stand up from the seat, let the student get up from the seat by himself and only assist when asked.
8. Once the student is standing and has good balance, the guide reestablishes contact by offering her arm.

Procedure for Auditorium Seating with a Guide

1. The guide pauses at the appropriate row.
2. The student aligns himself alongside the guide. This position ensures that the guide and student are aligned side by side to enter the row of seats and allows for lateral movement. The guide should be closest to the row

of seats so that she can enter the row first, leading the student as they sidestep together.

3. The guide initiates the lateral movement into the row.

4. The student uses his free hand to lightly trail the back of the seats directly in front of him, making sure not to contact the back of anyone's head in the row in front and being cautious not to step on the toes of anyone already seated in his row.

5. The guide stops at the appropriate seat and positions the student in front of his designated seat.

6. The student releases his grasp of the guide, and with the back of his legs, squares off against the edge of the seat.

7. The student uses the back of his hand to clear the seat prior to sitting down.

8. To exit, the guide reestablishes contact with the student as they rise out of their seats. They may need to switch places so that the guide leads the student out of the row if they need to exit from the same direction they entered.

9. The student resumes proper guide position, the guide initiates lateral movement down the row to exit, and they sidestep out of the row together. Once again, the student can use his free hand to trail the back of the seats in front of him until he reaches the aisle.

Protective Techniques

Protective techniques shield the body from areas not previewed by a cane and offer safety when a cane is not being used. Protective techniques focus on two main areas of the body: the upper body and the lower body. The hand and forearm provide advanced warning of potential obstacles in a person's path of travel and serve as a buffer between the initial point of contact with the obstacle and the person's body. There may be times when either the upper or lower body needs to be protected, such as while walking in areas with low-hanging branches, but often both techniques will be utilized simultaneously to provide protection to both the upper and lower body, particularly while crossing open areas.

Protective techniques are especially important when students travel short distances without their canes, such as through a kitchen where cabinet doors may be open both above and below the counter, or in a classroom, where tables, chairs, or other obstacles might be in their path of travel. Additionally, the upper-body protective technique shields students' heads while they are bending down to pick up dropped objects from the floor. Protective techniques should be used selectively in areas where students know there are head-level obstacles or obstacles at waist or thigh level, or in unfamiliar areas where upper- or lower-level obstacles are suspected. Protective techniques are typically used for short periods of time since they can be awkward and difficult to sustain physically for long amounts of time, particularly for younger children. Use of a cane typically eliminates the need for lower-body protection, but upper-body protection is useful even with a cane because a cane cannot provide information about head- and shoulder-level obstacles.

Upper-Body Protective Technique

The upper-body protective technique is also called the forearm protective technique or the upper-hand-and-forearm protective technique.

Procedure

1. With the palm of the hand facing outward and away from the student and with the fingers held together, the student raises his arm up to shoulder height and moves it across and toward the opposite side of his body. The student's fingertips extend just beyond the shoulder on the opposite side of his body to ensure the forearm protects the student's face.

   a. If the arm does not go all the way across the body, the open side of the body is not protected.

2. While the hand is elevated just above shoulder level, the student extends it outward about 8 to 12 inches in front of his face (or less for young students whose arm length may be shorter). The arm should be bent at the elbow, forming an angle of about 120 degrees (see Figure 6.6). This extension creates a buffer space to allow the student to respond to any obstacle the hand or forearm contacts.

   a. If the hand stays flat on the student's forehead or shoulder, there is no breaking distance since the hand and the head are at the same place and will both contact the obstacle at the same time.

   b. It is important to keep a straight line from the elbow to the fingertips and not allow the wrist to bend back toward the body, so that the student receives the necessary protection from the fingers and palm of the hand contacting any obstacles or hazards first.

3. The student continues walking forward in this position until he believes he is clear of all head-level obstacles.

   a. For example, if walking under trees, the student knows he has cleared overhanging branches when he is no longer stepping on dried leaves or when the leaves are no longer present.

4. The upper-body protective technique is also used when retrieving dropped objects that are near obstacles, such as tables. As a student lowers himself toward the floor, he keeps his hand extended at a more upward angle across his face, and outward so his hand or forearm finds the table edge or other head-level obstacle while bending over. The table edge provides a reference point so the student can safely pass below it.

   a. On the way up from the floor, the student leads with his hand—palm out—directly above his head so that his hand finds the table edge or another obstacle before his head makes contact with it.

Adaptations

- When working with young children, it is helpful to come up with a prompt that all team members can use to let the child know when to use upper-body protection (e.g., bumper up or hands out). The child should practice using upper-body protective technique before moving on to soft objects or a wall to demonstrate his skills. Both arms may need to be used initially (Sapp, 2004c). Practicing with crepe paper or balloons hung from the ceiling at head level can create a meaningful yet safe environment in which to learn this technique.

- The position of the arm can be slightly modified if it is known that head-level obstacles, such as overhanging branches, will be encountered. In this case, the fingers can be angled up more, at about a 45-degree angle, so that the arm covers the forehead and the top of the head for better protection from overhead hazards.

Figure 6.6 A student using upper- and lower-body protective technique.

- Use of a modified upper-body protective technique is also useful when leaning over to examine and clear a seat before sitting down in case there are any head-level obstacles protruding out from above the seat (e.g., displays extending out from the wall).

Lower-Body Protective Technique

The lower-body protective technique is also called the lower-hand-and-forearm protective technique.

Procedure

1. With the back of the hand facing outward (away from the student) and the palm facing toward the body, the hand is lowered in a diagonal position across the waist and toward the thigh on the opposite side of the body (see Figure 6.6).
2. While the hand and arm are positioned across the body, the student extends them outward about 8 to 12 inches (or less for young students whose arm length may be shorter). This extension creates a buffer space to allow the student to respond to any obstacle the hand or forearm contacts before the lower body arrives at the obstacle (see Figure 6.7).
   a. If the hand and forearm stay flat on the lower torso, there is no breaking distance since the hand and the body are at the same place and will both contact the obstacle at the same time.
3. The fingers should be held together and relaxed, and slightly curved back toward the body, with the thumb tucked in, so that the back of the hand gently contacts the obstacle.
4. The student continues walking forward in this position until he believes he is clear of all waist- or lower-level obstacles.

Adaptations

- For taller students, it may be necessary to extend the lower arm by holding a folding cane, rolled-up magazine, or other long object for the technique to work and to ensure that the arm does not pass above the low obstacle (e.g., a desk or table).
- The height of the student is an important factor to consider when deciding which

Figure 6.7 A student using lower-body protective technique to avoid a waist-level obstacle.

Gabriella Davis

protective technique to use. For example, an obstacle such as a table that requires use of the lower-body technique for an older student may require use of the upper-body technique for a toddler.

Trailing

Trailing allows students to maintain a straight line of travel down a hallway or in a classroom, determine their position in space, and locate helpful landmarks and clues. Trailing a wall and staying in constant contact with the wall to lo-

cate a destination such as a classroom door provides students with an awareness of details and landmarks specific to that environment. Students use trailing to orient themselves to a new environment during room familiarization and to practice locating specific places within a controlled environment prior to being introduced to cane travel. Trailing also can be used to determine a student's position in space and to maintain a parallel line of travel to a surface. Additionally, trailing can be used to enter or leave an unfamiliar room when there is not sufficient room for effective cane use.

Trailing a Wall

Procedure

1. The student faces the desired direction of travel. The student should be parallel to the wall or surface being trailed.
   a. In hallways and corridors, trailing typically takes place along the right-hand side so that the student moves with the flow of pedestrian traffic.
2. The arm nearest the wall or surface being trailed should be positioned at a 45-degree downward angle, extending at the elbow and with the palm facing downward (see Figure 6.8).
3. The trailing hand is positioned so that the fingers are slightly bent, or flexed, with the palm and fingers cupped and the fingers close together and pointing toward the ground. The cupping of the hand allows it to act as a shock absorber. The thumb should be tucked so it does not get caught on anything. This hand position, along with a slightly relaxed arm, prevents fingers from getting jammed.

4. The pinkie finger and ring finger are placed against the surface to be trailed, using light pressure so that the hand can easily glide over any irregular surfaces.

5. The trailing arm needs to remain far enough in front of the body so that the arm arrives first, thereby protecting the body from bumping into any obstacles at mid-body height. This position also allows students to locate objects that may jut out from the trailing surface, providing enough time to respond and navigate around them. Allowing the arm to drift to the side or back eliminates the effectiveness of the trailing technique in protecting the body.

Adaptations

- The arm or hand position may vary slightly to accommodate the best location on the surface for trailing. For example, if there is chair rail molding positioned waist high along a hallway, it can be used as a guide for trailing.

- If the trailing surface is rough, the student can turn his hand to trail the wall using the back of the hand and fingernails rather than just the pinkie and ring fingers, maintaining light contact with the trailing surface. The lighter the contact with the surface being trailed, the easier it is for the student to maintain a steady pace and avoid injury.

- In a room with benches, chairs, or wall cabinets projecting outward into the room, protective techniques may need to be used along with or instead of the trailing technique. When protective techniques are used, the student's elbow that is closest to the wall can be in light contact with the wall. The use of protective techniques while trailing is dependent on the objects students may encounter.

- When trailing is not being used for protection, but to locate landmarks (e.g., when using a cane), trailing with the palm of the hand closer to the side of the body at an upward angle may be more functional. In this case, the cane is carrying out the task of trailing for protection.

- For toddlers, cruising along furniture or walls using two hands and then one hand is a precursor to trailing (Sapp, 2004b).

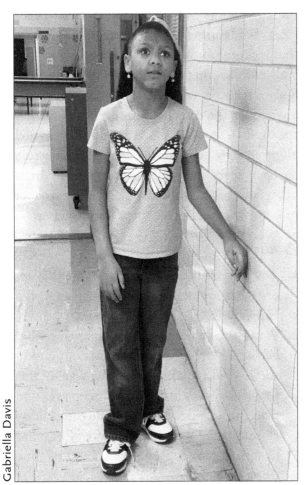

Figure 6.8 A student trailing a wall.

Gabriella Davis

Alignment Techniques

Alignment techniques assist students with positioning for travel in a straight line. Students can use two different alignment methods to get started on a route: squaring off (perpendicular alignment) and direction taking (parallel alignment).

Squaring Off (Perpendicular Alignment)

Squaring off, or perpendicular alignment, is a useful technique for crossing a hallway to locate a destination or during room familiarization (see the next section in this chapter). Squaring off can also be used at a curb to establish a straight line of travel by aligning the feet in a perpendicular manner to the drop-off or by using auditory cues such as traffic sounds to align. It is best to teach squaring off indoors, using walls for alignment. Students should place their backs against a wall prior to learning the squaring-off technique to ensure they understand how to position their backs flat, or square, against the wall.

Procedure

1. The student places his back, with two or more body parts (e.g., shoulders and heels), against the wall to help him project a straight line of travel.
   a. The student's line of travel is perpendicular to the wall to which he has squared off.
2. Using the wall as a point of reference, the student projects a straight line of travel into the open space, away from the wall, and walks forward to the other side of the hallway.

3. Once the student is comfortable squaring off against walls in the hallway, he can move on to larger distances, such as crossing small rooms.

Direction Taking (Parallel Alignment)

In *direction taking,* or parallel alignment, students place themselves lateral to a wall and use trailing to gain a straight line of travel by mentally projecting a travel path forward from the trailed surface when the surface contact ends (e.g., when crossing an open hallway and there is a break in the wall to get to the other side). Students can also bring the shoulder that is closest to the parallel wall up against the wall itself so that the shoulder or side of the body is square with the wall line. With parallel alignment, the direction of travel is parallel to the wall. It is best to start teaching parallel alignment by projecting a line of travel across an open space in a hallway to try to find the other side; for example, by placing the student in a hallway with a plus-shaped intersection.

Procedure

1. The student trails along a wall line that approaches a plus-shaped intersection in the hallway.
2. When the student reaches the intersection, he finds a break in the wall and an end to surface contact with the trailing wall. At this point the student will need to pause and place his shoulder and the side of his body closest to the wall against the wall (similar to squaring off with his back, but this time using his side).
3. Once aligned with his side against the wall, the student proceeds forward, projecting a

straight line of travel forward from the trailed surface in the same direction he is walking.

4. When the student reaches the other side of the intersection, he finds the continuation of the wall line he was originally trailing.

5. Once the student has demonstrated the ability to cross without veering, he can try to cross the opening without pausing to place his shoulder or side on the wall, using only the natural alignment that occurs with trailing and walking.

   a. The student can use the starting wall as a guide for staying parallel to help him find the wall on the opposite side of the open intersection.

6. Eventually, the student's use of auditory skills will allow him to sense where the wall is. The student will no longer need to stay close to the wall in order to walk parallel with it.

Adaptations

- It is not uncommon for veering to occur initially when using parallel alignment. Micro-corrections of the feet or body position are often needed to maintain a straight line of travel if veering occurs frequently. For example, if the student is trying to cross an open intersection in a hallway but veers into the middle of the opening, he can try to position himself more toward the wall line and away from the center of the intersection. Knowledge of a clock face can aid with spatial orientation in such a correction. Instead of walking forward toward what would be 12 o'clock, the student can point his body more toward the right, to one o'clock, to correct his line of travel and accommodate for the veering that occurred to the left.

- Students can also utilize parallel alignment while crossing streets by using auditory cues from traffic sounds to project a straight line of travel across a street or when using a cane and trailing a grass line to travel parallel to the grass or sidewalk in more advanced travel.

Room Familiarization

Room familiarization helps students obtain information about the layout of a room and develop a sense of orientation within it, such as a classroom that they will be in for the school year. To gain knowledge about this room's layout, students use a room-familiarization process. Although this process takes some time, its thoroughness provides information that allows students to understand locations of objects within the room and the relative positions and relationships among these objects, thereby facilitating safe and independent movement. For example, where is the teacher's desk in relation to the student's desk? Where is the science center in relation to the classroom door? There are two types of room layouts: open and closed. Open rooms are rooms that have most of the furniture around the perimeter of the room (e.g., living room). Closed rooms are rooms that have furniture placed both around the perimeter and in the middle of the room (e.g., classroom with desks).

Initially, students travel around the perimeter of the room, then they continue to the center of the room to learn what the interior contains and how objects are arranged within it. If students are sure that the room is free of elevation changes (e.g., a step-down or ramp), they may choose to trail a wall with one hand while using the opposite hand and arm for upper- or lower-body protective technique. Students should walk slowly as they explore a room to safely encounter and travel around obstacles. Students who use a long cane may feel more comfortable holding the cane in the hand furthest from the wall for preview of the room or if they anticipate unexpected changes in elevation. If not using a cane, lower-body protective technique (perhaps with an arm extension object in the hand) is helpful when using basic skills to explore a room. The systematic process described below typically takes multiple lessons to complete and can be somewhat laborious, but it is a useful strategy for students to learn for times when they need to independently explore an unfamiliar space that they will be frequenting. This technique would typically not be used for a room that a student visits occasionally.

Exploring the Perimeter of a Room

Procedure

1. The student identifies one landmark as a starting point and memorizes it so he can confidently identify it as his home base. (The door to the room can often be used as a starting reference point.)

2. From the starting point, referred to as home base, the student begins by traveling along the entire length of the first wall, all the way to the first corner. The student may begin in either direction, going around the room in a clockwise or counterclockwise pattern. Along the way, the student keeps track of what he finds and considers the most significant features of the wall or along the wall so that a name can be assigned to that wall,

such as "the window wall" or "the cabinet wall." It can also be labeled "wall 1" or the "north wall" if the student knows cardinal directions. If objects or obstacles are encountered along the wall line, the student trails around the obstacles and returns to the wall line so that he can continue following the wall until reaching the first corner. Again, the obstacles may be features significant enough to use in naming the wall, such as "the couch wall."

3. From the end of the first wall, the student returns to his home base.

4. From home base, the student trails along the first wall until he reaches the first corner again, then turns and continues along the second wall until he reaches the corner marking the end of the second wall.

5. The student names the second wall based on its characteristics or the labeling system the student chose and then returns to his home base.

   a. On the trip back, the student can begin to anticipate some of the landmarks found along both the second and the first walls.

   b. Some students, particularly those with intellectual disabilities, may need to learn the route around the room first and then the reversal of the route. The reversal may be considered a whole new route from their perspective.

6. The student continues exploring the third and fourth walls, making sure to return to his home base after adding each new wall, and labeling walls three and four after each trip.

7. After the student finishes exploring the fourth wall, he returns to his home base (see Figure 6.9).

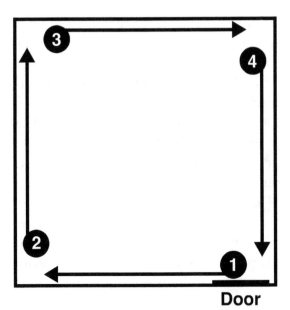

Door

Figure 6.9 Example of the path a student would travel to explore the perimeter of a room.

Adaptations

- A student may find multiple doors in the room that resemble the door he is using as his home base. The doors may have the same handle shape and be built from the same materials, so the student must become familiar with his own starting point and focus on what makes this home base distinctive.

- Most rooms have four walls, but occasionally, a room will have a different number of walls. If this is the case, the student will also find that the corners are not all 90-degree turns, and that may provide clues to the room's shape.

- When exploring the perimeter of a room, it is helpful to try to identify the approximate halfway point on each wall to help with spatial mapping. Using landmarks or clues can assist in this process (e.g., the fire extinguisher is located approximately in the middle of wall 2).

Exploring the Interior of a Room Using a Grid Pattern

Procedure

1. Starting at a corner at one end of the room, the student moves approximately one arm's length away from the wall at his side. The student then squares off against the wall behind him and walks forward across the middle of the room to the opposite side using protective techniques or a cane.

2. When the student reaches the other side of the room, he turns around to face the wall from which he started, moves a short distance away from the side wall, squares off, and heads back to the original wall from which he started, thus creating a grid pattern.

3. The student continues this process, going back and forth from one side of the room to the other, moving over about three feet each time, until he has explored the entire room. The back-and-forth pattern is similar to mowing a lawn or vacuuming a room.

4. If the student wants to be thorough, he can repeat the process between the other two walls to cover the entire room by first walking across the room and then walking up and down the room. In this case, the student's path might resemble the square configuration of graph paper.

   a. When using this grid pattern, the student explores every square inch of the room and knows the placement of objects within it.

5. If the student encounters an object or piece of furniture in his path, he needs to trail around it and try to realign himself on the original path when he reaches the other side

of the obstacle to continue his line of travel toward the opposite wall.

Adaptations

- The student can stand at home base after exploring the room's perimeter and interior and be asked to point to different places or items in the room to assess if he is developing the skills of mental mapping and spatial awareness. Having the student verbally describe what is located along each wall and in the center of the room also ensures that he has created a cognitive map of the room that matches the physical layout of the room.
- Having the student create a tactile map of the room after completing room familiarization is another good way to evaluate the student's spatial memory of the room layout.

Systematic Search Patterns

Finding Dropped Objects

Systematic *search patterns* help students locate and retrieve dropped objects on the floor, such as keys, phones, and toys, or find objects on a surface. Using a systematic search pattern allows a student who is blind or visually impaired to retrieve a dropped object more reliably than a random search. Often, in a random search, the student's hand will come very close to the object but will feel nothing; therefore, the student will move his hand away from that spot thinking the area was checked and nothing was found. This strategy often results in frustration or someone else picking up the object for the student.

By using a systematic search pattern, students can effectively cover every square inch of a space and minimize the chance of "just missing" the dropped object. When retrieving a dropped object, students should be encouraged to use all available sensory information (e.g., the sound of keys hitting the floor, proprioceptive awareness of slope for object that may roll, tactile awareness of different floor materials) to understand as much about the location of the dropped object as possible, which can minimize the area that needs to be searched. If students are able to use their hearing to track the object, such as when a penny falls on the floor and then rolls, pausing and listening to the coin's path offers an initial indication of where to begin the search.

Systematic search patterns can also be used to find objects on a table, desk, or other surface (e.g., kitchen counter). In this case, cupping the hands with the fingers curled under while exploring the surface is a preferred way of locating an object, as opposed to spreading the fingers out or having the hand flat on the surface, since cupping the hands reduces the chance of spilling something or knocking things off the surface. Having a starting point as a reference and knowing where that point is facilitates a systematic search pattern as the searched area expands. It is normally best to practice the different search patterns on a tabletop first before using them to locate dropped objects on the floor in order to identify a preferred pattern or patterns to use.

Procedure

1. The student listens when the object is dropped and turns his body in the direction of the sound, trying to localize the sound, if possible. He then uses upper-body protective technique while lowering his body toward

the floor or ground to protect himself from contacting obstacles located above his head.

2. The student begins to move his hand in a circular pattern (or use any search pattern he desires; see Figure 6.10 for examples of different search patterns), with each successive circle slightly bigger than the one before, and continue this concentric-circle pattern until he finds the object or reaches as far as his arm can stretch.

a. If the student has not found the object, the student should try the pattern on the opposite side with his other hand, making overlapping circles of increasing circumference as far as his arm can reach.

b. It is important for the student to keep one hand in the same place as the starting reference point so he knows where he started each search pattern and to prevent him from haphazardly searching the same area more than once, thus increasing the probability of finding the dropped object.

3. If the student can listen to the sound when the object contacts the floor, more often than not, he will be able to locate the object through a search using first one hand and then the other. If not, the student needs to move his body to one side of the original search location and repeat the process, first with one hand and then with the other. If the student still has not located the object, he should move to the opposite side of the original search location and repeat the search procedure until the object is found.

4. The area around the feet should also be checked before moving too far to search, as the object may be right under the student's feet.

5. It is advisable for the student to wash his hands after searching on the floor for an object.

Adaptations

- Rather than using a concentric-circle pattern, there are a variety of other search patterns the student can use (see Figure 6.10). When using any search pattern, it is important to have a starting point as a reference to avoid exploring the same area when searching. Systematic search patterns will lead to quicker success in finding dropped objects and reduce frustration on the part of the student.

- Students can make slightly overlapping forward and backward passes with their hands across a surface where they anticipate the dropped object to have fallen. A way to extend the search is to use a long cane placed flat on the floor. By laying the cane on the floor, the entire length of the cane is in contact with the surface being explored. The student moves his cane forward and to the sides slowly so that the cane can contact the dropped object somewhere along its length. The student then moves his other hand down the length of the cane to locate the object.

Additional Techniques

Car Familiarization

Car familiarization enables a student to safely locate the proper door on a vehicle and to efficiently enter and exit a variety of vehicles. Car familiarization is necessary for a student to learn to safely locate the door of a parked car,

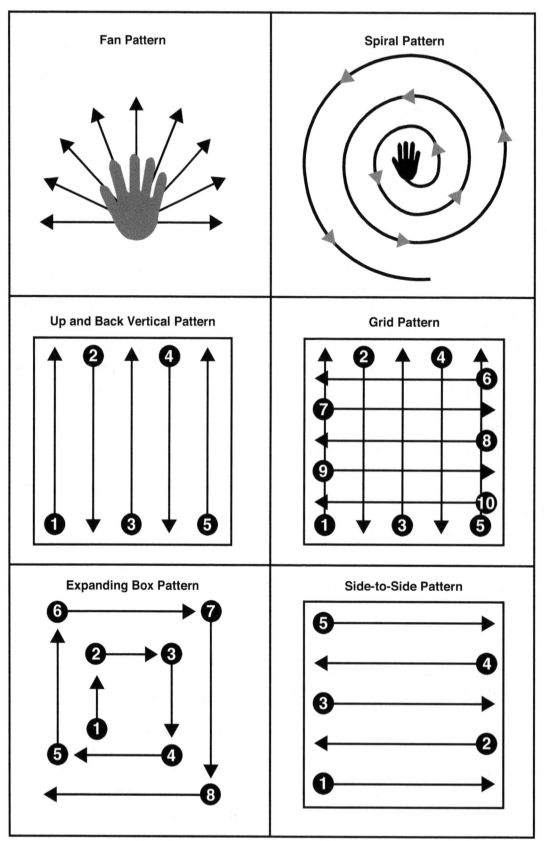

Figure 6.10 Students can use a number of different search patterns to locate dropped objects.

seat himself in the car, close the door, and fasten his seatbelt independently and confidently. This skill provides the student with independence and reduces the need for family members or caregivers to perform this task for the student. Before teaching the car-familiarization technique, it is helpful, but not necessary, for the student to demonstrate proficiency in the following skills: protective techniques, trailing, opening and closing doors, direction taking, search patterns, examining objects, contacting objects, placement of cane, and clearing a seat and sitting down.

It may be helpful to have the student repeat the steps a few times prior to beginning the task. For example, the student can verbally describe the steps and discuss what is different between entering a car and entering a truck and state his preferences.

Procedure

1. The student contacts the car and determines the direction it is facing to locate the proper door. This task is completed first with the student making contact with the car and then using trailing techniques along the car, with verbal cues as needed for safety, to help him find the car's front windshield and wipers.
2. Once the front windshield and wipers are found and the direction of the car is established, the student locates the doorjamb between the front and back windows using trailing.
3. With the back of his hand, the student locates the door handle just below and to the right of the doorjamb.
4. With his free hand, the student contacts the edge of the roof.

a. This action allows the student to know where the roof edge is when he enters the car and negates the need for upper-body protection to avoid bumping his head.
5. The student contacts the back of the seat, clearing the seat using the back of his hand, and turns and sits down.
6. The student verbally notifies others when he is ready to close the door to avoid slamming someone else's hand in a door as it is closed.
7. When exiting the car, the student opens the door and maintains contact with the door.
8. With his free hand, the student once again contacts the roof and proceeds to exit, verbally notifying others prior to closing the door.

Adaptations

- If the vehicle is a truck or sport utility vehicle with a running board and a high entrance step, the student who uses a cane can locate the running board by anchoring his cane as he does when ascending stairs or traveling up a curb. The student uses his cane to explore the height and depth of the running board. Then the student opens the door, locates a grab handle inside the door and takes hold, stepping up onto the running board and slowly turning around to lower his head and sit in the seat. In this situation, it is difficult, if not impossible, to sweep the surface of the seat prior to sitting down since both hands are involved in lifting the body up into the truck.
- It may be necessary to teach the student to use upper-body or lower-body protective technique as well as cane trailing so the student does not collide with the side mirrors extending from the vehicle when trailing along its side.

- If the student is young or small in stature, he may need to lift his hand a bit higher as he trails the car or truck.
- Some students may need to spend considerable time on concept development prior to understanding the different types of vehicles and their features. Use a variety of model cars and trucks paired with experiences exploring actual vehicles to help with conceptual understanding of part-to-whole learning.
- Students who use canes need to make sure that their canes are completely inside the vehicle before closing the door. If riding in very small cars, a folding cane may be easier to manage.

Storing or Stowing a Long Cane

Knowing how to properly store or stow a long cane keeps the cane in a known location and helps the student retrieve it easily when needed. It also keeps the cane clear from walkways to prevent others from tripping over it. One important factor to consider when working with a student on seating is how he will handle his cane. If the student uses a folding cane, it can be folded and placed in his lap, put in a holster located on his belt, put in a backpack or purse, or placed under the chair in which the student sits. Often a student will place his cane on the table. This placement creates some challenges, especially if the table is one on which food is eaten. A helpful strategy is to remind the student that even though the grip of the cane is in his hand, the cane tip travels everywhere the bottom of the shoe does. Proper etiquette dictates a person should keep one's shoes off the table and the same applies to the cane tip. If a student is working with a rigid cane, the strategies are different.

General Procedures

1. The student lays the cane on the floor perpendicular to the direction he is facing and places a foot or both feet on the cane to prevent it from rolling away if someone bumps the cane while it is on the floor.
2. If the student is seated at a table or in an auditorium with other individuals around him, the student should alert those around him that the cane is being placed on the floor so people do not accidently trip over it.
3. Alternatively, the student can place the cane tip on the floor while the upper portion of the cane rests on the student's shoulder. The tip should be positioned slightly below the front tip of the foot so that it does not extended beyond the front of the foot. This will prevent the tip and cane from inadvertently extending into a walkway.

Procedures for Vehicles

With vehicles ranging from subcompact cars to large vans, entering and sitting in a vehicle with the cane can certainly be tricky, with multiple rows and seat belts to navigate through en route to the seat.

1. A rigid cane can be laid on the floor of a van parallel with the sliding door, or if the van is large enough, it can be laid on the floor parallel to the seat row in which the student is sitting.
2. In a small vehicle, the rigid cane can be placed between the side of the seat and the door or wall of the vehicle, extending from the floor of the front seat to the back seat, but still clear of other passengers.
3. When vehicles are large enough, the angled shoulder to floor technique, in which the

cane tip is placed on the floor while the upper portion rests on the student's shoulder, is also an option.

Adaptations

- For students using a folding cane, the cane should be used in combination with protective techniques.
- When a student is in an environment with other individuals who also use canes and the student needs to retrieve his cane, it is important to have a way of identifying and verifying that the cane is indeed the student's. This can be accomplished by applying a braille name label, hanging a keychain on the cord, or placing a rubber band just below the grip.

Summary

People who are blind or who have low vision use various techniques and devices (e.g., guide, cane, dog guide) to travel safely. This chapter explained the different ways guides can safely walk with individuals with visual impairments, as well as other techniques that can be used by students who are blind or visually impaired to familiarize themselves with a new room, protect themselves when they are trying to locate dropped objects, or store their canes while riding in a car. It is important for all O&M partners (e.g., teachers, paraeducators, family members, therapists) working with students who are blind or who have low vision to know these basic O&M skills and use correct mobility techniques to reinforce the use of these skills on a daily basis to ensure safe and efficient travel.

References

Fazzi, D. L., & Barlow, J. M. (2017). *Orientation and mobility techniques: A guide for the practitioner* (2nd ed.). New York, NY: AFB Press.

Goodman, W. (1989). *Mobility training for people with disabilities: Children and adults with physical, mental, visual and hearing impairments can learn to travel.* Springfield, IL: Charles C Thomas.

Jacobson, W. H. (2013). *The art and science of teaching orientation and mobility to persons with visual impairments* (2nd ed.). New York, NY: AFB Press.

LaGrow, S. J., & Long, R. G. (2011). *Orientation and mobility: Techniques for independence* (2nd ed.). Alexandria, VA: Association for Education and Rehabilitation of the Blind and Visually Impaired.

Sapp, W. (2004a). *Guide techniques for toddlers.* Chapel Hill: University of North Carolina at Chapel Hill, FPG Child Development Institute, Early Intervention Training Center for Infants and Toddlers with Visual Impairments.

Sapp, W. (2004b). *Hand trailing for toddlers.* Chapel Hill: University of North Carolina at Chapel Hill, FPG Child Development Institute, Early Intervention Training Center for Infants and Toddlers with Visual Impairments.

Sapp, W. (2004c). *Upper body protection for toddlers.* Chapel Hill: University of North Carolina at Chapel Hill, FPG Child Development Institute, Early Intervention Training Center for Infants and Toddlers with Visual Impairments.

Wiener, W. R., Welsh, R. L., & Blasch, B. B. (Eds.). (2010). *Foundations of orientation and mobility* (3rd ed., Vols. I–II). New York, NY: AFB Press.

7

Orientation and Mobility Systems and Tools

Nora Griffin-Shirley

**Questions to Guide Your
Reading of This Chapter**

➤ What are the orientation and mobility systems and tools used by children with visual impairments?

➤ What are some advantages and disadvantages of different orientation aids and mobility systems and tools?

➤ What purpose do optical devices play in the lives of children with low vision?

The ECC [expanded core curriculum] area of assistive technology includes much more than instruction in the use of devices; it encompasses a broad spectrum of educational services and strategies to provide access for students to participate equally in learning and daily living activities. (McNear & Farrenkopf, 2014, p. 189)

According to the Individuals with Disabilities Education Improvement Act (2004), *assistive technology* refers to "any item, piece of equipment, or product system, whether acquired commercially off the shelf, modified, or cus- tomized, that is used to increase, maintain, or improve functional capabilities of a child with a disability" (34 C.F.R. § 300.5). Referred to as high- or low-tech devices, assistive technology is available to assist children who are visually impaired to travel in their homes, schools, and communities. Global positioning system (GPS) devices, digital maps, and bioptic telescopic systems are considered high-tech devices because they use integrated circuitry or computer-based instruments. Low-tech devices (e.g., sunglasses, visors, canes, or teacher-made maps) do not have integrated circuitry (Presley, 2010). Tools can be classified into orientation aids or mobility devices (see Sidebar 7.1 for definitions of key terms). Orientation aids are tools that assist individuals who are visually impaired in knowing where they are, whereas mobility devices help this population with their ambulation. Often, medical, education, or rehabilitation teams decide what assistive technology individuals with visual impairments should use (e.g., a doctor-prescribed wheelchair). This chapter will describe orientation and mobility (O&M) systems and tools—both low- and high-tech devices—and their advantages and disadvantages.

SIDEBAR 7.1

Key Terms

Adaptive mobility device (AMD) Handmade or commercially purchased device, other than the long cane, that protects individuals who are blind or visually impaired while they travel and provides them with information about the surface upon which they are walking. Often used as a transition to the long cane.

Assistive technology Equipment or products that increase, maintain, or improve the functional capabilities of individuals with disabilities.

Dog guides Specially trained service dogs that assist individuals who are blind or visually impaired in orientation and mobility.

Electronic orientation aid (EOA) Device used for orientation and navigation that helps individuals who are blind or visually impaired find their way in unfamiliar environments.

Electronic travel aid (ETA) Mobility device that converts visual information into tactile or auditory sig-

nals, or both, and extends the range of sensory awareness of the traveler with a visual impairment beyond the fingertip, cane, or dog guide. Also referred to as electronic travel device.

Long cane Piece of equipment that can be made from different materials that identifies individuals as blind, clears the area in front of them while they walk, and provides information about the surface upon which they are walking.

Optical devices Tools that aid individuals with low vision in performing tasks and seeing better at near and at far.

Orientation aids Tools that assist people with visual impairments in learning spatial concepts and the spatial layout of their environments.

Orthopedic equipment Mobility devices that support, stabilize, and assist individuals with visual impairments and physical disabilities.

Orientation Aids

Orientation aids support individuals with vision loss in learning spatial concepts and the spatial layouts of the environments they encounter. Orientation aids include manipulatives, models, verbal aids, maps, and electronic orientation aids such as geographic information systems (GIS), GPS devices, digital maps, and sound beacons (see Sidebar 7.2).

These orientation aids can be helpful for individuals with visual impairments who wish to learn the spatial layout of large geographic ar-

eas (e.g., a college campus, a subway system) and for students with cognitive challenges when learning simple routes. Additionally, teaching map-reading skills at a very young age is crucial for children with visual impairments, especially those who are congenitally blind, to develop cognitive mapping skills (Bentzen & Marston, 2010).

Manipulatives

Manipulatives are objects of varying shapes and sizes that are used to assist children with visual

---

SIDEBAR 7.2

Orientation Aids

Some of the orientation aids listed below may be used for other functions, but the definitions provided here are specific to O&M for people who are blind or visually impaired.

Accessible pedestrian signal (APS) A device used to provide accessible information—through audible, tactile, or other means—to individuals who are visually impaired about when a walk signal is on at a lighted intersection.

Audio map An audio-recorded verbal description of a route.

Compass An accessible device that provides cardinal directions (north, east, south, west) and intermediate directions (northeast, southeast, southwest, northwest) in digitized speech or braille output.

Geographic information system (GIS) An electronic database that collects, analyzes, and depicts geographic information.

Global positioning system (GPS) An electronic technology system that uses navigational satellites to communicate with receivers to determine a person's position within the environment.

Manipulatives Objects of varying shapes and sizes used to help children who are blind or visually impaired learn environmental and spatial concepts.

Map A multidimensional depiction of an area that assists individuals with vision loss in familiarizing themselves with their communities and areas of interest. Maps come in tactile, digital, or large-print formats.

Model A three-dimensional representation of a structure, area, or concept.

Talking sign An infrared wireless communication system that assists individuals who are blind while they travel by providing voice messages to a hand-held receiver with information about their location.

---

impairments in learning environmental and spatial concepts. They range from small toys (e.g., blocks) to large objects (e.g., traffic cones) (Fazzi & Petersmeyer, 2001). O&M specialists can have students measure a route's distance using traffic cones or pedometers or build multistory buildings from LEGOs to illustrate the concept of a big city.

Models

Whether commercial or homemade, models are three-dimensional representations of real objects, groups of objects found together in the environment, or spatial layouts (see Figure 7.1).

Examples of models include a doll's house, an architectural rendering of a skyscraper, a simulation of a cul-de-sac, or a representation of a school building or the training neighborhood used for O&M instruction. Industrial-arts programs in high schools sometimes construct models for students with visual impairments to use. Models are especially helpful for students who may have trouble reading maps and need something more concrete, such as a doll's house that illustrates how the first floor of a home is connected to the second floor (to illustrate to a child how the floor of a second-floor bedroom can be the ceiling of a first-floor living room) (Bentzen & Marston, 2010). Models

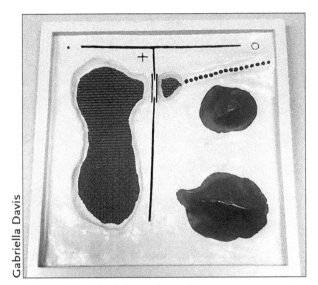

Figure 7.1 Models such as this one representing two hills and a small body of water may be helpful for students who have trouble reading maps.

Gabriella Davis

may also be introduced prior to teaching the concept of maps.

When designing models, scale is an important factor to consider. For example, if constructing an intersection, it is important to make sure the small cars used to learn traffic patterns are in proportion to the street widths (Bentzen & Marston, 2010). It is crucial that a model does not become a substitute for the real object. A model of a truck can be presented to a student who is blind but should be followed by having the student tactilely explore many different makes and models of trucks during an O&M lesson. It is also important to make sure the student understands the concepts of miniature and scale when using models.

Verbal Description

A verbal, braille, or written description of a route or an environment, given to or developed by a student who is visually impaired, is an ori-

entation tool that offers students additional ways to travel within the environment (e.g., route maps). The description can include details about landmarks, techniques to use in specific situations, and various directional information (e.g., "Walk two blocks north and then four blocks west" or "Turn left so that Main Street is now in front of you"). For students who may not be literate or who cannot read braille, audio maps—audio-recorded verbal descriptions of routes—can be used and carried inconspicuously while traveling.

Students with visual impairments can also request a verbal route description from other pedestrians. During O&M instruction, students are taught techniques such as how to request information, where to stand to seek assistance from pedestrians, how to interpret whether the information provided by others is useful, and what questions to ask to receive accurate information. Role-playing is commonly used as an instructional strategy to learn how to solicit verbal assistance prior to requesting information from a pedestrian on a route.

Tactile and Large-Print Maps

Commercial or handmade tactile or large-print maps assist students with visual impairments in familiarizing themselves with their communities and new areas of interest. Optical devices can be utilized by students with low vision to view commercial print maps; these maps may also be available in tactile format for students who are blind. It may be necessary for students to access maps of their city, public transportation system, and airline routes to plan their trips.

When constructing maps, a student's vision, tactile sensitivity, intellectual functioning level, and prior experience with map reading should be taken into consideration. Informational content, size and scale, schematization, symbols, information density, labels, and use of grids, overlays, and underlays are other factors to keep in mind when designing maps (Bentzen & Marston, 2010). O&M specialists and their students can make maps from household items (e.g., puff paint, cardboard, needlework magnetic board with magnets, Wikki Stix, buttons, textured fabric, Velcro; see Figure 7.2). For an elementary-age student who is blind, a single, straight, raised line on a piece of paper can represent a simple I route (a route with no turns) from her desk to the classroom door. A large-print map of a student's classroom and school layout on a white piece of paper with symbols labeled with a wide, black felt-tip pen can be used to familiarize a student with low vision to his or her new school at the beginning of a school year.

Students are taught how to read maps by O&M specialists. Map-reading skills include being able to identify symbols, scanning maps in a systematic fashion, tracing line symbols, and recognizing shapes (Bentzen & Marston, 2010; Pogrund et al., 2012; see Figures 7.3a and 7.3b). For example, before an O&M lesson, Mr. Page, an O&M specialist, creates a tactile map of Judy's neighborhood using a commercial map-making kit (see the Resources section in the online AFB Learning Center). During the lesson, Judy completes the map by adding symbols representing the landmarks she will use to help orient herself to the neighborhood.

Electronic Orientation Aids

Electronic orientation aids (EOAs) assist students with visual impairments with orientation when

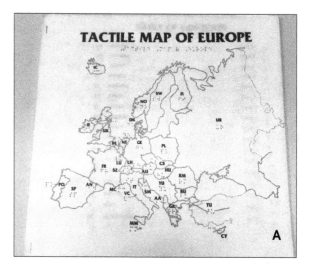

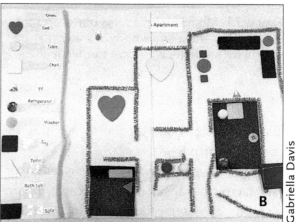

Figure 7.2 Tactile maps can be created from a variety of items, such as a map of Europe consisting of raised lines on felt paper (A) or a map of an apartment made from pipe cleaners, Styrofoam, and other home items (B).

planning routes or while traveling (Dakopoulos & Bourbakis, 2010). Known as navigation aids, EOAs include GIS and GPS devices, compasses, directional devices such as accessible pedestrian signals, and accessible signage, to name just a few (see Figure 7.4). These devices do not replace a cane. EOAs assist with wayfinding by providing detailed information regarding street names, addresses, intersections, and points of interest; accessing databases to provide the stu-

Figure 7.4 Electronic orientation aids such as compasses assist students with visual impairments with orientation when traveling and planning routes.

Figure 7.3 Map-reading skills are important for students to learn to orient themselves to their environment. A student can study a tactile map prior to an O&M lesson (A) and then utilize the tactile map during the O&M lesson (B).

dent with routes (Roentgen, Gelderblom, Soede, & de Witte, 2008); and storing route information recorded by the student. The student can record the route information while being familiarized to the route by an O&M specialist, other professional, caregiver, or pedestrian. The recorded information can also be reviewed at a later time, as needed.

A GIS is an electronic database that allows geographic information to be captured, stored, and manipulated to produce digital maps (virtual images of an area). These digital maps can be displayed through visual or auditory means, or through braille displays, and accessed by people who are blind or visually impaired (Bentzen & Marston, 2010; see Figure 7.5). Often, they are used together with a GPS device to determine, via satellites, the exact location of where a student is located, where the student wants to go, and how to plan a route to get to the desired

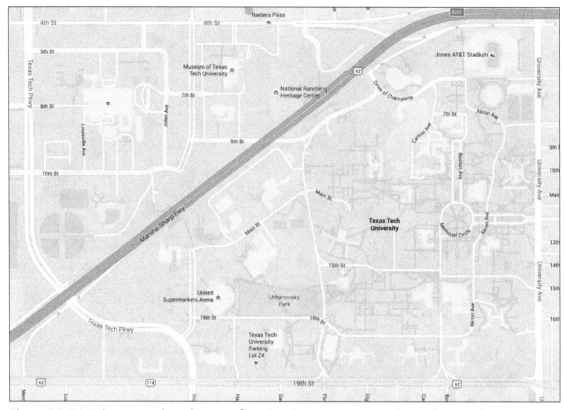

Figure 7.5 Digital maps, such as this one of a university campus, can assist students in determining their location and planning routes to desired destinations.

destination. The GPS is referred to as a position locator device (Dakopoulos & Bourbakis, 2010). After downloading database and location information onto their braille notetakers, students can use the information to plan routes, find out where their favorite stores are, and where their friends' houses are and how to get there. Detailed information can then be used and shared with other students who are blind or visually impaired (Bentzen & Marston, 2010).

Using a GPS and GIS in tandem enables students with visual impairments to input information about their community, including the stores, restaurants, malls, and other locations that are important to them. This information can be shared with others to create a database of disability-friendly areas. Frequently used routes can be reviewed and retraced, assisting travelers with visual impairments with wayfinding.

Talking, electronic, and braille compasses are also useful orientation aids. These accessible compasses provide users who are visually impaired with information about cardinal directions (north, east, south, west) and intermediate directions (northeast, southeast, southwest, northwest) either through digitized speech or braille output. For example, George wants to go to the store that is two streets south of his home. He uses an electronic compass to show him where south is in relation to his home. George starts heading in a southerly direction and then stops after crossing one street to check his compass to make sure he is still heading south. These compasses can be stand-alone devices or available as applications (apps) for mobile technology.

Directional devices such as accessible pedestrian signals can be relatively easy for individuals with vision loss to locate since they are typically found in established locations at intersections. Accessible pedestrian signals provide audible and vibrotactile information accessible to pedestrians who are blind or visually impaired about when the Walk signal at an intersection is on. They may also have a pushbutton locator tone, a tactile arrow aligned with the direction of travel, and automatic volume adjustment (Fazzi & Barlow, 2017). For example, Mary, who is blind and a cane user, is approaching a corner with an accessible pedestrian signal. She can hear the device emitting an audible tick, tick sound, allowing her to establish its location and walk toward it as she prepares to cross the street. The signal tells Mary when the Walk sign is on for the street she is about to cross. However, even with this additional auditory information, Mary must still use good cane skills and listen for traffic sounds to decide when it is safe for her to cross the street.

Accessible signage and talking signs that utilize infrared light transmitters and handheld receivers have also been developed. In these devices, the receiver is aimed at a talking-sign transmitter by a person with a visual impairment, and an audible message is emitted. This technology has been used in buildings to locate rooms and rapid transit systems to indicate stops (e.g., a voice message saying, "South entrance, Canal Street") (Smith & Penrod, 2010).

Many factors (e.g., maturity of the student, ability to communicate and move, area in which the student is going to travel, cognitive level) need to be considered when O&M specialists decide whether to provide training for students with EOAs (Griffin-Shirley & Page, 2012). However, curricula have been developed for children with visual impairments, including those with intellectual disabilities, to gain competency with EOAs (Greenberg & Kuns, 2011). The amount of vision a student has also needs to be taken into account because if the student is able to visually detect landmarks and obstacles, the student will not need a device to do it for him or her (Smith & Penrod, 2010).

With all the advantages orientation aids provide, they also have disadvantages (see Table 7.1). In addition to the disadvantages listed in the table, other drawbacks include the training needed to be able to use the devices, the cost of the devices, and "the interface of these systems" with the student with a visual impairment (Smith & Penrod, 2010, p. 271). Maintenance and repair of EOAs is also a potential disadvantage. For future development and improvements of these aids, the following questions should be addressed:

- How large should equipment be?
- What software is easiest to use?
- What information should be presented for the different types of potential users who are visually impaired (e.g., those who need information for route planning versus those who need a more detailed overview of areas of interest)?

Mobility Systems and Tools

Mobility systems and tools are classified into various types and include guide technique, the long cane, dog guides, adaptive mobility devices, orthopedic equipment, and electronic travel aids. These mobility systems allow students

TABLE 7.1

Advantages and Disadvantages of Orientation Aids

Tool	Advantages	Disadvantages
Tactile Maps and Models	• Can be used to tactilely explore an entire area at one time • Can be used to tactilely explore the relationship of the parts to the whole • Can be used in a program of independent study • Can be used to plan routes to a destination, alternate routes to the same destination, or round-trip routes • Can be carried on lessons to reinforce the actual environment • Can reinforce shapes and patterns	• Size distortions • Unable to fully reproduce the actual environment • Some concepts cannot be taught with a map or model • Students may become overly dependent on the map or model • Instructors may use the model in place of the actual environment
Verbal Descriptions	• Provide information specific to the route or routes students travel	• If an audio map or description, the device that recorded or stored the information may not be available if battery dies
Electronic Orientation Aids (EOAs)	• Allow students to spatially update while traveling • Students do not need to rely on other pedestrians for assistance in orientation • Assist with route planning and mapping, which can reduce travel time and stress • Can aid in use of public transportation • Facilitate orientation	• Dependent on battery life of device • Tall objects or building may interfere with signals from some EOAs • Usually used with a cane or dog guide and not independently, unless the student has enough functional vision

Source: Adapted from Smith, D. L., & Penrod, W. M. (2010). Adaptive technology for orientation and mobility. In W. R. Wiener, R. L. Welsh, & B. B. Blasch (Eds.), *Foundations of orientation and mobility: Vol. I. History and theory* (3rd ed., pp. 241–276). New York, NY: AFB Press.

to find and avoid obstacles, scan areas the students are traveling, and assist with orientation and landmark identification (Smith & Penrod, 2010). The purpose of mobility tools is to provide advance information about the path of travel, thus leading to safe movement.

Guide Technique

Guide technique is a procedure for providing appropriate assistance to a person with a visual impairment to travel safely and efficiently with a guide (Fazzi & Barlow, 2017; see Figure 7.6).

Gabriella Davis

Figure 7.6 A front view of a student and guide using guide technique.

The guide provides the student with a visual impairment with protection from obstacles in the environment and is responsible for orientation while the student gets used to moving through the environment (LaGrow, 2010). Students can attend to sensory information around them without the fear of injuring themselves as they walk with another person using guide technique. For example, if a student is walking in a school hallway on the way to lunch, the student can listen for the sounds of the cafeteria (e.g., children's voices, trays being slid along the food line, food being emptied into trash cans) and notice the smell of food

cooking while the guide ensures the student's safety. (See Chapter 6 for more information on specific guide techniques.)

Long Canes

Canes have been used by people who are blind or visually impaired for centuries (see Chapter 1 for more information on the history of canes). They can be made from different materials (e.g., wood, fiberglass, aluminum, carbon fiber); come in different colors (e.g., white, metallic silver, multicolored); serve different purposes (e.g., obstacle protection, drop-off and texture detection, identification of an individual who is blind); and have different shapes, sizes (e.g., adjusted to a person's chin or nose or 2 inches above a person's sternum; taking into account a person's stride length, walking speed, arm length, and gait pattern, after which the cane length may need to be shortened or lengthened), and components (e.g., crook, grip, shaft, tip) (Jacobson, 2013). There are also a variety of tip choices for canes based on the needs of the student. They include nylon pencil-, marshmallow-, teardrop-, or mushroom-shaped tips; metal glider tips; roller ball tips; recoil spring tips; Bundu Basher curved tips for wilderness or rural travel; and even cane tips for snow and sand travel (e.g., the Dakota Disk). *Long canes* can be rigid or folding (see Figures 7.7a and 7.7b). The primary purposes of using a long cane are identification, protection, and information gathering (Hill & Ponder, 1976). Cane usage identifies individuals as blind, clears the area in front of them while they are walking, and provides information about the surface upon which they are walking.

For each student, the O&M specialist will decide which cane is most appropriate for the

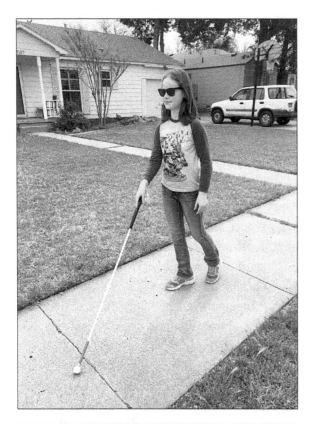

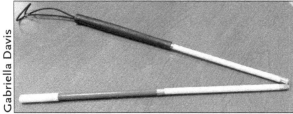

Gabriella Davis

Figure 7.7 Student walking with straight, rigid cane (A) and a folding cane with its joints and pieces folded (B).

student's travel needs, the preferred length of the cane, and the different cane techniques the student will need to learn. Early introduction of canes to toddlers and preschoolers has many potential positive outcomes, such as increased movement and exploration, improved posture and gait, decreased fear of injury, improved concept development, and acceptance of the cane by the child and others (Anthony, Bleier, Fazzi, Kish, & Pogrund, 2002). Once children with

visual impairments learn to use their canes, they are responsible for how and when they are used, their maintenance, and their replacement (Jacobson, 2013). Students may need a variety of canes for different uses, such as a folding cane for airplane travel and a straight cane for daily use.

All children with vision loss have a right to receive O&M services from a certified O&M specialist. Due to a national shortage of O&M specialists, there is increasing pressure on other professionals to provide O&M services to children with visual impairments (Mason & Davidson, 2000). However, teachers of students with visual impairments and other professionals should not be issuing canes for students, but rather monitoring and reinforcing their students' proper cane usage.

Dog Guides

Dogs assist humans with work, serve as pets, and can be used for therapeutic purposes. Teaching dogs to help guide people who are blind was first documented by Johann Wilhelm Klein in 1819. Since that time, dogs have been formally trained to assist people who are blind; these dogs are referred to as *dog guides*. In 1929, The Seeing Eye, the first school for training individuals who are blind to use dog guides, was established (see Chapter 1 for more information on the history of dog guides). There are currently 20 dog guide training schools located throughout North America (American Foundation for the Blind, n.d.; National Federation of the Blind, n.d.).

Dogs guides are placed with individuals who are visually impaired as young as 16 years of age. Their purpose is to guide individuals who are blind or visually impaired in the areas in which they travel (see Figure 7.8). Training is provided both to the dog guide and the person who is blind. It is preferable for a person to have O&M training prior to obtaining a dog guide. O&M specialists can inform their students about the use of dog guides and where they can receive training. O&M specialists can also teach students how to utilize their hearing to pay attention to acoustic information in the environment they may otherwise miss (Franck, Haneline, Brooks, & Whitstock, 2010). Once a student has received a dog guide, the O&M specialist may provide orientation to both familiar and unfamiliar environments. Sidebars 7.3 and 7.4 discuss the roles of the O&M specialist and the teacher of students with visual impairments when working with students who are interested in receiving a dog guide. When comparing the lists, it is clear the roles of these professionals overlap.

Adaptive Mobility Devices

For toddlers, students with visual impairments and additional intellectual or physical disabilities, and seniors, O&M specialists may suggest the use of an *adaptive mobility device* (AMD; Jacobson, 2013). Serving the same purpose as a cane, AMDs can be commercially purchased or handmade using plastic and PVC pipes or other materials (Pogrund et al., 2012). AMDs are highly individualized for each student (see Figure 7.9). Generally, AMDs are not meant for long-term use, but rather as a transition to the cane. However, some children with visual impairments will always use an AMD as a substitute for a cane (Smith & Penrod, 2010) because they may not be able to learn to use a cane as a result of an intellectual, behavioral, or physical impairment.

Gabriella Davis

Figure 7.8 Dog guides lead individuals who are blind or visually impaired in the areas in which they travel.

It is the role of the O&M specialist to demonstrate how to use the device at home, at school, and in the community to members of the student's educational team. Educational team members and caregivers should inform the O&M specialist if the student is not using the AMD appropriately so further instruction by the O&M specialist can be provided (Smith & Penrod, 2010).

Orthopedic Equipment

Students with visual impairments and physical disabilities may often require a prosthesis (an artificial limb), an orthosis (a brace-like tool that assists a child in accomplishing a daily living

---

SIDEBAR 7.3

Role of the O&M Specialist

When instructing students who are interested in receiving a dog guide, O&M specialists can:

- Familiarize students with dog guide schools, the training they provide, and the application process.
- Invite representatives from dog guide schools to speak to their students about the use of dog guides.
- Find a dog guide user to talk with their students about his or her personal experiences using a dog guide (e.g., advantages, disadvantages, upkeep, cost).
- Collaborate with teachers of students with visual impairments whose students have also expressed an interest in using a dog guide to obtain more information for all students.
- Teach students how to utilize their hearing for acoustic information in the environment they may otherwise miss.
- Instruct students in understanding time-distance judgment and how it may change depending on whether students use a dog guide or a cane.
- Attend a dog guide school for professional development.

SIDEBAR 7.4

Role of the Teacher of Students with Visual Impairments

When instructing students who are interested in receiving a dog guide, teachers of students with visual impairments can:

- Familiarize students with dog guide schools.
- Invite representatives from dog guide schools to speak to their students.
- Find a dog guide user to talk with their students about his or her personal experiences.
- Collaborate with the O&M specialist of students who have expressed an interest in using a dog guide.
- Develop a braille literacy exercise in which students read a book about dog guides.
- Have students conduct a computer search on the topic of dog guide usage to improve their computer skills.
- Encourage parents of young children who are blind or visually impaired to get a dog so the children can become well versed in the care and feeding of a dog.
- Encourage students to gain experience and have responsibility for caring for themselves as well as animals, including cleaning up after dogs.
- Visit a dog guide school so students can experience the selection and training of dogs to work with individuals who are blind firsthand.

---

skill), or other *orthopedic equipment* such as wheelchairs, forearm crutches (e.g., Lofstrand crutches), scooters, one-handed support devices (e.g., side-style hemis, one-arm walkers; see Figure 7.10a), and walkers (see Figure 7.10b).

When teaching students with physical disabilities, it is important to keep in mind that if they can accomplish a task with their own body parts, that is preferable to using a device. For example, for a student who has cerebral palsy, using a limb may keep it from atrophying (Hallahan, Kauffman, & Pullen, 2012). The student's educational team can address this issue and provide advice on what activities of daily

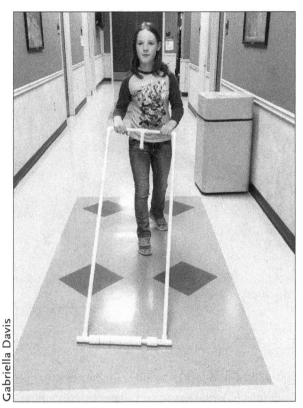

Gabriella Davis

Figure 7.9 Adaptive mobility devices, whether purchased commercially or handmade, are individualized for each student.

living should be completed with or without equipment and tools.

Ambulatory devices (e.g., crutches, posterior walkers with the child walking in front of the device) help students improve the quality of their walking, but for students who lack postural control, a wheelchair may be necessary. Power chairs with head and trunk supports, trays, and specially constructed cushions may also be used by students. For very young children, special strollers that support the child's back and keep the hips aligned, car seats, and beds may also be suggested (Hoon & Tolley, 2013).

O&M specialists will need to teach students who are visually impaired and who have orthopedic problems how to use a long cane in conjunction with the mobility devices they use for support. Collaboration with physical and occupational therapists is important when working with a student who needs a mobility cane in addition to another support device. This collaboration helps to identify the equipment that works best with a long cane and addresses the student's travel needs beyond the school. For a student with an impaired hand, a modification of the cane grip may be needed for the student to be able to use the cane appropriately. Physical and occupational therapists teach students how to use this orthopedic equipment while O&M specialists instruct students how to travel with this equipment in different locations.

This equipment is prescribed by physicians, occupational therapists, or physical therapists. Other professionals in the field of vision education should be familiar with this equipment and its proper use for their students and should collaborate regularly with the prescribing specialist. Teachers of students with visual impairments monitor the use of orthopedic equipment and mobility devices within the environments in which they work with their students. All professionals working with students need to confer with one another about the suitability and use of such equipment. A transdisciplinary service delivery model is typically used with children with visual impairments and additional disabilities who use this type of equipment (Pogrund & Fazzi, 2002; Smith & Levack, 1997). Often, O&M specialists will role release to individuals that work with students on a daily basis, such as classroom teachers, paraeducators, and parents. With this practice, O&M specialists train other service providers in the proper use of this equipment and then monitor the progress of these

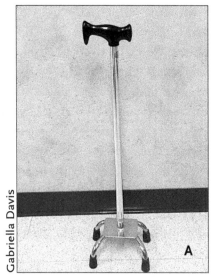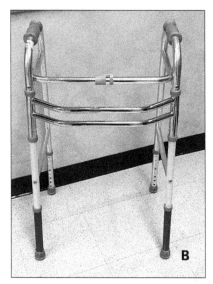

Gabriella Davis

Figure 7.10 Orthopedic equipment can include one-handed support devices (A) and walkers (B).

professionals with students who are blind and who have physical disabilities (Smith & Levack, 1997). (See Chapter 11 for a detailed explanation of transdisciplinary teams and role release.)

Jamie is a high school student who is totally blind and has cerebral palsy. Depending on where Jamie needs to travel, she uses a long cane, a support cane, and a wheelchair. For long distances, Jamie uses her manual wheelchair and her long cane. For short walks, her one-handed support device and long cane are enough. Her O&M specialist has taught Jamie to be proficient in the use of all her mobility devices.

Jamie is on her high school's speech and debate team. In the past, the team has won state championships and gone on to national competitions. Since Jamie is a great debater, she needs to travel with the team to a variety of venues. Her O&M specialist, her debate team coach, and her parents consult with one another to plan for her team trips. Additionally, Jamie has taught all her team members how to guide her when she is using her wheelchair.

(See the online AFB Learning Center for information on how to guide a student who is blind and using a wheelchair.)

Electronic Travel Aids

Tools that convert visual information into tactile information, auditory information, or both, and which enable people who are blind to interpret this information are called *electronic travel aids* (ETAs; Blasch, Long, & Griffin-Shirley, 1989). ETAs are sometimes also referred to as electronic travel devices. ETAs provide safety where a cane or dog guide cannot, give information concerning obstacles or landmarks in a person's line of travel, aid with familiarization to new environments, and minimize stress (Roentgen et al., 2008). Some ETAs can replace a cane or dog guide (e.g., UltraCane) while others should be used with a mobility device (e.g., Sonic Pathfinder, Miniguide, Hand Guide, K-Sonar; see the Resources section in the online AFB Learning Center) (Smith & Penrod, 2010). Prior to exposure to ETAs, students should first become proficient in cane travel or in use of a dog guide (Roentgen et al., 2008).

Training to become proficient in the use of ETAs is usually provided by O&M specialists and dog guide trainers. ETAs are used more intermittently than regularly by individuals with visual impairments when moving. ETAs may be used in areas where upper-body hazards are known to exist, in unfamiliar areas as an additional precaution, or when looking for specific landmarks for orientation purposes. Some ETAs are not able to detect objects located on the ground, so the cane is still the best option for detecting these objects (Smith & Penrod, 2010).

Generally, ETAs are expensive and require additional training and motivation on the part of the student to become proficient in their use. Additional disadvantages include breakage, coordination needed to use a handheld device, limited range, weather-resistant considerations since these devices are usually electronic, and modification or alteration of the traditional hand position required for cane use (Smith & Penrod, 2010; see Table 7.2).

Optical Devices

Many children with visual impairments have some useful vision. An O&M evaluation, conducted by an O&M specialist, can determine students' functional vision in both familiar and unfamiliar settings with varied lighting conditions while accomplishing different mobility tasks (e.g., finding the principal's office, purchasing an item in a store, walking a block). During an O&M evaluation, students may use *optical devices* that have been prescribed by an optometrist specializing in low vision. O&M specialists or teachers of students with visual impairments may recommend a clinical low vision evaluation if a student has not had one. Data from the O&M evaluation concerning functional vision is important to share with the low vision specialist.

Initial instruction in how to use and maintain optical devices is provided by the low vision specialist, with education professionals and caregivers reinforcing this instruction at home, in school, and in the community. Generally, teachers of students with visual impairments teach children how to use these devices within the classroom setting while O&M specialists train them to use the devices in travel situations. Collaboration between the low vision specialist, teacher of students with visual impairments, O&M specialist, and caregivers can help motivate children with low vision to properly use their devices when completing academic, mobility, or daily living tasks. Students may feel embarrassed using optical devices in their classrooms; therefore, education professionals may find it necessary to help these students cope with the psychological aspects associated with using optical devices.

Optical devices for students with low vision include (Zimmerman, Zebehazy, & Moon, 2010):

- Eyeglasses and contact lenses that bring objects into focus and are used for near and distance viewing and reading tasks

TABLE 7.2

Advantages and Disadvantages of Mobility Systems and Tools

Tool	Advantages	Disadvantages
Guide Technique	• Generally readily available • Relatively easy to train a guide to meet a student's needs • Enhances socialization opportunities	• May create dependence on other people if only mode of mobility, which may limit mobility at times • May have negative implications for feelings of independence and self-worth • Walking with an untrained guide can cause insecurity and even injury
Long Canes	• Allow investigation of the environment • Reliable, long-lasting, and not significantly affected by unfavorable weather and temperature conditions • Require minimal maintenance; no accessories • Easy to accommodate to traveler's physical specifications and special needs • Provide echo-ranging cues and force-impact information • Provide information about ground textures • Relatively inexpensive (e.g., range from free to $60)	• Do not provide adequate protection to the upper part of the body • Do not always provide complete mobility coverage, even with excellent technique • Can trip pedestrians in congested areas if used inappropriately • Cane tips need to be replaced if they break or wear out • High winds can interfere with control of the cane • Canes that are too short or too long may provide inadequate preview and detection information • Extensive training may be required for some people to learn to use a cane properly
Dog Guides	• Social benefits; dogs can serve as icebreakers for social conversations • Protect the entire body • Allow a person who is blind to get to most destinations independently • Increase user's speed of travel (most dogs travel at a speed of 2–5 mph)	• Have a high cost and degree of maintenance (e.g., food, walking, grooming, vet costs) • Require extensive training (minimum of 4–6 weeks, full time) • Some social aspects may be negative, especially if people speak to the dog first rather than the person • Dogs have a limited life span (working life is usually 7–9 years); emotional loss of previous dog; retraining with new dog • Limited clientele: users need to be active (must walk or use the dog daily) and in good enough shape to keep up with the dog, responsible (typically at least 16 years of age or older), and have reduced visual status

TABLE 7.2

Tool	Advantages	Disadvantages
Adaptive Mobility Devices (AMDs)	• Offer more sensory feedback for the student to increase motivation to move (e.g., noise, weight, vibration) • Provide more security while moving through space, so can get students moving more easily • Promote concept development, problem solving, and self-confidence • May be used to provide motor memory as a transition to use of a cane • Can be handmade or commercially purchased	• Handmade devices may not be constructed safely and may cause a safety issue • Need to be rebuilt as child grows • Can be cumbersome in some environments • Very conspicuous; often misunderstood and seen as an orthopedic device
Orthopedic Equipment*	• Assists with mobility, thus fostering independence • Lightweight • Can be used in variety of environments (e.g., beach, city, ranch) • Easy to transport via personal vehicle • Additional hardware exists (e.g., wheelchair packs, cup holders, portable hand controls) to help travelers using orthopedic equipment	• Need a prescription to obtain equipment • One size does not fit all; needs to be adjusted for growth of child or change in physical status of person • Cost; equipment is usually expensive • May need different types of equipment for different tasks (e.g., walker for walking, scooter for long-distance travel)
Electronic Travel Aids (ETAs)	• Provide a degree of sensory information about the environment, which, even under ideal circumstances, would not be possible to obtain using only a long cane or dog guide • Make noncontact trailing and tracking possible; allow for more information and earlier detection • Provide options to either avoid or make contact with objects, or use them for orientation purposes • Some help with correction from a veer, allow for increased pace, protect against overhangs, and provide greater confidence in travel	• Very expensive (several hundred to several thousand dollars) • Most require extensive training before they can be used efficiently • Most are not weather-resistant (rain and snow may also provide false warning signals) • Require battery recharging • Handheld devices do not allow for a free hand when traveling using a cane • Devices with auditory output may interfere with use of environmental auditory landmarks or cues

(continued on next page)

TABLE 7.2 (*continued*)

Tool	Advantages	Disadvantages
	• Allow for object detection of overhanging obstacles when using a cane	• Some devices will not receive reflections from clear plate glass in windows or doors (unless very dirty or an object is within range behind the glass) • Some beams will not pick up objects less than 9–18 inches high; glossy and highly polished surfaces may affect forward beam reflection
Optical Devices*	• Low-tech, or nonoptical devices (e.g., sunglasses, visors, hats), are easy to use and inexpensive • Socially acceptable, and some are cosmetically appealing • Provide more access and independence for students with low vision if used when needed • Can help reduce eye fatigue	• Some high-tech devices (e.g., bioptic systems, telescopes, magnifiers) may require a prescription from an optometrist with low vision training, who may not be available in a specific area • Can be expensive • Require maintenance to change bulbs and batteries • Some are cosmetically unappealing and conspicuous, so students may reject using them • May require two hands to use • Limited field of view • May cause fatigue • Users may need more lighting while using some devices • Users may need to adjust reading speed while using devices

*These areas include many different devices. Advantages and disadvantages tend to be specific to each device. This section provides general advantages and disadvantages.

Sources: Portions of this table were adapted from Smith, D. L., & Penrod, W. M. (2010). Adaptive technology for orientation and mobility. In W. R. Wiener, R. L. Welsh, & B. B. Blasch (Eds.), *Foundations of orientation and mobility: Vol. I. History and theory* (3rd ed., pp. 241–276). New York, NY: AFB Press; and Zimmerman, G. J., Zebehazy, K. T., & Moon, M. L. (2010). Optics and low vision devices. In A. L. Corn & J. N. Erin (Eds.), *Foundations of low vision: Clinical and functional perspectives* (2nd ed., pp. 192–237). New York, NY: AFB Press.

• Magnifiers that enlarge images and print for near tasks such as reading and writing (see Figure 7.11)
• Telescopes and monoculars that bring distance objects into closer view and are used for short-term distance viewing such as reading street signs and building numbers and viewing traffic lights (see Figures 7.12a and 7.12b)
• Bioptic telescopic systems, which are telescopes mounted into eyeglass lenses, positioned above or below an individual's direct

line of sight when facing forward, that can aid in a variety of tasks

- Night vision goggles, which can be handheld or worn on the head to assist with distance viewing for people with night blindness

In addition, a variety of nonoptical devices can also assist students with low vision to enhance their usable vision and to help reduce glare, both indoors and outdoors. They include:

- Hats, visors, sunglasses that help reduce glare (Note: Special permission from school administrators may be needed to allow students to wear hats inside a school)
- Apps that can be used to enlarge print or images or provide more light for reading materials
- Wide-angle flashlights that can provide additional lighting in dimly lit or dark areas

During O&M lessons, students can also use these devices for reading and distance viewing. For example, Bianca uses her telescope to locate the sign for Garcia's Restaurant. Once inside, she uses her phone's magnifier and flashlight apps to enlarge the text on the menu and provide better illumination to read the menu.

Students with eye conditions like retinitis pigmentosa, which can cause night blindness, can benefit from night vision systems or wide-angle flashlights, which can provide additional lighting in dark areas and help promote safety. Night vision systems illuminate the area in which a student with low vision is walking, thus improving distance vision. Some have a camera that "takes a nighttime image and projects it onto a screen for the viewer with enhanced brightness and contrast" (Zimmerman et al., 2010, p. 228).

Gabriella Davis

Figure 7.11 Magnifiers, such as this handheld one, enlarge print for near tasks such as reading.

Some O&M specialists and occupational therapists receive additional training to teach students with low vision how to drive. Some of these students will use bioptic telescopic systems to aid them in driving. These students usually need to take both a driving test and an eye exam on an annual basis to renew their driver's licenses.

Optical devices can be cumbersome, expensive, cosmetically unappealing, and may require additional training. For some students, these disadvantages outweigh the advantages of using the devices (see Table 7.2). Students in middle and high school will often reject the use of such optical devices, even when they may be

Gabriella Davis

Figure 7.12 One type of optical device is a monocular (A), which students can use to read information located at a distance, such as an address on a house (B).

beneficial, because they do not want to feel different from their peers. It is important to be sensitive to the perceptions of adolescents regarding the use of optical devices even when educational team members feel it is in the best interest of these students to use the devices. Often, as students get older and their self-confidence develops, they will realize the value of these devices and begin to incorporate them into their daily routines.

Future Technological Developments

With the advancement of research involving the brain, computer science and technology, sight-substitution systems, metallurgy and plastics (e.g., use of thermoform for prosthetic limbs), and neurocognitive prosthetics (e.g., cochlear implants), the tools for children with visual impairments, including those with additional disabilities, are changing rapidly (Hallahan et al., 2012; Hoon & Tolley, 2013). A major challenge for teachers of students with visual impairments, O&M specialists, related service personnel, and general educators is learning how to assess their students for this new technology and determining how to get educational systems to purchase and maintain the devices. Family members are faced with advocating for new technology as their children grow and mature. In the past, it has been very difficult for some children to receive the equipment they need and to maintain and replace that equipment. A systemic change involving the government and medical and educational systems is needed to adequately address access to new technology that can improve the lives of children with visual impairments.

Summary

O&M systems and tools include low- and high-tech devices to assist children with visual impairments in remaining oriented and traveling as safely and independently as they can in their home, school, and community settings. A team of experts decides which devices are best suited for students with visual impairments to use for their mobility needs and for other activities of daily living. As integral members of the educational team who complete evaluations and suggest the most appropriate devices, O&M specialists are responsible for training students in the use of O&M devices and systems. In some cases, teachers of students with visual impairments will also evaluate and teach children with visual impairments how to use their devices, as well as monitor and reinforce their use. Additionally, other education professionals and caregivers should reinforce the use of these devices so that they are integrated into students' daily routines. Collaboration among all professionals and caregivers is necessary if students who are blind or visually impaired are going to use their O&M systems and tools to meet their travel needs.

References

American Foundation for the Blind. (n.d.). Dog guide training: AFB directory of services listings. Retrieved from http://www.afb.org/directory.aspx?action=results&CategoryID=54

Anthony, T. L., Bleier, H., Fazzi, D. L., Kish, D., & Pogrund, R. L. (2002). Mobility focus: Developing early skills for orientation and mobility. In R. L. Pogrund & D. L. Fazzi (Eds.), *Early focus: Working with young children who are blind or visually impaired and their families* (2nd ed., pp. 326–404). New York, NY: AFB Press.

Bentzen, B. L., & Marston, J. R. (2010). Orientation aids for students with vision loss. In W. R. Wiener, R. L. Welsh, & B. B. Blasch (Eds.), *Foundations of orientation and mobility: Vol. I. History and theory* (3rd ed., pp. 296–323). New York, NY: AFB Press.

Blasch, B. B., Long, R. G., & Griffin-Shirley, N. (1989). Results of a national survey of electronic travel aid use. *Journal of Visual Impairment & Blindness, 83,* 449–453.

Dakopoulos, D., & Bourbakis, N. (2010). Wearable obstacle avoidance electronic travel aids for blind: A survey. *IEEE Transactions on Systems, Man, and Cybernetics—Part C: Applications and Reviews, 40*(1), 25–35.

Fazzi, D. L., & Barlow, J. M. (2017). *Orientation and mobility techniques: A guide for the practitioner* (2nd ed.). New York, NY: AFB Press.

Fazzi, D. L., & Petersmeyer, B. A. (2001). *Imagining the possibilities: Creative approaches to orientation and mobility instruction for persons who are visually impaired.* New York, NY: AFB Press.

Franck, L., Haneline, R., Brooks, A., & Whitstock, R. (2010). Dog guides for orientation and mobility. In W. R. Wiener, R. L. Welsh, & B. B. Blasch (Eds.), *Foundations of orientation and mobility: Vol. I. History and theory* (3rd ed., pp. 277–295). New York, NY: AFB Press.

Greenberg, M. D., & Kuns, J. (2011). *Finding your way: A curriculum for teaching and using the BrailleNote with Sendero GPS 2011.* Fremont: California School for the Blind.

Griffin-Shirley, N., & Page, A. (2012). Part 3: Appendices. Assistive technology used in O&M. In R. Pogrund, D. Sewell, H. Anderson, L. Calaci, M. F. Cowart, C. M. Gonzalez, . . . B. Roberson-Smith (Eds.), *TAPS—Teaching age-appropriate purposeful skills: An orientation and mobility curriculum for students with visual impairments* (3rd ed., pp. 211–223). Austin: Texas School for the Blind and Visually Impaired.

Hallahan, D. P., Kauffman, J. M., & Pullen, P. C. (2012). *Exceptional learners: An introduction to special education* (12th ed.). Upper Saddle River, NJ: Pearson.

Hill, E., & Ponder, P. (1976). *Orientation and mobility techniques: A guide for the practitioner.* New York, NY: American Foundation for the Blind.

Hoon, A. H., & Tolley, F. (2013). Cerebral palsy. In M. L. Batshaw, N. J. Roizen, & G. R. Lotrecchiano (Eds.), *Children with disabilities* (7th ed., pp. 423–450). Baltimore, MD: Paul H. Brookes.

Individuals with Disabilities Education Improvement Act (IDEA), 20 U.S.C. § 1400 (2004).

Jacobson, W. H. (2013). *The art and science of teaching orientation and mobility to persons with visual impairments* (2nd ed.). New York, NY: AFB Press.

LaGrow, S. J. (2010). Improving perception for orientation and mobility. In W. R. Wiener, R. L. Welsh, & B. B. Blasch (Eds.), *Foundations of orientation and mobility: Vol. II. Instructional strategies and practical applications* (3rd ed., pp. 3–26). New York, NY: AFB Press.

Mason, C., & Davidson, R. (2000). *National plan for training personnel to serve children with blindness and low vision.* Reston, VA: Council for Exceptional Children.

McNear, D., & Farrenkopf, C. (2014). Assistive technology. In C. B. Allman & S. Lewis (Eds.), *ECC essentials: Teaching the expanded core curriculum to students with visual impairments* (pp. 187–247). New York, NY: AFB Press.

National Federation of the Blind. (n.d.). Guide dog schools resource list. Retrieved from https://nfb.org/resource-list-guide-dog-schools

Pogrund, R. L., & Fazzi, D. L. (Eds.). (2002). *Early focus: Working with young children who are blind or visually impaired and their families* (2nd ed.). New York, NY: AFB Press.

Pogrund, R., Sewell, D., Anderson, H., Calaci, L., Cowart, M. F., Gonzalez, C. M., . . . Roberson-Smith, B. (2012). *TAPS—Teaching age-appropriate purposeful skills: An orientation and mobility curriculum for students with visual impairments* (3rd ed.). Austin: Texas School for the Blind and Visually Impaired.

Presley, I. (2010). The impact of assistive technology: Assessment and instruction for children and youths with low vision. In A. L. Corn & J. N. Erin (Eds.), *Foundations of low vision: Clinical and functional perspectives* (2nd ed., pp. 589–654). New York, NY: AFB Press.

Roentgen, U. R., Gelderblom, G. J., Soede, M., & de Witte, L. P. (2008). Inventory of electronic mobility aids for persons with visual impairments: A literature review. *Journal of Visual Impairment & Blindness, 102*(11), 702–724.

Smith, D. L., & Penrod, W. M. (2010). Adaptive technology for orientation and mobility. In W. R. Wiener, R. L. Welsh, & B. B. Blasch (Eds.), *Foundations of orientation and mobility: Vol. I. History and theory* (3rd ed., pp. 241–276). New York, NY: AFB Press.

Smith, M., & Levack, N. (1997). *Teaching students with visual and multiple impairments: A resource guide.* Austin: Texas School for the Blind and Visually Impaired.

Zimmerman, G. J., Zebehazy, K. T., & Moon, M. L. (2010). Optics and low vision devices. In A. L. Corn & J. N. Erin (Eds.), *Foundations of low vision: Clinical and functional perspectives* (2nd ed., pp. 192–237). New York, NY: AFB Press.

8

Environmental Accessibility

Jennifer L. Cmar and Sandra J. Rosen

> ### Questions to Guide Your Reading of This Chapter
>
> ➤ Which laws and guidelines for environmental accessibility are applicable to children with visual impairments?
> ➤ How do barriers, hazards, and obstacles affect independent travel for children with visual impairments?
> ➤ What are some considerations for conducting environmental assessments?
> ➤ Which modifications are commonly used to alleviate problematic environmental factors?

And not just the right thing; it's profoundly the right thing to do, because the one argument for accessibility that doesn't get made nearly often enough is how extraordinarily better it makes some people's lives. (Krug, 2006, p. 171)

Most individuals, whether sighted or visually impaired, travel in a variety of environments on a daily basis. When thinking about environments in the context of orientation and mobility (O&M) for children with visual impairments, a broad scope of physical spaces—both familiar and unfamiliar—should be considered, including homes, dormitories, schools, rehabilitation centers, office buildings, stores, and transit centers. Environments can help or hinder children's development, activity, and participation (Pivik, 2010). An optimal environment promotes development and purposeful movement for children with visual impairments (Levtzion-Korach, Tennenbaum, Schnitzer, & Ornoy, 2000). Sometimes, modifications to an environment are necessary to provide access, reduce hazards, and promote safety for children with visual impairments.

This chapter provides an overview of issues related to environmental assessment, adaptations, and modifications to promote O&M for children with visual impairments. First, relevant laws and frameworks for environmental accessibility and design are introduced. Those are followed by a discussion of the aspects of environments that may be considered barriers, hazards, or obstacles for children with visual impairments. The chapter then moves to the considerations for assessing environments to promote O&M and common environmental modifications. Finally, avenues for involvement of O&M specialists in advocacy efforts are provided.

Environmental Accessibility and Design

Legislation and Accessibility Guidelines

The Architectural Barriers Act (ABA) of 1968, one of the first U.S. laws addressing environmental accessibility, requires access to federal buildings and other facilities that are built or altered using certain federal funds. ABA standards are established by the General Services Administration, the Department of Defense, the Department of Housing and Urban Development, and the U.S. Postal Service.

The Americans with Disabilities Act (ADA) of 1990 prohibits discrimination based on disability in areas of employment, public accommodations, public services, public transportation, and telecommunications. The ADA aims to ensure access to the built environment for individuals with disabilities and requires removal of physical barriers to accessibility (Story, Mueller, & Mace, 1998). ADA standards for *accessible design*, established by the U.S. Department of Justice and the U.S. Department of Transportation, apply to state and local government facilities and places open to the public (see Sidebar 8.1 for definitions of key terms).

SIDEBAR 8.1
Key Terms

Accessible design Features added to existing products or environments with the goal of eliminating barriers and promoting usability by individuals with disabilities.

Barrier Aspect of the environment that stops an individual's progress, such as a barricade, or prevents an individual with a visual impairment from accessing the environment safely and independently. A barrier can also be something that is missing from the environment, such as the absence of a sidewalk or lack of braille on elevator buttons.

Compatibility factor Environmental feature that can positively or negatively affect access for individuals with specific disabilities, depending on the techniques or devices used.

Environmental assessment Process of systematically analyzing areas to identify barriers and hazards and provide recommendations for eliminating them.

Environmental modification Change to an environment that enhances functioning and promotes safety and independence.

Hazard Potential source of harm present in the environment, such as an overhanging tree branch extending across the sidewalk, that poses a danger if not avoided and not detected by someone using a long cane or proper mobility techniques.

Obstacle Environmental element that is in the way of an individual's path of travel, such as a trash can on the sidewalk, that can be negotiated by an individual with a visual impairment using a long cane or proper mobility techniques.

Truncated dome Paver or tile that has small flattened domes raised in a polka-dot fashion above its surface that can be detected tactilely.

Universal design Framework that promotes the design of products and environments to be usable by all people, regardless of age, size, ability, or disability.

ABA Accessibility Standards were established in 1982 and ADA Accessibility Guidelines (ADAAG) were established in 1991. To promote uniformity, the ABA and ADA guidelines were consolidated into the ADA-ABA Accessibility Guidelines in 2004 (United States Access Board, 2004). These requirements for minimum acceptable standards for accessible design apply to new construction and modifications of public use areas. Sidebar 8.2 provides an overview of the relevant guidelines for individuals with visual impairments.

Universal Design

Universal design is the concept of constructing products and environments to be usable by people of all ages and abilities to the greatest extent possible (Mace, Hardie, & Place, 1991;

Story et al., 1998). The seven principles of universal design, as established by The Center for Universal Design (1997), are described in Table 8.1.

The framework for universal design emerged from the realization that design changes for individuals with disabilities are beneficial for everyone (Story et al., 1998). For example, high-contrast, large-print signs intended for people with low vision are easier for everyone to read, especially in busy visual environments, extreme lighting conditions, and adverse weather conditions (Story et al., 1998). Additional examples include *truncated domes* on the edges of subway platforms (see Figure 8.1) and auditory announcements of approaching trains at subway stations. Truncated domes are a type of tactile paver or tile that has small domes raised in a polka-dot fashion

TABLE 8.1
Principles of Universal Design

Principle	Description
Equitable Use	The design is useful and marketable to people with diverse abilities.
Flexibility in Use	The design accommodates a wide range of individual preferences and abilities.
Simple and Intuitive Use	Use of the design is easy to understand, regardless of the user's experience, knowledge, language skills, or current concentration level.
Perceptible Information	The design communicates necessary information effectively to the user, regardless of ambient conditions or the user's sensory abilities.
Tolerance for Error	The design minimizes hazards and the adverse consequences of accidental or unintended actions.
Low Physical Effort	The design can be used efficiently and comfortably and with a minimum of fatigue.
Size and Space for Approach and Use	Appropriate size and space is provided for approach, reach, manipulation, and use regardless of user's body size, posture, or mobility.

Source: Reprinted from The Center for Universal Design. (1997). *The principles of universal design* (Version 2.0). Raleigh: North Carolina State University. Copyright © 1997 NC State University, The Center for Universal Design.

Accessibility Guidelines

The following is an overview of relevant guidelines for individuals with visual impairments. The section numbers in parentheses refer to the appropriate sections in the ADAAG (first number) and combined ADA-ABA guidelines (second number).

Protruding Objects (Section 4.4; Section 307)

- Overhangs above cane-sweep height (more than 27 inches from the ground) cannot protrude more than 4 inches.
- Objects within the sweep of canes (at or below 27 inches) or above 80 inches can protrude from the wall any amount.
- Fixed barriers detectable by canes must be placed below areas such as the underside of stairwells that provide less than 80 inches of vertical clearance.

Elevators (Section 4.10; Section 407)

- Audible signals are required to provide information about which elevator car is arriving, which direction the car is headed (one sound indicates up, two sounds indicate down), and to identify floors as they are passed.
- The floor number must be indicated on both doorjambs, in raised and braille characters, at 60 inches above the ground.

Detectable Warnings (Section 4.29; Section 705)

- Truncated domes are required at curb ramps and other locations where pedestrian and vehicle areas are not easily distinguishable.
- Truncated domes are required along the edges of transit boarding platforms.

Signage (Section 4.30; Section 703)

- Raised and braille characters are required on signs that designate permanent rooms and spaces (e.g., restrooms, exits, rooms, floors).
- Raised and braille characters are not required on temporary signs (e.g., building directories, "out of service" signs).
- Tactile signs should be placed on the latch side of doors.
- For non-tactile signs, character height is determined by viewing distance. Character height for capital letters on overhead signs—those placed at 80 inches or higher—must be at least 3 inches.
- For both tactile and non-tactile signs, contrast between the characters and their background and a non-glare finish (e.g., eggshell, matte) are required; sans-serif fonts are preferred.

ATMs and Transit Fare Machines (Section 4.34; Section 707)

- Machines should be speech enabled and include braille instructions for initiating speech mode, which should be easy to access.
- Each function should have at least one tactilely distinct input control.
- Function keys should contrast visually from background surfaces.
- Numeric keys should have a 12-key ascending or descending layout, in which the number 5 is tactilely distinct.

Sources: United States Access Board. (2004). ADA and ABA accessibility guidelines. Retrieved from https://www.access-board .gov/guidelines-and-standards/buildings-and-sites/about-the-ada-standards/background/ada-aba-accessibility-guidelines -2004; United States Access Board. (n.d.). A guide to ADAAG provisions. Retrieved from https://www.access-board.gov /guidelines-and-standards/buildings-and-sites/113-ada-standards/background/adaag/422-a-guide-to-adaag-provisions

Sandra J. Rosen

Figure 8.1 Design changes for individuals with disabilities, such as truncated domes on the edges of subway platforms, can be beneficial for all people.

above the surface of the paver that are detectable by a cane or underfoot. The domes are truncated, or flattened, on the top to make them easier for people to walk on. Although universal design and accessibility have some commonalities and are often used interchangeably, the two terms are not synonymous. Table 8.2 provides an overview of key differences between accessibility and universal design.

Architectural Barriers in the Environment

Since the development of accessibility and universal design guidelines, architects, engineers, developers, and designers have become more aware of design issues affecting accessibility and usability of environments; however, architectural barriers continue to exist in many environments. In discussing architectural barriers for individuals with visual impairments, a clarification of the distinctions between *barriers, hazards,* and *obstacles* is needed (see Sidebar 8.1). Barriers, hazards, and obstacles for individuals with visual impairments can be categorized in terms of physical and functional elements. Depending on a person's individual characteristics and repertoire of skills, physical hazards and obstacles that may affect safety, independent travel, and participation in society include the absence of sidewalks or pedestrian walkways, uncovered manholes, construction sites with head-level scaffolding, objects that protrude at head-level (e.g., signs, tree branches, guy-wires), and quiet vehicles. Functional obstacles and barriers involve the absence of spatial information or inconsistencies in placement and features of items at specific locations (Marston & Church, 2005). Functional obstacles and barriers may include:

- Bus stops, as they are found at different locations on a block and have inconsistent features (e.g., poles, benches, shelters) (Marston & Church, 2005)
- Elevator call buttons with unconventional design features, such as nonstandard shapes and sizes (Danford, 2003)

TABLE 8.2

Accessibility versus Universal Design

Accessibility	Universal Design
Added on to existing design	Incorporated into design from the outset
Used primarily by people with disabilities	Used by everyone
A civil rights issue	An inclusive approach
A finite concept	An ideal
Compliance with ADA Accessibility Guidelines (ADAAG)	No minimal level of compliance
Eliminates physical barriers	Promotes social participation

Sources: Adapted from Danford, G. S. (2003). Universal design: People with vision, hearing, and mobility impairments evaluate a model building. *Generations, 27*(1), 91–94; Iwarsson, S., & Stahl, A. (2003). Accessibility, usability and universal design—Positioning and definition of concepts describing person-environment relationships. *Disability and Rehabilitation, 25*(2), 57–66; and Levine, D. (Ed.). (2003). *Universal design New York 2.* Buffalo: State University of New York at Buffalo, Center for Inclusive Design and Environmental Access.

- Signage that lacks braille, tactile characters, or large, high-contrast print (Danford, 2003; Lahtinen, Palmer, & Ojala, 2014; Marston & Church, 2005)

- Inconsistent or illogical numbering systems (Levine, 2003)

The distinction between a hazard and an obstacle often depends on a person's skills and use of assistive devices. For example, an unanticipated drop-off can be a hazard to an inexperienced cane user. Similarly, a flight of stairs that has no handrails, open risers, and inconsistencies in the number, depth, or height of steps can be considered a hazard or an obstacle depending on a person's characteristics, experience, and mobility skills.

Unaddressed hazards and barriers may be evident in older buildings that have not been renovated to incorporate universal design or to comply with ADAAG (Steinman, Nguyen, Pynoos, & Leland, 2011). Compatibility factors are features of an environment that can promote or hinder access by people with specific disabilities using different techniques or devices. Some environmental features that are intended to promote accessibility for a particular group of people may be barriers or hazards for others. If that is the case, such an *environmental modification* is an example of having a negative *compatibility factor.* On the other hand, some modifications have a positive compatibility factor, meaning that they benefit all groups without creating a problem for anyone else (e.g., announcing a train arrival both visually and auditorily at a rapid rail station is useful for everyone). Some examples of environmental features that potentially have negative compatibility are:

- Curb ramps, which were designed to remove a barrier for wheelchair users who wish to cross the street. Curb ramps can make it difficult for individuals with visual impairments to tactilely identify the curb and thus increase their risk of walking into the street unintentionally (Bentzen & Barlow, 1995). Adding a raised lip and texture to the ramp that allows a wheelchair to easily roll over it and also provides tactile clues for a cane user approaching the corner is a solution that reconciles the negative compatibility factor.

- New installations of drinking fountains in public buildings, which often protrude from the wall. This placement leaves a space underneath the fountain, making it more accessible to wheelchair users. This raised wall placement, however, can pose a potential hazard for individuals who are visually impaired because the long cane can slide underneath the water fountain, not alerting the cane user to the presence of a waist-high hazard. A possible solution is to extend the sides of the water fountain down to the floor so they would be detected by a cane user without prohibiting a wheelchair user from drinking from the fountain.
- Accessible pedestrian signals (APS), which provide auditory information to let people who are visually impaired know when a traffic light has changed from red to green or that a Walk signal is displayed. While this information can be helpful to a nonvisual traveler, neighborhood opposition to these signals is sometimes raised due to concerns about noise pollution. Another concern about APS devices is voiced by consumer groups who feel that such devices provide the public with the impression that people who are blind or visually impaired are incapable of determining for themselves when it is safe to cross the street.
- Hybrid or electric ("quiet") vehicles, which are lauded by many people who value not

having the sounds of motors add to the general noise level in the environment. Quiet cars, however, can pose a significant safety hazard for people who cannot see or hear them coming. Tire noise is very minimal when such vehicles are moving slowly. Without engine sounds to alert a pedestrian who is blind to the movement of a vehicle nearby, there is a risk of unknowingly crossing into the path of a moving vehicle. A common example of such a hazard is when drivers back out of residential driveways and do not see pedestrians in the rearview mirror.

In the end, even the most carefully designed space may not provide accessibility to every person.

Environmental Factors

Various aspects of an environment can support or impede O&M for students with visual impairments. Examples of environmental factors that are important to consider include:

- Signage and maps: placement, consistency, format, accessibility
- Organization: consistency and placement of needed items; arrangement of furniture; labeling schemes for cupboards, storage areas, and appliances
- Safety: nonslip flooring materials; slippery surfaces or uneven terrain (Marigold & Patla, 2008); accessibility of emergency procedures; grab bars and railings; cluttered walkways and paths; loose rugs or electrical cords; head-level objects undetectable by a

Jennifer L. Cmar

Figure 8.2 Head-level objects undetectable by a long cane, such as areas underneath stairwells, are important safety considerations.

long cane, such as signs or open windows that protrude from walls, areas underneath stairwells (see Figure 8.2), and open cabinet doors; blended curbs (Bentzen & Barlow, 1995); sudden drop-offs on one or both sides of a walkway; truncated domes or other tactile warnings

- Lighting and glare: adequacy of lighting at various times of day in indoor and outdoor areas; available light sources (e.g., natural, artificial); sudden changes in illumination; strong shadows created by position of lighting; sources of glare (see Sidebar 8.3);

ability to control amount, location, and direction of light to support different tasks and accommodate fluctuations in vision

- Color and contrast: main color scheme present in environment; use of color to identify items; use of color to designate the purpose of an area in places with excessive visual clutter (e.g., color-coded signs in a library, such as purple for fiction, green for nonfiction); use of contrast to distinguish steps, doorframes, handles; effect of lighting on ability to discern and discriminate colors

Environmental Assessment

Environmental assessment is the process of systematically analyzing areas and surroundings in which individuals with visual impairments live, work, or attend school. O&M specialists provide this important service to identify barriers and hazards and to provide suggestions for modifications to enhance functioning and promote safety and independence. Formal and informal environmental assessments (see Figure 8.3) typically involve the use of questionnaires, interviews, or observations of how a person functions in a particular environment (Carignan, Rousseau, Gresset, & Couturier, 2008). Collaborative environmental assessment methods involve the perspectives of multiple stakeholders and include individuals with visual impairments in the evaluation process (Burgstahler, 2012; Pivik, 2010).

Environmental assessments should take into account the activities an individual needs to perform in a specific environment and how the individual interacts with different aspects of that environment (Carignan et al., 2008; Iwarsson & Stahl, 2003; Stevens-Ratchford & Krause, 2004). For example, can a middle school student with low vision locate and access the correct locker at school under current lighting conditions? Can a young adult who is blind locate all required ingredients and use the current appliances, without modification, to prepare breakfast in the kitchen at home? When conducting environmental assessments for students with visual impairments, consider the following aspects:

- Individual characteristics, including age, visual diagnosis, visual functioning, communication needs, assistive devices used, additional disabilities, and medical conditions
- Specific tasks that the student needs to perform in the environment
- The student's current functioning and task performance in the environment
- Environmental characteristics that support or impede O&M, such as obstacles, hazards, safety features, lighting, contrast, and accessible signage

Suggestions for Remediation of Environmental Factors

Children with visual impairments need to access all indoor and outdoor areas of their home, classroom, and school environments to the same extent as their sighted peers (Cox & Dykes, 2001). Results of an environmental assessment may indicate that modifications are necessary in those environments to promote safe, independent, and efficient movement. Children with cortical or cerebral visual impairment (CVI) are especially affected by environmental factors; differences in a child's functioning can often be attributed to characteristics of the environment rather than fluctuations in vision (Roman-Lantzy, 2018). The following sections offer suggestions and considerations for environmental modifications.

Signage and Maps

The following list provides suggestions for the design and placement of signs and maps to promote orientation for children with visual impairments:

FIGURE 8.3

Sample Environmental Assessment Form

Environmental Assessment Form

Date: _____ Assessor: _____

Background Information

Student

Name: _____ DOB: _____

School: _____ Grade: _____

Environment

Location: _____

General description: _____

_____

_____

Task(s)

Task(s) student needs to perform in this environment: _____

_____

Device(s) used by student: _____

_____

Description of student's current task performance: _____

_____

Analysis of Environment

Instructions: Observe the student performing tasks in the environment. In the following list, mark a + for items that meet the student's needs or enhance task performance. Mark a – for items that do not meet the student's needs, and provide recommendations for improvement of each problematic item. Use N/A for items that do not apply.

Signage and Maps

_____ Signage is placed in consistent locations.

_____ Signage is mounted at an appropriate height.

_____ Signage and maps have large print, braille, or raised characters.

_____ Signage and maps have appropriate color and contrast.

_____ Other (please specify):

Comments: _____

_____

Recommendations: _____

_____

FIGURE 8.3

Organization

_____ Areas are organized by function.

_____ Items are easy to reach.

_____ Items are stored in consistent locations.

_____ Personal items and storage areas are identifiable.

_____ Appliances are labeled with large print, braille, or tactile markers.

_____ Other (please specify):

Comments: _____

_____

Recommendations: _____

_____

Safety

_____ Area rugs, runners, and mats are secured to the floor.

_____ Electrical cords are removed from walkways or secured.

_____ Walkways are free of clutter.

_____ Emergency procedures, alarms, and exits are accessible.

_____ Grab bars and railings are installed where needed.

_____ A barrier is placed beneath any head-level objects.

_____ Doors, cabinets, and drawers are closed when not in use.

_____ Other (please specify):

Comments: _____

_____

Recommendations: _____

_____

Lighting and Glare

_____ Sufficient lighting is present.

_____ Areas are evenly lit.

_____ Windows are clean and not blocked by objects or shrubbery.

_____ Window coverings are adjustable.

_____ Sources of glare are minimized.

_____ Light bulbs are free of dust and in working order.

_____ Lighting is adjustable.

_____ Task lighting is positioned appropriately.

_____ Other (please specify):

(continued on next page)

FIGURE 8.3 (*continued*)

Comments: _____

_____

Recommendations: _____

_____

Color and Contrast

_____ Color is used for organization.

_____ Visual clutter is minimized.

_____ Adequate contrast is used on floors, walls, doors, and knobs.

_____ Color and contrast are used to mark stairs, steps, curbs, and drop-offs.

_____ Contrast is used to mark glass walls or large windows.

_____ Other (please specify):

Comments: _____

_____

Recommendations: _____

_____

Other

_____ Textured or contrasting flooring materials are used to define areas.

_____ Auditory or olfactory cues are present.

_____ Background noise is minimized.

_____ Other (please specify):

Comments: _____

_____

Recommendations: _____

_____

- Consider location, positioning, lighting, color, contrast, and glare.
- Include braille and print.
- Consider adding braille or tactile markings to handrails in stairwells to identify each floor number (Levine, 2003).
- Refer to the ADA-ABA Accessibility Guidelines for specific standards for placement and fonts.

- Use preferred colors and less complexity when designing signs and maps for students with CVI (Roman-Lantzy, 2018).

Organization

The following list includes suggestions for organizing environments to promote O&M:

- Organize areas by function.
- Organize cupboards and storage areas so that everything is within reach to minimize the risk of falling as a person reaches or bends down and the body's center of gravity shifts away from the base of support.
- Provide consistent locations for items and put things back in their proper places. Position items near where they will be used, and store the most frequently used items in easily accessible areas (Levine, 2003).
- Label controls on appliances with large print, tactile, or braille labels (Stevens-Ratchford & Krause, 2004).
- Many students with CVI benefit from predictable, uncluttered, and organized environments because they have difficulty navigating areas with excessive visual complexity (Cohen-Maitre & Haerich, 2005).
  - Involve these students in organizing or moving objects to promote predictability.
  - Store objects when not in use to minimize clutter.
  - Label storage areas with colors, words, or pictures to facilitate organization (McKillop et al., 2006).

Safety

The following list includes considerations for promoting safety in different environments:

- Items such as area rugs, electrical cords, and clutter can pose a tripping hazard if not properly secured or stored.
  - Rugs, runners, and mats should be securely attached to the floor or re-

moved. Double-sided carpet tape can be used to attach rugs to floors. Securely adhering a stiff piece of linoleum or plastic on the underside of each corner of a rug can keep the corners from turning up.
  - Keep electrical cords out of walkways and other high-traffic areas, or tape them securely to the floor or wall.
  - Remove clutter from main paths on the floor to minimize tripping hazards.
- Arrange furniture to provide clear and distinct travel routes. Alert students to changes in the layout of furniture and reorient them to the new layout. (See Chapter 6 for room-familiarization strategies.) Occasionally rearranging furniture can promote development of mental-mapping skills, as long as students are forewarned and assist with moving the furniture.
- Provide information about emergency procedures in an accessible format and offer training on evacuation procedures and exit routes (Cox & Dykes, 2001; Lahtinen et al., 2014).
- Ask all individuals who use a particular area to either keep doors and cabinets completely open or fully closed (Cox & Dykes, 2001). Place a barrier beneath protruding objects that are located at or near head level. Putting an enclosure around an open staircase that would be a hazard for a cane user is a remedy for such an environmental feature (see Figure 8.4).
- Install grab bars and railings where needed, especially in bathroom areas. Consult with an occupational or physical therapist to determine ideal placement for children with special physical needs or impairments.

Sandra J. Rosen

Figure 8.4 Placing barriers or enclosures beneath protruding objects reduces the hazard for cane users.

Lighting and Glare

Adequate and appropriately placed lighting can promote safety and independence in indoor and outdoor environments (Centre for Excellence in Universal Design, 2012). The appropriateness of lighting depends on a person's vision; two individuals may have very different lighting needs to perform the same task. Types of artificial lighting include fluorescent, incandescent, and light-emitting diodes (LEDs; see Table 8.3 for more information on artificial lighting). In general, lighting should illuminate the entire room evenly, and

task lighting can be added to areas where additional lighting is needed.

The following list includes additional suggestions for optimizing lighting and reducing glare.

- Maximize natural light by cleaning windows and keeping tree branches and shrubbery away from the outside of windows. Similarly, avoid placing items such as hanging plants in front of windows where they can block light. Install adjustable window coverings (e.g., curtains, blinds, or shutters) to allow for control of natural light.
- Strategically place adjustable lamps in areas where an extra light source is needed (Cox & Dykes, 2001). Position task lighting to avoid or minimize strong shadows and glare. Most often, the best task lighting comes from over the nondominant shoulder.
- Install dimmer switches on lights if additional adjustment is needed.
- Dust light bulbs periodically, and replace bulbs as soon as they burn out.
- In some public places, fluorescent ceiling lights can be modified to reduce glare by replacing or retrofitting the louvers or shields that cover the tubes.
- Place a covering with a matte finish over shiny surfaces to reduce glare. Similarly, use matte paint to minimize glare on walls. Other options to reduce glare include tinted glass, self-sticking window film that reduces glare, adjustable blinds and shades, and indirect lighting (Levine, 2003).
- Provide training in proper use of hats, visors, or absorptive lenses, such as NoIRS or UVShields, and in adjusting body position to avoid facing the light directly (Geruschat & Turano, 2002).

TABLE 8.3

Types of Artificial Lighting

Type of Light	Common Uses	Advantages	Disadvantages
Fluorescent			
Linear Fluorescent Lamps (tubes)	• Ceiling fixtures • Cabinet lighting	• Supply broad, even coverage • Provide bright light • Are economical • Newer electronic ballasts eliminate many problems associated with magnetic ballasts	• Contain small amounts of mercury • Not suitable for outdoor use in cold climates • Older types may flicker or make a buzzing sound • May cause headaches and eye strain • Can cause glare
Compact Fluorescent Lamps (CFLs)	• Ceiling fixtures • Lamps	• Emit less heat than incandescent lighting • Come in various bases and styles • Last longer than incandescent bulbs	• Contain small amounts of mercury • May not be suitable for extremely cold or hot climates • Take 1–3 minutes to reach full brightness • Are heavier than incandescent bulbs
Incandescent			
General	• Ceiling fixtures • Desk lamps • Floor lamps	• Provide high contrast • Bulbs available in many shapes and sizes • Do not flicker • Can be easily dimmed	• Can create shadows and glare • Can get hot • Do not last long
Halogen	• Floor lamps • Track lighting • Recessed ceiling fixtures	• Provide very bright, concentrated light • Good for spot lighting	• Can create bright spots and glare • Can get very hot • Some types are prone to bursting

(continued on next page)

TABLE 8.3 (*continued*)

Type of Light	Common Uses	Advantages	Disadvantages
Light-Emitting Diodes (LEDs)			
Light-Emitting Diodes (LEDs)	• Ceiling fixtures • Cabinet lighting • Desk lamps • Floor lamps	• Most energy efficient • Last a long time • Achieve full brightness instantly • Have low surface temperature • Have plastic covers • May have the ability to change colors	• Higher initial price • Produce less light than incandescent and fluorescent light sources • Gradual reduction in light output over time • Require ventilation

Sources: Adapted from Lighting Research Center. (n.d.). Lighting patterns for homes. Troy, NY: Rensselaer Polytechnic Institute. Retrieved from http://www.lrc.rpi.edu/patternbook/index.asp; and VisionAware. (n.d.). Video series: Better lighting for better sight. New York, NY: American Foundation for the Blind. Retrieved from http://www.visionaware.org/info/everyday-living/home-modification-/lighting-and-glare/videos-better-lighting-for-better-sight/1234

Color and Contrast

Color and contrast are simple and effective modifications that can be implemented in most school, home, work, and recreational environments. Color can be used to promote safety, accessibility, and participation in school, work, recreation, and leisure activities. Color may be used as a warning for potential hazards (e.g., placing a red sign on or near head-level scaffolding at a construction site), as a means of coding for location or identification (e.g., using yellow containers to store toys and blue containers to store school supplies), and as an aid in judging depth perception (e.g., adding a yellow strip to the edge of curbs or other drop-offs). Some children with low vision may have difficulty differentiating between certain groups of colors, such as dark blue, black, and dark brown. On the other hand, bright primary colors (e.g., red and yellow) are more saturated and are often more easily discerned than pastels or shades of colors. Consequently, many children with CVI show a marked preference for colors such as red and yellow.

Lighting influences color perception. When sufficient lighting is present, colors are more easily discerned and discriminated. Dim light can mute colors, bright light can intensify colors, and shady areas can cause objects to look more "gray" than their original color.

Contrast is another important consideration when assessing and modifying environments for children with low vision, especially when combined with the environmental effects of lighting and color perception. For children with reduced visual acuity, discerning and differentiating elements in environments without contrast becomes even more challenging. Contrast can be used to promote orientation and visual clarity, perception of space, and identification of obstacles, hazards, and environmental features

(Centre for Excellence in Universal Design, 2012). The following list offers suggestions for effective use of color and contrast in environments:

- Reduce visual clutter as much as possible. Objects are more easily discerned when viewed against a solid background. A patterned background may be more difficult to see due to the figure-ground effect, where objects appear to blend in with their background. Therefore, a solid-colored area rug is preferable to a rug with a busy pattern.
- Choose contrasting colors for walls, floors, and doorframes. Black and white provide the highest contrast, but a stark white background can create glare for some people. Black (or blue or dark brown) and yellow or beige are good options to consider since they provide excellent contrast and are less susceptible to glare.
- Use contrast in the selection and placement of table coverings, placemats, and shelf liners. Use lighter backgrounds for dark-colored objects, and darker backgrounds for light-colored objects. For example, a black plate is most visible against a light beige or white background, and a white plate is more visible against a darker table covering.
- Use color for organization and labeling.
- Mark the edges of stairs, steps, and curbs with a contrasting color; use a contrasting color on light switch plates, door handles, and railings to make locating them easier (see Figure 8.5). Mark glass walls or large windows clearly and permanently in a manner that contrasts with the background when viewed from both directions (Centre for Excellence in Universal Design, 2012).

- Place brightly colored objects or accessories on furniture to aid in identification. For example, a contrasting cloth can be placed on the back of a student's chair to make it easier to locate.
- Use preferred colors and high contrast to help students with CVI locate important items, but avoid using too many objects of the same color within an environment (Cohen-Maitre & Haerich, 2005). For instance, a bright yellow cup can be easily located against a black background, especially if it is the only yellow object in the room.

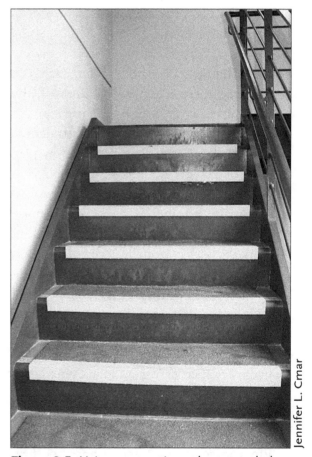

Jennifer L. Cmar

Figure 8.5 Using contrasting color to mark the edges of stairs, steps, and curbs makes them easier to locate.

- Use lighted objects paired with color (e.g., a red lava lamp) to promote visual attention in students with CVI who exhibit light-gazing behaviors (looking at light sources for extended periods of time) (Roman-Lantzy, 2018). The O&M specialist can wear a dark-colored smock when working with young students with CVI to provide contrast when using brightly colored or lit objects to encourage use of visual efficiency skills and reaching (Sheline, n.d.).

Sound, Touch, and Movement

The following list provides suggestions for maximizing the use of sound, touch, and movement in environments:

- Use sound to aid in orientation, such as a clock on the wall or wind chimes in the backyard near the door (see Figure 8.6).
- Use textured or tactile markers to denote specific areas (e.g., rug on floor in play area of classroom, tactile label on coat cubby).
- Minimize extraneous background noise (e.g., mute the television, place desks or other work areas away from busy corridors). This consideration is especially important for students with CVI who may be overwhelmed by busy or noisy environments (McKillop et al., 2006).
- Use colored objects with movement or reflective properties (e.g., balloons, pinwheels) to promote visual attention in students with CVI (Roman-Lantzy, 2018).

Environmental assessments and modifications are ongoing processes. Individual func-

Jennifer L. Cmar

Figure 8.6 Sounds, such as placing wind chimes near a door, can be used to aid orientation.

tioning and task performance must be reassessed periodically with regard to environmental characteristics. The appropriateness of existing modifications may be reevaluated, and temporary modifications should be phased out as skills develop (Lueck, 2004). To the extent possible, environments should be kept stable; predictable environments can increase safety and facilitate independent orientation. Natural environments cannot always be controlled; school classrooms, hallways, and outdoor areas are by nature uncontrolled environments. It is vital, however, to educate those who use these areas on the importance of maintaining consistency through actions such as closing cabinet doors and keeping items off the floor in walking pathways. These simple measures can go a long way in promoting safety, not only for students with visual impairments, but for all who use these areas.

Advocacy

O&M specialists participate in a range of advocacy efforts in local and national capacities to promote accessible environments. Common ways for O&M specialists to get involved include:

- Informing students of their rights and teaching them how to request modifications and file complaints when necessary
- Working with school administrators to suggest needed environmental modifications to increase student safety, access, and independence
- Acting as a liaison to traffic engineers, structural engineers, and designers to propose and implement accessibility solutions and livable cities
- Along with the student, discussing with city traffic authorities the need to install an APS at a specific intersection to facilitate the student's independence
- Providing input on revisions to accessibility guidelines and standards
- Helping businesses locate resources to improve the accessibility of their buildings
- Volunteering on access boards and advisory committees

- Participating in research related to accessibility and universal design

Other professionals, family members, and caregivers can inform O&M specialists of accessibility concerns, brainstorm potential solutions, and support students as they develop their self-advocacy skills.

Summary

The ADA-ABA Accessibility Guidelines are intended to ensure access to the built environment for all individuals with disabilities. The principles of universal design provide further guidelines on providing equal access to all people. When assessing environments, individual characteristics, environmental characteristics, the child's current functioning and task performance, and tasks that the child needs to perform should be taken into consideration. The suggestions for environmental modifications in this chapter are intended to provide an overview of common ways in which to modify environments; however, other options may be equally as useful or more useful for some children. O&M specialists provide instruction on strategies for traveling in various environments. This instruction may include safe negotiation of environmental hazards and alternative strategies for situations where modifications are not feasible and hazards cannot be eliminated. O&M specialists promote greater accessibility of environments by becoming involved in local, regional, and national advocacy efforts and by working with other educational team members, including families, to increase awareness of accessibility issues and solutions.

References

Americans with Disabilities Act of 1990, Pub. L. No. 101-336 (1990).

Architectural Barriers Act, 42 U.S.C. § 4151 (1968).

Bentzen, B. L., & Barlow, J. M. (1995). Impact of curb ramps on the safety of persons who are blind. *Journal of Visual Impairment & Blindness, 89*(4), 319–328.

Burgstahler, S. (2012). *Universal design in education: Principles and applications.* Seattle: University of Washington.

Carignan, M., Rousseau, J., Gresset, J., & Couturier, J. A. (2008). Content validity of a home-based person-environment interaction assessment tool for visually impaired adults. *Journal of Rehabilitation Research & Development, 45*(7), 1037–1051.

The Center for Universal Design. (1997). *The principles of universal design* (Version 2.0). Raleigh: North Carolina State University.

Centre for Excellence in Universal Design. (2012). *Building for everyone: A universal design approach. Internal environment and services.* Dublin, Ireland: National Disability Authority. Retrieved from http://universaldesign.ie/Built-Environment/Building-for-Everyone/4-Internal-Environment-and-Services.pdf

Cohen-Maitre, S. A., & Haerich, P. (2005). Visual attention to movement and color in children with cortical visual impairment. *Journal of Visual Impairment & Blindness, 99*(7), 389–402.

Cox, P. R., & Dykes, M. K. (2001). Effective classroom adaptations for students with visual impairments. *TEACHING Exceptional Children, 33*(6), 68–74.

Danford, G. S. (2003). Universal design: People with vision, hearing, and mobility impairments evaluate a model building. *Generations, 27*(1), 91–94.

Geruschat, D. R., & Turano, K. A. (2002). Connecting research on retinitis pigmentosa to the practice of orientation and mobility. *Journal of Visual Impairment & Blindness, 96*(2), 69–85.

Iwarsson, S., & Stahl, A. (2003). Accessibility, usability and universal design—Positioning and definition of concepts describing person-environment relationships. *Disability and Rehabilitation, 25*(2), 57–66.

Krug, S. (2006). *Don't make me think: A common sense approach to web usability* (2nd ed.). Berkeley, CA: New Riders.

Lahtinen, R., Palmer, R., & Ojala, S. (2014). Practice-oriented safety procedures in work environment with visually and hearing impaired colleagues. In K. Saranto, M. Castrén, T. Kuusela, S. Hyrynsalmi, & S. Ojala (Eds.), *Safe and secure cities: Proceedings of the 5th international conference on well-being in the information society, Turku, Finland, August 18–20, 2014* (pp. 109–119). Cham, Switzerland: Springer International.

Levine, D. (Ed.). (2003). *Universal design New York 2.* Buffalo: State University of New York at Buffalo, Center for Inclusive Design and Environmental Access.

Levtzion-Korach, O., Tennenbaum, A., Schnitzer, R., & Ornoy, A. (2000). Early motor development of blind children. *Journal of Paediatrics and Child Health, 36*(3), 226–229.

Lighting Research Center. (n.d.). Lighting patterns for homes. Troy, NY: Rensselaer Polytechnic Institute. Retrieved from http://www.lrc.rpi.edu/patternbook/index.asp

Lueck, A. H. (2004). Relating functional vision assessment, intervention, and outcomes for students with low vision. *Visual Impairment Research, 6*(1), 45–52.

Mace, R. L., Hardie, G. J., & Place, J. P. (1991). Accessible environments: Toward universal design. In W. F. E. Preiser, J. C. Vischer, & E. T. White (Eds.), *Design intervention: Toward a more humane architecture* (pp. 155–176). New York, NY: Van Nostrand Reinhold.

Marigold, D. S., & Patla, A. E. (2008). Visual information from the lower visual field is important for walking across multi-surface terrain. *Experimental Brain Research, 188*(1), 23–31.

Marston, J. R., & Church, R. L. (2005). A relative access measure to identify barriers to efficient transit use by persons with visual impairments. *Disability and Rehabilitation, 27*(13), 769–779.

McColgan, M. W. (2007). Lighting answers: Light pollution. Troy, NY: Rensselaer Polytechnic Institute, Lighting Research Center. Retrieved from http://www.lrc.rpi.edu/programs/nlpip/lighting answers/lightpollution/abstract.asp

McKillop, E., Bennett, D., McDaid, G., Holland, B., Smith, G., Spowart, K., & Dutton, G. (2006). Problems experienced by children with cognitive visual dysfunction due to cerebral visual impairment—And the approaches which parents have adopted to deal with these problems. *British Journal of Visual Impairment, 24*(3), 121–127.

Pivik, J. R. (2010). The perspective of children and youth: How different stakeholders identify architectural barriers for inclusion in schools. *Journal of Environmental Psychology, 30*(4), 510–517.

Roman-Lantzy, C. (2018). *Cortical visual impairment: An approach to assessment and intervention* (2nd ed.). New York, NY: AFB Press.

Sheline, D. (n.d.). Strategies for students with cortical visual impairment. Strategy to See. Retrieved from http://strategytosee.com/strategies-for-students -with-cortical-visual-impairment-handout/

Steinman, B. A., Nguyen, A. Q. D., Pynoos, J., & Leland, N. (2011). Falls-prevention interventions for persons who are blind or visually impaired. *Insight: Research and Practice in Visual Impairment and Blindness, 4*(2), 83–91.

Stevens-Ratchford, R., & Krause, A. (2004). Visually impaired older adults and home-based leisure activities: The effects of person-environment congruence. *Journal of Visual Impairment & Blindness, 98*(1), 14–27.

Story, M. F., Mueller, J. L., & Mace, R. L. (1998). *The universal design file: Designing for people of all ages and abilities* (Rev. ed.). Raleigh: North Carolina State University, College of Design, The Center for Universal Design.

United States Access Board. (2004). ADA and ABA accessibility guidelines. Retrieved from https://www.access-board.gov/guidelines-and -standards/buildings-and-sites/about-the-ada -standards/background/ada-aba-accessibility -guidelines-2004

VisionAware. (n.d.). Video series: Better lighting for better sight. New York, NY: American Foundation for the Blind. Retrieved from http://www .visionaware.org/info/everyday-living/home -modification-/lighting-and-glare/videos-better -lighting-for-better-sight/1234

9

Orientation and Mobility and the Expanded Core Curriculum

Vicki DePountis

Questions to Guide Your Reading of This Chapter

➤ What is the expanded core curriculum and why does it exist?

➤ How are orientation and mobility (O&M) and the expanded core curriculum related?

➤ How can O&M be incorporated into each of the other areas of the expanded core curriculum?

➤ How can professionals working with students with visual impairments on the expanded core curriculum reinforce O&M skills and concepts?

It takes an "O&M village" to realize greater success and improve students' achievement. (Fazzi, 2014, p. 272)

The components of orientation and mobility (O&M) include body concepts, environmental concepts, spatial concepts, perceptual and sensory skills, mobility skills, orientation skills, interpersonal skills, and decision-making skills (Fazzi, 2014). This chapter examines the ways these O&M components can be incorpo-

rated into all areas of the expanded core curriculum.

The Expanded Core Curriculum

A primary role of teachers of students with visual impairments is to adapt the academic core curriculum to make it accessible to students with visual impairments. However, visual impairment professionals have known for years that additional instruction is needed so that students who are blind or visually impaired can learn concepts and skills that their sighted peers learn incidentally. In 1996, Phil Hatlen proposed that the expanded core curriculum (ECC) be used to "systematically and sequentially" teach skills and concepts that are not addressed or not adequately addressed within the core curriculum for students with visual impairments (Hatlen, 1996). The ECC addresses the skills necessary for students with visual impairments to access the core curriculum, as well as the skills necessary for developmentally appropriate independent functioning within the school and community. For example, a child who is sighted may not need to be taught how to position his or her hand to shake another person's hand. In most cases, the child is simply told, "Shake my hand," and the visual cue of the outstretched hand directs the child to grasp it. However, performing the same exercise with a child who is blind will require additional instruction for the child to know how to position his or her hand. In addition, if the child has an intellectual disability, physical guidance may also be necessary. Although teachers of students with visual impairments lead the process of assessing student skills within the ECC, all members of the Individualized Education Program (IEP) team, through collaborative consultation, must determine appropriate and meaningful instruction. O&M specialists play a key role in this process for two reasons. First, O&M is one of the ECC domains and, second, O&M skills play an integral role in supporting all other ECC domains.

The ECC is composed of nine areas or domains: compensatory access, orientation and mobility, social interaction, career education, assistive technology, independent living, recreation and leisure, sensory efficiency, and self-determination (Hatlen, 1996; Sapp & Hatlen, 2010). These areas address students' functional and educational needs that result from their disabilities as required by the Individuals with Disabilities Education Improvement Act (2004), commonly referred to as IDEA. The previous example of hand shaking would be categorized as a social interaction skill. Some states have legislation that explicitly requires teachers of students with visual impairments to evaluate and instruct students with visual impairments in all areas of the ECC (e.g., ECC Bill, Texas Education Code C § 30.002, 2013). Collaboration between vision professionals, teachers, related services professionals, and

families is important for successful implementation of the ECC because many of the areas include skills that are most relevant in non-school settings (Sapp & Hatlen, 2010). Some ECC domains, like recreation and leisure and independent living skills, readily lend themselves to the integration of O&M components because O&M skills are integral to learning those areas. Other domains, like self-determination, require indepth knowledge of O&M components to find opportunities to introduce them into instruction.

Orientation and Mobility as Related to the ECC

As noted, O&M is one of the nine areas of the ECC. In addition, there is a lot of overlap between O&M and other areas of the ECC. As a result, many O&M components can be applied or reinforced during instruction in the other eight domains. Teachers of students with visual impairments, when working with students on literacy access, part of the *compensatory skills* domain, can find opportunities to incorporate the O&M components of body concepts, spatial concepts, and perceptual and sensory skills (see Sidebar 9.1 for definitions of key terms). O&M concepts such as body awareness and positioning, laterality and spatial relations, size and shape, and time and schedule concepts are taught systematically, often within artificial scenarios during O&M lessons. However, the ultimate goal is to apply these concepts to skills used by students with visual impairments in natural and meaningful scenarios. For example, a student may learn the concept of a room-numbering system in the hallway of her school. However, it may not be until the concept is

Key Terms

Augmentative communication devices Tools used to communicate and express thoughts by students with little or no functional speech.

Compensatory skills Knowledge and skills needed by students who are blind or visually impaired to access the core curriculum.

Electronic braille notetaker Portable device with a braille keyboard for inputting information and a speech synthesizer or refreshable braille display for outputting information.

Hand-over-hand Guidance of a student's hand by placing the student's hand underneath the teacher's hand to assist the student in completing a task.

Hand-under-hand Guidance of a student's hand by placing the teacher's hand underneath the student's hand to explore objects or guide the student through a task.

Imitation play Type of play in which young children engage by emulating the actions of others.

Object symbols Tangible symbols used to represent events, activities, or objects.

Parallel play Type of play in which a child plays near another child but not with that child.

Physical play Play that involves gross motor movement.

Screen reader Text-to-speech software with a speech synthesizer that offers auditory access to text on a computer.

Self-determination Skills that enable students to convey and advocate for their own needs and wants.

Sensory efficiency Skills that enable students to use all their senses as effectively as possible to access the world around them.

Sensory play Type of play in which children engage in an activity that stimulates one or more of their senses.

Sensory space Area that has been equipped with appropriate visual, auditory, and tactile objects to stimulate the senses.

Specialized keyboards Specially designed keyboards, which may be concave, convex, tilted, split, or otherwise configured, to be used by individuals with disabilities.

Tactile graphics Raised-line versions of print images that convey non-textual information to individuals who are blind or visually impaired.

Tactile symbol Form of communication, often used with students with multiple disabilities or those who cannot learn braille, that uses concrete and abstract symbols to teach students to gather information.

Video magnifiers Electronic devices that provide magnification by using a video camera to capture and project a magnified image on a screen for viewing at near or at a distance.

applied to getting to tryouts for the goalball team, a recreational activity, that the skills become meaningful to the student.

Body awareness and spatial and environmental concepts are used by students when navigating classrooms, participating in games, and traveling with their families. Time and scheduling concepts are used during the school day and for planning after-school activities. Incorporating these skills into other ECC areas ensures the skills are generalized so they can be applied as appropriate. Generalization, the process of applying learned skills to various situations (Roberts, 2001), is particularly critical for O&M concepts and skills. The purpose of O&M instruction is to teach skills that will be used to navigate and perform a wide range of everyday tasks in a variety of environments (Pogrund et al., 2012). Furthermore, integrating O&M skills throughout the ECC ensures that the skills will be maintained and refined over time, as developmentally appropriate.

Compensatory Access

Compensatory Skills

Compensatory skills are the knowledge and skills needed to access the core curriculum and support accurate concept development. The skills that teachers of students with visual impairments traditionally teach students with visual impairments fall into this area. Compensatory skills include use of braille, *tactile graphics*, object or *tactile symbols*, and audio materials (Hatlen, 1996) as appropriate for literacy. Additionally, in order to learn alongside their academic peers, students with visual impairments need strategies for organization and study skills, spatial concepts, and listening skills

and accurate concept development. Many O&M components, such as spatial concepts, are automatically incorporated while teaching compensatory skills. Others, like body concepts, can be reinforced during activities in which the student is already participating.

Incorporating O&M into Compensatory Skills Instruction

Braille Readiness Skills

The 1997 amendments to the Individuals with Disabilities Education Act (1990, 1997) state that a child with a visual impairment must be provided with braille instruction unless evaluations reveal that the use of braille is not appropriate. To be successful, a child must prepare to learn braille long before starting school. Many braille readiness skills, such as listening, sitting up, and fine motor skills, overlap or complement O&M skills. For example, a child will need to strengthen his or her hands and practice rotation skills of the wrist and hand to turn the paper feed knob on a brailler. These same skills can be reinforced by working on the O&M skill of turning door knobs. By maintaining awareness of O&M concepts and skills, teachers of students with visual impairments, parents, and other professionals can reinforce them when working on braille readiness skills. Table 9.1 lists some braille readiness skills and activities and the corresponding O&M components and skills they support. In addition, young children with visual impairments can be exposed to stories about body awareness, various indoor and outdoor environments, and travel.

Organization and Study Skills

Organization and study skills are particularly critical to the educational success of students

TABLE 9.1

O&M Components in Braille Readiness Skills

Braille Readiness Skills	O&M Component Reinforced
Fine Motor Skills	
Holds objects in each hand	Body concepts – laterality
Utilizes rotation skills	Mobility skills – turning knobs
Uses two hands cooperatively	Body concepts – purposeful movement
Shows hand strength and flexibility	Mobility skills – cane and AMD skills
Book and Story	
Purposefully traces marks in tactile book from start to end	Perceptual and sensory skills – tactile Spatial concepts – positional concepts
Holds book and turns pages	Body concepts – purposeful movement
Listening Skills	
Alerts to sounds	Perceptual and sensory skills – auditory
Follows two-step directions	Interpersonal skills – receptive language
Listens to interaction songs	Interpersonal skills – receptive language Perceptual and sensory skills – auditory
Concepts	
Identifies and names body parts	Body concepts – body parts
Shows understanding of object permanence	Spatial concepts – reaching
Searches for dropped objects	Spatial concepts – purposeful movement
Comprehends concepts of more or less, big or small, long or short, wide or narrow	Spatial concepts – quantitative concepts
Understands positional concepts with marks on page	Spatial concepts – object-to-object relationships, tactile scanning
Tactile	
Locates tactile mark on paper	Spatial concepts – object-to-object relationships, tactile scanning
Traces outline of shapes	Spatial concepts – geometric shapes, tactile scanning
Traces a continuous left-to-right line	Spatial concepts – directionality, tactile scanning
Examines objects by touch	Environmental concepts – tactilely exploring materials, kinesthetic awareness

Sources: Adapted from McComiskey, A. V. (1996). The braille readiness skills grid: A guide to building a foundation for literacy. *Journal of Visual Impairment & Blindness, 90*(3), 190–193; and Pogrund, R., Sewell, D., Anderson, H., Calaci, L., Cowart, M. F., Gonzalez, C. M., . . . Roberson-Smith, B. (2012). *TAPS—Teaching age-appropriate purposeful skills: An orientation and mobility curriculum for students with visual impairments* (3rd ed.). Austin: Texas School for the Blind and Visually Impaired.

with visual impairments. Without good organizational skills, students may spend valuable time searching for school supplies, assignments, and textbooks. In elementary school, students are introduced to various study skills including note taking, highlighting, underlining, and outlining. However, since these are visual skills, teachers of students with visual impairments will need to work with students to determine appropriate alternative strategies and tools students who are blind or visually impaired can use, such as recorders, braille notetakers, and magnifiers. O&M concepts that can support organization and study skills are consistent use of positional language and consistent placement of objects and assistive technology in study areas, backpacks, and lockers. For example, if the student is learning about the planes of the body and laterality during O&M instruction, the teacher of students with visual impairments, classroom teacher, parent, or others may apply these concepts to the student's backpack as follows: "The plane with the straps is the *back* plane of the backpack. The *back* of the backpack goes against your *back*. The magnifier belongs in the pocket on the *right* side of the backpack when the *front* of the backpack is facing you."

Spatial Concepts

Spatial concepts taught during O&M lessons can simultaneously be taught as compensatory skills for successful class participation. Students generally have classroom familiarization lessons during O&M sessions at the start of the school year. The ability to get to relevant areas of the classroom independently and quickly is important for participation in all activities. When classroom teachers are knowledgeable about the room-familiarization process (see Chapter 6), they can use consistent language to encourage students with visual impairments to get to the trash can, sink, cubbies, and other areas using their spatial skills. They will be more likely to say, "The water fountain is against the north wall of the classroom, to the right of the windows," rather than bring the student water each time.

The arrangement of objects in relation to one other, to the student, and within the space is evident in many classroom tasks. Reading fundamentals, such as left to right and top to bottom, are spatial concepts. Math and science shapes, angles, tables, graphs, and charts are frequently used to display information. When classroom teachers understand the importance of using accurate spatial language with children with visual impairments, they are more likely to use correct terminology instead of saying "over here" or "over there." They are also more likely to identify teaching moments where students can act out the concepts. For example, they may have students walk in between the rows of desk to experience the concept of parallel. Using concrete examples of spatial concepts benefits the student who is visually impaired as well as the other students in the class.

Listening Skills and Concept Development

Listening skills and part-to-whole concept development are important compensatory skills for both classroom and O&M success. Each time students remember multistep instructions during a class activity they are practicing remembering multistep directions for travel. If the teacher of students with visual impairments, classroom teacher, and O&M specialist agree to present instructions consistently, such as "Step 1 . . . , Step 2 . . . , Step 3 . . . ," it will reinforce the student's ability to remember instructions. Forward and backward chaining are two common part-to-whole strategies for teaching routes. In forward chaining, instruction begins at the starting point of a route, and each subsequent segment is added on. In backward chaining, instruction begins at the end point of a route, and each preceding segment is added on (Lewis & Allman, 2014). Each time a concept is presented in discrete pieces that are put together in class, forward and backward chaining are reinforced. Each step is one part of the whole process. In many situations, sighted children can visually perceive the whole with one glance, but children with visual impairments must listen to each discrete step and combine them to understand the whole process. When all professionals who work with students with visual impairments understand the need to explicitly list instructions and present new concepts using the part-to-whole approach, students become more efficient at learning to use part-to-whole strategies.

Social Interaction

Social Interaction Skills

Social interaction skills are essential for successful communication in personal and professional settings. They include verbal or signed communication and nonverbal communication such as facial expressions and body language. These skills are important throughout life for maintaining employment, developing positive self-esteem and strong relationships, and general acceptance in society. Most social interaction skills are learned visually, through observation, beginning in infancy. Children who are blind or visually impaired need systematic instruction in social skills. The components of social interaction include appropriate body language, social communication, effective conversation patterns, cooperation skills, interactions with others, social etiquette, development of relationships and friendships, knowledge of self, and interpretation and monitoring of social behavior (Sacks, 2014). Social interactions become more complex as children grow, and teaching many of these components provides opportunities to reinforce O&M skills (see Table 9.2 for examples of O&M components in social interactions).

Incorporating O&M into Social Interaction Instruction for Preschoolers

Social development begins in infancy through bonding experiences with parents and caregivers (D'Allura, 2002). The close gaze between an infant and a caregiver during feeding encourages continuous visual regard. Caregivers of an infant with a visual impairment must learn to respond to a different set of cues when the infant wants attention. Instead of crying and visually seeking the caregiver, the infant may be very quiet in an attempt to listen for the location of the caregiver (FamilyConnect, n.d.b). Although caregivers are learning to respond to different cues, they must teach their infants and toddlers to exhibit the same social cues as other children so they are socially accepted by their sighted peers as they grow. For example, during

TABLE 9.2

O&M Components in Social Interaction Skills

Social Interaction Skills	O&M Component Reinforced
Preschool	
Maintains eye contact	Body concepts – knowledge of body and facial parts
Keeps head up	Body and spatial concepts – posture
Turns head toward speaker	Perceptual and sensory skills – auditory
Nods or shakes head for yes and no	Body concepts – purposeful movement
Elementary and Middle School	
Decides to approach others	Perceptual and sensory skills – auditory
Approaches others	Orientation skills, mobility skills – distance, direction, cane skills
Turns toward different speakers	Body concepts – knowledge of body parts
	Orientation skills – self to others
	Perceptual and sensory skills – auditory
Participates in activities	Mobility skills – purposeful movement, motor skills, cane skills
	Orientation skills – self to others
Gets to activities	Decision-making skills – choosing attire, selecting route
	Orientation skills, mobility skills – distance, direction, cane skills
	Spatial concepts – map reading, building layout
Interacts in large crowds, as in a cafeteria or playground	Environmental concepts – cafeteria, playground
	Orientation skills, mobility skills – purposeful movement, distance, direction, pencil grip, cane skills
	Spatial concepts – self to others, spatial layout
Stands at appropriate distance	Body concepts – knowledge of body parts
	Interpersonal skills – social etiquette
	Spatial concepts – self to others
High School	
Responds to someone who says "Hi" in the hallway	Body concepts – knowledge of body parts
	Interpersonal skills – social etiquette
	Orientation skills – self to others
	Perceptual and sensory skills – auditory
Goes to sporting events and after-school activities	Decision-making skills – choosing attire, selecting route
	Environmental concepts – neighborhoods, structures
	Orientation skills, mobility skills – distance, direction, cane skills
	Spatial concepts – map reading, building layout

(continued on next page)

TABLE 9.2 (*continued*)

Social Interaction Skills	O&M Component Reinforced
Participates in study groups	Decision-making skills – choosing books and study materials Environmental concepts – quiet areas Interpersonal skills – social etiquette, requesting assistance Orientation skills, mobility skills – indoor travel, cane skills and storage
Socializes	Decision-making skills – choosing appropriate attire Environmental concepts – malls, stadiums, coffee shops, homes Interpersonal skills – social etiquette Orientation skills, mobility skills – self to others, cane skills Perceptual and sensory skills – applying meaning to auditory information

Sources: Adapted from Sacks, S. Z. (2014). Social interaction. In C. B. Allman & S. Lewis (Eds.), *ECC essentials: Teaching the expanded core curriculum to students with visual impairments* (pp. 324–368). New York, NY: AFB Press; and Pogrund, R., Sewell, D., Anderson, H., Calaci, L., Cowart, M. F., Gonzalez, C. M., . . . Roberson-Smith, B. (2012). *TAPS—Teaching age-appropriate purposeful skills: An orientation and mobility curriculum for students with visual impairments* (3rd ed.). Austin: Texas School for the Blind and Visually Impaired.

feeding time, the caregiver may wait until the infant positions his or her face toward the caregiver before providing the bottle. When caring for more than one infant or toddler, it is helpful to look for opportunities to position the toddlers next to each other during typical social activities such as eating (see Figure 9.1). They can be encouraged to listen for each other's voices, turn their heads toward each other, and communicate.

Caregivers should also provide auditory descriptions of activities and the body parts involved. In addition, as infants with visual impairments grow and become mobile, O&M specialists can teach them to explore their surroundings and follow simple travel requests, such as, "Come here. Sit down. Find the ball on your right." These skills prepare toddlers for positive social interactions with other preschoolers.

Incorporating O&M into Social Interaction Instruction for Elementary and Middle School Students

As children grow, they have opportunities to engage in different types of social interactions. Each stage of development builds on the preceding set of skills. For example, toddlers will predominantly interact with their family members, rarely having to decide whether to approach another person. Once they reach elementary-school age, children have opportunities to make friends with peers and interact with teachers. Social interactions become more complex and include a variety of gestures. Students with visual impairments will not always see social gestures such as "high fives" and "thumbs up." This age is a good time to start teaching students to let their friends know that they cannot see gestures. Us-

Vicki DePountis

Figure 9.1 Positioning toddlers next to each other during social activities such as eating encourages them to listen for each other's voices, turn their heads toward each other, and communicate.

ing self-advocacy skills, students with visual impairments can ask their friends to role-play social situations and show the students with visual impairments any relevant gestures for those interactions. The O&M specialist can encourage students with visual impairments, as appropriate, to teach their friends to guide them so that they can socialize as they travel on campus.

Incorporating O&M into Social Interaction Instruction for High School Students

During adolescence, students participate in an increasing number of complex social situations. They may be required to interact with others in study groups, on teams, as spectators, on dates, during parties, and just casually in passing (Sacks, 2014). Students with visual impairments will need to be taught more advanced social skills, including the nuances associated with platonic and romantic relationships. Some high school students with visual impairments have a solid understanding of body and spatial con-

cepts. In these cases, the O&M specialist can inform all professionals and caregivers who work with these students that providing verbal directions before and during new social situations is sufficient for learning corresponding social interaction skills. An O&M specialist working with a student with a visual impairment who also has additional disabilities will need to inform others of the student's unique words, signs, or gestures for following body movements and directional instructions. For example, a student with an intellectual disability usually turns right when the right arm is stroked. It will be helpful for individuals working with that student on the skill of facing a speaker to know this and other physical prompts for communicating directional movement. Sharing this individualized information about O&M for each student with as many people as possible who interact with the student increases the likelihood that O&M skills will be integrated during teachable moments in social interactions. Better still, encourage the student to self-advocate and teach his or her friends guide techniques, how to use positional language, and how to physically demonstrate gestures and facial expressions.

Career Education

Career Education Skills

Children become familiar with the concept of employment by observing family members and friends, as well as people in the community, in the media, and in school. Career education ensures that students with visual impairments of all ages have hands-on opportunities to experience jobs they may not be aware of otherwise because they cannot observe people working in those jobs. Students also learn work-related skills such as punctuality, assuming responsibility, following directions, applying social skills in the workplace, and working as part of a team. Research has shown that although transition services are not required to begin until a child is 16 years old (IDEA, 2004), intervention that begins in the preschool and elementary grades is more likely to lead to positive employment outcomes (Crudden, 2012; Wolffe, 2014).

Career exploration must include examination of the travel skills needed to get to and from a work site or campus. A case study by Mask and DePountis (2018) reports that even when campus travel is mastered, successfully navigating a city's mass transit system to get to and from work is a recurring obstacle for individuals with visual impairments. Therefore, O&M skills and concepts should be incorporated into teaching children of all ages about career education.

Incorporating O&M into Career Education Instruction

Career-related foundational knowledge and skills, such as following directions, maintaining schedules, and sorting and storing items, begin in preschool (Wolffe & Rosenblum, 2014). Maintaining defined spaces for objects and activities within a classroom helps ensure children with visual impairments use their O&M skills and can participate as independently as possible. Children with visual impairments learn to be responsible for returning items to their proper place using trailing skills, protective techniques, and landmarks within the room (see Chapter 6 for more information on these techniques). They may use a calendar system with *object symbols* to determine where to go for the next activity on the schedule (Blaha, 2001). During role-playing or imaginative play, children with visual impairments should have as many tactile representations of various workspaces with bold colors as possible. Positional language, such as "The cashier stands behind the register," should be used to describe the setting while the child is physically guided to the correct place to experience the job.

In elementary school, children begin taking personal responsibility for themselves and their possessions, and children may be asked to complete chores at school and at home. At this age, career education focuses on increasing career awareness. Education professionals should work closely with O&M specialists to determine which jobs are appropriate for students with visual impairments to accomplish independently. Students who are learning to read tactile or large-print maps may be provided with tactile or large-print drawings of areas within the classroom so they can retrieve and replace task-related items. The O&M specialist can work with the classroom teacher to determine what errands the student can complete independently on campus.

This age is also when children start exploring their interests and abilities and imagining themselves in various careers. During field trips, teachers should take time to discuss the roles of those employed within locations they are visiting. Many cities have children's museums with areas dedicated to exposing young children to various work settings (Wolffe & Rosenblum, 2014). It is important to discuss all field trips with the O&M specialist to determine whether O&M lessons can be integrated into the field trips.

By the time a child is in late elementary school, the child should have some awareness of the concept of a job and why people work, as well as self-awareness regarding interests and capabilities. Secondary school, with needs assessment beginning in middle school, is the time for students to gain a more comprehensive understanding of job-seeking and job-related activities (Texas School for the Blind and Visually Impaired, 2007). It is even more important for students with visual impairments to participate in paid or volunteer work activities, including the process of job searching. Professionals should take these opportunities to discuss how the student might obtain an interview.

In middle school and high school, it is important for students to visit job sites in which they may have career interests. Students can apply their orientation skills to determining the locations of the work and volunteer sites. There are opportunities for using cardinal directions, tactile maps, and GPS devices. Students can use environmental concepts, mobility skills, interpersonal skills, and decision-making skills to plan and execute, as developmentally appropriate, entire trips to and from the various work sites. Multiple volunteer opportunities and work experiences, appropriate social skills, and efficient independent travel skills are some of the factors associated with paid employment for young adults with visual impairments (McDonnall, 2011).

Assistive Technology

Assistive Technology Skills

In special education, assistive technology is a very broad term defined by IDEA (2004) as "any item, piece of equipment, or product system, whether acquired commercially off the shelf, modified, or customized, that is used to increase, maintain, or improve functional capabilities of a child with a disability" (34 C.F.R. § 300.5). There are generally three purposes for assistive technology: access to information, communication, and personal productivity (McNear & Farrenkopf, 2014).

For students with visual impairments, assistive technology typically includes *electronic braille notetakers*, braillers, magnification software, *video magnifiers*, *screen readers*, tablets, long canes, GPS devices, and optical devices. Students with visual impairments who have additional disabilities may also need assistive technology such as sensory spaces, switches, communication systems, and adaptive mobility devices. These devices may be used in any setting and to access all areas of the ECC. Instruction in use of the assistive technology must begin at a young age, and evaluation must continue throughout a child's growth and development. Ongoing training should be provided to everyone who interacts with the child.

Incorporating O&M into Assistive Technology Instruction

Assistive technology devices allow students to access the core curriculum in school and at home to help complete their homework. Devices may support inputting information, such as *specialized keyboards*, or outputting information, such as text-to-speech software. Adults may use such devices to perform tasks on their jobs or browse the Internet to learn about activities around town. Instruction in the use of these tools is critical, and O&M concepts can be valuable motivators. For example, a student who is learning to use JAWS, a screen reader, to access the Internet may be more motivated to do so if tasked with determining what public transportation will get him to the mall. He can use assistive technology to practice decision-making skills when planning the trip.

Assistive technology that enables reading and writing, and access to science, technology, engineering, and mathematics content, as well as images and graphs, is considered communication technology, as are *augmentative communication devices*. When teaching students use of these devices, such as choice-making software activated by a switch, professionals should maintain consistent placement of devices and describe them using spatial and body concepts. Saying, for example, "Your switch is in front of your right hand" will reinforce O&M concepts. Very young children with multiple impairments will begin to understand body-to-object positions when defined sensory spaces are used consistently. A *sensory space* is an area that has been equipped with appropriate visual, auditory, and tactile objects to stimulate the senses. A child may start by unintentionally contacting tactilely interesting items. Through repetition, the child will learn that, for example, the beads are in front of his right hand and the Slinky is next to his left hand (see Figure 9.2). The knowledge that familiar objects are close by will motivate the student to move toward them.

Vicki DePountis

Figure 9.2 This sensory space is equipped with objects to stimulate the child's senses, such as beads and a Slinky, which motivate the child to move toward them.

Students with visual impairments have unique needs, and there are many assistive technology tools available to help them manage their personal productivity. When assistive technology specialists work with teachers of students with visual impairments, O&M specialists, and other members of a student's educational team, it is more likely that each member will find opportunities to integrate skills across all aspects of the student's life. Some students may benefit from electronic travel aids used in conjunction with their cane when traveling around campus. Others may find wayfinding games that use GPS technology a rewarding way to address the recreation and leisure area of the ECC.

Independent Living

Independent Living Skills

Independent living skills are sometimes referred to as daily living skills. These are the many skills necessary for living with as much independence as possible, and many of these skills are learned through observation. Independent living skills include personal hygiene and grooming, food preparation and eating, time and money management, clothing care, and household maintenance (Hubbard, 2015). Students with visual impairments may not be aware that their peers are engaging in daily living skills and that they are expected to learn these skills as well. Parents of a child who is blind or visually impaired may organize the child's room and keep it tidy, thinking this will promote independence since the child can find items more easily. However, if the parents do not demonstrate the organization and cleaning process to the child, the child will not be able to take care of his or her possessions without help. Results of one study that compared the mastery of independent living skills of children with visual impairments and sighted children revealed that children with visual impairments were mastering about half as many skills as their same-age sighted peers (Lewis & Iselin, 2002). Instruction in this area, as in all areas of the ECC, will vary depending on the amount of useful vision a child has.

Incorporating O&M into Independent Living Instruction

Independent living skills are tasks and routines that require movement through an environment and interaction with objects in that environment. Orientation skills are needed to determine the locations of the requisite objects, and mobility skills are essential to get to them safely. Instruction in independent living skills is therefore the perfect opportunity to reinforce O&M skills. It is important to verbally direct students through tasks using spatial concepts, landmarks, and body concepts. Many of the skills needed for independent living require motor skills that are often taught and reinforced by the O&M specialist (e.g., the hand strength needed to hold a cane is also necessary to open a door or jar). By collaborating with the teacher of students with visual impairments and family members to determine appropriate goals for independent living skills, the O&M specialist can look for opportunities to integrate O&M components into independent living skills instruction on a daily basis. Table 9.3 provides an overview of the O&M components that can be incorporated into teaching independent living skills.

One strategy is to provide information to other team members in a relevant location where a task will be taking place. For example, if a student who is blind and has autism is learning how to put on deodorant, the relevant positional and body concepts can be taped to the wall next to the location of the deodorant. Then, as the caregiver prompts the student through application of the deodorant, the caregiver can read the steps taped to the wall. Steps may include: "Reach down with your right hand to find deodorant"; "Clasp with both hands"; "Pull to take off cover"; and "Raise your left arm up high." In this case, all caregivers will be more likely to use the same language, thereby consistently reinforcing body concepts, spatial concepts, and mobility skills. The same instructions can be revised and placed on the door of the student's gym locker so that paraeducators working with the student can also use the same language.

TABLE 9.3

O&M Components in Independent Living Skills

Independent Living Skills	Body Concepts	Decision-Making Skills	Environmental Concepts	Interpersonal Skills	Mobility Skills	Orientation Skills	Perceptual and Sensory Skills	Spatial Concepts
Stores toys, clothing, personal items in same locations	X							X
Sorts items based on tactile information							X	
Participates in putting items away in all parts of the home					X	X		X
Participates in shopping and selecting personal grooming items		X					X	
Visits health and beauty stores	X		X		X	X	X	
Meets with a hairstylist to learn about hair care, styles, and preferences	X			X				
Uses grooming products such as deodorants, toothpaste, makeup, and lotions	X						X	
Lays out an outfit						X		X
Selects the correct size	X	X		X				
Goes to a store or mall		X	X		X	X		X
Dresses for the weather		X	X					
Sorts clothes for laundry							X	X
Goes to the laundry area, laundromat, or dry cleaner			X		X	X		X
Hangs clothing in an organized manner						X		X
Uses a washer and dryer		X						X
Sets the table		X				X		X
Passes food	X			X		X		X
Has table manners	X			X			X	X
Accesses the menu				X				
Goes to a restaurant			X		X	X		
Gathers ingredients in the kitchen					X	X		X
Gathers utensils and appliances					X	X		X
Heats food using oven or stovetop							X	X

TABLE 9.3

Independent Living Skills	Body Concepts	Decision-Making Skills	Environmental Concepts	Interpersonal Skills	Mobility Skills	Orientation Skills	Perceptual and Sensory Skills	Spatial Concepts
Locates the microwave					X	X		X
Changes linens						X	X	X
Puts things away					X	X		X
Uses a vacuum					X	X		X
Sweeps and mops					X	X	X	X
Goes to stores and makes purchases		X	X	X	X	X	X	X
Goes to banks and conducts business		X	X	X	X	X		X
Makes a purchase from a vending machine		X			X	X		X
Uses an ATM to withdraw money		X	X		X	X		X

Source: Adapted from Bardin, J. A. (2014). Independent living. In C. B. Allman & S. Lewis (Eds.), *ECC essentials: Teaching the expanded core curriculum to students with visual impairments* (pp. 283–302). New York, NY: AFB Press.

Recreation and Leisure

Recreation and Leisure Skills

Recreation and leisure—sometimes called recreation, fitness, and leisure—refers to people engaging in activities of their choosing, for pleasure, during their free time. These activities may be sedentary, such as reading, knitting, or playing video games, or physical, such as jumping rope, playing golf, or dancing. It can also include individual or team sports. For very young children, play is the most critical component of recreation and leisure. As children grow, the following components increase in importance: physical activity; health, fitness, and individual sports; team and spectator sports;

and leisure activities and hobbies (Allman, Lewis, Lieberman, & Ross, 2014).

In addition to being enjoyable, physical activities provide opportunities to remain fit and healthy. People's recreation and leisure preferences are largely determined by what they have been exposed to at home, in their community, and in the media. Children with visual impairments need systematic instruction in recreation, fitness, and leisure activities because of the lifelong impact of this area of the ECC. Without the ability to observe the activities in which siblings, friends, and classmates are engaged, children with visual impairments often do not have the necessary repeated exposure to new activities for them to become fun. Children with deafblindness or multiple disabilities need additional support to engage in recreational activities, and staff may not always be skilled in providing it (Lieberman & MacVicar, 2003). Lifelong benefits of recreational activities may include improved cardiovascular function, better ability to sleep, more social engagement, lower chance of injury, and improved self-esteem. In addition, exposure to a variety of movements improves body awareness, flexibility, strength, and stamina, all of which can improve independent living skills, social skills, and O&M skills (FamilyConnect, n.d.a).

Incorporating O&M into Recreation and Leisure Instruction

O&M skills are most relevant in more active recreational activities such as *physical play* and individual and team sports. Success in teaching skills in this area of the ECC will be greatly enhanced if the teacher of students with visual impairments, O&M specialist, and physical education teacher collaborate and work together. In many cases, simply informing school personnel and family members about the importance of providing verbal directions and instructions during recreation and leisure activities can ensure that O&M concepts are reinforced so that students can participate independently. Table 9.4 provides information about common recreation and leisure activities for all ages that incorporate O&M components.

For infants and preschoolers, recreation and leisure are synonymous with play. The social gazes of infancy evolve into social games such as peek-a-boo. Many of these social games reinforce O&M components such as body concepts and mobility skills. When individuals who interact with children with visual impairments are aware of the importance of O&M for young children, they are more likely to choose social games that provide opportunities to reinforce O&M components. Toddlers with sight also engage in *imitation play*, interactive play, *sensory play*, and physical play (Allman et al., 2014). Imitation play often occurs during *parallel play,* when two toddlers are playing with similar toys, such as toy trucks. One toddler visually observes and then imitates the actions of the other toddler. Imitation play also occurs when young children imitate the activities of adults and within turn-taking games such as rolling a ball. When the child has a visual impairment, it is important that descriptive language and physical prompting replace the visual information. Children with deafblindness or other disabilities will need even more physical prompting. It is important to ask individuals who are blind if it is okay to touch them before using any physical prompts, and *hand-under-hand* guidance is a preferred and more respectful method of physical prompting than *hand-over-hand guidance.* Caregivers can describe the positions of the toys as well as the positions and movements of the child's body and body parts, and the child's body in relation to the toys. Interactive play may include tickling games with caregivers and games such as "Pat-a-Cake." Sensory play involves interacting with toys or objects to produce interesting sounds or experience various textures. Activity gyms can be created to stimulate visual, tactile, and auditory experiences. Physical play, or games requiring gross motor skills such as riding on a rocking horse, running, and jumping, may need to be systematically taught to children with visual impairments (Anthony, 2013).

As students get older and the choices for recreation and leisure activities increase and be-

TABLE 9.4

O&M Components in Recreation and Leisure Skills

Recreation and Leisure Skills	O&M Component Reinforced
Infants, Toddlers, and Preschoolers	
Participates in social games such as "Pat-a-Cake" and "Head, Shoulders, Knees, and Toes"	Body concepts – knowledge of body and facial parts Mobility skills – purposeful movement
Imitates and takes turns with toys, such as passing a ball back and forth	Mobility skills – catching, pushing Orientation skills – awareness of position in room Spatial concepts – self to others, body-to-object relationships
Enjoys sensory experiences like activity gyms	Perceptual and sensory skills – auditory, tactile Spatial concepts, orientation skills, mobility skills – reaching, purposeful movement, crawling or creeping
Partakes in physical play and games requiring gross motor skills, such as ride-on toys, rocking toys, and hide-and-seek	Body concepts – correct positioning of body parts Mobility skills – moving body appropriately to play Orientation skills – location in room Spatial concepts – riding straight, fast or slow, near or far
Elementary, Middle, and High School Students	
Participates in physical play games requiring gross motor skills, such as bicycle riding, racing, dancing, and jumping rope	Body concepts – correct positioning of body parts Mobility skills – pedaling, jumping, running Orientation skills – location in gym, or on playground, track, or trail Spatial concepts – up or down, around, fast or slow, near or far, straight or curved, in front or behind; self to others; body-to-object relationships
Joins in physical play such as ball-playing games and team sports	Body concepts – holding, kicking, throwing Decision-making skills – when to pass, strategies for getting to practices and games Interpersonal skills – communicating with teammates or coaches, requesting assistance or modifications Mobility skills – running, kicking, spinning, hopping, throwing, jumping, gymnastics Orientation skills – location on field, court, arena, or stage Spatial concepts – self to others, body-to-object relationships, object-to-object relationships

Source: Adapted from Allman, C. B., Lewis, S., Lieberman, L. J., & Ross, M. A. (2014). Recreation and leisure. In C. B. Allman & S. Lewis (Eds.), *ECC essentials: Teaching the expanded core curriculum to students with visual impairments* (pp. 371–381). New York, NY: AFB Press.

come more complex, they will require more O&M skills. The O&M specialist should work closely with the physical education teacher and teacher of students with visual impairments to ensure activities are modified, or opportunities to engage in alternative activities are provided. For example, if a sixth-grade physical education class regularly plays basketball, the teacher of students with visual impairments may suggest placing an audible beacon on the basketball hoop. The O&M specialist can spend a lesson determining the hoop location with the student with a visual impairment using positional language, body concepts, and tactile maps. The physical education teacher can observe this lesson, and the two professionals can work together to determine what layup arrangement and guide assistance will maximize the student's participation as well as ensure everyone's safety. According to the AccesSports model developed by Paul Ponchillia (1995), the following steps must be taken to analyze activities to accommodate a student's needs (Lieberman, Ponchillia, & Ponchillia, 2013; Ponchillia, 1995):

1. Consider all of the student's current skills and disabilities, and the effects of the environment.
2. Examine targets, goals, equipment, boundaries, and the rules of the activity for potential barriers to play for the student.
3. Select auditory, tactile, or visual adaptations.
4. Select modifications to rules of play.
5. Evaluate and modify as necessary.

Yoga has long been considered a recreation and fitness activity with unique benefits for individuals with visual impairments, and regular practice can improve proprioceptive function (Mohanty, Pradhan, & Nagathna, 2014) and visuospatial memory (Eyre et al., 2016). At its core, yoga unites breath, body, and mind in ways that best suit the needs of the individual (Pogrund et al., 2012). Mindful movement fosters the development of accurate body concepts and attention to proprioceptive input, the keys to body awareness (DePountis & Okungu, 2016). Practicing yoga regularly helps individuals understand their ability to position and move their bodies within a defined space (Maloney, 2016; see Figure 9.3). Not only can this information provide a starting point to improve mobility, it can decrease the likelihood of injury from engaging in activities that individuals know are beyond their capabilities.

Older children and adults can also benefit from a tai chi exercise program as part of their O&M training. Tai chi combines a series of postures and controlled movements to maintain mobility and improve balance and overall well-being. Both yoga and tai chi can become lifelong recreation and fitness activities (Miszko, Ramsey, & Blasch, 2004). The skills needed for sports and activities in which individuals who are blind or visually impaired can participate, such as swimming, jujitsu, tandem biking, skiing, beep baseball, goalball, and bowling, among others, overlap with motor skill development, coordination, spatial awareness, concept development, and other skills that are also required for safe and efficient O&M (See Chapters 2, 3, and 5 for information on concept development, motor development, and spatial orientation, respectively.)

Sensory Efficiency

Sensory Efficiency Skills

Sensory efficiency is a very complex area because it permeates all parts of life, and therefore, all

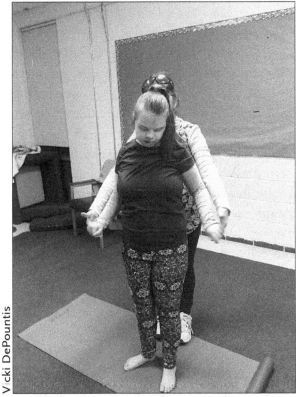

Vicki DePountis

Figure 9.3 Yoga can improve proprioceptive function, visuospatial memory, and accurate body concepts and positioning for individuals with visual impairments.

other domains of the ECC. It is also one of the components of O&M. There are seven sensory systems that allow human beings to detect information related to their bodies and their environments. These include the visual, audi-tory, tactile, gustatory, olfactory, proprioceptive, and vestibular systems (see Chapters 3 and 5 for more information on sensory systems). Perception occurs when one or more systems detect a stimulus inside or outside the body. When individuals have good sensory efficiency, all the sensory systems work together to provide the brain with quick and detailed information so that perception of the stimulus is accurate and meaningful (Foley & Matlin, 2010). For example, the olfactory system may detect the smell of smoke. If the system is efficient, it will accurately identify the odor as smoke as opposed to dust or wildflowers. In addition, and perhaps more importantly, the brain will deduce the meaning of the smell—that there may be a fire. The ability of the olfactory system to identify the odor accurately, distinguish it from similar odors such as that of a barbecue, and attach meaning to the odor—smoke means possible danger—are all learned responses. Sensory efficiency can be improved, and for students with visual impairments, learning to support any remaining vision with information from all other senses can have a significant impact on environmental access.

Incorporating O&M into Sensory Efficiency Instruction

O&M specialists routinely integrate sensory efficiency skills into their lessons. For example, by asking students to notice odors and sounds in the environment to help them with orientation, the O&M specialist is encouraging students to use their sensory systems. The tactile system can detect changes in terrain and temperature. O&M specialists can also use movement games to stimulate the proprioceptive and vestibular systems. The vestibular system, located in the inner ear, informs the brain about head position related to balance, while the proprioceptive system continuously informs the brain about how various parts of the body are positioned, as proprioceptors (sensors in the joints, muscles, and tendons) provide feedback to the individual. (See Chapter 3 for more information on the vestibular and proprioceptive systems.)

When everyone who works with the student understands the meaning and purpose of sensory efficiency skills, they are more likely to take advantage of teachable moments, or to seek out scenarios that provide teachable moments, role models, and opportunities for practice. O&M skills can then be incorporated into those teachable moments in meaningful ways.

When working with preschoolers, a teacher who understands sensory efficiency may spray a lemon scent before the start of a lesson on making lemonade. The smell will cue all the students in the class, including those who are deafblind, that a lemonade-preparation lesson is about to begin. When the student who is deafblind notices the scent, he or she can be guided to the food-preparation station of the classroom. The student may have to locate and stop at the "grocery store" area of the room to get some lemons for the activity. In elementary school, a classroom teacher who is aware of sensory efficiency principles is more likely to notice and incorporate smells from the cafeteria into lessons. The teacher can designate the student who is blind as the line leader for lunch. On field trips, various olfactory, auditory, visual, and tactile cues can act as starting points for discussions on environmental concepts, followed by the development of routes with landmarks for travel. For example, a field trip to a mall provides opportunities to identify the food court based on odors, the ice skating rink based on temperature, and different stores based on the music playing at each one.

Self-Determination

Self-Determination Skills

O&M skills can have a big impact on the ability to access all that the world has to offer. In this respect, its incorporation into the self-determination area of the ECC is important. *Self-determination* consists of students reflecting on their interests, values, and motivations, and understanding potential barriers to achieving goals. Goal-setting, problem-solving, and decision-making skills enable students to set meaningful goals and assess where they will need more skills, knowledge, and assistance. According to Wolffe and Rosenblum (2014), important components of self-determination include self-knowledge, self-advocacy, assertiveness, problem solving and goal setting, and self-directed behavior. Without sufficient O&M skills, students may limit goal setting to familiar destinations. In addition, it has long been known that the ability to travel has a great deal of impact on student confidence, which in turn, affects goal setting (Tuttle & Tuttle, 2004). When working with students on self-determination, teachers of students with visual impairments and O&M specialists should encourage students to consider travel skills necessary to achieve goals. It is important to note that most ECC domains have observable established norms. For example, the social interaction gesture of nodding means "yes," and the rules and skills required for playing in team sports are consistent. Self-determination is based on the student's preferences and self-perceptions. Questioning and trust are essential to understanding and identifying the gaps in self-determination skills that affect a student's values and motivation. The barriers to attaining those self-determination skills can then be identified. In Table 9.5, for example, only students who value choosing their own outfits every day may benefit from learning to request assistance and express preferences in a store.

Incorporating O&M into Self-Determination Instruction

Self-advocacy is the component of self-determination that inspires a student with a visual impairment to call a museum before a school trip to inquire about audio tours and tactile exhibits. O&M lessons often require making phone calls to obtain information. Calling is a common way of requesting assistance, which is an interpersonal skill. Students may have to call public transportation companies to get timetables, malls to get store hours, businesses to get exact addresses, and stores to inquire about prices or items in stock. When the teacher of students with visual impairments or other professional is aware of the broad content of O&M skills training, he or she will know whether the student has had opportunities to practice these interpersonal skills. If so, the teacher will be less likely to gather the information for the student and will incorporate O&M skills into the self-advocacy lesson. Communication among all members of the child's educational team is critical because teaching self-determination skills requires identifying teachable moments. *Empowered*, a self-determination curriculum for students with

visual impairments published by the Texas School for the Blind and Visually Impaired (Cleveland et al., 2007), has a wealth of ideas on how to teach skills in this important ECC area.

Self-advocacy begins at a very young age. Caregivers can either encourage the child to make his or her needs known, or they can take care of everything before a request is even made. Most caregivers are somewhere in the middle of these two extremes. Over time, caregivers will begin to understand the child's means of communication. If they notice that a child frequently wants certain items, those items can be placed where the child can retrieve them independently. Allowing for choice making is the most basic self-determination skill. It is important to take the child's visual skills and mobility skills into account when determining how to arrange items in the house or classroom. If the child cannot immediately find an item, he or she should be encouraged to look for it in a systematic fashion. However, the item should not just be handed to the child. The "fairy godmother syndrome," whereby items seem to magically appear out of nowhere, does not promote self-determination or concept development. Following these simple steps from a young age allows children to be as independent as possible and to advocate for their needs when they cannot meet them on their own.

As children grow, it is important that they learn how to refuse assistance, whether because they want to be as independent as possible or because they are not comfortable with the offer. Of all the professionals who work with students with visual impairments, the O&M specialist is often the most likely to be in a situation where the need for skills in refusing assistance is evident. Students must learn through experience

TABLE 9.5

O&M Components in Self-Determination Skills

Self-Determination Skills	Potential Barriers	O&M Component Reinforced
Self-Advocacy: Ages Birth–3		
Chooses a toy for play time	Visual impairment impacts ability to visually locate a toy	Spatial concepts – toy is positioned in consistent location to enable independent selection and retrieval
Self-Knowledge: Ages 4–7		
States full name and address	Limited conceptual understanding of the meaning of an address	Environmental concepts – understanding of residential areas and address systems
Assertiveness: Ages 8–13		
Plans a weekend activity with friends	Caregiver unable to provide a ride	Interpersonal skills – negotiating with friends to carpool with one of them
Self-Advocacy: Ages 14–16		
Selects own clothing	Visual impairment impacts ability to visually distinguish clothing in a store	Decision-making skills – choosing to request assistance in a store
Problem Solving and Goal Setting: Ages 17–21		
Sets academic goals	Unorganized study area No quiet study area available at home Inability to drive to meet with tutor for help with a specific subject	Decision-making skills, interpersonal skills – using Internet and phone to locate and interview potential tutors Environmental concepts – locating and traveling to coffee shop to meet tutor Interpersonal skills – requesting assistance, arranging for later pickup from school Orientation skills, mobility skills – independently going to school library, using public transportation and a GPS device Spatial concepts – determining appropriate location and position of books, supplies, and assistive technology

Sources: Adapted from Wolffe, K. E., & Rosenblum, L. P. (2014). Self-determination. In C. B. Allman & S. Lewis (Eds.), *ECC essentials: Teaching the expanded core curriculum to students with visual impairments* (pp. 470–475). New York, NY: AFB Press.

when it is wise to request assistance and when to refuse assistance, without being demanding or passive (FamilyConnect, n.d.b). It is equally important for students to learn how to proactively ask for assistance when needed. Learning how to be interdependent, yet still in control, is another important self-determination skill. The O&M specialist should keep other team members informed about the student's skill level in this ECC area so they can take advantage of teachable moments when they present themselves.

Summary

A common saying among O&M specialists is "O&M is everything, and everything is O&M." Our bodies are always someplace, and the position of our bodies is always related to the positions of other people or objects. O&M concepts and skills are relevant to any activity in which individuals engage. The ECC is designed to teach students with visual impairments the skills they need to participate fully in the same activities as their sighted peers. In order to participate in any activity, students with visual impairments need to understand where their bodies are in relation to the objects and people engaged in the activity. Teaching all areas of the ECC provides opportunities to reinforce O&M skills. O&M skills are most meaningful when students can utilize them during activities in which they are meant to be used. Furthermore, since O&M skills are taught to enable students with visual impairments to participate as independently as possible in all activities of daily living, integrating O&M throughout ECC activities is the most natural way to teach those skills.

References

Allman, C. B., Lewis, S., Lieberman, L. J., & Ross, M. A. (2014). Recreation and leisure. In C. B. Allman & S. Lewis (Eds.), *ECC essentials: Teaching the expanded core curriculum to students with visual impairments* (pp. 369–410). New York, NY: AFB Press.

Anthony, T. A. (2013). Early childhood development: Movement and play in early childhood. In L. J. Lieberman, P. E. Ponchillia, & S. V. Ponchillia, *Physical education and sports for people with visual impairments and deafblindness: Foundations of instruction* (pp. 159–186). New York, NY: AFB Press.

Blaha, R. (2001). *Calendars for students with multiple impairments including deafblindness.* Austin: Texas School for the Blind and Visually Impaired.

Cleveland, J., Clinkscales, R. M., Hefner, N., Houghtling, D., Kubacak, C., & Sewell, D. (2007). *Empowered: An activity based self-determination curriculum for students with visual impairment.* Austin: Texas School for the Blind and Visually Impaired.

Crudden, A. (2012). Transition to employment for students with visual impairments: Components for success. *Journal of Visual Impairment & Blindness, 106*(7), 389–399.

D'Allura, T. (2002). Enhancing the social interaction skills of preschoolers with visual impairments. *Journal of Visual Impairment & Blindness, 96*(8), 576–584.

DePountis, V. M., & Okungu, P. A. (2016, April). *Using structured movement routines with music to improve body awareness for students with multiple impairments.* Poster presentation at the Council for Exceptional Children Convention and Expo, St. Louis, MO.

ECC Bill, Texas Education Code C § 30.002, Education for Children with Visual Impairments S.B. 39 (2013).

Eyre, H. A., Acevedo, B., Yang, H., Siddarth, P., Van Dyk, K., Ercoli, L., . . . Lavretsky, H. (2016). Changes in neural connectivity and memory following a yoga intervention for older adults: A pilot study. *Journal of Alzheimer's Disease, 52*(2), 673–684.

FamilyConnect. (n.d.a). Recreation, fitness, and leisure and the expanded core curriculum. New York, NY: American Foundation for the Blind. Retrieved from http://www.familyconnect.org/info/education/expanded-core-curriculum/recreation-fitness-and-leisure/123

FamilyConnect. (n.d.b). Social interaction skills and the expanded core curriculum. New York, NY: American Foundation for the Blind. Retrieved from http://www.familyconnect.org/info/education/expanded-core-curriculum/social-interaction-skills/123

Fazzi, D. L. (2014). Orientation and mobility. In C. B. Allman & S. Lewis (Eds.), *ECC essentials: Teaching the expanded core curriculum to students with visual impairments* (pp. 248–282). New York, NY: AFB Press.

Foley, H. J., & Matlin, M. W. (2010). *Sensation and perception* (5th ed.). New York, NY: Pearson.

Hatlen, P. (1996). The core curriculum for blind and visually impaired students, including those with additional disabilities. *RE:view, 28*(1), 25–32.

Hubbard, P. (2015). *Addressing the ECC: Independent living skills*. Austin: Texas School for the Blind and Visually Impaired.

Individuals with Disabilities Education Act (IDEA), Pub. L. No. 101-467 (1990).

Individuals with Disabilities Education Act Amendments of 1997, Pub. L. No. 105-17 (1997).

Individuals with Disabilities Education Improvement Act (IDEA), 20 U.S.C. § 1400 (2004).

Lewis, S., & Allman, C. B. (2014). Instruction and assessment: General principles and strategies. In C. B. Allman & S. Lewis (Eds.), *ECC essentials: Teaching the expanded core curriculum to students with visual impairments* (pp. 31–58). New York, NY: AFB Press.

Lewis, S., & Iselin, S. A. (2002). A comparison of the independent living skills of primary students with visual impairments and their sighted peers: A pilot study. *Journal of Visual Impairment & Blindness, 96*(5), 335–344.

Lieberman, L. J., & MacVicar, J. M. (2003). Play and recreational habits of youths who are deaf-blind. *Journal of Visual Impairment & Blindness, 97*(12), 755–766.

Lieberman, L. J., Ponchillia, P. E., & Ponchillia, S. V. (2013). *Physical education and sports for people with visual impairments and deafblindness: Foundations of instruction*. New York, NY: AFB Press.

Maloney, K. (2016). *Yoga for children with visual and multiple impairments: Fun movement activities inspired by yoga*. Austin: Texas School for the Blind and Visually Impaired.

Mask, P. R., & DePountis, V. M. (2018). The impact of transition services in facilitating college degree completion for students with visual impairments: Post-bachelor's degree perspectives. *Journal of Postsecondary Education and Disability, 31*(1).

McComiskey, A. V. (1996). The braille readiness skills grid: A guide to building a foundation for literacy. *Journal of Visual Impairment & Blindness, 90*(3), 190–193.

McDonnall, M. C. (2011). Predictors of employment for youths with visual impairments: Findings from the second National Longitudinal Transition Study. *Journal of Visual Impairment & Blindness, 105*(8), 453–466.

McNear, D., & Farrenkopf, C. (2014). Assistive technology. In C. B. Allman & S. Lewis (Eds.), *ECC essentials: Teaching the expanded core curriculum to students with visual impairments* (pp. 187–247). New York, NY: AFB Press.

Miszko, T. A., Ramsey, V. K., & Blasch, B. B. (2004). Tai chi for people with visual impairments: A pilot study. *Journal of Visual Impairment & Blindness, 98*(1), 5–13.

Mohanty, S., Pradhan, B., & Nagathna, R. (2014). The effect of yoga practice on proprioception in congenitally blind students. *British Journal of Visual Impairment, 32*(2), 124–135.

Pogrund, R., Sewell, D., Anderson, H., Calaci, L., Cowart, M. F., Gonzalez, C. M., . . . Roberson-Smith, B. (2012). *TAPS—Teaching age-appropriate purposeful skills: An orientation and mobility curriculum for students with visual impairments* (3rd ed.). Austin: Texas School for the Blind and Visually Impaired.

Ponchillia, P. E. (1995). AccesSports: A model for adapting mainstream sports activities for individuals with visual impairment. *RE:view, 27*(1), 5–14.

Roberts, A. (2001). Teaching transferable compensatory skills and processes to visually impaired adults [Practice notes]. *Journal of Visual Impairment & Blindness, 95*(4), 234–237.

Sacks, S. Z. (2014). Social interaction. In C. B. Allman & S. Lewis (Eds.), *ECC essentials: Teaching the expanded core curriculum to students with visual impairments* (pp. 324–368). New York, NY: AFB Press.

Sapp, W., & Hatlen, P. (2010). The expanded core curriculum: Where we have been, where we are going, and how we can get there. *Journal of Visual Impairment & Blindness, 104*(6), 338–348.

Texas School for the Blind and Visually Impaired. (2007). *EVALS: Evaluating visually impaired students.* Austin, TX: Author.

Tuttle, D. W., & Tuttle, N. R. (2004). *Self-esteem and adjusting with blindness: The process of responding to life's demands* (3rd ed.). Springfield, IL: Charles C Thomas.

Wolffe, K. E. (2014). Career education. In C. B. Allman & S. Lewis (Eds.), *ECC essentials: Teaching the expanded core curriculum to students with visual impairments* (pp. 411–469). New York, NY: AFB Press.

Wolffe, K. E., & Rosenblum, L. P. (2014). Self-determination. In C. B. Allman & S. Lewis (Eds.), *ECC essentials: Teaching the expanded core curriculum to students with visual impairments* (pp. 470–509). New York, NY: AFB Press.

10

Special Considerations for Students with Visual and Multiple Impairments

Stacy M. Kelly and Tracy Hallak

Questions to Guide Your Reading of This Chapter

➤ Why is orientation and mobility (O&M) for students with visual and multiple impairments important?

➤ What are the special considerations involved in the evaluation process for students with visual and multiple impairments?

➤ What are some effective instructional strategies for teaching O&M to students with visual and multiple impairments, and how does team collaboration facilitate generalization of skills for this population?

➤ How can O&M specialists ensure safety in the environment while encouraging purposeful movement for students with multiple impairments?

Only through freedom and environmental experience is it practically possible for human development to occur. (Montessori, 1949)

Students who have multiple impairments have two or more concomitant (coexisting) disabilities. For students who are visually impaired, these additional disabilities may include autism, developmental delay, hearing impairment or deafness, intellectual disability, orthopedic impairment, other health impairment, specific learning disability, speech or language impairment, attention deficit hyperactivity disorder, or traumatic brain injury. Any combination or any number of these disabilities may be present along with a visual impairment. Concomitant disabilities among students with visual impairments may result from pre- or postnatal trauma, accidents at any point after birth, inherited conditions, or other factors determined by diseases or syndromes with associated eye conditions. Furthermore, students with visual and multiple impairments comprise a large portion of the population of students who are visually impaired. The research shows that approximately 65 percent of school-age students who are visually impaired have visual and multiple impairments (Dote-Kwan, Chen, & Hughes, 2001; Hatton, 2001). Therefore, orientation and mobility (O&M) specialists, school professionals, and caregivers must be prepared to serve these students and meet their particular learning needs.

Philosophies and Assumptions

The unique nature of each child with visual and multiple impairments is another major consideration for O&M specialists working with these students. The effect of additional disabilities on physical, neurological, cognitive, and sensory functioning requires O&M specialists to adapt nearly every aspect of their professional role when working with students who have visual and multiple impairments. For O&M specialists serving students with multiple impairments, these adaptations include alternative approaches to evaluation strategies and tools, instructional strategies, O&M skills, and safety. There are also specific aspects of *positioning* and *handling* that must be considered by O&M specialists when providing services to students with visual and physical impairments (see Sidebar 10.1 for definitions of key terms). Collaboration is an essential component of providing meaningful O&M services to these students. O&M specialists, family members, general educators, and many other special education service providers must work together to support the educational challenges of students with visual and multiple impairments. (See Chapter 11 for more information on collaboration and teams.)

In the past, the field of O&M has not always recognized the value of O&M instruction for students with multiple impairments. If students were not mobile or were not able to travel independently, O&M was often not recognized as a necessary related service for this population. In recent years, the benefits of O&M instruction, albeit not many of the traditional O&M skills and approaches, have been shown to be significant for these students, even those with

the most severe disabilities (Banda, Okungu, Griffin-Shirley, Meeks, & Landa-Vialard, 2015; McGregor, 1998). When O&M is viewed as body and spatial awareness and purposeful movement, and not simply as independent travel in the community, the possibilities of O&M instruction are infinite. All students with visual impairments, no matter what other disabilities they may have, deserve an O&M evaluation by

---

SIDEBAR 10.1

Key Terms

Biobehavioral state Level of alertness and arousal, ranging from deep sleep to hysteria, which varies throughout the day.

Drop-offs Changes in level that may be located in front, behind, or to the side of a traveler, such as stairways, elevator shafts, curbs, or train platforms.

Handling Techniques involved in safely lifting or transferring individuals or their equipment.

Motor plan Ability to develop a mental strategy to carry out a movement or action, including sequencing movements, coordinating body and limbs, attaining sufficient speed, and possessing needed strength.

Muscle tone Degree of muscle tension or resistance, ranging from hypertonia (high muscle tone) to hypotonia (low muscle tone).

Orienting response Learned, automatic reaction to a stimulus.

Positioning Process of placing individuals with physical disabilities in a position that allows them to use their abilities and, and at the same time, be comfortable in a lying, sitting, or standing position.

an O&M specialist and services to meet their individual needs. The spectrum of O&M services for students with multiple impairments needs to be broadened to include creative and innovative strategies to meet the unique needs of these students so they can become as independent as possible. The following case study describes Alyssa, a student with visual and multiple impairments.

Alyssa, a 15-year-old girl who has septo-optic dysplagia and microphthalmia, uses an adaptive mobility device (AMD) as a result of her additional disabilities. Alyssa has no light perception. A global developmental delay, intellectual disability, and speech impairment have been identified as Alyssa's additional disabilities. She does not appear to have an auditory impairment; however, she does not respond to auditory information. Based on this information, Alyssa's Individualized Education Program (IEP) team has determined that Alyssa functions as deafblind and bases her educational programming on this prognosis.

Alyssa uses a tactile system for communication with her special education teachers, therapists, and specialists that includes routines and a variety of calendar boxes. However, her tactile system has evolved over the years. When Alyssa was in middle school, she used a tactile schedule with her O&M specialist and other special education teachers that involved a "finished" box upon completion of tasks and activities. Alyssa is now in high school and uses a BIGmack switch (a large button-shaped activation surface to simplify selection processes) connected to an iPad and a tactile symbols board (board with objects or parts of objects attached to a background) that displays a wide range of activities and choices that guide her experiences throughout the school day, including her O&M

lessons. Alyssa regularly uses an AMD (see Figure 10.1) to improve her purposeful movement and independence in travel. The O&M specialist has implemented several modifications to Alyssa's O&M program to address her functional diagnosis of deafblindness and multiple disabilities. A transdisciplinary team–based approach to O&M instruction provides Alyssa with a set of foundational skills that broadens her awareness of the environment. This awareness has resulted in Alyssa's increased motivation, independence, and safety.

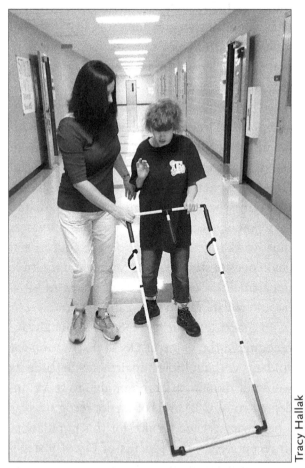

Figure 10.1 Using an adaptive mobility device improves a student's purposeful movement and independence in travel.

Tracy Hallak

Evaluation Strategies

As mentioned in the previous section, many students with visual impairments who receive services from O&M specialists also have additional impairments (Dote-Kwan et al., 2001; Hatton, 2001). The presence of additional disabilities affects the O&M evaluation process. Developmental checklists and assessment tools used with other populations are often not sensitive enough to provide useful information for program planning and intervention with children who have visual and multiple impairments (Blaha, Shafer, Smith, & Moss, 1996; see Chapter 1 for more information on evaluation tools).

The most important component for evaluating students with visual and multiple impairments is observation (see Appendix A for more information on data collection and direct and indirect methods). Each child will have a unique set of developmental skills; therefore, most evaluation tools and checklists will be inadequate. When assessing students, the O&M specialist and teacher of students with visual impairments should observe and note the following: integration of reflexes, orienting response, anticipation, habituation, *muscle tone*, processing time for motor planning, response to additional sensory information, primary sensory preference, the *biobehavioral state* of the child, and the planning category in which the child is functioning (Mercer, n.d.; Nelson, van Dijk, Oster, & McDonnell, 2009; Rosen, 2010a; Smith & Levack, 1997a).

The practitioner should observe the student on multiple occasions in a variety of settings and, whenever possible, at different times of the day. A separate observation form should be completed for each time of the day the student is observed. (See Figure 10.2 for a sample observation form that can be used to evaluate students with multiple impairments.) For example, first observe the student in a classroom in the morning, making note of each item from the observation form as well as classroom routines. Later in the week, observe the student in the middle of the day, in the cafeteria or at recess, repeating this process with a new observation form. Finally, observe the student in the afternoon, perhaps during an after-school program, using a third observation form. These observations may be used to determine the planning category for each student as well as how to collaborate with the transdisciplinary team on programming. The planning category determines the student's current level of functioning and governs the development of appropriate intervention strategies.

The second most important evaluation strategy is to interview family members and caregivers, special education teachers and assistants, and other related service personnel who spend time with the student. Getting their perspectives on the student's needs, strengths, preferences, and reinforcers is important in planning an O&M program for these students. For example, is there a skill these team members would like the student to learn that would reduce or eliminate the need for one of them to do it for the student? What motivates the student? What activities are preferred by the student? What does the student already do well?

Reflexes

Assessment of reflexes is important. The presence and strength of reflexes are important indicators of neurological functioning (Krapp &

FIGURE 10.2

Sample Observation Form

Observation Form for O&M Evaluation

Biobehavioral state (circle observed levels of arousal)

      Deep sleep   Intermediate sleep   Active sleep   Drowsiness   Quiet awake

      Active awake   Fussy awake   Mild agitation   Hysteria

Student planning category (note observed level of interaction and comment on what was observed)

    Biobehavioral category: _____

    Resonance category: _____

    Object category: _____

    Linguistic category: _____

    Functional skills category: _____

Observation of muscle tone (describe)

    Hands: _____

    Legs: _____

    Overall muscle tone: _____

Integration of reflexes observed

    ATNR   Yes_____ No_____

    STNR   Yes_____ No_____

    Other: _____

Observation of processing time necessary for motor planning

    Activity: _____

    Length of time: _____

Demonstrates orienting response to (mark all that apply and describe)

    Name/environmental sounds   Yes_____ No_____ Wait time_____

    Describe: _____

    Familiar toy (visual/auditory)   Yes_____ No_____ Wait time_____

    Describe: _____

    Touch   Yes_____ No_____ Wait time_____

    Describe: _____

FIGURE 10.2

Anticipation demonstrated (of activity, routine, etc.)

      Yes_____ No_____ Wait time_____

      Describe activity/routine: _____

      Observed behavior: _____

Habituation

      Demonstrates ability to filter out undesired distraction   Yes_____ No_____

      Setting: _____

      Length of time sustained: _____

      Inability to continue attending to desired response   Yes_____ No_____

What happens when sound is introduced? (e.g., quieting, localizing, self-stimulation, agitation)

_____

_____

Observed primary sensory preference (circle)

Auditory   Tactile   Visual   Gustatory   Olfactory   Vestibular   Proprioceptive

Additional observations:

Wilson, 2005). Primary reflexes that do not integrate may interfere with a child's ability to develop an appropriate foundation for stability and mobility as well as higher cortical functioning. Intervention is the key to integrating primitive reflexes and can be accomplished by creating activities that are "out of the pattern" (Rosen, 2010a). To decrease reflexive patterns that should no longer be present, activities should be designed that allow the child to move out of that pattern. For example, to decrease the asymmetrical tonic neck reflex (ATNR) that has not integrated, it might be helpful to create an activity that requires the child to bring both hands to midline or reach across the midline. Careful observation of the quality of movements, with an emphasis on determining whether primitive reflexes interfere with voluntary movement, will help establish the need for therapeutic intervention. If there are any concerns, the child should be referred for an evaluation by a physical therapist. (See Chapter 3 for an overview of reflexes and their relationship to O&M.)

Orienting Response

An *orienting response* is an automatic response to a stimulus, such as hearing one's name in a crowd and turning toward the source. The orienting response prepares the nervous system for further learning. Once the student's attention has been gained, the nervous system is prepared to receive additional input (Silverrain, 1989). When evaluating the student, observe to see if the student responds to his or her name, a familiar voice, or a familiar toy. It is important to evaluate what or who the student orients toward and how that manifests itself (Nelson et al., 2009). Some students may become quiet while others may get excited and move in response to the stimuli. This orientation may look different for each learner.

Habituation

Habituation can be thought of in two different ways. The first way is that the student no longer responds to previous sensory stimuli. For example, the student may orient to a musical toy, attend to it during the first and second times it is presented, but no longer respond or attend to it when presented again. The ability to maintain attention to a stimulus may be very limited for a student who is visually and multiply impaired.

The second way is habituation of the orienting response, which may occur when the stimulus is of no consequence or is meaningless to the student, such as background noise. Students with visual and multiple impairments may be unable to habituate to nonessential auditory stimuli, resulting in sensory overload. For example, a student may be unable to disregard the sound of the other children in the room and attend to a desired activity, which can result in overstimulation, causing the student to "shut down." When evaluating a student with multiple impairments, it is important to do so in a quiet, controlled environment by systematically introducing stimuli. This strategy will allow the evaluators to observe what the student attends and habituates to, and what causes overstimulation.

Anticipation

According to van Dijk, orientation is essential for learning (Nelson et al., 2009). The orienting response can lead to anticipation of activities. For example, a child hears her mother's voice and quiets in response in order to gather information. If the mother always comes to the child and picks her up, the child begins to anticipate this activity. Anticipation is an indication of memory and may provide associations between events (Nelson et al., 2009). Vision is typically the system through which preparation for changes occurs. Without vision, anticipation may be initiated through a routine, a predictable chain of related events that structure activities (Smith & Levack, 1997a). Anticipatory stimuli can be a sound, a touch, movement to a specific location or into a specific position, or the presence of a specific individual.

Interviewing the parent or caregiver and other service providers offers valuable information about what elicits a response from the child. Through the interview process, and during observations, the evaluator can identify what routines, if any, have been established and in what way the child with visual and multiple impairments demonstrates anticipation of each routine. It may be necessary to explain to parents that a routine is a daily event, such as bath time, mealtime, or bedtime (Smith & Levack, 1997a).

Sensory Preferences

All children, regardless of their developmental level, use sensory information to learn about their bodies, their environment, and spatial and environmental concepts (Rosen, 2010a). Sensory input and movement are linked and form the foundation for the gross and fine motor skills necessary for travel (Rosen, 2010a). Identifying the sensory preferences of children with visual and multiple impairments is important (see Appendix A for information on preference assessments). The inclination to move is based on how well sensory information is received and interpreted by the brain. There are seven types of sensory input to the brain: visual, tactile, vestibular, proprioceptive, auditory, olfactory, and gustatory (Rosen, 2010a; see Chapters 3 and 5 for information on sensory systems).

During the evaluation, it is important to observe if the student with multiple impairments responds to a variety of visual, auditory, or tactile stimuli. Nelson et al. (2009) refer to these as learning channels. The evaluator can determine if the student prefers one sense more than another and if he or she can attend to more than one sense at a time. Too much sensory information may cause the student to withdraw, shut down, or become fussy.

Some students with visual impairments respond best to visual stimuli. In the case of cortical or cerebral visual impairment (CVI), some students often have very specific visual preferences. Often, a student with CVI may prefer a color such as red or yellow and may respond to familiar monochromatic items. Movement of the visual target is also a key component of visual stimuli for students with CVI. (See Chapter 4 for more information on CVI.)

Audition may be the primary learning medium for some children. These children may quiet when attending to a particular sound, such as their mother's voice, or may turn in the direction of a familiar noise. Other children may respond to a familiar sound by becoming active with anticipation after hearing the sound. Some children who have CVI may respond specifically to familiar voices or musical stimuli.

Some students with visual and multiple impairments may respond best to touch. There are six types of sensory information provided by touch: deep touch, light touch, vibration, pain, temperature, and two-point touch, which is the ability to identify the number of points of contact of an object (Rosen, 2010a). The types of touch a student with visual and multiple impairments may respond best to are deep touch, light touch, vibration, and temperature. Deep touch can be very calming. Light touch can include the feel of different textures. Some students with visual and multiple impairments prefer deep pressure but will resist a light touch. Other students will attend to vibrating toys or demonstrate a tactile sensitivity toward fuzzy objects. Having a working knowledge of the sensory preferences of the learner will facilitate instructional programming and will help assess the learner's responsiveness during activities.

Muscle Tone and Motor Planning

Alexander, Boehme, and Cupps (1993) suggested muscle tone can be an indicator of motoric readiness for movement. While observing students with visual and multiple impairments, it is important to pay close attention to overall muscle tone, especially of the hands and legs. (See Chapter 3 for information on muscle tone.) Motoric influences include hypertonia (high muscle tone), hypotonia (low muscle tone), limited proprioceptive awareness, poor integration of primitive reflexes, and poor integration of mature reactions (Rosen, 2010b). Any student with a condition that has affected the brain, such as stroke, cerebral palsy, or hydrocephaly, may exhibit hypertonia or hypotonia. Hypertonia or hypotonia may be an indicator of an immature central nervous system or permanent motoric impairment. Problems with muscle tone will affect the ability of students with visual and multiple impairments to *motor plan* and may have implications for posture, gait patterns, balance, and using a long cane or AMD (Sapp, 2004). The student's voluntary movements in a variety of positions should be systematically observed. Some positions allow for more freedom and ease of movement while other positions may be more restrictive for a particular student. Some positions are more stimulating and allow the student to attend more fully (Blaha et al., 1996).

When working with students who have hypertonia, quick movements or sounds may activate a startle reflex that interferes with motor planning. Students with hypertonia may have decreased stamina and poor proprioception. Students with hypotonia may lack a stable postural foundation, resulting in a head lag or inefficient gait.

Students with congenital blindness often have difficulties with motor planning. There are several factors that may contribute to this difficulty: visual awareness, sensory integration deficits, and additional impairments. It is important to provide many opportunities for self-initiated movement throughout the day and allow adequate wait time for the child to

motor plan. It is always critical to wait, and then wait some more, when observing or instructing this population of students.

Biobehavioral State

Individuals function at a variety of biobehavioral states throughout the day. Biobehavioral categories include deep sleep, intermediate sleep, active sleep, drowsiness, quiet awake, active awake, fussy awake, mild agitation, and hysteria (Smith & Levack, 1997b). The ability to manage the biobehavioral state is often an issue for students with multiple impairments. Some students with multiple impairments are unable to maintain an alert state for an extended period of time. Other students with multiple impairments may become fussy or hysterical when offered too many sensory stimuli. These responses may result from students with multiple disabilities not exhibiting the typical developmental state and having difficulty achieving and maintaining alert states. Determining the time of day when students with multiple impairments are most likely to be in a quiet awake or active awake state helps with program planning and intervention. It is also important to determine the length of time students with visual and multiple impairments are able to maintain this level of alertness.

Planning Categories

While observing students with visual and multiple impairments throughout the day in a variety of environments, the O&M specialist and teacher of students with visual impairments should assess not only the biobehavioral state of the student but also the planning category. A planning category is determined based on observations and evaluation of the student. Once the student's present level of performance is determined, the teacher of students with visual impairments or O&M specialist will use that information to plan a program to address the student's specific needs. Mercer (n.d.) describes seven planning categories: biobehavioral, resonance, object, linguistic, functional skills, semi-independent, and independent. For the purposes of this chapter, the first five categories will be discussed since students in the semi-independent and independent categories typically function at a higher level and will benefit from more complex instructional strategies than the ones provided here.

Biobehavioral Category

Some students with visual and multiple impairments remain at the biobehavioral level, which is the most basic of planning categories. Students functioning at this level frequently demonstrate minimal awareness of their surroundings. They typically have a low response to stimuli or are overstimulated very easily. This state may result in a fussy or hysterical response or in the student going to sleep. The student is unable to modulate his or her physiological state for extended periods of time. Activities and routines should be created that will keep the student engaged and alert for increasing amounts of time. Careful consideration should be given to the environment and position of the student so that the student attends to only one stimulus at a time. Students often experience sensory overload when there are too many demands on the central nervous system. Determining the preferences of the student will help in planning activities that are motivating and engaging. An adequate amount of wait time should be provided for the student to respond.

Resonance Category

Students with visual and multiple impairments at the resonance level are just beginning to realize there is a world around them. At this level, movement and physical proximity to the student are needed to engage the student in coactive routines. While the student is unable to attend to a person or activity across the room, he or she may be engaged in physical contact in close proximity to others. Students at this level cannot communicate with space between themselves and the person providing intervention. When left alone, students with visual and multiple impairments at the resonance level may retreat into self-stimulatory behaviors. Routines and activities for this student should include hand-under-hand activities that allow the student to stay engaged and provide opportunities for purposeful movement, choice making, and communication. Maintaining a controlled environment will minimize sensory overload.

Object Category

Students with visual and multiple impairments functioning at the object level demonstrate emerging symbolic communication. They are beginning to understand that objects represent real events or activities. Objects used for communication are typically real representations of the activity, but they can be modified into tactile representations of the activity or routine. Using object symbols, tactile symbols, and calendar systems are good ways to communicate with students at this stage (Blaha, 2001). Students with visual and multiple impairments at the object level often demonstrate more mature anticipatory responses and emerging social interactions and are more tolerant of novel stimuli. Activities and routines for these

Tracy Hallak

Figure 10.3 Using a switch and tablet aids in promoting choice-making activities for students at the object level.

students should include choice making (see Figure 10.3) and opportunities for communication and participation.

Linguistic Category

Students with visual and multiple impairments functioning at the linguistic level typically exhibit a sophisticated linguistic system which may include verbal or sign language, or augmentative communication. These students typically demonstrate emerging problem-solving skills and have a more comprehensive understanding of the relationships between concepts. Routines and activities for these students should provide opportunities for concept development, problem solving, and communication.

Functional Skills Category

Students with visual and multiple impairments at the functional skills level may need some assistance in independent living skills and may have difficulty establishing a social circle, but are more likely to have highly developed social-interaction patterns. They typically have a limited number of recreation and leisure interests. Older students at this level may be able to read at the second- or third-grade level, perform simple arithmetic, and have more mature organizational concepts, such as time (weeks, months, years).

Instructional Strategies

Transdisciplinary Teams

Traditional O&M strategies and techniques typically have little success with students who have visual and multiple impairments (Perla & Ducret, n.d.). The transdisciplinary service delivery model is especially important when working with this population of students (Friend & Cook, 2010). According to Smith (1998), the components of transdisciplinary teaming include collaborative evaluation and IEP development, natural and frequent instruction, role release, and documentation. Collaborative planning and sharing of data amongst team members helps team members stay connected and focuses attention on strategies that are working and those that are not. This team approach facilitates consistent intervention and program planning across all domains and increases the chances of generalization, or use of skills in multiple settings. (See Chapter 11 for more on collaboration and transdisciplinary teaming.)

It is essential that O&M specialists, teachers of students with visual impairments, and other professionals collaborate on the evaluation process and instructional strategies to promote effective individualized planning. Once the strategic planning for a student with visual and multiple impairments has been established, the transdisciplinary team should design a program that meets the individual needs of that student.

Communication

According to Siegel-Causey and Ernst (1989), the service provider should strive to develop nurturance, enhance sensitivity, increase opportunities, sequence experiences, and utilize movement. These strategies are especially important when working with a student who is deafblind or multiply impaired because they lead to improved communication and instruction. Nurturance can be provided through positive interactions, support, and focus on the student's interests. These strategies result in an increased bond between student and teacher. Sensitivity can be enhanced by responding to the student's readiness to interact, his or her level of communication (see Instructional Programming later in this chapter), and the student's biobehavioral state. Increasing opportunities can be accomplished by offering choices, creating a need for requests, and giving the student opportunities to interact by providing wait time. Sequencing experiences and routines requires consistency and repetition, which are essential to increasing the student's anticipation and participation in a given activity. It is important to utilize movement by responding to movement as a behavior of communication. Movement as a form of communication should be used, and movements

that match the student's immediate ability should be selected.

Active Learning and Defined Spaces

Much of the learning in O&M for students with visual and multiple impairments occurs through practice of activities that have little resemblance to traditional O&M (Skellenger & Sapp, 2010). It is important to work toward the development of sequential sensorimotor skills whenever possible. Motor activities can be provided for students performing at all developmental levels in a variety of environments. Some instructional strategies include defined spaces, routines, and calendars. LilliWorks (n.d.) suggests that it is up to the parent, therapist, or educator to keep finding the right situation or environment to interest and engage a student.

It is through movement that learning takes place, and one of the basic principles of active learning is that everyone can learn. Nielsen (1992) coined the terms "Little Room" and "active learning" to promote these concepts. A Little Room is a structure with three walls and a Plexiglass ceiling laid over a child. Objects are suspended from the structure by pieces of elastic to provide maximum opportunity for contact when the child moves. This type of defined space is designed to have a variety of objects with different sounds, textures, and colors (when appropriate) that the child can enjoy. One of the purposes of the Little Room is to amplify the sounds made when the child contacts the objects (Smith, n.d.a). The objects should be placed in the same location, in proximity to the child, so that any movement will result in contact with a desired object. Over time, the child will begin to use self-initiated purposeful movement to explore a desired object. O&M specialists must understand the additional disabilities of their students and take positioning and equipment into consideration when designing a defined space. For example, defined spaces designed for students with CVI should limit the number of objects, emphasize the preferred color of the student, and minimize novelty.

While similar to a Little Room, defined spaces can be created in a variety of naturally occurring environments, can vary in design, and can be as simple as a child's crib, pack-n-play, or blanket. The key factor is that the sides or edges of the area are defined and predictable during each encounter. The purpose of a Little Room or defined space is to provide opportunities for orientation, sensory input, and motor planning.

Providing a defined space in which students with significant multiple impairments have opportunities to explore and control their motor abilities helps develop purposeful movement, anticipation, and an understanding of space. As students with visual and multiple impairments begin to roll, crawl, or creep, the space can be expanded to allow for further exploration. Defined spaces can be designed for a student with multiple disabilities in a wheelchair by providing a large enough area to fit the wheelchair, and in which the student can be positioned in such a way that objects are within reach on each side and from above (see Figure 9.2 in Chapter 9). Understanding learner preference is an important aspect of creating defined spaces.

Students with visual and multiple impairments should never be left alone in a defined space or Little Room. However, it is also important to avoid interfering with students by talking or adding additional stimuli during their exploration time. Motor planning and processing can be easily disrupted if students are disturbed during this time. Students and their movements should be observed, noting their likes and dislikes. When making changes, it is best to modify one object or item at a time to minimize novelty and encourage exploration.

Calendars and Routines

A calendar box or board is a type of communication system that organizes a child's day and supports the development and use of communication. A long box with an open side and top, it is divided into sections to represent regular events in the child's routine. An object is placed in each section to represent a specific event, and the child learns to anticipate the sequence of events by looking at or touching the next item in the box (Erin, 2017). Calendar systems may be created using real objects, tactile symbols, pictures, print, or braille (see Figure 10.4). Calendars assist the child in developing a sense of time (e.g., morning versus afternoon) and sequence (e.g., past, present, future; first, second, third). Children who are not ready for a daily calendar can begin with routines.

Calendars can be created for a routine, a day, a week, or even a month, depending on the individual needs of the student with multiple impairments. Calendars help students understand time, develop a system for communication, and provide emotional support (Blaha, 2001). For many learners, the calendar will use concrete objects that represent the past, present, and future. A calendar helps build security for students by extending the perspective and awareness of the learner to include events. Calendars enable students to anticipate what is coming next, and in doing so, help minimize fears and

Tracy Hallak

Figure 10.4 Calendar boxes organize a child's day by using objects and symbols to represent events in the child's routine.

anxiety about upcoming events. Calendars also allow students with visual and multiple impairments to have some control over their day when offered choices of when to do activities.

Routines are themselves a teaching tool. They are activities that take place during the day or week that are meaningful to the child. Activity routines provide consistency from one setting to the next and may elicit a higher participation level from the child within the activity. Routines can be incorporated into naturally occurring environments at home and at school. It is important to work closely with the family and other service providers and instructors to ensure the activity is implemented the same way each time.

Routines provided within natural contexts facilitate learning by teaching specific skills with consistency and repetition (Smith, n.d.b). Routines provide predictability, consistency, anticipation, and practice. When learners with visual and multiple impairments or students who are deafblind are able to anticipate what is coming next, this predictability can maximize their participation in the routine and provide opportunities for communication and purposeful movement. Choice making increases self-determination and can be incorporated into any routine. Allowing students with multiple impairments to choose the order of activities in the routines encourages motivation and participation. When planning routines, O&M specialists should incorporate activities that help develop muscle tone, use sensory information, and support concept development.

Routines should always have a clear beginning and end. A "finished box" is any container that a child can consistently use into which the child can place the symbol or object representing a completed activity (see Figure 10.5). This step provides closure for the child and assists with transition to the next activity. Implementing a finished box as an instructional strategy can facilitate important aspects of a routine, such as structure, predictability, and control.

Moss and Shafer (2006) state that during daily routines such as bathing, diapering, and feeding, the child begins to establish a memory and can anticipate the steps in the routine. Working closely with caregivers in the home will help them to understand the value of consistency and how the child develops concepts and generalizes those concepts to new environments. Routines at school may be developed around classroom activities or specific academic goals or O&M lessons. A well-designed routine

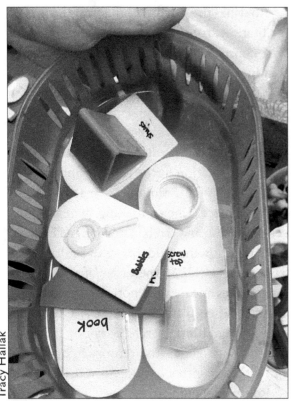

Tracy Hallak

Figure 10.5 Placing symbols or objects that represent a completed activity into a finished box provides closure for the child and assists with transition to the next activity.

will offer the teacher a way to begin an activity and meet the needs of the individual student by providing modifications to the activity.

Adjusting the level of difficulty of a routine is easy once a routine is established. It is important not to utilize the exact same routine indefinitely once a student has mastered it so that ongoing growth can occur. After the routine is mastered, it can be modified by adding novelty. The novelty may be a change in the time of day, the environment in which the routine is practiced, or the person who is facilitating the routine. One component of the routine can be omitted or changed as well. Communication within routines can be supported by utilizing

time delays, offering choices, and creating a need for requests. Routines also make student progress easier to document. It is important to review a routine on a regular basis to see if the student is making progress toward the desired goal. Careful data collection is essential to demonstrate student progress, even if in small increments (e.g., the need for fewer prompts to perform a skill). Calendars and routines may be used with children at every developmental level.

Prompting

Prompts are cues that encourage a student to initiate or complete a task (Fazzi & Naimy, 2010). For students who need prompting, a hierarchy of prompts, ranging from nonphysical to physical, and least to most intrusive, can be used (Fazzi & Naimy, 2010; Rosen & Crawford, 2010; Sacks, 2016). The prompts that do not involve physical contact from the instructor include natural prompts, gestures, indirect verbal prompts, and direct verbal prompts. The prompt that requires the least assistance is something that occurs naturally in the environment and does not involve input from the instructor. An example might be the school bell ringing to indicate that it is time to go to lunch. A gesture can be used with students who have low vision and includes actions such as pointing to the bathroom door as a reminder to students that it is coming up on the right. An indirect verbal prompt is a suggestion by the instructor. An example may be the instructor saying, "It is time for lunch." This prompts the student to get the cane and go to the door. A direct verbal prompt occurs in the form of a command. For example, the instructor might say, "Please get your cane and meet me at the door."

In addition to nonphysical prompts, there are prompts that involve varying degrees of physical contact. They include object prompts, modeling, light physical prompts, and full physical prompts. An object prompt may include handing the student his or her cane or AMD to indicate that it is time to start an O&M lesson. Modeling is an instructional method that involves showing a student the desired behavior, such as demonstrating upper- and lower-body protective techniques for the student to see or touch. Modeling the desired behavior by using more physical contact requires less independence on the part of the student (Fazzi & Naimy, 2010). A light physical prompt, such as a tap on the shoulder to indicate the direction to turn or as a reminder to stop, is used to support instruction. Physically assisting and guiding the student through a desired motor task is the most invasive type of prompt. It is important to always ask permission before physically contacting a student. If the student has limited or no language abilities, the instructor should tell the student that he or she will need to physically contact the student to assist in performing a task.

It is best to use hand-under-hand rather than hand-over-hand prompting when physical guidance is needed, as this strategy is more respectful to the learner. Hand-under-hand guidance involves the instructor placing the child's hand on top of the instructor's own, allowing the child to feel the motion with gentle guidance, while hand-over-hand guidance involves the instructor placing the child's hand under the instructor's hand to assist the child in completing a task. Whenever possible, the instructor should work from behind the child so that the instructor's hands and the child's hands move in the same direction. The instructor should verbally describe what is happening throughout the activity. Children who are reluctant to participate in an activity often have more freedom and feel more secure when given the opportunity to participate using hand-under-hand guidance.

Students with additional disabilities may benefit from more frequent prompting to ensure that skills are learned correctly (Fazzi & Petersmeyer, 2001). A task analysis of the routine or skill should be completed to determine when prompts are needed to assist the student. It is a good idea to begin with the least invasive prompt so the student does not become dependent on the use of prompts. As the student learns the skill or routine, prompts should be faded—gradually reduced until eventually eliminated—to reduce the student's reliance on prompts, increase confidence in using natural cues, and encourage independence. Prompts should be decreased slowly and systematically to reduce errors. If errors occur, the instructor should return to the previous level of prompting and start the process again.

Instructional Programming

When developing an instructional program, it is important to keep the whole child in mind, not just the visual impairment (Skellenger & Sapp, 2010). Many children will demonstrate attributes across more than one planning category (see Evaluation Strategies earlier in this chapter), and additional disabilities may limit potential for some skills. Multiple disabilities have a bigger impact and present more challenges than the addition of each disability alone, and each combination of disabilities presents a unique challenge (Sauerburger, Siffermann, & Rosen, 2006). Knowing this information, one of the roles of O&M specialists and teachers of students with visual impairments is to provide programming and experiential opportunities that facilitate increased concept development and maximum participation while allowing students with visual and multiple impairments to function as independently as possible in their environment.

Routines, repetition, and consistency are critical to program planning. Routines allow students with visual and multiple impairments to anticipate the next step and participate in an activity, and they promote independence and higher-level motor-planning skills. In addition, routines can become a type of dialogue and topic of conversation between students with multiple impairments and their instructors. Choice making and participation in an activity allow students to communicate while also encouraging purposeful movement.

Instructional Strategies for Learners at the Biobehavioral Level

The learning objective for children at this level is to help them maintain a quiet awake or active awake biobehavioral state so that they may participate in activities that are designed as interventions for longer periods of time (Smith & Levack, 1997a). One of the primary roles of the O&M specialist will be to collaborate with the educational team on motor planning and providing multiple opportunities for purposeful movement throughout the day. Defined spaces provide opportunities for children with visual and multiple impairments to begin to experience and gain an understanding of space and orientation. One intervention strategy can be the use of a defined space designed to meet an individual learner's preferences and motor abil-

ities. Allowing significant wait time for learners with visual and multiple impairments to motor plan is critical, especially in a new environment or in one that incorporates novel items. Some professionals working with this population may be inclined to hurry the learner who needs additional processing time to meet an objective or complete a task, but providing enough wait time is essential. Introducing simple routines will allow children with multiple impairments to anticipate what is going to happen and will help them regulate their biobehavioral state. This anticipation will, in turn, increase the window of time for intervention strategies.

Instructional Strategies for Learners at the Resonance Level

The goal for students functioning at this level is to realize that there is a world beyond them. When working with students at this level, it is important to be in close physical proximity to the students, or even in physical contact with them (Mercer, n.d.). When presenting a familiar or favorite toy, the toy should be positioned close to the student and in the most desirable visual field if the student has some functional vision. It may be necessary to move the toy or object to draw the student's visual attention. Encouraging orientation and reach helps students begin to understand space and learn the concept of a world beyond themselves.

Movement is also a key intervention strategy since body awareness is fundamental to O&M instruction. Simple routines that include close contact can be very effective, as can a song such as "Itsy, Bitsy Spider." These strategies can involve hand motions and repetitions, or holding the child and rocking, then stopping and waiting for the child to move or make a verbalization to indicate the desire for more. Providing the child with opportunities for choice making, participation, communication, and purposeful movement leads to awareness of the child's surroundings and the ability to affect his or her environment. Once a routine is mastered, a new routine can be introduced.

Instructional Strategies for Learners at the Object Level

Developing an organizational system should be a goal when program planning for students functioning at the object level. Time concepts, sequencing events, and spatial and environmental concepts should all be components of O&M instruction. Students with visual and multiple impairments that are just beginning to understand objects as representations of activities would benefit from an activity calendar that demonstrates each step in a routine, such as a grooming or eating routine. An activity calendar is similar in design to a daily calendar and has objects specific to a routine organized from left to right in sequential order. The planning category will help determine if real objects, tactile symbols, pictures, or braille are appropriate for sequencing the routine.

Students with visual and multiple impairments may also benefit from an object calendar that links events throughout the day, such as circle time, center time, O&M time, speech time, and lunchtime. An object calendar is a calendar box that uses real objects or parts of objects essential to the activity or event (e.g., a spoon to represent lunchtime). Routes to the locations of these activities can be embedded into the object calendar. Tactile symbols may also be used to represent instructors, such as the teacher of students with visual impairments or O&M specialist, so that students begin to associate the time of day or the day of the week with

their instructor. As students progress in their ability to form time and environmental concepts, the organizational system should also evolve. Objects should begin to represent larger chunks of time (day or week) and more complicated environmental concepts such as home, bus, or store (Blaha, 2001).

Instructional Strategies for Learners at the Linguistic Level

When program planning for this type of learner, teachers of students with visual impairments and O&M specialists should incorporate "who, what, when, where, and why" types of questions into their instruction. O&M specialists may ask their students to talk about the landmarks they will encounter on a route or the clothing that they need to wear for an outdoor lesson. Teachers of students with visual impairments can support their students in a similar manner by incorporating problem-solving skills into the curriculum. When this strategy is used, higher-level thinking skills evolve into problem solving for social situations, self-determination, and independent living skills, and can be incorporated into the educational program of students with visual and multiple impairments. It is important that other team members at school and at home also incorporate these skills into the student's daily routines to promote generalization.

Instructional Strategies for Learners at the Functional Skills Level

Teachers of students with visual impairments and O&M specialists often work closely together in planning instruction in the expanded core curriculum for students who have visual and multiple impairments. Independent living skills, self-advocacy, job experiences, and using public transportation are just a few of the areas that need to be addressed to assist these students in attaining maximum independence. Calendars and routines, along with tactile symbols and introduction to braille or print literacy, may be very useful for students who are functioning within this category. In addition, students can learn to use verbal skills, if they have them, to increase their independence by interacting with or gaining assistance from others at school and in the community. Exposure to objects and tactile symbols labeled in braille or print is one possible way to foster foundational literacy skills and to transition to a higher level of literacy for this population.

Instructional Strategies for Learners Who Are Deafblind

Loss of both vision and hearing has a significant impact on concept development and environmental awareness. It can also isolate students who are deafblind from those around them. Most learning for students identified as deafblind is through touch (Lolli, Sauerburger, & Bourquin, 2010). Deafblindness may occur as a result of syndromes such as Usher, Alstrom, or CHARGE, which often have additional associated conditions. Deafblindness can also be the result of prenatal or congenital complications such as rubella, cytomegalovirus, microcephaly, or maternal drug use. Postnatal events such as severe head injury, asphyxia, meningitis, or other infections can also result in deafblindness, as can complications from prematurity (National Center on Deaf-Blindness, n.d.). When program planning, it is important to take these other contributing factors into

consideration. Being deafblind is more complex than adding blindness and deafness together. The combined loss of two sensory channels creates instructional challenges for teachers who work with these students.

Communication and learning styles need to be taken into account when working with students who are deafblind. Some students may use gestures, communication devices, object or tactile signs, or sign language to communicate. Communication with a student who is deafblind also involves increased physical contact. Calendars and routines are excellent instructional strategies to incorporate when working with a student who is deafblind or who has intellectual delays. Calendar systems help improve communication and understanding of time concepts and provide emotional support to the student (Blaha, 2001). Object and tactile symbols may be created for use with or without the calendar. The symbols selected should be ones the student responds to consistently. The instructor should also consider the size of the symbol, its contrast, and its distance from the student, and whether the student is accessing the symbol tactilely or visually.

Modifications of O&M skills and techniques may be necessary for students who have combined vision and hearing loss. Most students who are identified as deafblind do not have total hearing and vision loss. Many students use functional vision, hearing, or both for travel purposes. Students should be taught to scan the environment using remaining vision and hearing whenever possible. Longer canes can provide additional feedback, preview, and reaction time. If there is insufficient information to determine if travel is safe, the student should get assistance or use an alternate route. Obtaining assistance and using alternate routes are also strategies to use with students who have total hearing and vision loss and thus do not have access to auditory and visual information. When traveling in public, students may use communication cards or booklets to solicit assistance when needed (Lolli et al., 2010). Communication cards are laminated cards with phrases that students can use to solicit aid from the public. These cards can say, "I am deaf and blind. Tap my hand if you can help me. I need to cross Main Street heading west" (Pogrund et al., 2012). If the student is traveling with a guide, it may be necessary to modify the grasp used for guide technique for communication purposes (Lolli et al., 2010).

Teachers of students with visual impairments and O&M specialists may also need to work closely with an intervener or interpreter (Texas Deaf-Blind Outreach, 2000). An intervener is trained in communication and support strategies specifically designed for students who are deafblind. Interveners often accompany a student who is deafblind on an O&M lesson to provide communication support. Specific O&M terminology may need to be provided to the interpreter or intervener in advance so that he or she will be familiar with the terms and will be able to communicate them clearly to the student. The teacher or O&M specialist should provide clear instructions to the interpreter or intervener.

Safety

Safety is at the forefront of the role of the O&M specialist in the lives of students with multiple impairments. The student with visual and multiple impairments needs to be safe, and school personnel need to protect themselves from accidents when interacting with the student. The safety measures described in the following sections are intended for the protection of the student as well as the protection of those providing the student with instruction or support throughout the school day.

Basic O&M Safety

There are several basic O&M techniques that should be implemented by the educational team to support students with visual and multiple impairments. It is imperative that the student with multiple impairments always use the railing when ascending or descending stairs. Proper instructor positioning is important to keep both the student and the instructor safe when ascending or descending stairs, and in all O&M techniques. Upper- and lower-body protective techniques should be demonstrated and taught to students and the educational teams that support them because they provide students with a way to keep themselves safe when traveling. A lot of hazardous clutter may not be easily detected by a mobility device, so the use of upper- and lower-body protective techniques helps locate obstacles that are not positioned in the path of a mobility device. For example, water fountains and fire extinguishers extend out from the wall and into the hallways of many school buildings. These items are positioned at such a height that it would create a safety concern if a student were to accidentally make contact or bump into them. Other basic O&M techniques, such as how to locate a dropped object safely using a systematic search pattern, apply to students with visual and multiple impairments as well. O&M specialists provide students with specialized training in these basic O&M techniques and that training is personalized to the abilities of students with visual and multiple impairments. (See Chapter 6 for more on basic O&M skills and adaptations.)

Canes and Adaptive Mobility Devices

For students with visual and multiple impairments that use mobility devices such as canes or AMDs, the cane or AMD supports safe travel. (See Chapter 7 for more on canes and AMDs.) Therefore, the cane or AMD should be with the learner at all times and not left behind at home or stored away in a locker or on a hook in the classroom. When using mobility devices, the cane tip or AMD should always maintain contact with the ground. If the cane is held in the air or misused, it becomes a safety concern for everyone around the student. The cane or AMD should be held out in front of the student. If the mobility device is held off to the side, it cannot be used to detect obstacles or drop-offs in the pathway of the learner, and it may cause other people to unexpectedly trip over it (Sapp, 2004). Rather than taking the cane or AMD away from the student who may be misusing it, all team members should work on a behavior plan to teach proper use of the mobility tool so the student can continue to improve his or her independence.

Route Travel

If a student will be traveling a route alone during the school day using rote memory, the route should contain adequate landmarks and the student should understand how to reverse the route. Additionally, the student should be taught skills to solicit assistance, if needed. Even if a student should not be traveling alone, it is still important to expose the student to environmental concepts and landmarks in all areas of travel in case there is a time when, for some unexpected reason, the student may end up on his or her own. Modifications to the length of the cane or AMD may be necessary based on the ability of the learner to process tactile information.

Operating a Wheelchair

There are many safety issues to consider when operating wheelchairs or motorized chairs. One of the first issues is the level of supervision. The level of supervision should be considered, clearly communicated to the student, and followed at all times. The level of supervision can range from an adult's hands on the chair at all times, to the adult observing a student traveling and making decisions with support, to the student traveling in a group with minimal assistance from the adult, and finally to the student traveling independently. Other safety issues include avoiding hazardous *drop-offs* such as stairways, elevator shafts, curbs, and train platforms. Falling down the stairs in a motorized chair can be a life-threatening event. The ability to detect drop-offs, make timely decisions, and effectively manage the wheelchair or motorized chair are all factors that need to be taken into consideration.

When working with students with visual impairments who use wheelchairs, it is important to collaborate with a physical therapist. The O&M specialist will need to provide the physical therapist with information about the student's best visual field. The physical therapist will then be able to adjust the wheelchair, including the headrest, height, and angle, to accommodate the student's best visual field. If a student has a slower response time due to motor-planning issues, it is important to work with the physical therapist to adjust the speed of the wheelchair, if it is a power chair, to allow the student more time to respond.

Students with visual impairments who use wheelchairs should never operate a wheelchair in reverse. Drop-offs such as stairways, elevator shafts, or train platforms cannot be detected when operating a wheelchair in reverse. For example, if a student boards an elevator by reversing the wheelchair into the elevator, there is no way for the student to know for certain that an elevator car is present and not just an open elevator shaft. The same serious risk applies to entering and exiting trains when going in reverse. If the train is not present, the drop-off to the train tracks is especially dangerous. The student can use other senses to inform these situations (e.g., hearing dings on an elevator to indicate it has arrived or hearing other people on the platform entering or exiting a train), but these are circumstantial forms of evidence as opposed to the ability to definitively detect moving objects and know for certain they are there. Rather than backing into an elevator or onto public transportation, a student with visual impairments using a wheelchair should enter going forward to better enable the student to confirm the presence of the platform he or she is boarding. Going forward on the platform provides the student the opportunity to physically detect the platform, using either functional vision or a cane. Once the student boards the platform, the student can turn him- or herself around so the student is once again facing forward in preparation for exiting. In these examples, it may seem easier or more convenient for the student to operate the wheelchair in reverse. However, it is a life-threatening decision to operate a wheelchair going backwards. The safety issues far outweigh the convenience. Students with visual impairments who use wheelchairs should only operate their wheelchairs going forward, never in reverse.

Another equally dangerous situation for a wheelchair user is a drop-off to the side of the chair. A 2-inch drop can cause a wheelchair to tip over. If the wheelchair user is also using a cane, it may be necessary to provide a longer cane so the learner can preview an area wider than the chair and have adequate response time to stop. Curb feelers may be used as a modification to wheelchairs to provide the learner with feedback about when the wheelchair is in contact with a wall and about the learner's distance from the wall (Rosen & Crawford, 2010). It is important to note, however, that curb feelers will not provide the learner with information about the actual distance between the wheelchair and the wall because curb feelers can be placed on different parts of the wheelchair and at different angles (Rosen & Crawford, 2010).

In addition, there are different ways that guide technique can be modified in a functional manner for people with visual impairments who use wheelchairs. For example, the guide can operate the wheelchair with input from the wheelchair user while utilizing positions similar to guide technique. Another modification is for the guide to walk next to the wheelchair while the person using the wheelchair holds on to the top of the guide's forearm. This technique requires the person who is visually impaired and using a wheelchair to have adequate arm strength and flexibility to hold onto the guide. Alternatively, if the person using the wheelchair has sufficient vision and reaction time, the wheelchair user can follow the guide. In this instance, the wheelchair user operates the wheelchair without touching the guide. It is important for the guide to remember that each movement he or she makes is a cue for the person using the wheelchair. Thus, the guide cannot use stairs or cut corners when guiding a person who uses a wheelchair. If capable, the wheelchair user can also be responsible for learning routes of travel, participating in guidance by directing the guide, and assisting with orientation and mental-mapping skills. Each of these techniques can serve as meaningful alternatives to the guide simply pushing the wheelchair from behind without engaging the learner who is using the wheelchair (Rosen & Crawford, 2010).

Instructional Strategies That Support Safety

Students with visual and multiple impairments may have a medical condition that affects their stamina or an additional disability that necessitates shorter lessons, breaks during lessons, extra wait time, or simplified communication. Additional wait time may be required for students to process what is happening in their immediate environment. Implementing a simplified and meaningful communication system that is personalized to each student is an important instructional strategy with direct impact on student safety. For example, students with multiple impairments who are nonverbal may use a thumbs-up signal to indicate to others when they think it is safe to cross a street or intersection and a thumbs-down signal to indicate when they think it is not safe to cross. This need for additional wait time, shorter lessons, breaks during lessons, or simplified communication may have a direct impact on the ability of students to travel safely and purposefully in their environment (Ambrose-Zaken, Calhoon, & Keim, 2010).

It is important for those working with students with multiple impairments on skills and concepts related to O&M to prepare for safety in advance of lessons or outings with their students. Safety gear, such as a helmet, may have to be worn by a student at all times. It is important to ensure proper fit and adjust safety gear as needed. For example, if the helmet strap is too tight, it may create an open sore, which may cause serious complications. Team members and parents can provide O&M specialists with information and guidance about required safety gear.

It is also important that all professionals working with a student recognize the warning signs and symptoms of seizures and know the proper steps to take if a student has a seizure (e.g., how to keep the student safe, who to call first if a seizure occurs during a lesson). School districts often train personnel in first aid, cardiopulmonary resuscitation (CPR), behavior management techniques, and other safety issues. These district-wide programs and trainings can be a valuable resource.

Prior to and during lessons, instructors should always have their cell phones charged, turned on, and ready to use, with emergency contacts (e.g., school offices, classroom teachers, parents) programmed and easily accessible. Also, professional liability insurance is recommended for O&M specialists in the event that something unforeseen occurs during a lesson.

Each of these safety concerns and supporting suggestions is intended for the safety and well-being of students with visual and multiple impairments and the professionals who support them as part of the educational team. It takes a collaborative effort among team members to implement educational programming that addresses the specific safety concerns of these students.

Positioning and Handling Considerations for Students with Severe Physical Disabilities

Teacher assistance and proper positioning may be required for optimal participation by students with severe physical disabilities in the learning environment and in daily activities. Positioning and handling suggestions should be routinely incorporated into daily activities. O&M specialists should collaborate with physical therapists to learn about the positioning and handling needs of their students with severe physical disabilities. It is important for O&M specialists to understand basic information about positioning and handling so they can follow safety procedures and communicate effectively with therapists to meet their students' individual needs. Knowledge of appropriate positioning and handling techniques allows O&M specialists to enhance students' efficient use of vision and teach motor skills in a safe manner.

Proper positioning keeps students from developing more severe motor problems, encourages students to move around and learn, and allows students to use their arms and upper bodies in the same way as if they were positioned in a stander (a piece of equipment that facilitates the standing position for students with physical impairments who cannot stand on their own). Providing variety in positioning prevents students with multiple disabilities from developing additional problems that can result from always keeping their legs or hands in the same position. Proper positioning may improve circulation, breathing, and digestion, and diminish the influence of abnormal posture or automatic, involuntary reflexes (see Sidebar 10.2

for suggestions on proper positioning). It is also important for team members who work with students with severe physical disabilities to consider their own safety when lifting and handling students by protecting their backs and using proper lifting techniques (see Sidebar 10.3), especially when working with students who use wheelchairs (see Sidebar 10.4).

SIDEBAR 10.3
Guidelines for Safe Handling and Lifting

When lifting or transferring students with multiple disabilities or their equipment, the person performing the lift or transfer should follow these guidelines:

- Maintain a wide base of support
- Pivot on legs; do not twist at the waist or the back
- Keep abdominals firm while lifting
- Keep the student or item close
- Keep the knees bent and the back straight
- Lift with the legs, not by bending the back
- Clear the area of extraneous materials that may be in the way
- Ask for assistance in lifting if the student or item exceeds one quarter of your body weight
- Consult with a physical therapist about the individualized needs of specific students

SIDEBAR 10.4
Guidelines for Safe Handling and Lifting of Students Who Use Wheelchairs

There are some additional guidelines that are important to remember when lifting and handling a student who uses a wheelchair. The following guidelines can make the movements smoother and safer:

- Always explain to the student being lifted what movement is going to occur next and what is expected of him or her.
- Always lock the wheelchair brakes prior to moving a student to or from a wheelchair.
- Make sure all seatbelts and straps have been unfastened prior to lifting. If lifting into a wheelchair, make sure all safety belts are fastened immediately.
- Encourage the student to assist according to his or her capabilities.
- When a student using a wheelchair takes public transportation, such as a bus, the bus driver should be the one to strap the student in, not the person assisting the student.

Summary

The education of students with visual and multiple impairments involves a different approach to orientation and mobility. O&M specialists and teachers of students with visual impairments are part of an educational team that delivers vision-specific content to students, their families, and other professionals who work with those students. As part of this collaborative effort, it is beneficial for O&M specialists to spend time observing students working with other special education service providers in a range of settings. O&M evaluation strategies and tools must also be modified; having a flexible approach to instructional delivery is important. O&M specialists who demonstrate high expectations for success paired with a willingness to try a variety of strategies often create new opportunities for students with visual and multiple impairments. Most important, there are many safety issues that must be addressed by O&M specialists and communicated to other team members to ensure students' safety in the environment while also encouraging purposeful movement. Students with multiple impairments benefit tremendously from O&M instruction that is tailored to meet their unique needs and that supports increased independence.

References

Alexander, R., Boehme, R., & Cupps, B. (1993). *Normal development of functional motor skills: The first year of life.* Tucson, AZ: Therapy Skill Builders.

Ambrose-Zaken, G., Calhoon, C. R., & Keim, J. R. (2010). Teaching orientation and mobility to students with cognitive impairments and vision loss. In W. R. Wiener, R. L. Welsh, & B. B. Blasch (Eds.), *Foundations of orientation and mobility: Vol. II. Instructional strategies and practical applications* (3rd ed., pp. 624–666). New York, NY: AFB Press.

Banda, D. R., Okungu, P. A., Griffin-Shirley, N., Meeks, M. K., & Landa-Vialard, O. (2015). Teaching orientation and mobility skills for students with autism and visual impairments in public schools: A data-based study. *International Journal of Orientation and Mobility, 7,* 34–43.

Blaha, R. (2001). Anticipation calendars. *Calendars for students with multiple impairments including deafblindness* (pp. 35–52). Austin: Texas School for the Blind and Visually Impaired.

Blaha, R., Shafer, S., Smith, M., & Moss, K. (1996, Fall). Thoughts on the assessment of the student with the most profound disabilities. *SEE/HEAR.* Retrieved from https://www.tsbvi.edu/seehear/archive/thoughts.htm

Dote-Kwan, J., Chen, D., & Hughes, M. (2001). A national survey of service providers who work with young children with visual impairments. *Journal of Visual Impairment & Blindness, 95*(6), 325–337.

Erin, J. N. (2017). Students with visual impairments and additional disabilities. In M. C. Holbrook, C. Kamei-Hannan, & T. McCarthy (Eds.), *Foundation of education: Vol. II. Instructional strategies for teaching children and youths with visual impair-ments* (3rd ed., pp. 309–349). New York, NY: AFB Press.

Fazzi, D. L., & Naimy, B. J. (2010). Teaching orientation and mobility to school-age children. In W. R. Wiener, R. L. Welsh, & B. B. Blasch (Eds.), *Foundations of orientation and mobility: Vol. II. Instructional strategies and practical applications* (3rd ed., pp. 208–262). New York, NY: AFB Press.

Fazzi, D. L., & Petersmeyer, B. A. (2001). Making learning meaningful and fun: Elements of innovative instruction. In *Imagining the possibilities: Creative approaches to orientation and mobility instruction for persons who are visually impaired* (pp. 65–90). New York, NY: AFB Press.

Friend, M., & Cook, L. (2010). *Interactions: Collaboration skills for school professionals* (6th ed.). Upper Saddle River, NJ: Pearson Education.

Hatton, D. D. (2001). Model registry of early childhood visual impairment: First-year results. *Journal of Visual Impairment & Blindness, 95*(7), 418–433.

Krapp, K., & Wilson, J. (Eds.). (2005). Neonatal reflexes. In *The Gale encyclopedia of children's health: Infancy through adolescence. Vol. 3. L-R.* Detroit, MI: Thomson Gale.

LilliWorks. (n.d.). 10 principles. Retrieved from http://www.lilliworks.com/sample-page/10-principles/

Lolli, D., Sauerburger, D., & Bourquin, E. A. (2010). Teaching orientation and mobility to students with vision and hearing loss. In W. R. Wiener, R. L. Welsh, & B. B. Blasch (Eds.), *Foundations of orientation and mobility: Vol. II. Instructional strategies and practical applications* (3rd ed., pp. 537–563). New York, NY: AFB Press.

McGregor, D. (1998). *Using verbal and physical prompts to teach the use of the long cane to a student who is visually impaired and has additional severe disabilities* (Doctoral dissertation). Texas Tech University, Lubbock, TX.

Mercer, D. (n.d.). Strategic programming for MIVI students: Takes knowing where each individual student fits within the strategic planning categories [PowerPoint presentation]. Nacogdoches, TX: Stephen F. Austin State University. Retrieved from http://www.slideserve

.com / tobias / strategic-programming-for-mivi -students

Montessori, M. (1949). *The absorbent mind*. Adyar, India: The Theosophical Publishing House.

Moss, K., & Shafer, S. (2006, Winter). Incorporating active learning theory into activity routines. *SEE / HEAR*. Retrieved from http://www.tsbvi.edu /seehear/winter06/learning.htm

National Center on Deaf-Blindness. (n.d.). Primary etiologies of deaf-blindness. Retrieved from https://nationaldb.org/library/page/2084

Nelson, C., van Dijk, J., Oster, T., & McDonnell, A. (2009). *Child guided strategies: The van Dijk approach to assessment*. Louisville, KY: American Printing House for the Blind.

Nielsen, L. (1992). Spatial relations and the "Little Room." *Future Reflections, 11*(2). Retrieved from https://nfb.org/images/nfb/publications/fr /fr11/issue2/f110214.html

Perla, F., & Ducret, W. D. (n.d.). Basic orientation and mobility for children with multiple disabilities: A starting point. *International Council for Education of People with Visual Impairment*. Retrieved from http://icevi.org/publications/icevix/wshops /0400.html

Pogrund, R., Sewell, D., Anderson, H., Calaci, L., Cowart, M. F., Gonzalez, C. M., . . . Roberson-Smith, B. (2012). *TAPS—Teaching age-appropriate purposeful skills: An orientation and mobility curriculum for students with visual impairments* (3rd ed.). Austin: Texas School for the Blind and Visually Impaired.

Rosen, S. (2010a). Improving sensorimotor functioning for orientation and mobility. In W. R. Wiener, R. L. Welsh, & B. B. Blasch (Eds.), *Foundations of orientation and mobility: Vol. II. Instructional strategies and practical applications* (3rd ed., pp. 118–137). New York, NY: AFB Press.

Rosen, S. (2010b). Kinesiology and sensorimotor functioning for students with vision loss. In W. R. Wiener, R. L. Welsh, & B. B. Blasch (Eds.), *Foundations of orientation and mobility: Vol. I. History and theory* (3rd ed., pp. 138–172). New York, NY: AFB Press.

Rosen, S., & Crawford, J. S. (2010). Teaching orientation and mobility to leaners with visual, physical, and health impairments. In W. R. Wiener, R. L. Welsh, & B. B. Blasch (Eds.), *Foundations of orientation and mobility: Vol. II. Instructional strategies and practical applications* (3rd ed., pp. 564–623). New York, NY: AFB Press.

Sacks, S. Z. (2016). Educating students with visual impairments who have multiple disabilities: An overview. In S. Z. Sacks & M. C. Zatta (Eds.), *Keys to educational success: Teaching students with visual impairments and multiple disabilities* (pp. 3–64). New York, NY: AFB Press.

Sapp, W. (2004). *Adaptive mobility devices and canes for toddlers: Suggestions for O&M specialists*. Chapel Hill: University of North Carolina at Chapel Hill, FPG Child Development Institute, Early Intervention Training Center for Infants and Toddlers with Visual Impairments.

Sauerburger, D., Siffermann, E., & Rosen, S. (2006, November). *Orientation and mobility for visually impaired persons with multiple disabilities including deaf-blindness*. Presentation at the 12th International Mobility Conference, Hong Kong, China. Retrieved from www.sauerburger.org/dona/ imc.htm

Siegel-Causey, E., & Ernst, B. (1989). Theoretical orientation and research in nonsymbolic development. In E. Siegel-Causey & D. Guess (Eds.), *Enhancing nonsymbolic communication interactions among learners with severe disabilities* (pp. 15–54). Baltimore, MD: Paul H. Brookes.

Silverrain, A. (1989). *An informal paper: Teaching the profoundly handicapped child*. San Antonio, TX: Education Service Center Region 20.

Skellenger, A. C., & Sapp, W. K. (2010). Teaching orientation and mobility for the early childhood years. In W. R. Wiener, R. L. Welsh, & B. B. Blasch (Eds.), *Foundations of orientation and mobility: Vol. II. Instructional strategies and practical applications* (3rd ed., pp. 163–207). New York, NY: AFB Press.

Smith, M. (1998, Spring). Joseph's coat: People teaming in transdisciplinary ways. *SEE/HEAR*. Retrieved from http://www.tsbvi.edu/seehear /spring98/joseph.html

Smith, M. (n.d.a). Dens. Austin: Texas School for the Blind and Visually Impaired. Retrieved from http://tsbvi.edu/143-mivi-general/1732-dens

Smith, M. (n.d.b). Routines. Austin: Texas School for the Blind and Visually Impaired. Retrieved from http://tsbvi.edu/203-resources/1733-routines

Smith, M., & Levack, N. (1997a). Behavioral state management for students with profound impairments. In *Teaching students with visual and multiple impairments: A resource guide* (2nd ed., pp. 251–266). Austin: Texas School for the Blind and Visually Impaired.

Smith, M., & Levack, N. (1997b). Orientation and mobility for students with multiple impairments. In *Teaching students with visual and multiple impairments: A resource guide* (2nd ed., pp. 414–440). Austin: Texas School for the Blind and Visually Impaired.

Texas Deaf-Blind Outreach. (2000). *A model of individual support to provide appropriate access to education for students who are deafblind.* Austin: Texas School for the Blind and Visually Impaired, Outreach Programs. Retrieved from http://www.tsbvi.edu/project-services/44-dbintervener/1886-interveners-for-students-with-deafblindness-in-texas

11

Collaboration in Orientation and Mobility

Shannon D. Darst and Rona L. Pogrund

Questions to Guide Your Reading of This Chapter

➤ What are the successful components of a professional learning community?

➤ What are the features of a collaborative educational team in an orientation and mobility (O&M) program?

➤ What are the three types of educational teams, and why is the transdisciplinary team the most desirable for an effective O&M program?

➤ In what ways are family members important team members in supporting an effective O&M program?

Coming together is a beginning. Staying together is progress. Working together is success. (Ford, n.d.)

Collaboration is the foundation of an effective service delivery system for students with visual impairments. Because orientation and mobility (O&M) is such an integral and overarching component in the lives of students with visual impairments, understanding and implementing effective collaborative practices among the

O&M specialist and other professionals who work with these students, as well as their families, is essential to the growth and progress of all students who receive services related to their visual impairment.

Professional Learning Communities

To understand collaboration among O&M specialists and other education professionals, a broad definition of collaboration is provided. *Collaboration* is an "interactive process that enables people with diverse expertise to generate solutions to mutually defined problems" (Idol, Nevin, & Paolucci-Whitcomb, 2000, p. 1; see Sidebar 11.1 for definitions of key terms). These people are co-equal partners (Friend & Cook, 2017) with a shared vision (Wiig, 1992). In the educational setting, collaboration occurs "when members of an inclusive learning community work together as equals to assist students to succeed in the classroom" (Powell, 2004, para. 9). These learning communities, commonly known as professional learning communities (PLCs; see Sidebar 11.2), are dedicated to improving teaching and learning through collaboration, reflective dialogue, and making their practice public. There are three integral questions that are the driving force behind the process that is the PLC. According to DuFour (2004, p. 6), these three questions are:

1. What do we want each student to learn?
2. How will we know when each student has learned it?
3. How will we respond when a student experiences difficulty learning?

For a PLC to be successful, collaboration must be more than just a set of guidelines set forth for the members who participate in the PLC process. Collaboration and the collaborative spirit must become the culture of the educational environment (see Figure 11.1).

Culture of Collaboration

For a successful culture of collaboration to occur, the following characteristics are needed (Friend & Cook, 2017):

- Each member's participation in collaboration must be voluntary.
- Parity among participants must be present during the entire collaborative process.
- Collaborative activities must be based on mutual goals that include all members of the collaborative team.
- Each member of the team has a shared responsibility of participation and decision making.
- All participants must share resources.
- All participants must share accountability for outcomes.

SIDEBAR 11.1

Key Terms

Collaboration Interactive process that enables individuals with diverse expertise to work together toward shared goals.

Interdisciplinary team Group of professionals from different disciplines who function as a team but work independently, yet share information and engage in joint planning.

Multidisciplinary team Group of professionals from different disciplines who function as a team but who perform their roles separately from one another, often resulting in a fragmented program.

Professional learning community (PLC) Group of educators who meet regularly, share expertise, and work collaboratively to improve teaching skills as well as student outcomes.

Role release Process whereby service providers train others in their area of expertise so that everyone on the transdisciplinary team, especially the primary interventionist, can implement suggested strategies and methods within the daily routines of the student.

Transdisciplinary team Group of professionals from different disciplines who function as a team and share roles, with one team member serving as the primary interventionist and implementing the team's suggestions.

Furthermore, Wiggins and Damore (2006) suggest that a positive attitude, a shared common philosophy toward educating students, such as the philosophy of the PLC process, and a shared common philosophy regarding students in special education can lead to successful collaboration among the educational team. Common

---

SIDEBAR 11.2

What Is a Professional Learning Community?

A *professional learning community* (PLC) is an ongoing process that is implemented by members and teams of professional educators. The attributes of a PLC are the focus on learning, the process by which a PLC functions, the collaboration and interdependence of the educators and teams within the process, the collective inquiry and action-oriented practices of the educators in the process, and the commitment of the educators and teams to continuous improvement of the components of the process, along with the systematic organization and cyclical implementation of the PLC's learning and improvement processes (DuFour, DuFour, Eaker, & Many, 2010).

The PLC process requires that all members be focused on learning and that each member have a specific responsibility in the process. The PLC process systematically identifies exactly what each student must learn, how each student's learning is monitored by every educator, how to support students' learning strengths, and how to effectively intervene to support struggling students (DuFour et al., 2010). This comprehensive process leads to a clear, standardized method of presenting information to students, checking for understanding and progress, and guaranteeing that each student will be able to meet the expectations of the next step in his or her educational journey because all the educators are working from the same set of expectations and goals.

The PLC process can only be successful with the dedication to collaborative and collective efforts of the individuals and the teams working together in the process. Members should all be focused on the end goal of student learning, and under the umbrella of that end goal, members should have a clear set of parameters within which they teach and assess student learning. This collaborative and collective effort includes sharing a common vocabulary and understanding of the PLC process, providing a clear statement of the need for the PLC process, identifying areas of strength and need in each learning environment, and having a systematic way to address these areas, with the goal of student learning as the driving force behind any choices made in the PLC process (DuFour et al., 2010).

The PLC process can easily be achieved if all members use the action-oriented steps of gathering data regarding each student's current level of performance, identifying the strengths and needs of each student, developing strategies to support areas of strengths and address areas of need, implementing the strategies, assessing the effectiveness of the strategies, and repeating the process while making forward progress toward student learning. By collaborating on a continuous basis, the standardized implementation of effective strategies can create a learning environment that becomes accessible to all students as the students come to understand a streamlined, defined method of learning.

---

philosophies among team members regarding teamwork, active communication, and complete participation from all members that results in growth from professional development can bolster openness and confidence in each member's role and value in the team model.

Common philosophies related to effective management and leadership that promote opportunities for all members to participate in joint activities, share and manage resources (e.g., time, materials), and foster collaborative efficiency can lead to a united and cohesive team.

Figure 11.1 For a PLC to be successful, collaboration must be more than just a set of guidelines, it must become the culture of the educational environment.

One of the key components for ensuring successful collaboration is guidance by a strong leader or supervisor who understands these concepts well and who can explain and teach team members how to create and support these characteristics on a consistent and ongoing basis. Ideally, this leader will be well trained in the roles and responsibilities of each team member. If the leader or any other member of the team is not fully aware of the roles and responsibilities of an O&M professional, the O&M professional must be able to articulate his or her job description and specific responsibilities to the team.

Along with a strong leader, each team member should consider his or her attitudes and beliefs as they relate to collaboration. Based on the research of Milteniene and Venclovaite (2012), collaboration can happen only when individual team members embrace the following concepts and ideals of collaboration: "readiness to learn from one another, identification of aims of education, definition and distribution of functions and roles, joint planning of activities, and joint discussion of the efficacy of these activities" (p. 112). The researchers note that, "It is important to receive colleagues' support and to use it in one's own practical activities, because it is through close collaboration that information is disseminated, knowledge is shared, and missing skills are developed" (p. 112). This idea leads back to the questions that drive the PLC; the goal for each team member is to address student learning, track and document progress, and address learning needs and deficits based on the results of student progress documentation.

The creation and implementation of collaboration in PLCs based on the characteristics and criteria listed should be the focus to address student need. Because of the nature of people and their differences, however, attention must be paid to the benefits and possible pitfalls that can impact effective collaboration. Huxham and Vangen (2005) arrived at a new theory of describing the process of collaboration. If ideal conditions occur in the educational collaborative process, Huxham and Vangen (2005) state that positive results, or collaborative advantage, will occur. Collaborative advantage encompasses the positive aspects that can come from collaboration, including new ideas, new relationships, shared resources, innovative solutions, strengthened networks, and increased legitimacy of the activities being conducted. The opposite of collaborative advantage is collaborative inertia. Collaborative inertia includes the negative aspects that can arise during the collaborative process, including endless discussions, stalemates, unproductive meetings, and lack of participation. Sometimes there are barriers to productive collaboration that include differing professional values, personality differences, time constraints, fear of losing one's expertise, and school politics. Acknowledging these potential barriers when they present themselves and bringing them to the team in a constructive manner is a good start to overcoming them (Robinson & Buly, 2007). As a member of the PLC and a professional in the field of O&M, the individual must be aware that these two opposing forces always exist during collaboration. All team members should be aware of the basic principles upon which collaborative advantage and collaborative inertia are built (see Sidebar 11.3) as well as any additional challenges that might impede successful collaboration (see Sidebar 11.4).

To ensure that a PLC is working effectively, some critical thinking questions can be asked of

---

SIDEBAR 11.3

Collaborative Advantage versus Collaborative Inertia

Collaborative Advantage

Collaborative advantage depends on collaboration design. Huxham and Vangen (2005) divide collaboration design into two parts: structure and process. The researchers state that structure includes how team members are represented and how much meaningful input each member has in the collaborative process. Process, according to the researchers, includes the team dynamic and the patterns of interactions among members. Structure and process are in a reflexive relationship during collaboration, meaning that the way a meeting is structured affects the process, and how the process works will affect the structure.

Collaborative Inertia

Collaborative inertia depends on the values that team members bring to the collaboration, as well as the information, concepts, and focus of the collaboration. Collaborative inertia can negatively affect the collaborative process if team members disregard the input or roles of other members, if some members do not strive to work collaboratively, thus alienating or ostracizing other team members, or if members become bored with a difficult or ambiguous concept or focal point and their disengagement impedes an ongoing working pattern among the other team members.

SIDEBAR 11.4

Challenges to Collaboration

Factors that can serve as barriers to successful collaboration include:

- Varying cultures and different team models among service delivery systems and professionals
- Differing professional values among team members
- Team members belonging to different professional organizations, attending their own conferences, and using their own jargon
- Personality differences among team members
- Team members being under time constraints and feeling overstressed
- Team members' fears of collaboration and of losing their expertise
- Team members being concerned about their social roles and about who is perceived as having the most power

Source: Adapted from Pogrund, R., & Griffin-Shirley, N. (2016). Fostering collaboration among professionals serving older people with vision loss. In N. Griffin-Shirley & L. Bozeman (Eds.), *O&M for independent living: Strategies for teaching orientation and mobility to older adults* (p. 228). New York, NY: AFB Press.

members (or potential members). These questions include:

1. How would your ideal PLC and team meetings be structured?
2. In what ways could meaningful input be shared by each PLC or team member in daily activities?

3. Ideally, how could PLC or team members interact in a way that fosters cooperation?
4. What are some of the patterns of interaction among team members (both effective and ineffective)? How could any one team member adjust his or her input to improve any negative patterns?

Types of Teams

With an understanding of the concept of collaboration in an educational environment, the next step is to establish the educational service delivery team. Members of the PLC are brought together in a structured team model to implement the collaboration needed to effectively serve each student with a visual impairment. Three different service delivery team models have been identified: the multidisciplinary team, the interdisciplinary team, and the transdisciplinary team.

Multidisciplinary Team

The *multidisciplinary team* is defined by Gargiulo (2015) as "a group of professionals from different disciplines who function as a team but perform their roles independent of one another" (p. 23). In this model, all professionals who work with a student with a visual impairment provide their expertise to the student independent of others on the team. The student is usually provided with each service in isolation from other services and in environments that belong to other service providers, including the classroom teacher. Parents or caregivers interact with each service provider separately. The only collaborative component to this model is that each team member is focused on service delivery for a student they all have in common.

Often, the strategies, accommodations, and modifications that are effective for each individual service provider may differ, creating a confusing and contradictory state of service delivery for the student. As a result of this, the programming may hinder the student's progress rather than support it. On the continuum of collaboration, the multidisciplinary team model is the least collaborative, least cooperative, least coordinated, and least integrative (Gargiulo, 2015), and often results in a fragmented program for the student.

The multidisciplinary team model allows for O&M training completely independent of any other skill areas identified in the results of evaluations provided by other education professionals on the student's team. The O&M specialist may communicate with the student's family members or caregivers to inform them of the O&M skills the student is learning, but this information may only be conveyed in a written report or at an Individualized Education Program (IEP) meeting. Due to this limited communication, the student and the O&M specialist are the only ones on the student's team who have been trained on and can properly reinforce the O&M skills being taught by the O&M specialist. The benefit of the multidisciplinary model for O&M specialists is that they have complete autonomy regarding identification of the skills that they teach to the student, as well as the strategies and methods used to teach new skills. The opportunity cost of this model, or the cost of foregoing the use of an alternative model, for the O&M specialist is that the student will not receive consistent reinforcement of the O&M skills taught during O&M lessons and may be taught conflicting O&M methods when working with other service professionals. This model is the least preferred model of service delivery for O&M instruction.

Interdisciplinary Team

The *interdisciplinary team* is defined by Gargiulo (2015) as "a group of professionals from different disciplines who function as a team but work independently; recommendations, however, are the result of sharing information and joint planning" (p. 23). In this model, all professionals who work with a student with a visual impairment come together as a team, bringing evaluation information into a sharing scenario and planning a more holistic list of services based on the student's strengths and needs, as documented in the results of each individual service provider's evaluation report. Many of the services that are provided to the student are still conducted within the boundaries of each service provider's role and responsibilities, but some techniques and strategies are supported in more than one educational environment. Some specialized services, like those provided by a physical therapist, speech-language pathologist, or occupational therapist, may still be provided in an environment independent from the domains of other service professionals. The team conducts meetings on a frequent, but not always consistent, basis and family members or caregivers interact with a team representative such as a general education teacher or special education teacher. The collaborative components of this model include a focus on the learning needs specific to each student, more open communication regarding the best practices for strategies, accommodations, and modifications, an effort to coordinate and collaborate on writing goals and objectives, and consistent support of skills learned across service areas. The programming becomes more effective and consistent for the student, and therefore, the student makes more progress toward accomplishing goals and objectives in all skill areas. This model falls in the middle of the continuum of being collaborative, cooperative, coordinated, and integrative (Gargiulo, 2015).

The interdisciplinary team model allows for O&M training in coordination with the skills the student is learning across other disciplines. The O&M specialist can share the best O&M strategies with other team members to create a more consistent support system for the O&M skills being taught. The O&M specialist communicates with other team members, especially the team representative, to convey information to the family members or caregivers to promote more consistent practice of O&M skills outside of the school environment. The entire team, including the student, should have a basic understanding of, and responsibility for, reinforcing O&M skills that are being taught by the O&M specialist. The benefit of the interdisciplinary model for the O&M specialist is that more consistent O&M strategies are practiced across the student's educational environments, including the home and community settings. The opportunity cost of this model for the O&M specialist is that team members may not always maintain the same level of implementation in using strategies with the student that are used by the O&M specialist. Ongoing observation and training of team members may require more time and effort on the part of the O&M specialist than would be necessary in a multidisciplinary model. However, despite this constraint, the interdisciplinary model is preferable to the multidisciplinary model of service delivery for O&M specialists.

Transdisciplinary Team

The *transdisciplinary team* is defined by Gargiulo (2015) as "a group of professionals from different disciplines who function as a team but work independently; however, they share roles, and a peer is identified as the primary interventionist" (p. 23). The transdisciplinary model takes the collaborative elements of the interdisciplinary model and adds two valuable components: role release and a primary interventionist (Gargiulo, 2015). The transdisciplinary model requires *role release*, meaning each service provider trains the other members of the team in their area of expertise regarding the strategies and methods used to teach the skills related to the goals and objectives of the student's IEP. Once each member of the team can implement the strategies and practices of the other team members with the student, one primary interventionist—typically the student's parent, case manager, homeroom teacher, or self-contained classroom teacher, depending on the setting—will support the communication and cross-discipline skill implementation for each student. Consultation among the team members should happen on a consistent and frequent basis to ensure that the student is generalizing skills and making progress on goals, as well as to brainstorm and troubleshoot any problem areas in the service delivery process. Family members and caregivers are equal partners on the team, and their input has as much weight on programming and service delivery as that of the educational service providers on the team. Direct, individualized service can be provided in isolation from other service areas when necessary, but the ideal situation calls for direct service to be provided within and throughout all of the student's other educational and service-provision environments. On the continuum of collaboration, the transdisciplinary model is the most collaborative, most cooperative, most coordinated, and most integrative (Gargiulo, 2015).

The transdisciplinary team model allows for O&M instruction to be provided to the student throughout his or her educational and personal life. Due to the cooperative "blurring of the lines" between each discipline, evaluations of individual service areas are conducted with as much input from all team members to obtain the most complete picture of the student's strengths and needs, which, in turn, provides a comprehensive foundation upon which the most pertinent goals and objectives can be created. The O&M specialist communicates with all members of the team, as well as directly with the student's family members or caregivers, to support consistent training and practice of O&M skills outside of the school environment. All members of the student's team are responsible for implementing and practicing the O&M skills written into the student's IEP by the O&M specialist. The benefit of the transdisciplinary model for the O&M specialist is that he or she becomes an active and integral part of the student's transdisciplinary team. A symbiotic relationship forms among the O&M specialist and the other team members, including the student and the family members or caregivers. This collaboration allows the O&M specialist to understand and practice how to integrate methods and strategies used by other team members, infuse skills learned in other areas of the student's educational and personal life into O&M instruction, and provide feedback to other service providers on skill progress and regression in areas other than O&M. This relationship also provides the O&M specialist the opportunity to

train other team members in how to implement and reinforce some basic and other more advanced O&M skills the student is learning as well as provide sensitivity training to those working with the student, which can help to integrate the most effective O&M methods into other skill areas. The opportunity cost of this model for the O&M specialist is the possible inconsistency in implementing strategies and skill practice across disciplines since the O&M specialist may not always be available to observe other team members implementing the skills in which they were trained and to provide them with feedback. As with the interdisciplinary model, the transdisciplinary model calls for extensive communication, observation, and training of all team members across many areas of the student's educational programming. These activities are time-consuming, especially in the beginning, but in the long run, the time and effort put in to create and maintain a transdisciplinary model can make a marked difference in a student's progress toward skill acquisition and generalization.

The transdisciplinary model is the optimal type of team model because it benefits all team members. In this model, the guiding philosophy is that all team members must commit themselves to teaching, learning, and working together across discipline boundaries (Woodruff & McGonigel, 1988). In the transdisciplinary model, families are active participants of the team. They, along with the other team members, conduct a comprehensive evaluation of the student and develop an Individualized Family Service Plan (IFSP) or IEP based on family priorities, needs, and resources. The team members are then responsible for implementing the plans. Communication is critical, so regular team meetings are held where the

Gabriella Davis

Figure 11.2 Collaboration and communication are vital to IEP planning since they allow information, knowledge, and skills to be shared.

transfer of information, knowledge, and skills can occur (Gargiulo & Kilgo, 2014; see Figure 11.2).

Team Members and Their Roles and Responsibilities

Fry (2001) outlines the roles and responsibilities of general and special education teachers and paraeducators in schools across five educational areas: instruction, evaluation, communication, leadership, and record keeping. The roles and responsibilities of two additional members of the transdisciplinary team, the O&M specialist and the teacher of students with visual impairments, have also been added and presented in a similar format outlining each educational area.

Since some O&M specialists may not be trained as certified teachers, the roles of the team members with whom the O&M special-

ist will collaborate in the transdisciplinary team model should first be explained. However, before looking at the specific roles and responsibilities of team members regarding O&M service delivery, more general roles and responsibilities are presented.

General and Special Education Teachers. The team leader of a transdisciplinary team will likely be a general education or special education teacher. The roles of these two team members are provided in Sidebars 11.5 and 11.6. These two sidebars explain how the general or special education teacher will function as part of the team. The general education teacher is primarily responsible for the academic instructional content and programming for any student in his or her classroom. The special education teacher fulfills the same responsibility, but the

---

SIDEBAR 11.5

Role of the General Education Teacher

Instruction

- Instructing individual students
- Providing small-group instruction
- Teaching the whole class
- Monitoring students' academic progress
- Implementing accommodations and modifications designed by the special education teacher

Evaluation

- Conducting formative and summative assessments of students, including grading assignments and projects
- Administering state and local standardized tests
- Developing appropriate exhibitions and demonstrations of student work

Communication

- Collaborating with the special education teacher on curriculum for class
- Providing feedback on effectiveness of strategies

- Attending IEP and planning meetings
- Communicating with families, parents, or caregivers
- Attending problem-solving meetings

Leadership

- Designing structure of the class, including the curriculum, classroom-management policies, physical design, and selection of materials
- Supervising paraeducators and peer tutors assigned to the class
- Providing information on curriculum and instruction to PLCs

Record Keeping

- Recording unit and daily lesson plans, activities, and homework
- Maintaining student grade and attendance records

Source: Adapted from Fry, N. (2001). Tying it together: Personal supports that lead to membership and belonging. In C. H. Kennedy & D. Fisher (Eds.), *Inclusive middle schools* (pp. 119–120). Baltimore, MD: Paul H. Brookes.

---

content and programming are based on each student's IEP.

Paraeducator. For many students who have multiple impairments or who need one-to-one assistance, the paraeducator, teaching assistant, or intervener is often with the student for more time during each school day than any other team member (except for the parent or caregiver). Because the paraeducator tends to be the person with whom the student interacts most often throughout the school day, the paraeducator's primary role is to support imple-

mentation of IEP programming and strategies. The general roles and responsibilities of the paraeducator, teaching assistant, or intervener are provided in Sidebar 11.7.

O&M Specialist. Along with the general roles and responsibilities of the O&M specialist outlined in Sidebar 11.8, Correa, Fazzi, and Pogrund (2002) list the following responsibilities of the O&M specialist (p. 431):

- Conducting home or school environmental assessments to suggest modifications to

enhance motivation for movement or to provide additional safety during independent movement
- Completing specialized assessments
- Providing in-service training for staff and students, including the proper use of guide technique
- Securing adaptive materials and equipment related to O&M

Since these responsibilities require extensive training and certification in O&M, they cannot be shared with other team members. (More specific strategies and techniques taught by the O&M specialist to other team members are described in the section on Teaming Strategies to Support O&M Instruction later in the chapter.) As O&M specialists grow more comfortable working as members of a transdisciplinary team and providing direct and collaborative consultation services for the student and other team members, they should consider building awareness and support for the O&M program (see Sidebar 11.9).

Teacher of Students with Visual Impairments. The teacher of students with visual impairments is the team member responsible for delivering skill-related content in the areas of the expanded core curriculum (ECC) to the student with a visual impairment, including supporting O&M skills. The teacher of students with visual impairments also supports the transdisciplinary team model by working with classroom teachers and others on the student's team to implement accommodations and modifications across all learning environments. The general roles and responsibilities of the teacher of students with visual impairments are outlined in Sidebar 11.10.

SIDEBAR 11.6
Role of the Special Education Teacher

Instruction
- Instructing individual students
- Adapting materials and instruction
- Providing small-group instruction
- Teaching the whole class
- Monitoring students' academic work
- Coordinating support for individual students, including medical and behavioral needs

Evaluation
- Grading students' performance
- Developing appropriate exhibitions and demonstrations of student work
- Administering educational tests

Communication
- Attending IEP and planning meetings
- Communicating with families, parents, or caregivers
- Attending problem-solving meetings
- Providing information about inclusion

Leadership
- Training and supervising paraeducators
- Coordinating peer tutors
- Facilitating the use of related-services professionals

Record Keeping
- Developing the IEP
- Maintaining records of students' performance
- Maintaining record of curriculum accommodations and modifications

Source: Adapted from Fry, N. (2001). Tying it together: Personal supports that lead to membership and belonging. In C. H. Kennedy & D. Fisher (Eds.), *Inclusive middle schools* (pp. 119–120). Baltimore, MD: Paul H. Brookes.

SIDEBAR 11.7

Role of the Paraeducator, Teaching Assistant, or Intervener

Instruction

- Following instructional plans as implemented by the general education teacher
- Implementing accommodations and modifications as designed by the special education teacher
- Providing specialized assistance to assigned students as necessary, including personal care
- Re-teaching skills to individuals and small groups

Evaluation

- Assisting and supporting general and special education teachers with evaluation of student performance
- Administering state and local standardized tests
- Collaborating with the general and special education teachers to report student progress

Communication

- Providing feedback to team members on success of strategies

- Assisting the general and special education teachers in communicating with students, families, parents, or caregivers
- Maintaining effective and open communication with school personnel
- Honoring confidentiality of student information

Leadership

- Facilitating social relationships between students
- Creating a positive and reinforcing environment for students
- Modeling effective communication strategies for other staff

Record Keeping

- Maintaining logs and time sheets as required to document contact time
- Maintaining records of students' performance
- Maintaining record of curriculum accommodations and modifications

Source: Adapted from Fry, N. (2001). Tying it together: Personal supports that lead to membership and belonging. In C. H. Kennedy & D. Fisher (Eds.), *Inclusive middle schools* (pp. 119–120). Baltimore, MD: Paul H. Brookes.

Parents and Family Members. The key to working with a student's family members and caregivers is to remember that the parent or direct caregiver is always the expert regarding the student. For the majority of students on an O&M specialist's caseload, the parent or caregiver has known the student since birth, and thus has had the most experience with the student. In the transdisciplinary model, parents or caregivers should have input in the same five areas of instruction, evaluation, communication, leadership, and record keeping as do other team members.

The first role of the parent or caregiver is that of an instructor. Parents and caregivers are usually a child's first teachers, beginning at birth. Parents and family members teach social interaction skills, independent living skills, communication skills, and even O&M skills from the first day of the child's life. The parent's role of instructor can be bolstered by having the O&M specialist provide specific

Role of the O&M Specialist

Instruction

- Instructing individual students
- Adapting materials and instruction

Evaluation

- Developing and conducting an O&M evaluation
- Assessing development of concept, motor, and sensory skills, and other skill areas of the expanded core curriculum

Communication

- Attending IFSP, IEP, and planning meetings
- Communicating with families, parents, or caregivers
- Communicating with other team members
- Providing feedback on effectiveness of strategies

Leadership

- Designing and implementing ongoing in-service education activities in the area of O&M for all team members
- Developing and implementing O&M activities to be used with family members
- Establishing community relationships to educate the general public about the O&M capabilities of students

Record Keeping

- Developing the IFSP or IEP
- Maintaining logs and time sheets as required to document contact time through use of data-collection methods
- Maintaining records of students' performance
- Updating student progress and current levels of performance

Building Awareness of O&M

Fazzi and Naimy (2010) suggest different ways in which an O&M professional can go above and beyond in creating and sustaining a highly successful O&M program and educating school and community personnel about O&M instruction for students with visual impairments. These activities include:

- Describing the purpose of various lessons to all team members, including the student and family
- Volunteering to prepare one of the school bulletin boards that is rotated throughout the year
- Inviting a team member or administrator to observe a lesson in the community
- Providing opportunities for families, colleagues, and administrators to participate in various activities of independent living or learn guide technique wearing a sleep shade or low vision simulator
- Assisting a student in preparing a presentation to his or her class about O&M accomplishments
- Contacting the local police department or other city or county government entities to notify them about O&M lessons taking place in their community
- Supporting local merchants and explaining why there will be students with visual impairments participating in lessons in their stores or places of business
- Volunteering to conduct an in-service training for the local public transportation company

Source: Adapted from Fazzi, D. L., & Naimy, B. J. (2010). Teaching orientation and mobility to school-age children. In W. R. Wiener, R. L. Welsh, & B. B. Blasch (Eds.), *Foundations of orientation and mobility: Vol. II. Instructional strategies and practical applications* (3rd ed., pp. 212–213). New York, NY: AFB Press.

SIDEBAR 11.10

Role of the Teacher of Students with Visual Impairments

Instruction

- Instructing individual students
- Instructing a student alongside his or her peers in a classroom setting
- Adapting materials and instruction
- Supporting O&M skills

Evaluation

- Developing and conducting a functional vision evaluation and learning media assessment
- Cooperatively assessing all areas of the ECC

Communication

- Attending IFSP, IEP, and planning meetings
- Communicating with families, parents, or care-givers
- Communicating with other team members
- Providing feedback on effectiveness of strategies

Leadership

- Designing and implementing ongoing in-service educational activities in the areas of the ECC for all team members
- Developing and implementing ECC activities to be used with family members
- Establishing community relationships to educate the general public regarding the vision-related capabilities of the student

Record Keeping

- Developing the IFSP or IEP
- Maintaining logs and time sheets as required to document contact time
- Maintaining records of students' performance through use of data-collection methods
- Updating student progress and current levels of performance

---

training and modeling to ensure that the acquisition of O&M skills continues throughout the child's life.

Parents and caregivers should also be equal partners on the evaluation team. Although most parents and caregivers will not use formal assessment and evaluation protocols, they can play an equal role in the evaluation process by offering "insight into how their child learns, what his or her interests are, and other aspects of the child that only a parent [or caregiver] can know" (U.S. Department of Education, 2000, sec. 7). Again, as a part of the transdisciplinary team, the parent or caregiver should understand the roles and responsibilities of the other team members. That understanding comes from be-

ing a part of the evaluation process for each individual discipline. Conducting a parent interview to find out the family's O&M priorities for their child should be a part of any O&M evaluation.

Parents and caregivers participate on the team in the area of communication. Parents and caregivers foster effective communication by sharing information about the student's experiences and activities at home. Parents and caregivers can also "offer insight or help the school explore possible reasons as well as possible solutions" (U.S. Department of Education, 2000, sec. 11) if the student is experiencing problems during the school day. In this way, the parent or caregiver should be able to communicate to the team leader and to any other team members the significant incidents that might affect the student on a short-term or long-term basis, including changes in living situation, health, and routine. The parent or caregiver should also be an effective listener as part of the communication component of team participation. Having a parent or caregiver be open and trusting of the other team members is crucial to ensuring continuity and consistency in service provision and implementation across environments.

Finally, parents and caregivers should be the leaders regarding what works and what does not work for the child. As previously noted, parents, caregivers, and other family members are the experts when it comes to their child. Parents, caregivers, and family members are leaders in the transdisciplinary team because they are the experts on their child's strengths and needs, especially in the context of the child's home life, the family's cultural beliefs and values, and their involvement in the community.

As for the responsibilities of parents, caregivers, and family members, Noe, McCaffery, and Meagher (2011) suggest they should schedule IEP and other meetings when they are able to attend, learn and understand the process, share information about the student, ask questions when there is something they don't understand, offer suggestions, and inform the rest of the team about what they believe the student needs to succeed. These responsibilities are based on establishing trust and honest communication practices among all members of the team. Acknowledging the expertise of parents, caregivers, and family members and reassuring them that the entire team is focused on the student's learning and progress are important steps to building trust and creating open, active lines of communication.

Role of Team Members in Use of a Cane or Adaptive Mobility Device

As with all other aspects of the O&M service delivery model, role release should be practiced and each team member should be trained on the purpose and use of a cane or adaptive mobility device (AMD) by the O&M specialist. As stated in Sapp (2004), the O&M specialist "should use professional judgment to determine when a child should begin using a cane [or AMD] outside of O&M lessons and should monitor the child's progress in using the cane [or AMD] with other adults" (p. 7). After a thorough O&M evaluation is completed, the O&M specialist will determine whether the child with a visual impairment needs to use a cane or AMD. "Determining when a child is ready to use a cane [or AMD] . . . depends on several factors: the child's level of skill with the cane [or device]; the willingness of the adult to allow the child to use the cane [or device]; and the ability of the adult to monitor cane [or AMD] use and give appropriate feedback" (Sapp, 2004, p. 7). Other team members, especially parents and caregivers, can offer input on the child's readiness for a cane or AMD, and the O&M specialist can provide the instruction needed to effectively train each member of the team on how to support device use. The responsibility of determining the child's readiness and the amount of team training needed lies with the O&M specialist.

Thorough training and ongoing monitoring by the O&M specialist is necessary to ensure that basic cane or AMD skills are supported and reinforced correctly. All team members, including parents, caregivers, school staff, and anyone who works with the student with a visual impairment on a consistent basis, should be trained in basic O&M skills such as guide technique, trailing, and protective techniques, along with any modifications or adaptations needed for a particular student, so that all team members can provide continuous and consistent support in O&M skills across living and learning environments (see Chapter 6 for more information on basic O&M skills). Along with basic O&M skills, the O&M specialist should also train each team member in the specific skills the O&M specialist is currently working on with the student, especially as they apply to cane or AMD use. These skills can include proper grip, appropriate storage of the device, and appropriate use of the device in various settings.

The student using a cane or AMD should be provided with many opportunities to practice using the device in as many learning environments as possible, including in a preschool or school setting, in the student's local community, and in the student's home. Paraeducators and classroom teachers are the primary team members who can encourage appropriate and consistent use of cane or AMD skills throughout the student's school day. The O&M specialist should create a priority list for the school staff that includes locations in the learning environment where the student should be using the cane or AMD. As the student becomes more proficient in the use of the cane or AMD in familiar environments, such as frequently visited classrooms, restrooms, the cafeteria, and the gym, more unfamiliar learning environments can be added to the list.

One key to student success in using a cane or AMD is to "involve parents in lessons with the [cane or] AMD as much as possible, to allow them to see the benefits of the [cane or] AMD for their child" (Sapp, 2004, p. 6; see Figure 11.3).

This involvement can require the O&M specialist asking parents or caregivers "to think of times each day when the child can use the [cane or] AMD and encourage them to let the child use the [cane or] AMD as often as possible" (Sapp, 2004, p. 6). It is important to remember that "Some children and families will be ready to use a cane as soon as it is introduced, though the child will benefit from continued instruction from the O&M specialist. Other children will require several instructional sessions with an O&M specialist before they are ready to use a cane [or AMD] with their parents [or caregivers]" (Sapp, 2004, p. 7). Video recording lessons at school and sharing the child's success in O&M with his or her family helps to demonstrate correct techniques while increasing the family's confidence in their child's abilities.

———

Kyle, an 8-year-old student with 20/80 vision with best correction in both eyes, aphakia, and peripheral field loss is being introduced to a long cane for use in familiar settings, including various locations in his school. For the past two years, Kyle has been using his functional vision as well as guidance from a staff member to travel around school, but this year, in third grade, students are expected to change classes independently at least five times during the school day. Kyle is now traveling from his classroom to three unfamiliar locations on campus, including outdoor travel to the gymnasium, which is a free-standing building separate from the main school building.

Strategies that can be used to ensure Kyle's successful use of his cane during transitions include performing multiple walk-through lessons to familiarize Kyle with all the routes he will use on a daily basis, working with Kyle on his organizational skills so he can travel from class to class with his

Rona L. Pogrund

Figure 11.3 Collaboration includes the O&M specialist involving parents in O&M lessons so they can observe their child using a cane or AMD.

personal materials (e.g., backpack, books, technology) while using his cane, repeating practice lessons focused on efficient basic cane use, and training Kyle's team members on skills needed to support his cane use during transitions. The team members who will need training include his general education classroom teachers, any staff members who might accompany Kyle or his class during transitions, and Kyle's parent or guardian. Ideally, Kyle's classmates should also receive a brief explanation about how Kyle uses his cane as a tool for travel and how to safely interact with Kyle while he is traveling with his cane. Training should occur before the school year starts (i.e., during professional development week) or during the first week of

school, with follow-up and refresher trainings taking place as needed during the school year. Training should take place in the environments in which Kyle will be using his cane, including hallways, outside walkways, classrooms, and any other areas of the school where Kyle will travel.

Collaborative Program Planning

When an O&M specialist is planning for O&M service programming, other team members and possible opportunities for collaboration should be considered. Some of the critical issues that must be considered in O&M program planning include (Bina, Naimy, Fazzi, & Crouse, 2010, p. 395)

- the population served;
- the ages, developmental levels, and needs of the clients and students;
- the size and geographical area to be served;
- the goals and objectives of the mobility program;
- the parameters, philosophy, and framework of the agency or school in which the O&M program must operate as a result of statutory, regulatory, or governance constraints;
- available resources based on budget limitations; and
- program evaluation to ensure accountability for student outcomes, state and federal mandates, and accreditation standards.

A student's O&M service needs should drive the amount of direct and collaborative consultation recommended on the student's IFSP or IEP. Student need, as shown in the results of a thorough O&M evaluation, should take priority over all other factors to appropriately address a student's O&M requirements. Collaborative consultation is just as important as direct service and should be included in recommended service time, despite the O&M specialist's concerns that collaborative consultation time takes away from available direct service time (Dettmer, Knackendoffel, & Thurston, 2013). To maximize efficient use of both direct service and collaborative consultation time, the O&M specialist needs to consider how to incorporate role release in collaborative consultation to help meet the student's needs, even if factors like a large caseload, agency or school regulatory constraints, and limited resources might

reduce the amount of time the O&M specialist spends delivering direct services to the student.

A key team member who should be included in the process of collaborative program planning is the student. Students of any age and any level of functioning can provide input on program planning, regardless of developmental level and communication capabilities. Input from the student is acquired through demonstration of O&M skills, as well as through all attempts and forms of communication, including verbal and nonverbal communication. The O&M specialist and other team members can support the growth of a student's self-determination and self-advocacy skills by including the student in the program planning process. When a student agrees to identified goals and objectives, the student will be more motivated to work toward meeting them in future lessons. All students receiving O&M services should be included in the IEP meeting and should participate in meeting decisions to the greatest degree possible.

One lesser-known form of collaboration in an O&M program is collaboration with the administration of the school district or agency. Getting administrators to understand the unique nature of O&M instruction—the need to go off campus for lessons, the need to travel to and from community destinations, the need for longer lessons for bus travel—can be a challenge that requires ongoing collaboration between the O&M specialist and the administration. Developing and maintaining "superior O&M services within any organizational structure or physical environment is accomplished by employing well-qualified O&M staff, ensuring effective communication, providing ongoing staff development and supervision designed to improve instructional effectiveness, maintaining an environment that is oriented to the student, and providing adequate fiscal support" (Bina et al., 2010, p. 432).

Finally, the O&M specialist and other team members can foster collaboration in a student's community by interacting with and training community members and stakeholders in the local area. Interaction with community members includes modeling appropriate interactions to foster student independence in community-based instruction, as well as encouraging students to practice independent skill building with community members. Training can include providing basic information about vision loss, explaining how to best assist a student with a visual impairment in a public setting, and promoting ways in which community stakeholders can encourage self-determination and independence in students when they are in the community.

─────────

Malia, a 13-year-old student with cortical visual impairment (CVI) and additional disabilities is transitioning to high school in three months. Malia has been using an AMD in her middle school for the past two and a half years. Her self-contained special education classroom staff in middle school has been successfully trained on how to support Malia using an AMD, and Malia has mastered her goals for using the AMD during transitions inside the school with some staff support and prompting. Malia's current O&M evaluation indicates that she has the potential to use the AMD independently with continued support and practice. Possible new goals for Malia in high school include learning new routes inside the school, using her AMD with support for transitions inside the school, and using her AMD with staff support during community-based instruction.

Prior to Malia starring high school, it is important for the O&M specialist to meet with the administration of the high school to explain what O&M is, describe how Malia will be using her AMD on her new campus, and to gain their support and listen to any safety or other concerns they may have. Such communication can facilitate a smoother transition since everyone will understand Malia's needs as well as be able to address any concerns on the part of the administration. Other team members who should be consulted regarding the new goals and recommendations for Malia include the special education teacher, paraeducators in her classroom, high school teachers and staff who will work with Malia during transitions inside the school building, Malia's teacher of students with visual impairments, and her parent or guardian. Other factors that will need to be considered include any obstacles in the routes Malia will use inside the high school, the time it takes Malia to travel inside the school using her AMD, Malia's ability to remember and follow new routes, opportunities for Malia to participate in community-based instruction, the training needed to ensure Malia's team can support her using the AMD in school and in the community, and the type and amount of direct and collaborative consultation O&M service time that will be needed to support Malia in meeting these recommended goals.

Referral for an O&M Evaluation

It is recommended that all students with visual impairments, no matter their age, other impairments, degree of vision, or cognitive ability, be referred for an O&M evaluation. This referral for evaluation applies to infants, toddlers, preschoolers, school-age students, students with multiple impairments, and students who have low vision. An O&M evaluation should be requested as part of a full individual initial evaluation for visual impairment–related concerns, as well as every three years, concurrent with the student's full individual reevaluation. A full individual initial evaluation and full individual reevaluation include multiple evaluations of various aspects of the student's current levels of functioning, the results of which determine if the student has met the criteria outlined in the Individuals with Disabilities Education Act (IDEA) of a student with a disability. Other instances when an O&M evaluation should be requested include a change of placement (e.g., from home to a school placement), transition to a new educational setting, and any other instances when a student experiences a change in visual functioning, orientation, or mobility (see Chapter 1 for more information on O&M evaluations). All team members may have input in the referral.

Joint Evaluations with O&M Specialists and Other Team Members

Once a student has been referred for an O&M evaluation, comprehensive and detailed data should be gathered from multiple sources to ensure that the results of the evaluation show a clear picture of the student's current strengths and needs related to O&M skills. Collaboration on data collection is essential to obtaining comprehensive results. Information for the O&M evaluation should be gathered from the following sources, including information from other team members (Russo & Liefert, 2003):

- Interviews with the student, parents or caregivers, other family members, instructional or school staff, and other related service staff

- Review of available student medical records, including eye examinations and reports completed by ophthalmologists and optometrists
- Review of student's IEP and full individual evaluation
- Review of student's related service and instructional evaluation reports (if available), including reports from a speech-language pathologist, physical therapist, occupational therapist, behavioral specialist, school psychologist, transition specialist, teacher of students with visual impairments, previous O&M specialist, adapted physical education teacher, and any other related service or professional support personnel who work with the student

In addition, discussions need to take place with ophthalmologists, optometrists, or other medical professionals regarding the student's visual and medical information, such as visual diagnosis, age of onset, visual acuity, visual fields, level of vision loss (and, if applicable, hearing loss) whether the student is functionally blind, legally blind, has color vision, or has photophobia, as well as the student's prognosis, treatment recommendations, and any precautions or suggestions. Finally, the teacher of students with visual impairments can provide information about the student's sensory modality and learning channels, accommodations and modifications, and learning media assessment results.

Other possible components of the O&M evaluation that require collaboration include the CVI Range, functional or adaptive skills inventory, developmental skills checklist or inventory, information pertaining to deafblindness (intervener input, communication strengths and needs), and a rating scale that can support a recommended amount and type of O&M service based on the evaluation data. Specific information related to skill areas that needs to be reviewed includes current levels of performance in various environments (home, school, familiar and unfamiliar community settings, and in a variety of lighting conditions, including night travel), psychological and learning strengths and needs, motor skills, sensory awareness and sensory integration, orthopedic strengths and needs, spatial concept development, literacy and learning media information, basic academic skill strengths and needs, orientation skills, body image, use of vision, basic O&M techniques, cane skills, street crossings, making appropriate judgments, maintaining appropriate conversations, soliciting and refusing assistance, use of public transportation, use of O&M devices (including electronic travel aids), and planning travel routes (Pogrund et al., 2012; Russo & Liefert, 2003; see Appendix B).

Writing IFSPs and IEPs

All IFSPs and IEPs, including transition plans, begin with a focused outcome: what skills and knowledge does the family—and, when appropriate, the student—want the student to be able to acquire and generalize in the short term and in the long term? All the goals and objectives from the very beginning of service provision to the transition to adult life should be centered around these desired skills and knowledge.

For IFSP planning, consideration of the skills and knowledge desired by the family is central to any program development. "One of the first steps in the process is to decide when and how frequently . . . to incorporate a goal or objective into [O&M] programming" (Deiner, 2013,

p. 172). Along with input from the family, goals and objectives should be based on results of an extensive O&M evaluation. The expected outcomes of the goals and objectives should be based on the student's current levels of performance; that is, the student's strengths and needs in each area of the goal's focus.

The O&M goals and objectives in the IEP should reflect the student's current level of O&M skill functioning, which can be found in the results of documented progress from the IFSP and from a current O&M evaluation. O&M goals and objectives in the IEP should reflect an array of input from team members as well as student strengths and needs related to O&M. "Cultural expectations, student age [and developmental] level, cognitive and physical capabilities, family resources and safety concerns, community norms, and environmental access play an important part in determining how independence and interdependence might be achieved for a given student" (Fazzi & Naimy, 2010, p. 214). At each annual IEP review meeting, the O&M goals and objectives should be reviewed and updated to ensure they reflect the student's progress and current skill needs. Additional collaboration with the student's entire team before each IEP meeting, as well as during periods of progress reporting, is needed to find gaps in skill acquisition and to address unforeseen setbacks that can occur due to circumstances outside of O&M direct service time. The information acquired from this collaboration, along with documentation of student progress or regression, should be the basis upon which all O&M goals are assessed and determined to be mastered, discontinued, or revised for the new IEP year.

As mandated by IDEA (2004), transition planning and transition services must be discussed and included in a student's IEP beginning at age 16. Ideally, this discussion on transition should begin much earlier so that the focus of programming is geared toward success after school ends. Information needed to effectively plan for a student's transition includes data from transition evaluations, suggested measurable postsecondary goals, options for continuing training or education as an adult, opportunities for employment, and suggested independent living skills. These pieces of information will be discussed by the student's IEP team on at least an annual basis as the student approaches the transition from school to adult life. Some key factors to consider when a team is planning a student's transition are the differences between public school service provision and adult service provision. Public school service provision addresses the needs of the whole child, is provided by a single entity delivering all services, is typically driven by a parent, caregiver, or family member, and is delivered free of charge to the student and the family (Heartland Area Education Agency, 2008). On the other hand, adult service provision is provided based on one or more disability-specific eligibility categories, is supplied by separate agencies that address different areas of skill building and need, is typically driven by the individual rather than a family member or caregiver, and does not have a guaranteed source of funding (Heartland Area Education Agency, 2008). When a student's team is planning for transition, these differences should be taken into consideration when setting goals for the student as well as determining the priority and timeline of skill areas that will need to be addressed. When planning for transition, the O&M specialist needs to consider the aspects of the student's adult life that may be affected by O&M skills, including career and vocational goals, transportation and independent travel goals, self-determination and self-advocacy, and independent living skills. The O&M specialist and other team members should work with the student's state-provided transition counselor (if one is available in the student's current state of residence) to build a support network for the student that will bridge the gap between school service provision and adult service provision.

Teaming Strategies to Support O&M Instruction

The teaming strategies most useful in supporting O&M instruction throughout all learning environments include preparation, team training, modeling, reviewing, and consistent, continuous support.

Preparation

The O&M specialist must prepare O&M instruction information using practical language and concepts and disseminate it to all team members. The key to preparation is to think about the basic information each team member will need to understand before training and modeling can take place. Information, including explanation of recommended goals and objectives, justification of these goals and objectives, types of devices and assistive technology recommended to meet the goals and objectives, strategies for use of these devices, and specific vocabulary used with the student, should be clarified during initial and follow-up team meetings for members to fully understand how they can support O&M skill building throughout all areas of the student's daily life. Teaming strategies may also include in-service or specific team training from the O&M specialist in areas that deal with the effects of various visual impairments on independent travel skills, use of assistive technology related to O&M, and integration of O&M skills into other areas of the ECC (see Chapter 9 for more information on incorporating O&M into other ECC areas).

Team Training

Once this information is explained by the O&M specialist and understood by each team member, the O&M specialist should train all team members in the conceptual implementation and support of the skills and concepts that he or she is teaching the student. These skills and concepts should be analyzed and broken down into specific steps, which will then be taught to any team members who will be supporting the student in learning and practicing these skills and concepts. For example, the O&M specialist may be teaching the student how to identify specific landmarks in the student's school. Each team member who travels with the student in the school should be taught appropriate techniques for locating landmarks as well as the vocabulary used to describe location techniques and the landmarks themselves. The O&M specialist should train the team using three different learning styles—training with visual information, auditory information, and kinesthetic information—to ensure that all team members can learn the techniques and strategies needed to support the student's learning.

Modeling

After all team members have been trained in a conceptual understanding of the strategies, the O&M specialist should then model the teaching techniques and strategies that best meet the student's needs to each of the team members (see Sidebar 11.11). For example, the O&M specialist may interrupt the student and classroom teacher while they travel from the classroom to the bathroom. The O&M specialist can model how to help the student learn about the landmarks at or near the bathroom while the classroom teacher observes the O&M specialist and the student working together. After the O&M specialist has modeled the appropriate techniques and strategies, the classroom teacher and the O&M specialist should switch roles. This role reversal will allow the classroom teacher the opportunity to repeat the techniques and strategies used by the O&M specialist in a real-world setting with the student. The O&M specialist should observe the interaction of the classroom teacher and the student and note consistent and inconsistent implementation of the modeled techniques and strategies. If any of the techniques and strategies are not implemented correctly, the O&M specialist should review them with the classroom teacher.

Reviewing

Once the O&M specialist and another team member switch roles and the modeled activity is implemented with the student by the other team member, the O&M specialist and the other team member should review both the positive and negative aspects of the activity. Specific notes should be provided by the O&M specialist in order for the other team member to clearly understand what was taught correctly and what techniques and strategies need to be refined to be consistent in teaching the student. Modeling, observation, and review are steps that may need to be repeated to ensure that the student is receiving consistent instruction across learning environments.

Having other team members use low vision simulators that imitate the visual impairment of the student with whom they are working provides valuable insight into the O&M needs of the student. Using blindfolds with team

---

SIDEBAR 11.11

Suggested O&M Strategies

The O&M specialist will model specific techniques and strategies to the student's team during role release. These strategies can then be used by team members to support the student's O&M skills.

- Use specific terms when verbalizing directions instead of using vague, nonspecific terms (e.g., "Make a 90 degree turn to your left at the end of the hall" versus "Turn to your left when you get there"; or "The hook for your cane is to the right of the door at shoulder level before the bookshelf" versus "Put your cane over here").
- If the student knows left and right, degree turns, or cardinal directions, use these terms to facilitate specific spatial orientation when providing directions.
- Communicate ahead of time about the sequence of landmarks, cues, or obstacles on a route, or when the student is learning the layout of a room, to develop mental mapping of the route or space.

- Use one instruction at a time when asking the student to follow directions (unless it is known that the student can retain more than one instruction at a time) and check for understanding by having the student repeat the directions.
- Use proper guide technique when walking with the student and encourage the use of correct technique if the student is walking with a peer as a guide.
- Limit physical prompting, but if necessary, always use hand-under-hand technique when physically guiding a student to do something; be sure to ask permission before touching the student (e.g., "Is it okay if I move your hand to show you where the door is on the tactile map of our classroom?").
- Encourage good posture and body positioning in social situations (e.g., remind the student to hold his or her head up and face his or her nose toward the person speaking to show interest).
- Use verbal directions rather than pushing or pulling the student.

---

members when teaching proper guide technique can be a useful strategy for reinforcing how to guide their student who is blind. Reversing roles and blindfolds so that the team member learns to be the guide is another valuable experience since the team member receives feedback from the O&M specialist while practicing the technique. Although some professionals may feel that blindfolding other team members is a good way for them to empathize with their students, it is important to be mindful that if using occlusion extensively in

short-term training situations without the use of a guide, this activity may also have potential negative consequences, such as reinforcing fear of blindness in team members, which can result in members being more overprotective when working with the student.

Consistent and Continuous Support

Once each team member is comfortable with providing consistent skill and concept support to the student without oversight by the O&M specialist, the O&M specialist should continue to communicate and occasionally observe each team member during teaching moments with the student to ensure that continuity and consistency in skill and concept implementation takes place over the long term. Training other team members does not remove the ultimate responsibility of the O&M specialist in ensuring that goals and objectives are met; therefore, ongoing monitoring of skill use by the student and O&M skill reinforcement by other team members is essential (Smith, 1998). As the student's O&M skills develop and the student meets his or her goals and objectives, the O&M specialist and other team members should set new goals and objectives, and they should repeat the teaming strategies of preparation, team training, modeling, reviewing, and consistent, continuous support when addressing the new goals and objectives. This cycle should continue throughout the student's time in an educational setting.

Collaboration with Families from Diverse Cultures

When working in a transdisciplinary team model, the O&M specialist must take into consideration the cultural practices, beliefs, and value systems of students, families, and other team members. These factors can affect how team members, especially families, view the appropriateness of interventions recommended by the O&M specialist. Understanding cultural norms is important in being sensitive to the views and needs of the student and the family (Turnbull, Turnbull, Wehmeyer, & Shogren, 2015). For example, in some cultures, a family may not want to foster independence in a child who is blind or visually impaired, especially as

it relates to mobility and travel, so understanding that aspect of the family's culture may help the O&M specialist and other team members when planning the child's IEP. When working with young children or students in a home setting, all team members, including the O&M specialist, must be "sensitive to cultural beliefs and value systems in designing home-based interventions or interventions with a parent [or caregiver] component" (Rathvon, 2008, p. 37). Speaking frankly, but sensitively, with the families of children from diverse cultural backgrounds about the family's expectations for their child can also help to make a connection and open the lines of communication regarding the role of the O&M specialist in the child's learning and growth. The O&M specialist can also bolster sensitivity and understanding of the cultural considerations of a student by enlisting the help of "school staff or community individuals from the same cultural/ethnic/linguistic background as the referred student in the intervention assistance process" (Rathvon, 2008, p. 37). The culturally competent O&M specialist may have to shift perspective to find a balance between professional beliefs (creating and supporting independent travel in a student who is blind or visually impaired) and the family's cultural beliefs.

See Sidebar 11.12 for a summary of the important elements discussed in this chapter that promote effective collaboration in an O&M program.

Summary

Orientation and mobility is essential for individuals who are blind or visually impaired; O&M skills facilitate access to the world around them.

Key Elements for Effective Collaboration in an O&M Program

- Collaboration is an interactive activity among multiple educational team members, with the focus of that activity being student learning, student skill retention, and student skill generalization.

- Collaboration takes place within a team comprised of members who are committed to creating a culture of positive interaction, open and active communication, goal setting, and continuous improvement in the learning and teaching processes.

- Professional learning communities create the process of collaboration, and they are the driving force behind student learning and consistent teaching for all members involved.

- There are three models of collaboration in an educational setting: multidisciplinary, interdisciplinary, and transdisciplinary. The transdisciplinary team model is the ideal model for those working with students with visual impairments.

- The transdisciplinary model requires role release. Each service provider will train the other members in their area of expertise regarding the strategies and methods used to teach the skills related to the student's current IFSP or IEP goals and objectives.

- Every team member, including the student and the student's family or caregivers, has a specific role in teaching, implementing, and supporting O&M skills. The O&M specialist takes the lead role when O&M skills and concepts are the focus of the team.

- Parents, caregivers, and families play a crucial role in supporting O&M skill and concept acquisition and generalization. The O&M specialist should establish a relationship with students' families and caregivers to foster consistent skill and concept development in the home and after-school learning environments.

- The O&M referral and evaluation process, program planning, and IFSP or IEP development is a collaborative effort among all team members, with the O&M specialist serving as the leader and expert on matters related to O&M skill and concept development. These processes should be worked into the larger framework of educating the whole student, and all team members should be equal partners in determining the best practices for meeting the student's needs in all skill areas.

- The foundation of the transdisciplinary team model is training all members of the team in the most effective teaching techniques and strategies in each learning area. The O&M specialist is responsible for training all team members in the consistent use of techniques and strategies related to the O&M skills and concepts being taught to the student with a visual impairment.

- Cultural diversity is an important component to consider when working in the transdisciplinary team model. Students, families, and other team members may all have varied practices, beliefs, and values that will affect their expectations and goals for the student with a visual impairment. The O&M specialist should be sensitive to the diverse viewpoints of all team members when managing implementation of O&M skills.

Teaching O&M without working in a collaborative team model is counterproductive to the purpose of O&M. If the O&M specialist works directly with the student without involving others on the educational team, the skills taught will likely not be integrated into the daily routines of the student. Generalization of these skills will be limited if others in the school and home settings are not reinforcing and supporting the skills learned on a regular basis in a functional context. It is collaboration with other team members that increases student progress toward meeting O&M goals and objectives. Having partners in O&M is what makes it successful for the student, and it is equally important for the O&M specialist to have mutual respect for the expertise and perspectives of the other members of the educational team.

References

Bina, M. J., Naimy, B. J., Fazzi, D. L., & Crouse, R. J. (2010). Administration, assessment, and program planning for orientation and mobility services. In W. R. Wiener, R. L. Welsh, & B. B. Blasch (Eds.), *Foundations of orientation and mobility: Vol. I. History and theory* (3rd ed., pp. 389–433). New York, NY: AFB Press.

Correa, V. I., Fazzi, D. L., & Pogrund, R. L. (2002). Team focus: Current trends, service delivery, and advocacy. In R. L. Pogrund & D. L. Fazzi (Eds.), *Early focus: Working with young children who are blind or visually impaired and their families* (2nd ed., pp. 405–441). New York, NY: AFB Press.

Deiner, P. L. (2013). *Inclusive early childhood education: Development, resources, and practice* (6th ed.). Belmont, CA: Wadsworth Cengage Learning.

Dettmer, P., Knackendoffel, A., & Thurston, L. P. (2013). *Collaboration, consultation, and teamwork for students with special needs* (7th ed.). New York, NY: Pearson.

DuFour, R. (2004). What is a professional learning community? *Educational Leadership, 61*(8), 6–11.

DuFour, R., DuFour, R., Eaker, R., & Many, T. (2010). *Learning by doing: A handbook for professional learning communities at work* (2nd ed.). Bloomington, IN: Solution Tree Press.

Fazzi, D. L., & Naimy, B. J. (2010). Teaching orientation and mobility to school-age children. In W. R. Wiener, R. L. Welsh, & B. B. Blasch (Eds.), *Foundations of orientation and mobility: Vol. II. Instructional strategies and practical applications* (3rd ed., pp. 208–262). New York, NY: AFB Press.

Ford, H. (n.d.). Henry Ford 150 quotes. Retrieved from https://media.ford.com/content/fordmedia/fna/us/en/asset.download.document.pdf.html/content/dam/fordmedia/North%20America/US/2013/07/17/Henry_Ford_150_quotes.pdf

Friend, M., & Cook, L. (2017). *Interactions: Collaboration skills for school professionals* (8th ed.). Upper Saddle River, NJ: Pearson Education.

Fry, N. (2001). Tying it together: Personal supports that lead to membership and belonging. In C. H. Kennedy & D. Fisher (Eds.), *Inclusive middle schools* (pp. 119–120). Baltimore, MD: Paul H. Brookes.

Gargiulo, R. M. (2015). *Special education in contemporary society: An introduction to exceptionality* (5th ed.). Thousand Oaks, CA: SAGE.

Gargiulo, R. M., & Kilgo, J. L. (2014). *An introduction to young children with special needs: Birth through age eight* (4th ed.). Belmont, CA: Wadsworth Cengage Learning.

Heartland Area Education Agency. (2008). *Transition resource guide.* Johnston, IA: Author.

Huxham, C., & Vangen, S. (2005). *Managing to collaborate: The theory and practice of collaborative advantage.* Abingdon, UK: Routledge.

Idol, L., Nevin, A., & Paolucci-Whitcomb, P. (2000). *Collaborative consultation.* Austin, TX: PRO-ED.

Individuals with Disabilities Education Improvement Act (IDEA), 20 U.S.C. § 1400 (2004).

Milteniene, L., & Venclovaite, I. (2012). Teacher collaboration in the context of inclusive education. *Special Education, 2*(27), 111–123.

Noe, M., McCaffery, M., & Meagher, R. (2011). Individual education play (IEP). In *IEP workshop: Building teacher-parent partnerships*. Verona, WI: Attainment Company.

Pogrund, R., Sewell, D., Anderson, H., Calaci, L., Cowart, M. F., Gonzalez, C. M., . . . Roberson-Smith, B. (2012). Part 2: Comprehensive initial and ongoing evaluation. In *TAPS—Teaching age-appropriate purposeful skills: An orientation and mobility curriculum for students with visual impairments* (3rd ed.). Austin: Texas School for the Blind and Visually Impaired.

Powell, W. (2004). Chapter 5: Collaboration. In O. Kusuma-Powell & W. Powell (Eds.), *Count me in! Developing inclusive international schools*. Washington, DC: U.S. Department of State, Overseas Schools Advisory Council. Retrieved from http://www.state.gov/m/a/os/43980.htm

Rathvon, N. (2008). *Effective school interventions: Evidence-based strategies for improving student outcomes* (2nd ed.). New York, NY: The Guilford Press.

Robinson, L., & Buly, M. R. (2007). Breaking the language barrier: Promoting collaboration between general and special educators. *Teacher Education Quarterly, 34*(3), 83–94.

Russo, J. R., & Liefert, F. K. (2003). Report writing. In S. A. Goodman & S. H. Wittenstein (Eds.), *Collaborative assessment: Working with students who are blind or visually impaired, including those with additional disabilities* (pp. 298–316). New York, NY: AFB Press.

Sapp, W. (2004). *Adaptive mobility devices and canes for toddlers: Suggestions for O&M specialists*. Chapel Hill: University of North Carolina at Chapel Hill, FPG Child Development Institute, Early Intervention Training Center for Infants and Toddlers with Visual Impairments.

Smith, M. (1998, Spring). Joseph's coat: People teaming in transdisciplinary ways. *SEE/HEAR*. Retrieved from http://www.tsbvi.edu/seehear/spring98/joseph.html

Turnbull, A., Turnbull, R., Wehmeyer, M. L., & Shogren, K. A. (2015). *Exceptional lives: Special education in today's schools* (8th ed.). New York, NY: Pearson.

U.S. Department of Education. (2000). *A guide to the individualized education program*. Jessup, MD: ED Pubs. Retrieved from https://www2.ed.gov/parents/needs/speced/iepguide/index.html

Wiggins, K. C., & Damore, S. J. (2006). "Survivors" or "friends"? A framework for assessing effective collaboration. *TEACHING Exceptional Children, 38*(5), 49–56.

Wiig, E. H. (1992). *Language intervention for school-age children: Models and procedures that work*. Chicago, IL: Riverside.

Woodruff, G., & McGonigel, M. J. (1988). Early intervention team approaches: The transdisciplinary model. In J. Jordan, J. Gallagher, P. Hutinger, & M. Karnes (Eds.), *Early childhood special education: Birth to three* (pp. 163–182). Reston, VA: Council for Exceptional Children.

Epilogue

Rona L. Pogrund

The future is uncertain . . . but this uncertainty is at the very heart of human creativity. (Ilya Prigogine, as quoted in Clarkson, 2002, p. 87)

This book provides a basic foundation of the field of orientation and mobility (O&M) for students who are blind or visually impaired. It provides a wealth of information for future O&M specialists and the many professionals and partners who work with these students in the school setting, as well as for their family members. In addition to this foundational knowledge about O&M, the basic skills that other educational team members can teach or reinforce have also been included in this book. Related professionals such as teachers of students with visual impairments, physical therapists, low vision specialists, adaptive physical educators, occupational therapists, speech-language pathologists, and others will gain valuable insight from this book on how they can collaborate and become partners with O&M specialists in supporting the O&M skills needed by students with visual impairments. By having knowledge about the field of O&M, family members, caregivers, classroom teachers, rehabilitation personnel, interveners, and paraeducators can encourage these students to generalize their use of O&M skills at home and in the community. O&M specialists alone cannot provide optimal O&M services to their students. They need other partners on the education or rehabilitation team to support students in the necessary O&M skills they are learning. Instruction from O&M specialists has little impact if the O&M skills learned are not expected, practiced, and reinforced by everyone who has contact with the student.

As noted throughout the book, almost every area of O&M has evolved from its origin centuries ago and become more formalized after World War II. Since then, the transformation of O&M has continued at a rapid pace. The populations who benefit have broadened, O&M tools have changed, alternate skills and instructional strategies have emerged, different instructional philosophies have been developed, the built environment has advanced, technology has entered the field, and the profession of O&M has evolved. Orientation and mobility has been recognized in federal law and in many state laws as a relevant and important service that individuals who are visually impaired both require and deserve to help them become as independent as possible and to prepare them for career, college, and adult life after leaving the educational system or upon entering the rehabilitation system.

The field of O&M faces many challenges in the future as it continues to grow into a viable

289

profession. Personnel preparation programs are constantly evolving to meet the challenge of preparing O&M specialists to meet the needs of the growing populations of young children and older adults with visual impairments. Both of these expanding groups of individuals are in need of O&M services. There is a strong retention rate in terms of O&M specialists staying on the job for many years, but there is a generation of baby boomer O&M specialists who are at or near retirement age. As these professionals leave the field, there needs to be a pipeline of newly trained O&M specialists to replace them. The challenge facing the service of older adults—the fastest growing population of people who are blind or visually impaired—is even greater than finding enough personnel to work with children from birth to 22 years of age.

Even if there are enough trained and certified O&M specialists to serve all of the populations in need, the funding to hire enough personnel in both the education and rehabilitation systems is an ongoing challenge. Over time, as priorities change in the political climate, they have a direct impact on available funding for services such as O&M. Individuals with visual impairments are a low-incidence population as compared to larger groups in special education and the broader general education community. Because of funding limits, even when O&M needs are identified, service times are often reduced because instead of hiring additional personnel, more work is added to the O&M specialist's caseload. Providing O&M services based on need should be the standard for all students. Until Medicare, Medicaid, and private insurers acknowledge the value of including O&M services, along with vision rehabilitation therapy and low vision therapy, for reimbursement—just as audiology services, physical therapy, speech therapy, and similar services are currently covered as essential services for adults who are blind or visually impaired—there will not be enough services provided. With the population of individuals with age-related visual impairments on the rise, the need for O&M services will only continue to increase in the decades ahead. Advocacy is needed at both the federal and state levels to change the current situation and prioritize a service that fosters independence, self-sufficiency, and self-confidence, and that improves the quality of life for both children and adults with visual impairments.

The ongoing changes in the populations served will require O&M professional preparation curricula to continue to evolve to meet the needs of an even larger variety of students. New strategies will need to be developed that better meet the needs of individuals who are visually impaired and who have comorbid conditions and multiple impairments such as brain disorders, deafblindness, autism, and others. Students with cerebral or cortical visual impairment, the most common diagnosis of children with visual impairments, create new O&M challenges because their vision fluctuates throughout the day and from day-to-day, with each student's visual impairment manifesting in a different way. Personnel preparation programs may find it challenging to adequately prepare future O&M specialists to meet the needs of their many students within the currently offered coursework.

Keeping up with technology in O&M is another ongoing challenge facing the field. There are new navigational devices and mobility tools being developed each year, some helpful and some merely ideas of creative inventors who want to help people who are blind. With so much new technology and other innovative O&M ideas, there is, unfortunately, little accompanying research being done to evaluate whether these pioneering systems are indeed valid and beneficial for users. There are few research studies being conducted in O&M in general since most of the research of developing evidence-based practices is typically conducted by university faculty, who are already stretched thin with teaching and O&M program coordination. Research also requires funding, and there are few resources available to fund O&M research and few researchers trying to obtain what little funds are available through federal grants and private foundations. Research is a challenge for a field as small as O&M. However, there is some excellent work being done to begin establishing evidence to support the evaluations, instructional interventions, and tools used by O&M specialists and their students.

The prospects for the field of O&M lie in the many possibilities for the future. New generations of innovative and passionate professionals will create new O&M paths that will continue to shape the field. Just as it has progressed over the past decades, O&M will continue to grow as a vital field that more and more people will recognize as the key to accessibility and equality. Without mastery of O&M skills, a person who is blind or visually impaired is limited in many areas such as self-confidence, employment options, social interactions, recreational opportunities, self-determination, and independence. Orientation and mobility is a basic freedom that is the right of all individuals with visual impairments. Including the voices of students and their families, along with the many partners who support success in O&M, will ensure that the O&M skills learned will continue to facilitate this freedom for all individuals who are blind or visually impaired.

Reference

Clarkson, P. (2002). *The transpersonal relationship in psychotherapy: The hidden curriculum of spirituality.* London, UK: Whurr Publishers.

Appendix A

Data-Based Decision Making and the Role of Preference Assessments

Devender R. Banda and Nouf M. Alzrayer

Importance of Data-Based Decision Making in Educational Settings

The 2004 Individuals with Disabilities Education Improvement Act, commonly known as IDEA, and the 2001 reauthorization of the Elementary and Secondary Education Act, commonly referred to as No Child Left Behind, require teachers to use practices founded on scientifically based research to improve student outcomes. The 2015 Every Student Succeeds Act used a similar term in place of scientifically based research: evidence-based practice (EBP). EBPs are strategies developed through an accumulation of rigorous experimental research studies published in peer-reviewed journals. The published articles are then systematically reviewed through a set of parameters (e.g., type of design used, data-collection methods, data reliability, intervention fidelity, replication of results) and are analyzed (e.g., via meta-analysis or qualitative descriptive reviews) to assess the impact of an intervention on student outcomes. EBPs are typically disseminated for practice and research through technical-assistance centers (e.g., What Works Clearinghouse), professional associations (e.g., National Center on Deaf-Blindness,

American Speech-Language-Hearing Association), and peer-reviewed journals.

EBPs are often reported in the field of learning disabilities, autism, intellectual disabilities, and emotional and behavioral disorders. However, in the field of orientation and mobility (O&M), this task is challenging because of the limited number of research studies conducted through rigorous designs due to the low incidence of individuals with visual impairments (Banda, Griffin-Shirley, Okungu, Ogot, & Meeks, 2014). Research and practice in the field of O&M is predominantly based on expert clinical opinion, ongoing practice, and anecdotal evidence. An important part of building an evidence base is maintaining ongoing data collection to evaluate student outcomes and using research designs to objectively determine the impact of an intervention (Odom et al., 2005). The following sections describe various data-collection methods and provide an overview of simple single-subject designs to inform O&M specialists how to begin using these methods in their O&M lessons with students with visual impairments. The importance of including students' preferences is also explored. Finally, a case study is provided at the end that summarizes all the components presented in this appendix.

Data Collection

Data collection is a vital part of initial and ongoing evaluation of outcomes for students with visual impairments. Data assists professionals in making instructional decisions on a continuous basis and communicating the results to parents, administrators, and other stakeholders (e.g., special education teacher, general educator, school nurse). Typical data collection in classrooms involves standardized or norm-referenced assessments, criterion-based assessments, and direct observation. In special education, ongoing assessment through direct observation is an important part of assessment, program planning, and evaluation.

Types of Data-Collection Methods

There are two types of data-collection methods used in education and social sciences: indirect and direct. Indirect methods involve gathering information about target behaviors by eliciting information from teachers, caregivers, and other personnel who are knowledgeable about the child. Indirect methods include interviews, reviews of records, questionnaires, and rating scales (Miltenberger, 2012). On the other hand, direct methods include observing and recording a specific behavior as the child exhibits or performs that behavior (e.g., observing how a toddler who is blind holds his or her adaptive mobility device).

There are some advantages and disadvantages of indirect methods. Indirect data-collection methods are a good starting point to achieve a better understanding of a particular behavior (Heflin & Alaimo, 2007) and require minimal or no training and time to conduct them (Fisher, Piazza, & Roane, 2011). Another advantage is

that indirect methods can help an O&M specialist establish the best time and place to collect data through direct observation methods (Miltenberger, 2012). Despite these advantages, there are limitations to these methods that O&M specialists should keep in mind. Indirect data-collection methods rely on individuals' memories and perspectives to gather information about specific behaviors (Fisher et al., 2011). Therefore, this information can be unreliable or invalid when planning a program to assist the student. Direct data-collection methods can provide O&M specialists with more accurate information about a target behavior or task (Miltenberger, 2012). Using both indirect and direct data-collection methods helps to create a comprehensive picture of a student's behaviors.

Indirect Data Collection

Interviews. Interviews are one of the most common methods to collect data on target behaviors. An O&M specialist can gather information about a behavior by conducting an interview with a student or his or her caregivers (e.g., parents, teachers, staff). In a structured interview, an O&M specialist asks a specific set of questions in the same order across multiple interviewees (Fisher et al., 2011). Follow-up questions may be asked if the O&M specialist needs to gather additional information. A disadvantage of the interview process is that it may provide inaccurate information about a target behavior (Fisher et al., 2011). An interviewee can answer the questions based on what he or she suspects the interviewer expects to hear, or an interviewee might provide incorrect or vague answers to questions posed by the interviewer. For example, a parent may state that his or her child frequently uses a cane at home, but it is evident that the child rarely takes the cane home and generally leaves it in the classroom. Additionally, interviews may involve the recollection of past events that may have little relevance to current target behaviors or teaching activities.

Rating Scales. The main purpose of rating scales is to gather information about the student's skills or target behaviors through yes or no questions or Likert scales (i.e., strongly agree to strongly disagree). One advantage of rating scales is that they can provide O&M specialists with quantifiable information about a target behavior that can be more useful as compared to qualitative information. However, a disadvantage is that, similar to interviews, rating scales are based on recall and the O&M specialist's views or perspectives, which can often be unreliable or invalid.

Direct Observation Methods

Direct observation and ongoing data-collection methods are efficient for tracking student behaviors for the purposes of evaluation and development of interventions. These methods provide an unambiguous way to communicate results to others (Kennedy, 2005). In order to collect data on a target behavior, the student's behavior must be observed and recorded as it occurs, such as observing a student who is blind gripping his or her cane while on the school playground. Several important steps should be followed when conducting direct observations (Miltenberger, 2012):

1. Observe the student by being close enough to see or hear the target behavior.
2. Write a precise definition of the behavior in measurable and observable terms. A clear measurable and observable definition will help others record the same behavior in different settings or at different times. For example, "the student's index finger is extended and pointing toward the ground while the thumb and remaining fingers are curled loosely around the cane."
3. Select the time period when the behavior is most likely to occur (e.g., any time the student uses his or her cane at school). The indirect methods described in the previous section are a great source of information in helping to select the observation periods.
4. Determine the place or setting in which to conduct the observations. Observations can be conducted either in natural or analog settings. In natural settings, the observations take place where the target behavior typically occurs. For example, Ms. Harris, the O&M specialist, observes Janie while she is traveling from her classroom to the playground at recess and monitors how Janie uses her cane on the playground. In analog settings, the observer records the student's behavior in a controlled or clinical setting (e.g., in an observation room with a two-way mirror). (Analog settings are not typically used in O&M.)
5. Select which type of observation to conduct, either a structured or unstructured observation. Structured observations require arranging an activity in which the observer records the target behavior. For example, an O&M specialist can record how many times Joseph correctly read the street signs with his monocular on a three-block route around his school. Unstructured observations occur during natural routines (e.g., bath time, mealtime, playtime) and typically involve no interactions or instructions from the observer.

6. Choose a recording method, which will likely vary across behaviors.

Event or Frequency Recording. In an event or frequency recording, the number of occurrences of a target behavior during a specific observation period are counted. In other words, this method is a simple frequency count of a behavior. The O&M specialist can also report the number of times a behavior occurred during a particular time period (i.e., rate), such as the number of words read per minute. Event recording is an effective method to use when the goal is to increase or decrease occurrences of a particular behavior. This method is best used with discrete behaviors that have a clear beginning and end (e.g., lifting a cane off the walking surface during touch technique, reading words with a monocular, telling time with a braille watch). Event recording is an easy method to employ and is an appropriate method to use with various behaviors. However, event recording is difficult to use for high-frequency behaviors (e.g., stereotypic behaviors such as hand flapping) or behaviors that last a longer period of time (e.g., out-of-seat behavior or time it takes to find a location on a tactile map).

Duration Recording. This recording method is used when the main goal is to record the amount of time that a behavior occurred (Cooper, Heron, & Heward, 2007). For example, recording the amount of time it takes for a student to walk across the hall using a protective technique. Duration recording can be used with behaviors with high frequency rates (e.g., number of times a student flaps his or her hands) or task-oriented continuous behaviors (e.g., time spent working on a reading passage) (Cooper et al., 2007). For duration recording,

the behavior must be operationally defined so that onset and offset of the target behavior can be clearly recorded. For example, the onset of an off-task behavior would be a student leaving his or her seat without permission, and the offset would be the student sitting back in the seat. A teacher can use a stopwatch to report the time a student engaged in a behavior. The recorded duration data can be reported in two ways: average duration and total duration (Alberto & Troutman, 2012). Average duration can be used when a student engages in a behavior regularly. For instance, an O&M specialist can report the average time a student is off-task as defined by not sweeping the cane side to side while traveling from the bus stop to the front door of the school. Total duration recording refers to the amount of time a student engages in a behavior during a specific period. For example, a teacher can record how long a student was engaged in appropriate play during recess. In O&M, duration recording can be used for the length of time a student holds the cane, walks from home to school, or completes a GPS assignment.

Latency Recording. Latency recording measures the amount of time that elapses between the presentation of a stimulus (e.g., asking a question) and the beginning of the behavior (e.g., student's response) (Alberto & Troutman, 2012). It is the amount of time that elapses between the teacher's command and the student's initiation of the response. This method is very useful for recording compliance-related behaviors (e.g., how long a student takes after the classroom teacher asks the student to get his or her cane or how long it takes a student to start walking when asked to go to the bathroom). This method is usually used when the goal is to decrease the amount of time it takes the student to respond to instructions. Initially, in O&M instruction, the student may not be motivated to comply with instructions, and it may take longer to initiate a task. Latency recording can be used in such cases to motivate the student to respond quickly using a variety of reinforcers that the student prefers (see Sidebar A.1).

SIDEBAR A.1
Preference Assessment

A preference assessment is a set of procedures used to identify a student's preferred items or activities (Lohrmann-O'Rourke, Browder, & Brown, 2000). These preferred items can be edibles (e.g., drinks, snacks), toys (e.g., cars, Legos), or activities (e.g., using an iPad, listening to music, playing games, reading a braille book, playing with an adult). Preference assessments offer a good starting point for developing training programs that focus on either increasing desirable behaviors or decreasing undesirable behaviors (Roscoe & Fisher, 2008). It is important to include preferences since they can motivate students to participate in O&M training programs. For example, allowing a student to listen to his or her favorite music for 5 minutes as a reward for using a cane to walk to recess will motivate the student to use the cane in the future.

Conducting a Preference Assessment

There are two steps involved in conducting a preference assessment (Cooper et al., 2007). In the first step, the O&M specialist needs to identify potentially preferred items from parents, caregivers, teachers, and the student. This identification can be done through interviews and questionnaires. For example, an O&M specialist can ask a parent to list the toys or food items the student likes.

In the second step, the O&M specialist observes the student's preferences by presenting the items or activities from the list of preferred items obtained in the first step. This step can be accomplished in different ways. One way is to present all the preferred items at once and observe the student's interaction with each item. During the observation, the O&M specialist can record which items the student picked and how long the student interacted with each item. For example, the teacher may list a teddy bear as a preferred toy if the student frequently selected and played with this toy during most of the observation time. Instead of presenting all the items at once, the teacher can also present a single item or activity at a time and see if the student selects the item or engages in the activity. Or, the O&M specialist can present two preferred items or activities and record which one the student picks. For example, if the student frequently chooses to play with an action figure when given a choice between the action figure and a car, then the O&M specialist will record that the action figure is a preferred item. Another way to conduct a preference assessment is to present an array of multiple preferred items and instruct the student to pick one item. After the session, the teacher can make a list of highly preferred items or activities from most to least preferred. For example, if the student picks a gummy bear, popcorn, and a toy car multiple times, then the O&M specialist will list these items as the most highly preferred. On the other hand, if the student rarely or never picks pretzels, puzzles, or bubbles to play with, then these items will be listed as the least preferred items.

(continued on next page)

SIDEBAR A.1 (*continued*)

Importance of Preference Assessment in O&M Instruction

A preference assessment can play an important role when teaching beginning O&M skills to children with visual impairments as well as children with additional disabilities. A preference assessment is also an excellent way to keep a student motivated to complete O&M skills during a lesson. It is very important to conduct preference assessments often because students' preferences may change from time to time. For example, playing with cars can become uninteresting to a student after the student has played with them for several days. It is

also better to use activities as preferences instead of food. Food items should only be used with parental permission and faded over time, while activity preferences should be introduced as the student learns relevant O&M skills. Eventually, once the student has learned relevant skills, it is desirable to move from tangible motivators to more natural reinforcers. For example, when learning the route to the cafeteria, a preferred item such as a snack may be used initially, but eventually the motivation for the student to get to the cafeteria independently shifts to having lunch and spending time with friends.

Permanent Product Recording. This method is different than the other recording methods because it measures tangible items or environmental effects that are the results of behaviors (Alberto & Troutman, 2012). For example, a teacher can measure a student's progress in writing by recording how many words are spelled correctly in an essay, or the teacher can measure the number of times the student independently arrives to class on time. Teachers do not have to observe the students engaging in the target behavior directly. Instead, they can measure the outcomes of the behavior. Permanent product recording can be used in a variety of educational teachings, such as recording the number of words written in an essay, the number of correct answers in math homework, the number of correct responses on an English quiz, or the number of correctly identified rooms in a school hallway on a student-generated tactile map. Permanent product has certain advantages compared to other recording methods, such as the availability to perform another task while

the student engages in the target behavior, the potential to conduct accurate and valid measurements, and the ability to measure multiple complex behaviors.

Using Single-Subject Designs to Evaluate the Effectiveness of Interventions

AB Design

Data collection in and of itself is not helpful if there is not also a way to evaluate the data on a regular basis. The simplest method to evaluate student progress is to collect baseline data for three to four days, or until a stable pattern is visible, and then introduce the intervention. This method is known as an AB design (A = baseline; B = intervention) in single-subject methodology (Alberto & Troutman, 2012). For example, the O&M specialist can measure the distance traveled by a student with a cane and how long it takes without any prompts, which is the baseline phase. Data needs to be collected for three to four days, or until stability is achieved. During the intervention phase, the O&M specialist provides instruction through modeling, prompting, and other systematic teaching procedures (e.g., fading, reinforcement). Data is also collected during the intervention phase and then graphed in a simple line graph. Data from the baseline phase to the intervention phase is compared (e.g., change in level or trend) to see the effect of the intervention.

Figure A.1 shows that the student takes around 45 to 50 seconds to walk to a destination during baseline. During intervention, the student takes 20 to 25 seconds to walk to the destination. This indicates that it takes the student less time to walk in the intervention phase as compared to the baseline phase. However, a simple AB design can be problematic in terms of evaluating the intervention. It is possible that some other factors or variables can influence or muddle the intervention, such as environmental factors (e.g., noise in the classroom, fire drill) and the motivation of the student.

ABAB Design

To assess the real effect of the intervention, it can be withdrawn and reintroduced systematically through implementation of an ABAB design, in which the AB phase occurs twice (Cooper et al., 2007). In this design, the teacher collects baseline data and introduces the intervention to observe the effect of teaching. Once the effect of the intervention is visible, the teacher can withdraw the intervention to see if the student continues to perform at the current level or goes back to baseline. If the intervention is, in fact, responsible for the improvement, the student behavior will most likely return to baseline. The teacher can then reintroduce the intervention and observe if the behavior improves as in the earlier intervention period.

As shown in Figure A.2, during the first baseline phase (A), the student takes 40 to 45 seconds to walk. When intervention is introduced during the first intervention phase (B), the student takes 20 to 23 seconds to walk. In the third phase (A), the intervention is withdrawn to see if the student regresses to the original baseline

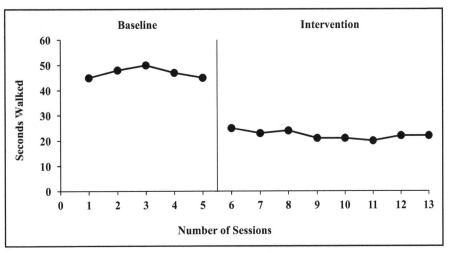

Figure A.1 Sample AB design: Amount of time it takes a student to walk to a destination, as displayed in a simple AB design graph.

phase. Data indicates that the student takes 43 to 46 seconds to walk to the destination. The intervention is reintroduced in the fourth phase (B), which clearly shows that the student takes 19 to 24 seconds to walk. In other words, if the student shows progress only during the intervention phases (B), the intervention is most likely responsible for the student's improvement. In the absence of intervention, the student's walking time remains at baseline levels. This method is one of the most effective ways to evaluate interventions. However, this approach may not work if the student learns the skill and it does not result in a complete loss of learning, which means that the second baseline data might look similar to the data in the first intervention phase rather than the data in the initial baseline. In such cases, more complicated designs can be utilized.

———

Matt is an 8-year-old boy with a visual impairment. Additionally, he has been diagnosed with a moderate intellectual disability. He attended an elementary school and received special education services in speech-language therapy, physical therapy, behavioral intervention, and O&M. Matt's IEP team, in consultation with Ms. Jones, the O&M specialist, would like to teach him to use a cane. He has no experience using a cane. Matt's behavioral analyst has conducted a preference assessment and determined that he likes playing with Legos and listening to music. The preference assessment was an important part of Matt's training program.

Ms. Jones planned to teach Matt to use his cane to walk from his classroom door to the playground. Initially, she collected baseline data on how many times Matt had to be told to sweep his cane from side to side to cover his body. During intervention, Ms. Jones provided one-on-one assistance and continued to collect data on Matt sweeping his cane from side to side. Additionally, she reinforced Matt's behavior by playing his favorite music or having him play with Legos immediately after the intervention session. Ms. Jones graphed baseline and intervention data using an AB design. She noticed an improvement in Matt's protection of his body by sweeping his cane side to

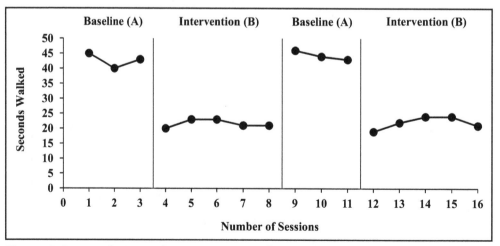

Figure A.2 Sample ABAB design: Amount of time it takes a student to walk to a destination, as displayed in a simple ABAB design graph.

side from baseline to intervention. Ms. Jones communicated the results to Matt's other teachers and the paraeducator in his class to have them reinforce the O&M training program on a daily basis as he traveled to and from the playground. The IEP team believed that conducting a preference assessment, defining the tasks in observable terms (e.g., number of verbal prompts), and collecting data on an ongoing basis was successful in evaluating the effectiveness of the O&M program.

Summary

Data collection is essential for measuring and tracking student progress. O&M specialists can use direct observation methods to collect student data and track their progress. Additionally, such data can provide O&M specialists with the means to communicate student progress to parents and administrators. Systematic data collection and evaluation of an intervention through single-subject designs can contribute to evidence-based practices (Odom et al., 2005). Federal law recommends that professionals use evidence-based practices to improve student outcomes in educational settings. Therefore, O&M specialists and other professionals need to utilize evidence-based practices when teaching students who are blind or visually impaired.

References

Alberto, P. A., & Troutman, A. C. (2012). *Applied behavior analysis for teachers* (9th ed.). Upper Saddle River, NJ: Pearson Education.

Banda, D. R., Griffin-Shirley, N., Okungu, P. A., Ogot, O. P., & Meeks, M. K. (2014). A review of intervention studies conducted with individuals with autism and sensory impairments. *Journal of Visual Impairment & Blindness, 108*(4), 299–309.

Cooper, J. O., Heron, T. E., & Heward, W. L. (2007). *Applied behavior analysis* (2nd ed.). Upper Saddle River, NJ: Pearson Education.

Elementary and Secondary Education Act (No Child Left Behind), Pub. L. No. 107-110 (2001).

Every Student Succeeds Act, Pub. L. No. 114-95 (2015).

Fisher, W. W., Piazza, C. C., & Roane, H. S. (Eds.). (2011). *Handbook of applied behavior analysis.* New York, NY: Guilford Press.

Heflin, L. J., & Alaimo, D. F. (2007). *Students with autism spectrum disorders: Effective instructional practices.* Upper Saddle River, NJ: Pearson/Merrill Prentice Hall.

Individuals with Disabilities Education Improvement Act (IDEA), 20 U.S.C. § 1400 (2004).

Kennedy, C. H. (2005). *Single-case designs for educational research.* Upper Saddle River, NJ: Pearson Education.

Lohrmann-O'Rourke, S., Browder, D. M., & Brown, F. (2000). Guidelines for conducting socially valid systematic preference assessments. *Journal of the Association for Persons with Severe Handicaps, 25*(1), 42–53.

Miltenberger, R. G. (2012). *Behavior modification: Principles and procedures* (5th ed.). Belmont, CA: Wadsworth Cengage Learning.

Odom, S. L., Brantlinger, E., Gersten, R., Horner, R. H., Thompson, B., & Harris, K. R. (2005). Research in special education: Scientific methods and evidence-based practices. *Exceptional Children, 71*(2), 137–148.

Roscoe, E. M., & Fisher, W. W. (2008). Evaluation of an efficient method for training staff to implement stimulus preference assessments. *Journal of Applied Behavior Analysis, 41*(2), 249–254.

Appendix B

Sample O&M Evaluation Report

Sunrise Independent School District
Orientation and Mobility Evaluation Report
Date of Report: July 29, 2011

Student Information

Student name: Twinkle Star Hill

Date of birth: July 31, 2006

Parent name(s): Jack and Jill Hill, father and mother

School: Elements Elementary, Sunrise ISO, Somewhere, TX

Grade: Kindergarten

Preferred language: English

Evaluator: Travis Trainer, certified orientation and mobility specialist

Date(s) of evaluation: July 7, 12, 18, and 20, 2011

Visual Information

Eye doctor: Dr. E. Y. Ball

Date of eye exam: May 5, 2009

Visual diagnosis:

Nystagmus (involuntary rhythmic side to side or up and down eye movements that are faster in one direction than the other direction)

Septo-optic dysplasia (smaller optic disks and pituitary problem that can lead to growth deficiency)

Optic nerve hypoplasia (small optic disks in both eyes which may cause reduced vision)

Age of onset: Birth

Prognosis: Permanent

Visual prescriptions: Safety glasses with plano lenses were prescribed

Acuity: O.D. (right): Count fingers; O.S. (left): 20/1200

Field restrictions: Some restriction evident, but not tested

(continued on next page)

Light sensitivity: Some sensitivity to bright lights, especially when going from inside to outside

Color discrimination: Normal

Medical Information

Hearing: Normal

Additional diagnosis: Septo-optic dysplasia that results in other accompanying characteristics, including a single anterior brain ventricle and short stature.

Other medical information: Height is shorter than typical for age. Student receives daily injections of a hormone stimulant.

Additional Information

Literacy medium/media used: Twinkle is just turning five and is receiving beginning braille instruction. She can tactually recognize all the letters of the alphabet but is not yet reading braille words.

Optical devices used: None

Student interview summary: Not conducted due to student age

Parent/guardian interview summary: Jill Hill, Twinkle's mother, reported that Twinkle began walking at the age of 15 months and is very active. Twinkle has always liked to explore things with both her hands and feet and shows little fear when in familiar or new environments. She has had O&M training since she was 13 months old, when her first O&M specialist introduced the use of a cane to the whole family. She likes her cane and calls O&M training "happy tapping." Her parents and teenage brother take turns walking in the neighborhood with her. During these outings, each person has a cane so that the older family members can model good cane use. When the family goes on outings in the community, Twinkle always takes her cane with her.

School personnel summaries: Twinkle's preschool teacher from last year reports that Twinkle was able to travel everywhere in the classroom on her own. While traveling with her white cane, she also followed well in a line when the class was traveling to other areas in the school, such as the cafeteria, office, gymnasium, and playground. On the playground, she was able to use all the equipment independently, including the slides, tunnels, swings, and climbing walls. The two skills she would like Twinkle to work on are riding a tricycle while pushing the pedals with her feet (she currently keeps her feet on the ground and walks while straddling the tricycle) and walking up and down stairs since the school she will attend for kindergarten is built on a hill and has several sets of stairs.

Previous O&M instruction received: Twinkle began receiving O&M training when she first moved into this school district at the age of 13 months (see Parent/guardian interview summary).

Evaluation Results

Evaluation tools/methods used:

- Evaluator observations
- *TAPS Comprehensive Initial and Ongoing Evaluation* (Pogrund et al., 2012)
- *Preschool Orientation and Mobility Screening* (Dodson-Burk & Hill, 1989)
- Consultation with classroom teacher and classroom assistant

- Consultation with mother
- Review of medical records

Evaluation locations/conditions:

- **Familiar/unfamiliar:** Twinkle was evaluated in the Open Door Preschool and in an unfamiliar adjacent building which houses the Early Childhood Intervention (ECI) offices.
- **Indoor/outdoor:** At the preschool, her travel skills were evaluated in her classroom, in the center's indoor central play area, on the main west playground, and the smaller south playground where the younger children play. In the adjacent building, she was evaluated in the reception area and the main floor hallways.
- **Day/night:** Twinkle was evaluated in the mornings prior to lunch and nap time at the Open Door Preschool in her classroom, in the center's indoor central play area, in the reception area of the ECI program (housed in the same building as the preschool), on the main west playground, and the smaller south playground. The window shades in one familiar classroom were drawn and the lights were off to simulate night travel. In June, Twinkle was also observed in her apartment during a consultation visit with her mother.
- **Lighting conditions:** Inside the school, overhead fluorescent lighting is used. For some indoor locations, there is also natural lighting from windows. On the playgrounds, there are patches of bright sunlight interspersed with shaded areas.

Attending behaviors:

Twinkle turned and walked toward a variety of noises. She was able to localize and track sounds. She noticed and identified smells such as leather, chocolate, cut grass, flowers, and so on. She was able to identify and label many environmental sounds. She was able to sit still to listen to a story or a half-hour movie or television show, if it was something she was interested in. She was beginning to respond to sound shadows and exhibited an emerging ability to use echolocation.

Expressive and receptive language skills:

Twinkle has made great progress the past several months in both expressive and receptive language skills. She spoke in short sentences, used adjectives and adverbs to describe items and actions, and followed one-, two-, and sometimes three-step directions, especially when the steps were related to each other (e.g., "Go to the reading center, find the laughing baby, and sit with her on the pillow"). Her voice was very soft and she sometimes talked into her chest so she often needed to be reminded to direct her face toward the head of the person(s) to whom she was speaking and to speak louder.

Motor skills/posture and gait/physical endurance:

Twinkle had a normal gait, although it became slightly wider than a mature gait when she was on an uneven surface. When she was unsure of the terrain or in new environments and not using her cane, she held her arms slightly up and out from her body. She usually walked with a normal heel-to-toe foot strike. Without her cane, she walked with her torso erect, but her head was frequently tilted downward and turned to the right side. She was able to run and seemed to delight in this activity. While running, her step length was short and somewhat choppy (up and down), causing her forward progress to be slower than usually seen when a child is running. With her cane, she kept her head erect and her vision directed

(continued on next page)

outwards, although the turn of her head to the right side remained. This head turn was probably to direct the dominant vision from her left eye into midline.

Twinkle liked to play with the other children in her classroom and especially liked to be out on the playground for extended periods of time. She walked around the playground, climbed on the various equipment, went down the slides, tried to ride a tricycle with adult assistance, loved to be pushed on the swings, and rarely chose to sit down when outside. She participated in all the indoor activities and did her best to follow physical movements that went along with songs or exercises, although she initially needed physical assistance as she did not clearly see the movements being displayed by the teacher and other students. Because she sometimes did not sleep well through the night at home (as reported by her mother), she was allowed to take a slightly longer nap in the afternoon, if desired. Because of this, O&M lessons were usually scheduled in the mornings.

Body imagery/awareness:

Twinkle was able to identify many of the more frequently referred to body parts on herself, another person, and her doll babies, such as head, arm, leg, knee, foot, eyes, nose, mouth, hands, fingers, etc. She was learning to follow simple directions that involved moving her body parts when given directions such as "use your foot to kick the ball" and "hold out your hands."

Spatial awareness:

Twinkle indicated good understanding of near spatial awareness by performing functional actions such as pulling out a chair to sit at a table and reaching behind herself into a basket to pull out toys. In order to learn the locations of centers within her classroom and equipment on the playground, she needed some initial guidance from adults who helped her explore areas and describe features by playing games such as, "Let's take the baby to the reading center, find a book, and sit on the pillow while we read it." She now travels confidently in her classroom, in the center indoor play area, and on the playgrounds, especially the larger playground where her class is taken daily. On the playground equipment, she knew how to travel from feature to feature, going up and down stairs and climbing walls as well as going down the two slides on her bottom and backward on her tummy. She ducked her head to avoid hitting overhead beams and the tops of the enclosed slides and tunnel. And she stopped at changes in surface to carefully step down or up, as needed. For the big step up to the playground, she turned sideways, held onto the retaining wall, and sidestepped up or down without difficulty.

Auditory awareness and use:

Twinkle followed simple verbal directions and could successfully travel toward a sound source. However, she was shy about asking others to indicate where they were by calling out to her. Since her distant vision is severely limited, she needs to learn to speak up and ask for auditory guidance when she cannot find someone.

Concept development:

- **Directional and positional:** Twinkle correctly identified whether she was traveling up or down a hill or stairs and followed directions using "in, out, around, over, under, through, between/in the middle of, beside, far, and near" correctly. She turned herself around and lay down when told to go down the slide feet first on her tummy and knew to move out of the way so that the next child could come down the slide. She followed directions to go forward and backward, and could move sideways but not always on command.

- **Laterality:** Twinkle responded correctly when asked to show or identify her left and right body parts. She is learning to follow directions that include left and right turns but sometimes completely circles around before proceeding in the correct direction. She did not yet know left and right on a person facing her.
- **Quantitative:** Twinkle was able to count to 100 with some errors and could consistently use one-to-one correspondence when counting up to 20 items.
- **Color:** Twinkle correctly identified red, blue, yellow, and green, especially when the colored items were placed on a contrasting or lighted background. She had more difficulty differentiating between colors which were close to each other on the color wheel and similar in intensity and/or hue, such as blues and purples, reds and oranges, blacks and browns, etc.
- **Cardinal directions:** Twinkle learned to identify the doors in her school as North, South, East, and West, but was not able to use these turns to identify which direction she was facing. She did not understand the relationships of the four cardinal directions to each other.
- **Environmental:** Twinkle correctly identified many environmental sounds such as a bus, car, motorcycle, lawnmower, leaf blower, airplane, water fountain, elevator doors, etc. She knew the names of environmental features such as curb, street, crosswalk, stop sign, sidewalk, bridge, hallway, corner, ramp, fence, dumpster, etc.

Use of vision:

Twinkle used her vision when traveling and was able to see and negotiate around most obstacles as well as follow a path and follow another student when traveling in a line. Twinkle was attracted by moving objects and was able to follow the trajectory of balls as small as one inch for a distance of 10 or more feet IF she had seen the beginning of their movement and there was good color contrast between the ball and the surface on which it was lying. However, when a 3-inch yellow ball was repeatedly placed 10 to 20 feet away on a brown surface, she often could not locate it, even when passing within inches of it. She was observed moving her head from side to side indicating an attempt to scan, but evidently the scanning was not efficient.

Use of low vision devices:

No low vision devices have been prescribed for her at the time of this evaluation. She should have a clinical low vision evaluation and be evaluated for a telescope for distant vision and magnifiers for near vision use.

Use of mobility devices:

Twinkle has received instruction in the use of a cane since she was 2 years, 9 months old. At that time, the classroom staff and Twinkle's mom were also issued canes and received instruction in basic cane use so that the adults could model cane use to Twinkle as described in the book *Independent Movement and Travel in Blind Children: A Promotion Model* (Cutter, 2007). Twinkle was able to walk for a distance of 50 feet while keeping the cane in front of her with the tip tapping the ground in a rhythmic pattern as she moved it back and forth in an arc. The arc width was not yet a consistent distance to her left and right sides, but she was gradually refining the cane movement to the proper width and placement. Staying in step has not yet been taught to her, but she did match the rhythm of her tapping to the rhythm of her footfall. Twinkle was able to use the cane to detect obstacles too small for her to see, as well as drop-offs. She was learning to hold the cane correctly as she went up and down stairs and could clear with the cane when stepping off of or onto curbs.

(continued on next page)

Travel skills:

- **Guide technique:** Twinkle knew how to walk with a guide and also how to guide someone else. Her family and the classroom staff have been instructed in guide techniques. Twinkle is not yet able to explain to others how to act as a guide for her.
- **Basic skills** (protective techniques, alignment techniques, trailing, search patterns): Twinkle was able to use search patterns when trying to find a dropped object. She knew and could successfully use upper- and lower-hand-and-forearm techniques, but rarely needed them since she is so short.
- **Cane skills:** (See comments under the section entitled "Use of mobility devices" in this report.)
- **Travel within home environment:** Within her apartment, Twinkle was able to travel independently, although all young children sometimes like extra help to find things. Twinkle's young age has precluded training in independent travel within the apartment complex.
- **Travel within the school environment:** Twinkle was well oriented to all frequented areas in her preschool environment. In the preschool, whenever Twinkle graduated to a new classroom, some individualized instruction was needed before she began independently traveling to all instructional and play areas.
- **Travel within the residential environment:** Twinkle has received instruction in residential areas around her preschool, so she knew many environmental concepts found in such areas. She located pertinent features such as driveways, sidewalks, corners at intersections, ramps, fire hydrants, etc., as she traveled around a block. She has not yet received instruction in crossing streets but is guided across by the O&M specialist. Prior to crossing with the instructor, she was learning to listen and look to the left and right as well as ahead and behind to determine if there was any oncoming traffic. However, she is not yet consistent in this determination.
- **Ability to gather and use information:** Twinkle used her auditory and tactual senses to gather information about her environment. She was able to count driveways or sidewalks to locate a specific destination and was learning to use landmarks and clues to maintain orientation.
- **Ability to problem solve:** Twinkle is an inquisitive, happy child who responded well to encouragement for trying tasks and praise for accomplishing tasks. Because of her reduced vision, physical guidance was needed to learn many tasks, but physical and verbal prompts should be faded as soon as possible so that she can learn the persistence and problem-solving skills that are needed to be successfully independent.

Eligibility Statement

As a child with a visual impairment, Twinkle Star Hill continues to qualify for direct training and consultation services with an orientation and mobility specialist.

Recommendations

1. Twinkle should participate in activities that use sound localization, including walking toward and away from various sounds. Identification of a variety of sounds can be included in these activities as well as awareness of sound shadows and use of echolocation. Additionally, she needs to learn to call out when trying to find others so that they can indicate their location by calling back to her.
2. Twinkle should continue to be oriented to her home environment by exploring her apartment complex. The locations of nearby features should be pointed out to her, such as mailboxes, apartments of

neighbors, the playground, pool, and office, so that she can begin to build a mental map of her home environment.

3. Efficient visual scanning techniques should be taught to Twinkle both inside and outside.

4. Activities that involve spatial and body awareness and use of positional words and phrases will help Twinkle use these concepts when following directions. Progress on these concepts and all other skills related to O&M instruction should be regularly noted in her own *TAPS Comprehensive Initial and Ongoing Evaluation* booklet (Pogrund et al., 2012).

5. Twinkle should learn to explain to others how to serve as a guide for her when needed. It is recommended that she begin by explaining the process to adults and then can proceed to explaining and demonstrating the technique to her classmates.

6. When Twinkle changes classrooms and/or schools, classroom staff and the O&M specialist should provide ample instruction in familiarizing her to new environments until she demonstrates the ability to travel independently to all regularly used areas, including areas in the classroom and throughout the school. During familiarization, Twinkle should be taught how landmarks and clues can help with maintaining orientation. Familiarization to the new school building and her classroom where she will attend kindergarten should be a high priority. While being familiarized to new environments, she should also be learning self-familiarization techniques so that she can eventually explore and mentally map new areas independently.

7. Instruction in basic cane use should continue, with an emphasis on maintaining the correct placement and width of the cane arc. Staying in step should be introduced by making it a game of "Kick the cane," so that it goes to the side that is opposite of the foot stepping forward. Recognizing when she is out of step and learning to get back in step can also be introduced, but mastery of these skills should not be expected until she is older. Adults should model the use of a long cane just as they model many other desired behaviors. Twinkle can walk next to adults while they tap and walk in step together. Singing a marching song could be incorporated into this activity.

8. Twinkle should receive instruction in cane use while ascending and descending stairs.

9. Verbal description of the environment and actions should be provided for Twinkle along with the opportunity to explore real items with all her senses whenever possible. For instance, when going to the grocery store with family members, she can feel various produce and compare their color, texture, shape, weight, and smell. At home, the exploration can continue by having her participate in washing and preparing the items, comparing the inside structure and texture, and noting any changes that occur as they are cooked, as well as how they taste. Comparing and contrasting similar and dissimilar items can become a regular game and will teach important skills that help her make sense of items with discriminating features not always visually apparent to her.

Travis Trainer, Certified Orientation and Mobility Specialist

Report dated and presented: July 30, 2011

Source: Reprinted with permission from Pogrund, R., Sewell, D., Anderson, H., Calaci, L. Cowart, M. F., Gonzalez, C. M., . . . Roberson-Smith, B. (2012). Part 3: Appendices. Evaluation report. In *TAPS—Teaching age-appropriate purposeful skills: An orientation and mobility curriculum for students with visual impairments* (3rd ed., pp. 283–292). Austin: Texas School for the Blind and Visually Impaired.

References

Cutter, J. (2007). *Independent movement and travel in blind children: A promotion model.* Charlotte, NC: Information Age Publishing.

Dodson-Burk, B., & Hill, E. W. (1989). *Preschool orientation and mobility screening.* Alexandria, VA: Association for Education and Rehabilitation of the Blind and Visually Impaired.

Pogrund, R., Sewell, D., Anderson, H., Calaci, L., Cowart, M. F., Gonzalez, C. M., . . . Roberson-Smith, B. (2012). Part 2: Comprehensive initial and ongoing evaluation. In *TAPS—Teaching age-appropriate purposeful skills: An orientation and mobility curriculum for students with visual impairments* (3rd ed.). Austin: Texas School for the Blind and Visually Impaired.

Index

Page references followed by *f*, *s*, or *t* indicate figures, sidebars, or tables, respectively.

CPSIA information can be obtained
at www.ICGtesting.com
Printed in the USA
LVHW010209210423
744933LV00028B/563

9 780891 287650